A
Primer
for
Playgoers

A Primer for Playgoers

Second Edition

EDWARD A. WRIGHT
CALIFORNIA STATE COLLEGE
AT LONG BEACH

LENTHIEL H. DOWNS
DENISON UNIVERSITY

PRENTICE-HALL, INC., Englewood Cliffs, New Jersey

Library of Congress Catalog Card No.: 68-57827

Current printing (last number):

10   9   8   7   6   5   4

Printed in the United States of America

PRENTICE-HALL INTERNATIONAL, INC., *London*
PRENTICE-HALL OF AUSTRALIA, PTY. LTD., *Sydney*
PRENTICE-HALL OF CANADA, LTD., *Toronto*
PRENTICE-HALL OF INDIA PRIVATE LTD., *New Delhi*
PRENTICE-HALL OF JAPAN, INC., *Tokyo*

Dedicated to those who through these pages may realize a fuller understanding and appreciation for the living theatre

Preface

Since the publication of *A Primer For Playgoers* (1958) and *Understanding Today's Theatre* (1959) the theatre, as all the world, has seen many startling innovations. One of the basic premises of both these earlier works was that the theatre had become too realistic, that both theatricality and imagination had been forsaken far too often. Our constant plea was for less realism and a return to the theatricalism that had been the very life blood of all great theatre from its inception. In the decade since then, there have been some impressive advances in these directions, although frequently both script and production seemed to be seeking change for the sake of change or cleverness rather than for artistic improvement. This was especially true in the area of playwriting, for in many instances there was an amazing lack of substance or clarity as well as any semblance of dramatic form. Under the vague plea of being avant garde, that haven of the young and frequently inexperienced, the search for "freedom" and "creativity" became only a world of obscurity or meaninglessness. Those dramatic principles that had proved of such great value for centuries were wholly disregarded. In this period of influence the more mature lovers of good theatre felt secure in their convictions that history would repeat itself—that these experiments would reach a peak of fashion then quickly fade—and restore the revered, proven principles of good theatre. The whole world is still in desperate need of new, imaginative, and trained playwrights who know and respect the theatre and its history, but there is evidence that, finally, the firm grasp of realism that has dominated the theatre for almost a century has been weakened.

In any theatre discussion, as in any dramatic production, there are many different ideas and minds at work. The ideas expressed in this book are not only those of the authors. Sincere thanks is expressed to all those who have permitted themselves to be quoted—from print and from verbal quotations. For what has been gleaned from other sources we are most grateful.

After spending many years in close association with the theatre and its personalities, comments that we remember have merged into our own ideas and experiences until the two sources are now integrally mingled. It is our hope that the reader will do likewise in forming his own standards of understanding the whole field that is theatre.

EDWARD A. WRIGHT
LENTHIEL H. DOWNS

Scripts

to be

Read

It is recommended for a class that the teacher require the reading of ten to twelve of the plays analyzed in Chapter Two as a minimal semester assignment. Many of them are available in inexpensive paperback reprints. All of them should be at hand for reference and reading in a school library. The following editions are suggested.

Sophocles, *Oedipus the King*. San Francisco: Chandler Publishing Co., Pocket Books; New York: Appleton-Century-Crofts, Crofts Classics.

Aristophanes, *The Birds*; Plautus, *The Menaechmi*, tran. Peter Arnott. New York: Appleton-Century-Crofts, Crofts Classics.

Everyman, in *An Anthology of English Drama Before Shakespeare*, ed. Robert Heilman. New York: Holt, Rinehart & Winston, Inc., 1952.

Shakespeare, *Hamlet*, ed. G. L. Kittredge. London: Blaisdell.

Molière, *Tartuffe*. New York: Appleton-Century-Crofts, Crofts Classics; also, *Eight Plays by Molière*. New York: Charles Scribner's Sons, Modern Library.

Ibsen, Henrik, *Ghosts and Other Plays*. Baltimore: Penguin Books, Inc.

Chekhov, Anton, *The Cherry Orchard*. Minneapolis: Univ. of Minnesota Press.

Shaw, George Bernard, *Major Barbara*. Baltimore: Penguin Books, Inc.

Pirandello, Luigi, *Naked Masks*, ed. Eric Bentley. E. P. Dutton & Co., Inc., 1952, Everyman's edition.

O'Neill, Eugene, *Dynamo*. New York: Horace Liveright, 1929.

Miller, Arthur, *Death of a Salesman*. New York: The Viking Press, 1940.

Dürrenmatt, Friedrich, *The Visit*, tran. Patrick Bowles. New York: Grove Press, 1962, Evergreen edition.

Pinter, Harold, *The Homecoming*. London: Metheun & Co., Ltd., 1965.

Friel, Brian, *Philadelphia, Here I Come!* New York: Farrar, Straus and Giroux, 1965.

Contents

III

The

Production

A
Primer
for
Playgoers

I

The

Audience

1

The Audience
and a Basis for
Dramatic Criticism

Every man, woman, or child who has expressed an opinion concerning a dramatic performance has, in a sense, proclaimed himself to be a critic. Whether his reaction has been good or bad, his opinion will have some effect on the thinking of those who have heard or read his comment, and what has been said will become a part of the production's history. The statement may have been inadvertent, biased, unfair, without thought or foundation, but once spoken or repeated, it ceases to be just an opinion and is accepted as a fact. Who has not heard, accepted, repeated, and been affected by such generalizations as: "They say it is terrible!" or "They say it is terrific!"

Another type of critic is the more powerful, and frequently only slightly more qualified, individual who is—often for strange and irrelevant reasons —assigned to cover an opening for the school or community paper. He may be completely lacking in the knowledge required of even a beginner in dramatic criticisms, but, again, "Anyone can write up a play." Yet the power of the written word takes over, and what this novice writes becomes the accepted authority for many. The hundreds of hours of work by the many persons involved in the production, their personal sacrifices, and their pride in their work—to say nothing of the financial outlay involved—far too often are condemned or praised for the wrong reasons or for no logical reason at all. As a further injustice, what the critic has written, although it is just a single opinion, becomes the only record of the production and so catalogs the event for the future.

It is doubtful if any other business or art is so much a victim of inept, untrained, illogical, and undeserved criticism as is a dramatic performance. Whether the remarks have grown out of prejudice, meager knowledge of the theatre, lack of understanding or sensitivity, momentary admiration or dislike for some individual participant, a poor dinner or disposition, an auditorium too hot or too cold, or any of a hundred incidents that could have occurred during the production itself does not matter. Those whose efforts are being discussed can console themselves only with the fact that criticism—good or bad—is much easier than creation or craftsmanship for the same reason that work is harder than talk.

Having been a part of the theatre—professional, community, and educational—for more than four decades, we are well aware that criticism of the critics is frequently heard, and that this criticism includes those who write the drama section for the national magazines or the large daily newspapers that report on opening night. This is inevitable, for total agreement on any phase of theatre is impossible. We live in a world without laws of logic or mathematical formulas to guide us. There are no yardsticks that will give us all the same answer, but there are yardsticks that should be familiar to all of us. In this book we propose to present and to discuss some of these criteria. If the amateur critics just referred to had been familiar with some basic dramatic principles and had used them honestly, there would be a greater feeling that justice had been done. Any intelligent theatre person knows that each member of the audience views what is before him with different eyes and so sees something different from his neighbor. How each member reacts will be determined by education, age, experience, nationality, maturity, background, temperament, heredity, environment, the rest of the audience, the weather, what he has done or eaten in the past few hours, or his plans for after the performance. This list of imponderables could go on indefinitely. Furthermore, if agreement on any one aspect of a given performance is impossible, then agreement is even more hopeless if different performances of the same play, in the same theatre, and with the same cast, are under discussion; for a different audience makes for a different production.

The future, fortunately, is not as hopeless as the previous paragraphs might indicate, and we look forward with optimism to a fairer and more just evaluation of the work that the various artists and theatre workers will contribute to future productions.

The United States today leads the world in all levels of theatre education. The better secondary schools carry full courses in theatre production, understanding, and appreciation. There are very few colleges or universities without dramatic programs. The more recognized institutions have made drama a part of their academic curriculum and offer degrees in Drama or Theatre through the doctorate. Tens of thousands of college students who had no previous knowledge of or interest in theatre are enrolling in courses that emphasize theatre understanding. They will be the audience of tomorrow and as such will be more demanding judges of what the artists are doing or trying to accomplish. There are also hundreds of community theatres, with new ones being organized every year. Many conduct classes in the various phases of theatre production. Repertory groups are being established in cities across the country. Statistics from Actors Equity Association show that there are more professional actors now employed by such companies outside New York than there are in the city itself.

Excellent books on playwriting, acting, directing, scene design, stage costuming, and lighting are currently on the market. The only part of the theatre experience that has been neglected is the audience—and this book is directed to the audience. The audience is that wonderful, fabulous, unpredictable, and powerful mass of individuals that no longer sees, hears, or reacts as individuals—that sometimes-lamb and sometimes-giant that meekly accepts or sharply rebuffs what is put before it. It is that barely discernible mass beyond the lights for whom everything has been done and for whom every artist has been working—that frequently generous and often thoughtless or downright rude mass of faces whose laughter or tears, silence or coughing can send the cast and crew into a seventh heaven or the depths of dejection. The audience is that all-powerful entity that keeps the play running or closes it on Saturday night, decreeing, too, when an actor is a star or a "has-been." The audience demands and expects to get just what it wants, and it is always positive in its "I know what I like" and "All I want is my money's worth."

We believe the last two quotations more accurately characterize audience attitudes when rephrased: "I like what I know" and "I get more for my money when I know why I have (or have not) got my money's worth." In other words, it may not be nearly so important to have liked or disliked a work of art as it is to know why one did or did not approve and to understand why others have or have not done so.

This book is directed to numerous groups: to those who have been active participants in the noncommercial theatre but who have been too close to develop the feeling of artistic detachment necessary for adequate critical evaluation; to the countless untrained playgoers who attend school and community theatre performances, as well as the smaller group who have an opportunity to enjoy the professional theatre; to those whose only dramatic fare has been the motion picture or the television screen; and to those who are beginning their appreciation of the theatre in the classroom. The object of this book is the whole potential audience that should enjoy live theatre.

Perhaps this is the most difficult time in all dramatic history to attempt such a work, for the primary distinction of our modern drama and theatre—and especially our current offerings—is that they possess no distinctive feature. At any time in the past, our task would have been far more simple. Today we have two extremes with every possible shade between. At one end of the spectrum we find the rose-colored spectacle of the large-scale musical or the "escapist" fare so popular on Broadway. This type of entertainment—the farces and comedies—is sought by the jaded business man and the "expense-account" theatregoer. At the other end we have the bitter, relentless, dark picture of the human condition, where man is only a victim struggling in an impossible world, his life a useless and purposeless span between a birth and a death he neither sought nor desired. In the first type we see a pretty-pretty version of an imaginary world we might dream of knowing; in the second, a world of negation—a universe in which any Deity that might once have existed now is dead. The very foundations of all past theatre—the belief that man is a creature of dignity, that he possesses a will and a destiny, that life is worth living and the world is rational—has given way to hopelessness and futility where man has no power or control over his life or destiny. Rather than trying to clarify existence, the goal of this theatre seems to be to further becloud it. The first speaks a language of clichés and fantasy; the second, a language that only a select few understand or pretend to understand.

The "illusion of reality" that has been theatre's chief goal for some one hundred years has given way to an overlapping of so many different "isms" that it is impossible to distinguish or name them all.

To show a proper respect for both the old and the new and to give each its proper recognition and prophesy what portions of the present avant-garde will live is no easy task. In all life, and especially in the arts, history has constantly shown the older generation frowning upon the new, often for no other reason than because it is new, and the younger refuting the old just because it is old. When the new is accepted, imitated, and established, it becomes a part of the traditional. Always its effect is felt, although it may or may not be an important improvement on the art itself.

Through the collection, organization, and presentation of facts, principles, and opinions that have grown out of the theatre's history, this book will present and attempt to develop at least one valid approach to appraising the work of all artists who have created the drama and brought it to life. At the risk of being both academic and pedantic, we will attempt to give the beginner some generally accepted principles of drama and the theatre. One of the earliest lessons a teacher learns is the necessity of giving the beginner some anchor at the very start. As his knowledge and experience develop, the student will learn that these early generalizations have many exceptions and that his appreciation is often enhanced by the artist's deviation from these early principles or assumptions. *Training consists of learning the rules. It is experience that teaches us the exceptions.*

Although the major portion of our discussions will be directed toward a standard for judging a dramatic production on the stage, much of what is said can be applied as well to both motion picture and television production. One cannot emphasize too strongly, however, the importance of a solid foundation and full understanding of those principles inherent in the mother of both—the live and legitimate theatre.

The word *theatre* includes both the motion picture and the television show. Since these two thespian offspring have taken over the mass audience, the parent—commonly called the legitimate theatre or the stage—has been forced to alter its methods. Frequently it has not been willing to do so and, consequently, has suffered both adverse criticism and financial loss. Each of the three media is powerful in its own right and each has its own potential, although frequently it is disappointing in its failure to realize that potential. In their techniques, and to a lesser extent in their form, the offspring differ from the parent. On the stage the actor has historically been the most important single entity, whereas, in both the cinema and television, the command position is dictated by the camera. In television there are the added differences in audience—age, size, and environment—as opposed to the stage or motion picture audience. These differences have psychological as well as mechanical and technical effects on the audience. The theatre has a history of approximately 2,500 years in the western world. The motion picture has been in existence only since about 1910, and television, since 1936. Each has come far, made fine contributions, and become established as a separate division of dramatic art. We would condemn a kind of intellectual snobbery that looks askance at these two mass media. They provide for many millions a kind of entertainment that brings them joy—a delight they might not find in the theatre we shall be discussing, even if a living theatre were available for them to attend.

The substance is basically the same for all three media, but within the limitations of this book it seemed unwise to include discussions of the cinema and television.

We regret that the two areas must be eliminated, for we respect both. But one admonition: Never try to compare the final result of any one medium with that of another. Each is sufficiently different so that it should be considered only in the context of that medium. For this reason, we shall, for the most part, avoid references to either motion pictures or television.

Although every effort will be made to point up those elements that can make for greater understanding and aesthetic enjoyment of the theatre, there is no guarantee that dramatic appreciation will follow. Appreciation itself cannot be taught. It is a by-product that grows from knowledge and understanding. It comes to the individual only after he has applied, first consciously, and later subconsciously, all that he can learn about form and technique, accepted principles and practices. It is an intangible asset that grows with experience and time. It is our fondest hope that through the pages of this book the reader may find a key to this great and enriching experience.

We are aware of the problems in discussing or explaining any art, and here we are faced with the complications of dealing with two arts at the same time—that of dramatic literature and that of the total stage production. Tyrone Guthrie says in his book *A Life in the Theatre*:

> I learned . . . that the script of a play, even of a great play, a masterpiece, is still only a part of the raw material of a performance. The script, the cast, the appurtenances of costume, make-up, scenery, properties and lights, and finally the audience—these are all ingredients which have somehow to be fused together into a single work of art. Of course, the script is nearly always the most important of these elements; it is the basis. But the script alone has no theatrical existence. It awaits the interpretation.[1]

Finally, our goals are: (1) to help each individual develop for himself an artistically honest standard for evaluating the dramatic production; (2) to provide a fairer means of judging the work of all those artists whose efforts are being witnessed; and (3) to build a better audience, which will in turn demand a better theatre.

We shall figuratively go backstage and try to see first what goes into the writing of a play, and then what goes into the total production—the finished work. Although we can only hope that some measure of appreciation may be the final result, it is our belief that *taste* can be improved. We would define taste as a mental perception of quality, a perception embodying *judgment*, a discriminative faculty—the act of liking or preferring something—and the sense of *what is appropriate, harmonious, or beautiful* in nature or art. Both taste and judgment will always be relative, and our goal is not to dictate a number of artistic fiats, but rather to improve the general taste of the reader so far as dramatic fare is concerned. Although we are convinced that public feelings are rarely reversed, we feel that within any entertainment medium there is the power to extend or retard the audience's desires or demands.

In our effort to better understand the theatre we shall rely on three sources of information: facts, opinions, and principles. The remainder of

[1]Sir Tyrone Guthrie, *A Life in the Theatre* (New York: McGraw-Hill Book Company, 1959), p. 17.

this book will fall into one or another of these three categories. We must recognize each of the three sources for what it is and consider its value to the theatre in general and to us personally in establishing our own basis for judgment. This is especially true in respect to opinions and principles.

Facts are the most easily recognized, although even they are often mistaken. The simplest examples are dates, pictures of actual productions, the names of playwrights, actors and technicians, the stories of plays, and the provable effects that certain individuals or works have had on later dramatic literature or theatre production. Familiarity with as many plays from as many different countries and periods as possible is desirable. It is very helpful to read the practical and theoretical works of those theatre craftsmen who have written about their profession. Knowing who has said what is to know a fact; but what was said is frequently just an opinion. However, opinions may be accepted as facts by certain individuals or even by history. And opinions may sometimes become generally accepted dramatic principles.

The following statements may be considered to be facts:

> ... Our Western theatre has its origin in the culture of the Greeks; it was part of their religious life some five hundred years before Christ. Aeschylus, Sophocles, Euripides, and Aristophanes were four of the greatest Greek playwrights.
> ... The Elizabethan Age in England, during the latter part of the sixteenth century and early part of the seventeenth, was one of the greatest literary eras of the English-speaking peoples, and William Shakespeare was its leader.
> ... Henrik Ibsen, a Norwegian, is considered to be the father of the modern drama. He wrote his greatest plays between 1860 and 1905, and he was the author of such social plays as *The Doll's House, Ghosts,* and *Hedda Gabler,* which were effective in bringing about changes in contemporary attitudes toward life and in the laws of our land.
> ... Many of the fourteen scripts discussed in Chapter II have withstood the tests of time and are accepted as literature *and* as theatre because they possess both the literary qualities and the theatricality that are necessary for successful production.
> ... Now more people in this country can say on any given morning, "I saw a play last night" than at any other time in history. Almost 90 per cent of all American homes have television sets, and between forty million and eighty million persons attend the motion pictures every week. In addition, there are thousands of stage productions by school, community, and professional groups across the country.

Of the three sources of information, *opinions* form the most abundant and the least reliable part, although they are often the most interesting and challenging. Certainly they provoke the most discussion. It will always be so, not only because the very nature of theatre is emotional rather than intellectual, but because our reactions and our personal preferences are based on the sum total of all that makes each of us an individual personality. Our opinions may be difficult for others to understand, and even we may find it hard to justify them by any standard other than "I just have a feeling."

It is not unusual for our best critics to disagree completely on what a specific play has said, even though the script is there to be read and studied.

For example, it is generally accepted that *The Cherry Orchard* by Anton Chekhov is one of the truly great plays of modern times. The author labels it a comedy, but that excellent authority John Gassner calls it "a wistful tragedy of personal defeat, symbolic of the decay of a class and a social order." Differences in point of view and background of author and critic are surely the answer. The play depicts the fall of the Old Regime in Russia and the rise of the peasant class. Chekhov belonged to the latter group. Mr. Gassner, however, sensed the tragedy that comes to those who are unable to adjust their lives to a new order and a new world and who must always live in the past, clinging to it long after it is gone. This failure on the part of the protagonist to adjust made the play, to Gassner, a tragedy. When *The Cherry Orchard* was first performed at the Moscow Art Theatre under the direction of the great Stanislavsky, it was played as a serious drama of character and without the comedic qualities that Chekhov desired.

Eugene O'Neill's *Anna Christie* has been called a tragedy, a melodrama, and a comedy, depending upon what the individual believes happened to the characters after the drama was ended by the playwright. *The Little Foxes*, by Lillian Hellman, has been labeled both a comedy and a melodrama.

In the opinions of excellent scholars the turning point of *Hamlet* has been placed in three different scenes: the Players' scene when Hamlet is finally convinced that the king is guilty; the scene where he could revenge his father's death by killing the king but does not do so because the king is at prayer; and the Mother's Bedchamber scene when the ghost makes his second appearance. Each opinion can be defended by its proponent.

If opinions vary so widely on a written script, it is little wonder that agreement by the best critics on a total production is rare indeed. Opinion on the most ephemeral of the theatre arts—acting—is usually so varied that a single characterization by a given actor may evoke the full critical gamut from "deplorable" to "brilliant," and the same vocal quality or physical action may be described as "sheer genius" or "amateurish and regrettable."

The most valued opinions are those that are the outgrowth of sound dramatic principles and are arrived at after the emotion of the moment has passed, and thought or reasoning has taken over. Such are the opinions that follow:

> ... The stage is more effective than either the motion picture or television because of its aliveness, its immediacy, and its personal touch. There are few experiences more exciting than playgoing.
> ... *Our Town* by Thornton Wilder and *Death of a Salesman* by Arthur Miller are two of the greatest American plays yet written, but Eugene O'Neill is still the greatest playwright our nation has produced.
> ... "Commercialism may not be entirely desirable in the theatre, but neither is pseudo-intellectual isolationism. There are those who turn their backs on the harsh reality of the public taste and indulge themselves in meaningless mumbo-jumbo under the gallant banner of avant-gardism, or the guise of 'raising the level of public taste.' These would-be reformers do not realize that such a goal cannot be accomplished by forcing on the public their own standards, or their own philosophy of art—particularly when there is no evidence that theirs is any better. No man has the right to say that this the public should see and this it should not. This would be a form of artistic fascism which is dangerous and should be deplored far more than commercialism. It is smug and theatre smugness can only breed stagnation."[2]
> ... "If the Absurdists are correct ... then the very forces which gave life and strength to the modern theatre have caused it to decline ... Once you assert that the meaning of life is absurdity, that the laws of logic are spurious, that action is meaningless, that individuality is illusory, that social interaction is unimportant, and that communication is impossible, you have denied every assumption upon which the art of the theatre as we have known it in the western world is based."[3]
> ... "Of all the arts the theatre is the most popular in its appeal, the most immediate in its impact, and the most complex in its nature."

[2]Russell O'Neil, *The Devil's Profession* (New York: Simon & Schuster Inc., 1964), pp. 65–66.

[3]Robert W. Corrigan, *The Modern Theatre*, Introduction (New York: The Macmillan Company, 1964), p. xviii.

... "Drama is the most perfect instrument Man has devised to record, vitally, and in dimension, the mystery and magic, the purpose and pattern of his life through the ages."

... "Why do so many contemporary plays seem to be preoccupied with soul-searching, pessimism, and the experience of alienation? ... because it is simply something that has to be done—we can add this further thought: Because the act of wrestling with the dark angel is the only honest exercise of faith, when all our other faiths have failed.

"Realistically we know that everything in the outside world is in an ethical shambles ... over one hundred million human beings have been killed in military action alone in this century, and the killing is still going on. Culturally we have outgrown the era of Romanticism which promised that a consuming love could be the source of all enduring values. And now our leading theologians are telling us that 'God is dead,' which is to say, we must face the chaos we have made, without the assurance of our traditional convictions.

"And so it is no wonder that in all three of these contemporary plays [The Night of the Iguana, Who's Afraid of Virginia Woolf, and After the Fall] the characters are unable to relate to themselves or to communicate with each other adequately; and it is no wonder that our theatre is going through a dark night of the soul, in much the same way as Jacob wrestled with his dark angel almost four thousand years ago."[4]

These are opinions. One may or may not agree with them. Any opinion can become the source of much discussion, and such discussions can be valuable to us all when the opinion has grown out of some sound dramatic principle.

Our third source of information is the most difficult. *Principles* are often variable and frequently open to question, debate, or change. The individual may accept a principle now and later alter or even discard it altogether. A principle is a specific point of view or conviction from which we make our start in analyzing a given piece of work. It is a springboard in our thinking. Eventually these beliefs become a part of us and are the substrata that determine our taste, the soil out of which our understanding and finally our appreciation may come.

Because we may have formulated different principles than have our acquaintances, we shall often find ourselves in disagreement on the worth of an artist's work or the total production. Before discussions become too

[4] William Packard, "The Theater: Stress on Soul-Searching in Plays Reflects the Era," *The Wall Street Journal*, August 8, 1966, Editorial page.

heated we should seek the lowest common denominator, namely the principle upon which we are basing our conclusions.

The fact that certain principles are listed on these pages does not suggest that the reader must accept them. Nor does it mean that they are precepts upon which others have arrived at their own conclusions regarding a dramatic performance. They can help the reader as the first step in building his own standard of evaluation, especially if he chooses to accept them until he has discovered others that he may prefer. They can become the anchors that any beginner so sorely needs. Remember, however, that *no principle is of more value than the integrity of the individual who applies it.*

Here, as a kind of foundation upon which we shall build our structure, we present and explain seven basic principles. They are the bedrock upon which most of the opinions stated on the following pages rest. These principles, we feel, are a valid start for any beginner who is interested in learning more about the theatre. They try to answer the following questions:

1. What is Art?
2. Of what is Art composed?
3. What is the purpose of Art?
4. How can I understand or evaluate Art?
5. Why is Theatre an Art?
6. What are the Theatre's obligations?
7. What are the obligations of the audience or the critic?

PRINCIPLE ONE: Art Is Life Interpreted By and Through the Personality of the Artist.

George Jean Nathan once said that if he were the Secretary of Culture he would burn all the books that attempted to define art. If such a ruling were to be enacted it would greatly reduce our libraries; indeed, we could fill many pages by listing what has been written in an effort to define art. For our purpose, the definition listed above seems most satisfactory. In the theatre every artist endeavors to picture life as he sees it. We credit two men for the definition. Francis Bacon said, "Art is man added to Nature"; and the great Japanese playwright and story-teller Chikamatsu Mongaemon (often called the Japanese Shakespeare) said, "Art is the layer that lies between the skins of truth and falsity—that which is false but not false, true but not true—that is what gives us joy."

Man's experience is not limited to the things he can see, hear, or touch. Unlike other animals he has the power of picturing in his mind what is not but what might be. He is able not only to accumulate, record, and profit by the experiences of the past but to imagine and devise different ways of doing things—to have new ideas.

All art implies selection on the part of the artist. The moment that man enters any situation we have the twin element of selection and emphasis rather than sheer representation, for man interprets, and no two persons see exactly the same picture. When man begins to create, to record, or to communicate what he has seen or felt *as he has experienced it*, art begins. He adds something to nature, and the result is neither true nor false, although the illusion may seem more real than life itself.

No artist is ever wholly natural—he only *seems* natural. The most interesting conversation in life could very well be unreal or unsatisfactory in the theatre, lacking emphasis, coherence, unity, climax, or continuity. The very characters we might shun in life are frequently found to be the most delightful or entertaining on the stage.

Let us imagine for a moment that an individual has had an experience in life that has given him great personal pleasure by affecting him either emotionally or intellectually. It may have been the discovery of a great truth, the realization of a philosophy, the appreciation of the beauty of a sunset, the song of a bird, or some humorous or serious aspect of daily life. In any event, the participant has an all-consuming desire to reproduce that experience so that it can be shared with others. He must first choose the art through which he will speak. What he wants to share may be most easily expressed by the dance, by a musical composition, a poem, a formal painting, or a cartoon. He could choose the short story, the novel, or the drama. Let us imagine that he has chosen and written the drama. Readers of this drama may find in it what the playwright meant to say, or they may discover some further experience of their own that they, too, wish to share. They produce the drama, which then becomes a play, and they in turn become actors, technicians, and director. In the work of each artist some facet of his own thinking, feeling, and background will appear, for the tree an artist paints is not nature's tree— it is his. The characters a playwright creates are not life's characters— they are his. St. Joan, Queen Elizabeth I, Abraham Lincoln, and Mary of Scotland have appeared countless times in literature. Each re-creation is different, although patterned after the same model, for each is the sum total of a different author's impression, technique, and imagination. In the art of acting, twenty Hamlets will be twenty different people, although they speak the same lines, for each actor must create the character through his own experiences and personality.

Every artist selects and emphasizes just what he desires us, his audience, to see, for we see life through his eyes. The playwright tells his story within his chosen framework, with characters, dialogue, and theme all slanted to portray life as he sees it. The actor creates the role in terms of his own physical, emotional, vocal, and intellectual qualifications. The various technicians do what must be done to sustain the mood, project the story, and enhance the production. Simultaneously the director as creator, interpreter, and coordinator translates all these elements into a harmonious whole. All work with the same goal—to share an emotional experience by picturing some aspect of life through their own personalities and to give the audience a memorable experience.

In art, we who make up the audience are given the opportunity of submitting to new and varied experiences, of momentarily stepping out of the world of reality and knowing the worlds that are inhabited by the great artists of the ages. We look, for the moment, at life through their eyes and their personalities.

Through art we may become acquainted with a whole new world. Brooks Atkinson has said this most effectively in the following quotation:

> Out of his imagination, exultancy, despair, revolt or passion the artist creates a world that has his own coherence and submits it as the truth. For the worlds of art are bewilderingly unalike. The tragic world of Sophocles, the tender, reverent world of Michelangelo, the gamy world of Chaucer, Shakespeare's vast world of intelligence and sensibility, the satirical world of Molière, the human world of Dickens, the mad world of Van Gogh, and the luminous world of Manet, the noble world of Beethoven, and the nervous world of Stravinsky, the electric world of Shaw, the dark world of O'Neill, the gusty world of O'Casey—these are some of the worlds available.[5]

PRINCIPLE TWO: Art Consists of Three Specific Elements— Substance, Form, and Technique.

An artist's substance is what he tries to say—his content, subject matter, the material of his creation, the aspects of life he wishes to emphasize or communicate, and the emotions, feelings, moods, or ideas he would share with his audience. After feelings or thought comes his form, and through this form the artist projects his substance.

Whatever means he may have chosen, the artist discovers certain principles that have been established as guides. This is his form—the channel through which his ideas or emotions will pass. By the form he intensifies what he has to say; he enhances his content. Form also goes under the names of rules, formulas, standards, conventions, patterns, and similar terms. As indicated above, we have chosen the word *principles*. History has proved that although rules or principles must never confine an art,

[5]Brooks Atkinson, "Note On Art," *The New York Times*, Sept. 8, 1957.

all art does constantly produce rules. They constitute the structure within and by which an artist will create. When he can be more effective by altering them or even establishing new principles he may do so. In 1912 William Archer called this "the part of original genius to override the dictates of experience." Ferdinand Bruentière said it very well in 1894 in his essay "The Law of the Drama":

> I leave the dramatist complete freedom in development—the truth is there are no rules—there never will be. There are only conventions which are necessarily variable, since their only object is to fulfill the essential aim of the dramatic work, and the means of accomplishing this vary with the place, the time, and the man.

If the artist does not have Archer's "genius" his own efforts to set up new guidelines may fail. If he does and is successful he may very well establish a new form or a new set of principles.

It was not until almost one hundred years after Aeschylus, Sophocles, and Euripides had completed their works that Aristotle analyzed the playwright's masterpieces and wrote his *Poetics*, which for centuries stood as the guide for other playwrights. In time Shakespeare and his fellow dramatists created an entirely new style of playwriting by disregarding the unities and formal rules of the Greek dramas. Thus a new formula was established and the Romantic style was born. Again in the mid-nineteenth century, the realistic drama became the most popular form. In our own time, various playwrights are striving to break with this realistic theatre. Such innovations are frequently called the avant-garde and are often both imaginative and interesting. If the experimentations are accepted, new principles come into being, for the theatre is a very pragmatic art—what works is good, and what is good is eventually accepted, thus becoming the theatre of the period. The only requirment is that the results be equally, or more effective than they would have been with the form that the artist has altered or forsaken.

So dramatic form has changed through the centuries; and it is these various forms with which artists are involved that these pages are chiefly concerned. The playwright with his words and meter speaks through the elements of drama: theme, plot, dialogue, mood, character, or spectacle. The play he writes will usually, although not always, fall into one of the four general types of drama—tragedy, melodrama, comedy, and farce. His aesthetic style may be classic, realistic, romantic, naturalistic, impressionistic, fanciful, epic, absurd, et cetera. The structure of his script will somehow include exposition, inciting moment, turning point, falling action, climax, and conclusion. When the script is brought to life in the theatre before an audience, each contributing artist expresses himself through a form that is a part of his contribution to the play.

The actor's approach represents the school and method he has chosen, his involvement with the technical, intellectual, and emotional areas of acting. The scene designer's form is reflected in the style of his scenery. It may be realism, simplified realism, impressionism, expressionism, or a combination of several. The costumer and the electrician have worked within certain bounds or conventions demanded by their fields. Even the director will have approached the whole production with an over-all design that encompasses certain principles or traditions. There is no final authority, no absolute standard, in the theatre, but there are principles that must be given recognition if the finished product is to show the planning, forsight, care, and selection that great art possesses. We recognize some recent philosophies to the contrary, but it is our opinion that real art is never unpremeditated, for it cannot exist without meaning, objectivity, and organization. All art is carefully worked out and designed by the artist, and this premeditation is the form and technique through which he expresses his ideas or emotions.

Technique, the method of fitting or blending the substance into the form, is the artist's personal means of accomplishing his end. It involves the selection and arrangement of the artist's materials for a particular effect. Form and technique are the elements that differentiate art from life, and technique is also the element that distinguishes one artist's work from that of another. It is sometimes called his personal style or quality, for it is essentially the artist's projection of himself. The three media—stage, motion picture, and television—are very much alike so far as substance and form are concerned, but they vary greatly in their techniques.

Two actors could not possibly play a role identically, nor could two playwrights write the same story in the same way, although both of them may deal with the same subject and follow the same principles—principles dictated by the form in which that subject has been interpreted.

Alexandre Dumas *fils*, the French playwright, once said: "Technique is so important that it sometimes happens that technique is mistaken for art." We are all familiar with stage, motion picture, television personalities who depend too much on their technique or showmanship for success. Such artists usually have a very short professional life, for substance and form are in the final analysis more important. Technique without content is not enough: An artist must say something. In the chapters dealing with the playwright, the actors, the technicians, and the director, we shall further distinguish among these three components of an art, for it is fundamental that one must have a knowledge of the various forms and techniques common to drama and theatre production, both past and present, if he is to understand the artistry of any dramatic production.

PRINCIPLE THREE: The Purpose of All Art Is to Give Aesthetic Pleasure, to Clarify Life Through the Communication of the Artist's Thoughts, Ideas, or Emotions.

It is the primary function of any work of art to stimulate the imagination through the senses. The physical experience of beauty, which lifts us out of ourselves and enables us to see more deeply into the great realities, has been called aesthetic pleasure; it is defined as an appreciation of the beautiful. Beauty has never been absolutely defined. Some feel that the artist merely records beauty that inheres in his subject matter. Others believe that beauty lies in the artist's skill, style, or technique in duplicating nature. Some would call it a "unity in variety" or the complete harmony of all the elements that the artist has used to express a central idea or theme.

Many moderns contend that beauty exists in the mind of the viewer or hearer, that the artist strikes some note bringing to the observer's mind a pleasurable experience or emotion that gives the aesthetic pleasure through recognition of a past experience. Another theory places the sense of beauty in the artist's personal interpretation of what he sees. This aesthetic approach has given us both *impressionism* and *expressionism*, as well as many other "isms" of modern art.

There are also some who unite their ethical or religious thinking with their aesthetic sense. They accept the theory that "Beauty is truth, truth beauty." Closely allied, but standing by themselves, are those who can derive aesthetic pleasure only when they perceive the presence of God or an emphasis on their own moral code combined with their art. In the theatre these individuals are often called the moralists, for they insist upon the presence of a great moral theme or lesson.

Certain intellectuals say that aesthetic pleasure can come only from an art object that challenges them to think, or furnishes a greater understanding of the world's problems. We contend that there is as much beauty in our theatre today as at any time in all history. We would not for a moment be classed with those pessimists who feel that the theatre is dying or those who constantly cry for the "good old days" and protest that "the theatre is not what it used to be." We agree with the man who said that poetry is present at that moment when one becomes conscious of the presence of the beautiful. By such a definition poetry certainly did not go out of the theatre with the death of Shakespeare or Jonson. It has only changed its emphasis. In many respects there is more poetry in our modern theatre than in Shakespeare's day. His poetry lay in the written text of the play; ours lies in the complete harmony of all the arts that are found in a dramatic production.

The Greeks sought their poetry in dialogue. The Medievalists found it in the theme of the liturgical play, expressing to the masses in understandable language the Biblical stories the priests could not give them in Latin. Renaissance Italy found beauty in the scenic, dramatic backgrounds of Leonardo da Vinci and other contemporary artists; Elizabethan England, in the incomparable language of Shakespeare; seventeenth-century France, in the superb pantomime of the *commedia dell' arte* which finally emerged in Molière's comedies of manners. The realists have found it in the completeness of their artistic representation of life on the stage. The expressionist finds it in the imaginativeness of his conception. Thus all have found beauty in the theatre, whether it be in the acting, the direction, the setting, the story itself, the work of the technicians or, as is possible today, in the harmonious coordination of the labors of all these contributing artists.

Closely related to the importance of aesthetic pleasure is the second phase of this principle: the clarity of the artist's communication. Count Leo Tolstoy said:

> Art is a human activity which is passed on to others, causing them to feel and experience what the artist has felt and experienced. . . . It is a means of communication between people, uniting them in the same feelings. . . . As soon as the spectators and the hearers are affected by the same feelings which the artist felt—that is art.

Although any artist must communicate something to the observer or the listener, the greatest aspect of art may be something we are unable to explain—even though it has moved us greatly. Communication is in the mind, the emotions, and the spirit, speaking clearly, understandably; and the observer has grasped the basic substance and, in a sense, appreciated both the form and technique of the artist. To attempt to relate that experience fully, or to transfer the ecstacy it has brought is futile. The most valuable aspect in art often cannot be explained, because the real meaning of any work of art is subjective. If this were not so, there would be little meaning in any art. Art exists to suggest ways in which truth may be approached. The artist's interpretation is subjective, for he only offers his comments on a given aspect of life. That comment, however, should be clear in its purpose and in its meaning. Whether the artist speaks to many or to few is another question. A well-known critic once said that if the artist was able to transfer to only one other person the essence of what he had felt or experienced, he had created a work of art. This concept is known as the Mandarin view. The Mandarins believe that as art becomes greater it is understood and appreciated by fewer and fewer people; they use the phrase "the higher the fewer." Their opponents contend that if the audience is so limited, the artist's communication is not as clear as it should have been. They argue that a Mandarin's work lacks the universality that art should possess. Believing that art belongs to everyone and that it should be shared, these theorists agree with Tolstoy, who said, "Exclusive art is bad art. Good art unites."

Aristotle wrote, "The aim of art is to represent not the outward appearance of things, but their inward significance; for this, and not the external mannerism and detail, is true reality."

Art, then, should clarify and not further complicate life. It is wholly possible that we may differ with the artist's opinion, his interpretation of life, or his conclusions. We may not like the way in which he has portrayed his feelings or thoughts; we may question the values involved. Indeed, we may debate whether or not they should have been expressed; but we should be clear as to the artist's purpose, his feelings, and his thoughts. We should feel that we know what he has been trying to say. This does not mean that someone else may not get from the work another idea or a different emotional response. People's backgrounds, points of view, and mental processes are so different that we may frequently interpret the same art work differently from others. A play should be a movement toward something. To permit an audience to leave the theatre without a clear idea of what that something is, or not knowing what the play is about—even if it is about doubt or nothingness—is indefensible.

Clayton Hamilton has further emphasized this principle thus:

> Art and Nature compete eternally with each other in the great task of making humanity aware of what is true and beautiful and good. They are the two teachers in our schoolroom of a world. . . . It would be difficult to judge decisively whether Art or Nature is the greater teacher. Nature has more to tell us, but Art is better skilled for utterance. Nature has so much to say that she has no patience for articulation. She thrills us with a vague awareness of multitudinous indecipherable messages; but she speaks to us in whispers and in thunders—elusive, indeterminate, discomforting. Art, with less to say, has more patience for the formulation of her messages; she speaks to us in a voice that has been deliberately trained, and her utterance is lucid and precise. She does not try, like Nature, to tell us everything at once. She selects, instead, some single definite and little truth to tell us at a time, and exerts herself to speak it clearly. We can never estimate precisely what it is that we have learned from Nature; but whatever Art has spoken to us, we know exactly what we have been told.[6]

[6]Clayton Hamilton, *Theory of the Theatre* (New York: Henry Holt & Company, 1939).

PRINCIPLE FOUR: A Valid Premise to Any Artistic Evaluation Could Logically Consist of the Three Questions of Goethe: "What Is the Artist Trying to Do?" "How Well Has He Done It?" "Is It Worth the Doing?"

As the cornerstone of our approach to art appreciation, as the premise to every decision we shall make regarding the work of any artist in or out of the theatre, we cannot emphasize too strongly the validity and the importance of the above principle, borrowed from the works of the great German Romantic playwright, philosopher, and critic, Johann Wolfgang von Goethe (1749–1832). Playwright, actor, scene designer, electrician, costumer, or director—every artist has the inalienable right to express himself as he may desire. We may not agree that his chosen way is best; we may not like what he says, his point of view, his form of expression, or his style. Yet it is the artist's right to work as he chooses, and as observers we should ask ourselves Goethe's three questions. To answer them well, one must be familiar with the artist and the period in which he lived, his other work, and the forms and techniques of the times. The third question, especially, demands a sense of values, some taste and discrimination, and a knowledge of theatre, past and present.

Although these questions may seem simple superficially, one soon realizes that they may be answered on many levels, and the more one learns about any art, the more valid these guides become in assessing examples of it. Pursued in depth, Goethe's questions bring to mind many other questions that will require much additional knowledge on the part of the critic. Some such questions, listed below, will be discussed in the following chapters.

What is the artist trying to do? What type of script has the playwright provided? Is it tragedy, melodrama, comedy, farce—or a combination of any of these? Is his goal sheer entertainment for the "tired businessman," or would he teach us some lesson? Is the play purely a commercial venture, or does it represent an effort at an artistic and worthwhile document? Has he chosen to amuse, instruct, propagandize, convince, delight, enthrall, excite, startle, or otherwise arouse his audience? In what style has he written? Has he used the conventional structure of the "well-made play?" What elements of drama have received his greatest attention? Does he have a theme? What questions does he raise or answer? To what age or cultural level does he appeal?

Has the director used the original text, an adaptation, a revision, a translation? Was the choice a wise one? Has he altered the playwright's emphasis on plot, character, mood, or theme? Has he cast wisely? Has the text of a familiar play received the director's own interpretation, an entirely new one, or the conventional one? Does the director seem to have emphasized the theme projected by the author; how has he treated it—seriously, facetiously, with tongue in cheek, lightly, satirically? What aesthetic or personal style is seen in the production? How has the director balanced empathy and aesthetic distance; reality and theatricality? How has he treated the production in color, line, mass, pace, rhythm? How has he used sound, lighting, and scenic effects to tell his story?

Has each technician cooperated with the director's interpretation, yet brought to the production his own particular gifts and talents? Have any of them detracted from or especially added to the production? Is any element in the designs symbolic?

Have the actors been impersonators or interpreters? Have they exploited their own personalities? Are they well rehearsed, adequate in imagination, vocal and physical training, emotional impact? What has each individually brought to the performance? Are they playing subtly, broadly, in a specific style? Are the characters drawn or played as stereotypes? Do the actors work as part of an ensemble? Are they fresh, easy, restrained, convincing? Do they mean to be?

How well has he done it? This is the critic's opportunity to place his judgment on the degree of success the artist has achieved. Here, we evaluate his technique, his methods, his talent, and his success in attaining goals such as those we have recognized in question one. We are now concerned with the effectiveness of the whole production, and that effectiveness is measured by the principles that we have chosen for yardsticks of our dramatic knowledge. We are now evaluating the artist's personal form and technique as outlined in Principle Two.

Is it worth the doing? Again the goal of the artist is brought into focus, but now we raise the question of value in time and effort on the part of both artist and viewer. We may ask: Was the script or production worth the time of the author—of all those involved? Did it merit the audience's time and money? Has the same thing been said or done too many times or better? Is the piece stage-worthy? Has it added to the stature or experience of any of the participants? Has the performance helped anyone in any way? Has it been done too often or too recently in this area? Was it worth reviving? Does it promote theatre in general or raise theatre standards? In short: What was its worth or its purpose?

PRINCIPLE FIVE: The Theatre Is a Meeting Ground of All the Arts and as Such Consists of Five Areas—Drama or Script, Actors, Technicians, Director, and Audience, Each of Which Must Be Properly Evaluated Before the Whole Production Has Been Seen.

For many years the fine arts were considered to include the dance, music, poetry or literature, sculpture, painting, drawing, and architecture. Some recent standard dictionaries have listed an eighth— dramatic art. In any event, the theatre is perhaps the one place where all the elements of all the fine arts meet on common ground. In the acting, we find the bodily movement and gesture that compose the dance. In the speech of the actors and the total sound of the performance, we find the rhythm, melody, and harmony of music. The drama itself, with its words and meter, is the poetry or literature. The line, mass, and color of the graphic arts—which include sculpture, painting, drawing, and architecture—are found in the scenery, lighting effects, and set décor. The theatre has always been closely associated with the aesthetic aspect of man's existence. Of late the importance of unity in the dramatic production has developed into the art of the theatre.

In approaching the subject from the historical angle, we find that in every race and in every civilization there is evidence that dramatic performance was an integral part of the two original arts—dance and music. The dance has often been called the mother of the arts and music the universal art. Drama came third, for primitive man gave vent to his feelings and emotions through the physical expression of the dance. He soon accompanied it with the rhythm of the tom-tom, and the first drama emerged when dialogue was added. Thus, drama and dramatic art became a part of man's daily life through primitive man's dramas of love, hatred, food-getting, initiation, sacrifice, and historical representation.

The work of every artist must reflect recognition of the pillars of the fine arts: unity, emphasis, rhythm, balance, proportion, harmony, and grace; but the director of the dramatic production must be especially aware of them. This will be more fully discussed in the chapter on the Director and Direction.

As students of both drama and theatre, we must recognize that the crafts as well as the arts become important ingredients as the actors, technicians, director, and audience are brought into the total picture. Many elements make a play, and a play is made for many people. Even the spelling of the word *playwright* rather than *playwrite* would indicate that a play is *made* rather than written—made by the contributing efforts of all who are responsible for the whole production. The theatre is a genuinely cooperative art. It is, in effect, a five-ring circus. Until the areas represented by the playwright, the actors, the technicians, the director, and the audience have been evaluated, we have not really seen the production. In many respects the audience is the most important contributor, for the others have from the beginning been working for its satisfaction, approval, enjoyment, and entertainment. Until the theatregoer has recognized and honestly judged the contributions of every artist involved, and understood the audience's reaction, he has not really seen a play.

PRINCIPLE SIX: The Theatre, as a Synthesis of the Arts, Exists for the Audience and Has Specific Obligations to That Audience Whose Time and Money It Accepts.

The theatre must always make its appeal to the audience rather than to the individual. This fact broadens the concept of what is beautiful and emphasizes our conviction that art, and certainly the theatre, must never restrict itself to an "art for art's sake" existence. Such a statement is utterly without validity, for the theatre belongs to the people and should exist for and speak to them. Poetry may make its appeal to 10 per cent of the population; for the drama to do so is suicide.

This responsibility need never discourage experimentation, growth, and change. On the contrary, it may stimulate them, for audiences are willing to learn and are ever seeking something new. Although audiences have always been receptive to change, the theatre artist, more than any other, may be compelled to move slowly. He must never forget that he is the servant of the many.

Every participant in the theatre finds a kind of elation or delight in his work. As much as any other individual these workers want to share that joy, for, as Tyrone Guthrie has pointed out, the joy of expression is normally greater if it can be shared. Sir Tyrone goes on to say:

> Some pleasures seem greater if they are shared with a limited and carefully selected group of participants, maybe with a single partner. This is the basis of what we may call the Mandarin view of art. According to this view, works of art acquire merit as they are enjoyable by fewer and better equipped connoisseurs, or Mandarins. The higher the fewer.[7]

There is agreement that the theatre exists for the audience; indeed, most people would insist that the theatre should give the audience what

[7]From A LIFE IN THE THEATRE by Tyrone Guthrie. Copyright © 1959 by Tyrone Guthrie. Used by permission of McGraw-Hill Book Company.

it wants. But each contributor talks in terms of a different audience—the audience that, in his thinking, *wants what he wants.*

The true lover of the theatre who would criticize producers or directors who cater to the lower dramatic taste and conceive the theatre to exist only as escape, just as severely would chide those who would sacrifice entertainment and cry out for only intellectual drama or theatre with a message. This latter group includes any who propose to use the theatre as an extension of the pulpit, the platform, or the classroom. Its members see the theatre not as an art in its own right, but as a tool for pointing up and dramatizing their own ideas. One side is as much in error as the other. The so-called purveyors of escapism may talk of "giving them what they want" and "show business" while the other faction cries out for "art theatre" or "social significance." The former group demands nothing of the audience, and the latter often asks too much. Eventually both are doomed to failure, for each is soon faced by a disappointed and steadily diminishing audience.

We contend that the audience goes to the theatre to be moved emotionally and that the theatre is first a chapel of emotion, with a play's emotional content more important than the intellectual.

If a theatrical experience can teach a truth of life, inspire the audience to do finer things, thrill them with poetry or literary quality, send them out better equipped to face life, or challenge them intellectually, then the experience has been truly worthwhile. Horace said very wisely in 34 B.C., "He who joints the instructive with the agreeable, carries off every vote by delighting and at the same time admonishing. . . ." Basically and foremost, however, the theatre must give its audience an emotional experience. One *feels* greatness before recognizing it intellectually.

It is the further obligation of the theatre to give the audience far more of life than its members could have lived in the period of time they spent in the theatre. It must accent the lessons and truths it presents, paint the characters so vividly that the audience may come to know and understand them. The story may parallel or may differ radically from life as experienced by the audience, but it must always furnish the vicarious experience and emotion that only the theatre can give.

Except for a very short period in the last century, man has always demanded that the theatre as an art *seem* real rather than *be* real; that it *reflect* life and not *be* life; that it be always an *illusion.* It is in this element of *seeming* that we find the real art of the theatre, although the exact degree has varied throughout the ages and among the many types and forms of drama and theatre. Shakespeare's admonition, "Hold the mirror up to nature," supposes a special kind of mirror—one that reflects for the audience just what the artist would have it see, but never allows that seeing to confuse art with life itself. John Gassner has called this "theatrical reality."

A fourth obligation of the theatre is always to make the audience *believe* what it sees—at least for the time being. The light of the morrow and the process of careful analysis may reveal certain implausibilities, but these must never be obvious during the performance. The emotion, spirit, and illusion of life must be present.

Finally, the theatre must at all times tell the truth about its people and about life. When it lies or the audience no longer believes it, at that moment it ceases to exist as an art. This does not mean that plays must be realistic in their style and the settings naturalistic, or even that the subject matter must be close to actuality. A fantasy can be just as true as the most realistic play if the characters in that fantasy and the setting against which it is played *are consistent with the laws of their imagined existence. The Tempest* and *The Blue Bird* are just as true as the most literal representation of life. And their truth or theme may be far more lasting in our memories.

To summarize, the theatre's five obligations to its audience are:

1. The theatre must make its appeal to the audience rather than to the individual.

2. The theatre must move its audience emotionally.

3. The theatre must give its audience more of life than they could live in the same period of time.

4. The theatre must *seem* real as it creates an illusion of life.

5. Theatrical illusion must be a truthful picture of life and one that the audience must believe—at least while in the theatre.

PRINCIPLE SEVEN: The Audience as Part of the Total Dramatic Experience Has Certain Obligations to the Artists Who Make Up the Theatre.

Throughout these pages the audience is foremost in our thoughts. Every artist is working in the hope of sharing an experience with the audience; of bringing to it some measure of entertainment, for which the audience will in turn give its sustained attention and immediate appreciation. This sought-for attention and appreciation make the audience an active participant in any dramatic production; it is as much a part of the success or failure of a production as is the contribution of any theatre artist.

The theatre has been described as a strange combination of imagination and reason. The nature of the ideal audience is half child, half adult, which knows something of both literary and stage values, but above all, possesses a respect for the theatre as an institution and as an art. Only then will an audience, like a child, give tangible evidence of its pleasure, its sympathy, its delight, and its exaltation. This giving is imperative if the fire of ecstasy is to be kindled for both actors and spectators. Cornelia Otis Skinner tells of having spent an unbearable hour and a half with an audience that refused to respond to the humor that had convulsed most audiences. The gloom of her dressing room was matched only by her own distress when she was visited by a woman who said, "Oh, Miss Skinner, it was so wonderful. It was all we could do to keep from laughing!"

Psychologists have pointed out that audiences, in general, have certain qualities that make them different from individuals. This principle has been further treated by John Mason Brown[8] and also by Clayton Hamilton in his essay "The Psychology of Audiences."[9] Each of these men has described the characteristics of an audience. The following is a summation of the metamorphosis that takes place when the average man becomes a part of an audience:

> He loses his higher and more personal sensibilities of intellect or character;
> . . . is less intellectual and more emotional;
> . . . is less reasonable and judicious;
> . . . descends several rungs in the ladder of intellectual maturity. He demands a struggle, is boyishly heroic, carelessly unthinking, easily credulous;
> . . . wants to take sides, to hiss or to applaud;
> . . . finds that emotion is contagious, does what his neighbor does;
> . . . is more sensuous, loves costumes, color, spectacle;
> . . . is more commonplace, demands the love of woman, home, country, right;
> . . . is more conservative;
> . . . is a little hard of hearing;
> . . . is unpredictable.

Someone has divided the theatre audience into three extremes—the escapists, the moralists, and the artsakists. The escapists want to forget the responsibilities and problems of their everyday life, asking only to be amused and clamoring for the lighter plays or musicals. They are referred to as the "tired businessmen," although they are found in all professions and sometimes, surprisingly enough, have brilliant minds.

Not long after *Death of a Salesman* had completed its road tour, a professor from a large university was heard to condemn that play be-

[8]John Mason Brown, *The Art of Playgoing* (New York: W. W. Norton & Company, Inc., 1936).
[9]Hamilton, *Theory of the Theatre.*

cause it had haunted him for days, and he seemed not to be able to put it out of his mind. Asked why he had not liked the play, he answered, "It had nothing to say." Those within hearing were quick to point out that Arthur Miller had said a great deal with his theme, showing that a man who builds his life and that of his family on a shallow, ethically unsound foundation is doomed to failure. The professor readily agreed, but said that what troubled him was that there were too many people in America exactly like Willy Loman. Then came the answer that would have been expected from anyone but so distinguished an educator, "To tell you the truth, when I go to the theatre, I want something light and entertaining."

The second audience type consists of those who demand that the theatre uplift, teach a lesson, preach a sermon, picture some part of life of which they personally approve. They would close their eyes to anything with which they do not agree, and insist that only "beautiful and nice clean plays be presented." We find these persons in every community, and they are one of the greatest problems that the director in the noncommercial theatre must face. They blind themselves to the fact that evil exists in the world, sometimes refusing to accept the theatre as a reflection of life. Members of this group, which we may call the *moralists*, are honest neither with themselves nor with the artists whom they criticize.

The so-called "artsakists" shudder at box-office success and disdainfully refer to all popular theatre as "show business." They deny that the theatre belongs to the people and would claim it for their own little group of supposed intellectuals. They smugly imply that popularity with an audience only signifies mediocrity and that courting it is far beneath the true artist.

To please these three extremes and the millions who lie somewhere between is not an easy task. In *The Art of Playgoing*, John Mason Brown says:

> Stand at the entrance to any theatre when the audience is assembling; look into its multitudinous face; study its varying expressions; attempt to gauge the separate minds which are mere cells in its composite brain; think of the conflicting interests, perceptions, backgrounds, vocabularies, sympathies, standards, convictions, consciences, and levels of sophistication from which his giant body is sprung, and the challenges and difficulties faced by dramatists in presenting such situations, ideas, and characters as will be comprehensible and acceptable to the crowd even when they are satisfactorily meeting our own quite different individual demands will be made clearer for us than any textbook or dramatic technique has ever been able to make them.[10]

[10]Brown, *The Art of Playgoing.*

The variety of what an audience may most appreciate is unlimited. Some may desire the lines of Sophocles or Shakespeare, and others, the lines of today's most popular motion picture actress. One may choose a play that propagandizes a religious or social theme, another an historical romance or biography. To some a line of pretty chorus girls backed by spectacular scenery and accompanied by lively music may have a far greater appeal than a stellar production of *Murder in the Cathedral*. One may clamor for revivals of the classics or a dramatization of a famous novel, the naturalness of Chekhov or the farce of Neil Simon, the preachments of Shaw, the epic theatre of Brecht, the searchings of Pirandello, the time relativity or fourth dimensional philosophy of J. B. Priestley, the negativism of the absurdists, or the intellectual challenge demanded of the theatre by Eric Bentley.

Forming as it does an integral part of the theatre experience, the audience has certain obligations. The *good* playgoer does not look upon the theatre as merely a temporary vacation from his personal problems. He asks that it provide more than escape, and he puts no limitations on the artist's conceptions or beliefs but permits him to use whatever material he may need to tell his story. Nor does he demand any particular style of entertainment. When he enters the theatre, he makes a certain surrender to it—not a blind surrender, for he retains his judgment and his taste. However, he accepts the theatre as make-believe, as a world built for him by many people; and he, as part of the audience, will try to evaluate their efforts.

The good playgoer realizes that the theatre is a synthesis of all the arts. He does not think only in terms of story, actors, scenery, or lighting, or costumes. He realizes that he may like one part of a production and be disappointed in another, and that condemnation or praise of the whole based on a single contribution is unjust. He appreciates the fact that the theatre is capable of moving him in many ways, but that the whole experience is a two-way proposition—a game that he, too, must play.

He knows that at the very heart of all theatre pleasure is what Shakespeare called "imaginary puissance" or a sort of temporary half-belief. This half-belief does not demand that he blindly accept one stage setting as "Hamlet's castle," or another setting as "the home of Willy Loman," but that he does not set up in his mind the argument that he is *not* seeing Elsinore or the home of Willy Loman. Coleridge once said, "True stage illusion consists not in the mind's judging it to be a forest, but in its remission of judgment that it is *not* a forest."

The *poor* theatregoer is sometimes disturbed when he sees people he knows playing parts that are contrary to his accepted beliefs, as in the case of the college professor who said to the director, "Please don't ever cast one of our fine young people in an objectionable role, for always afterward one is reminded of that character when he meets him on the street." Such individuals are utterly lacking in imaginary puissance. They refuse to give actors their rights as artists to be actors and to speak the lines of someone else.

Contrary to this narrow and wholly unjustified viewpoint, the good playgoer gives the actors, the scenic artist, and all those involved with the production the opportunity of taking him into their imaginary world. If actors, technicians, and director fail to accomplish their goal, after the playgoer has given them ample opportunity through his imaginary puissance, then the playgoer has the right to offer adverse criticism of them as artists. It will show more intelligence on his part, however, and give him greater personal pleasure if he is able to tell *why* they have or have not failed to accomplish their goals.

The good playgoer recognizes his own prejudices and tries to rise above them. He may not care for a given actor or for a particular type of dramatic event, but he does make an effort to judge honestly by giving every artist his right to work as he chooses.

The final obligation of the audience is our basic premise of dramatic criticism: the three questions of Goethe, cited as Principle Number Four.

The reader will do well to understand the five basic obligations summarized below, for they are the minimum essentials of being a good theatregoer. Each member of the audience should:

> 1. View each dramatic event with an ample supply of imaginary puissance;
> 2. Recognize his own personal prejudices;
> 3. Observe and evaluate the work of *all* the artists who have made the production possible;
> 4. Accept each artist's right to express himself as he desires;
> 5. Ask—always—the three questions of Goethe:
>> *What is the artist trying to do?*
>> *How well has he done it?*
>> *Is it worth the doing?*

So much for the audience itself, collective nature, and how it differs from the individual in what it demands of a performance; but none of this should be forgotten in any analysis we make of a production.

We shall now go a step further and consider the requirements of the good dramatic critic as opposed to the average playgoer. Although it is not our goal to create professional critics, people frequently have opportunities to express publicly their opinions on what they have experienced in the theatre. Although what they may say is still just an opinion, it does, under these circumstances, carry greater weight and should, therefore, be backed by greater knowledge.

We have already used the expressions "critic" and "dramatic criticism" too loosely and in doing so have added to the common confusion of these terms with "reviewer" and "play review." A similar error consists of saying, "I read a play," rather than, "I read a script," or "I read a drama." A *play* can only be seen and heard—in production with an audience present. This distinction will be further developed in the pages that follow, but it was necessary to mention it before establishing the true difference between the "reviewer" and the "critic." These two misconceptions are so deeply embedded in the minds of the general public that it would be useless for us to try to alter the common interchangeability of the terms, but we, as specialists, should be perfectly clear regarding the meanings of these terms.

Any statement concerning a dramatic event is, in essence, the re-creation of feelings into thought for, as John Gassner so ably put it: "Criticism consists of describing the inter-action that occurred during a dramatic performance when each of its three entities—the script, the production, and the audience—acted and was acted upon by the other two." If critical writing is to possess any authority, the author should possess some special personal qualifications. Ideal characteristics include an abiding love and respect for the theatre; as broad a background as possible in the history of theatre and dramatic literature; a knowledge of many plays; a wide experience with life on many levels; an acquaintance with people and their relationships with each other; the possession of taste and discrimination; an understanding of the form and techniques of all the artists involved; the ability to recognize creativity and talent wherever it may lie, and to distinguish between genius and mediocrity; a thorough knowledge of one's own prejudices as well as the ability to discount those prejudices; and a sincere appreciation of what the theatre has been, is, and can be. A flexible foundation of sound dramatic principles and convictions that preferably have grown out of a personal experience in some phase of practical theatre should underlie these traits.

The reviewer reports only what he saw and heard, and how he felt about what occurred and why. He should present reasons for his reactions and his opinions, as well as explain why they were different from those of the audience if that were the case. He frequently estimates how long it will run, or how successful it will be financially and otherwise. Some reviewers estimate what a production has done or may do for the careers of those involved. The reviewer may, and usually does, offer some judgment on how he feels a production will appeal to the general public or just what segment of the people will find it most entertaining or enjoyable. He should take into account the audience present and its contributions to the total effect. This estimate should include answers to the following questions: What sort of people, generally, make up the audience? What classes do they represent chronologically, socially, and mentally? Have they displayed an interest and appreciation? Do they seem to understand the play and what the various artists are trying to do? Is this interest held throughout the performance? Are there definite responses of tears, laughter, applause, or silence? Are the people emotionally moved, or bored? Do they cough, show restlessness, leave during the performance? Is the applause spontaneous, or politely perfunctory? To what type, group, or age does the play make its greatest appeal? Would you advise your friends to see it and why? A reviewer does not go much further.

The dramatic critic will do all this and much more. Dramatic criticism can be said to exist on at least three levels, which we define as the literary, the theatrical, and the practical.

In the literary approach, sometimes called the Aristotelian, one is interested primarily in the literary value inherent in the written drama, and critics have interpreted it in a variety of ways. Some critics are most interested in the script's philosophical or sociological aspects. Others have more concern with the academic aspects of the script, which concern the structure of the drama itself—the relation of form and style, or the techniques each artist has used to weld together substance and form. Others give greater thought to the language of the drama, its characterizations, or its theme.

Critical analysis may also be made from the viewpoint of history. The period in which the drama was written and first performed is taken into account, along with the size and shape of the physical theatre; the evolution of the playing area and seating arrangement, and the varying natures of the audience during the centuries of the theatre's existence.

The first level of dramatic criticism is concerned foremost with the written drama or the work of the playwright, and less with the play's theatrical effectiveness or its popularity with the audience.

The second level is more interested in what the theatre can do for the drama when it becomes a play; how well it acts; what its psychological impact can be in the theatre. Its followers evaluate the script as a theatre-piece as well as a literary work. As aestheticians they are primarily interested in the magic that can be experienced in the theatre through its creativeness and the artistic use of imagination, lighting, scenery, and sound. Their interest lies in the beauty to be brought and the aesthetic effect to be had on mankind, theatrically.

The third level considers mainly the practical and popular theatre whose first interest is in making money through the attraction of great crowds. This "show business" approach is sometimes referred to as Shubertian. (The name is derived from the famous New York producers who for many years made a business of the theatre.) Critics who view a production on this level are interested purely in its popular appeal. The production must be exciting entertainment, which usually means escape. It must attract great crowds. The theatre the critics endorse must cater to the masses and could sometimes be accused of sacrificing integrity and truth for popularity and appeal. It is the criticism we hear most frequently of the Broadway theatre as well as of the motion picture and television.

If Goethe's theory of art criticism is to be our premise, the true critic must make an effort to evaluate on all these various levels—the greatness in drama, the creation of aesthetic enjoyment through theatrical magic, and popular entertainment. He must recognize that all are occasionally found in a single production, that sometimes none are present, and that more often than not there are variations of values even on the same level. A vulgar piece often pretends to be better than it really is; the presence of tinsel, spectacle, and applause can often mislead us.

The good critic will, then, try to ascertain why a script was written or a production attempted or what the playwright or director was trying to say. He will analyze the sociological, psychological, and philosophical impacts the script might have had when written and if these could differ today. He may compare one production with previous ones, and the work of the playwright, the actors, the director, and technicians with previous work by them and by others in their respective areas. He will try to judge script and production in terms of art as well as entertainment. He may even reveal how he thinks various artists could have improved the work. He analyzes the audience and their reactions. He tries to discover and analyze the real values inherent, realized or unrealized.

The good critic considers the whole event in terms of unity, emphasis, balance, proportion, harmony, grace, and rhythm. He weighs all the evidence in trying to discover just where an entire work may stand in theatre or dramatic history. Ever aware that this is *Theatre*—a world apart whose object is to picture many worlds of many periods, moods, fantasies, and imaginings—he also knows that an illusion may appear in many different styles.

A good critic or even a reviewer should have some specific standard, some personal demands that he would require or look for in a production. In a recent National Theatre Conference symposium on dramatic criticism, respected professionals presented their own criteria for their work, as follows.

Henry Hewes of *Saturday Review* noted that he always asked himself four questions about each artist involved: "Is he sincere?" "Is he imaginative?" "Is he truthful?" and "Does he show originality?"

Thomas F. Driver, who has been drama critic for *The Reporter* and other magazines, said that the four qualities he has looked for in plays are: vitality in the artist's work, fidelity to reality (which is not the same as realism), control of the medium, and taste.

Harold Clurman, director, author, and theatre critic for *The Nation* said,

> Every play makes both a statement and an emotional impact; the critic's duty is to judge whether the statement has value, has relevance to human experience, as well as to describe the emotional impact so that his readers can feel it. The theatre as a whole must communicate. *What* is it communicating? This is as much the critic's job to determine as the director's. He must criticize in *depth*, realizing that the playwright's intention is primary.

John Beaufort of *The Christian Science Monitor* set forth his own "critical commandments" in this way, "The critic must respond—be modest—respect the public—beware of power, either real or imagined.— never sneer—never kill with a word—honor the creative spirit—welcome new talent—hail the audacious innovator—be kind to the producer, and above all—crusade for the living theatre."

Norman S. Nadel, drama critic for the Scripts-Howard Organization, although he did not speak at the meeting, submitted the following statement:

> My approach to the critical function might best be expressed in questions I ask myself, and for which I seek answers in the play and its production:
>
> 1. What is the intent? If comedy, which of several styles and functions? If drama, which kind? If it is a less easily categorized form, such as the intentional enigma of Edward Albee's *Tiny Alice*, I must be able to recognize it as such, and evaluate it accordingly.
>
> 2. Is the intent realized? If the play achieves its purpose, why and how does it achieve it? If not, why not? This leads to:
>
> 3. Analysis by parts—writing, directing, acting, ideological content, emotional values, character development, character relationship, physical mounting, proportions, etc.
>
> 4. Was it worth doing? Is there sufficient justification—as truth, character dissection, suspense, satire, fantasy, farce, preachment or whatever the one or several purposes?
>
> 5. For my total approach to the theatre as an art form and to each play in particular, I can best quote something by my good friend, the distinguished critic and theatre scholar, Dr. Joseph T. Shipley, author of *Guide to Great Plays*, a very useful reference work. He—and I— look for the three E's in ascending order: Entertainment, Enlightenment, Exaltation. An acceptable play can entertain. The worthy play enlightens in one way or another; we are informed—mentally and emotionally enriched by the experience. The great play—Shaw's *Saint Joan*, for example—exalts. The spirit is lifted up, inspired, ennobled.

The late John Gassner, who spoke at the meeting, would also have emphasized the latter part of Nadel's criteria. Gassner's advice to the critic suggested that he should possess the "resistant flexibility" commended by Colley Cibber, that he should combine critical severity with discriminating charity, that criticism involves a revelation after a conflict of minds. Further, one should always be conscious of the type of play, remember that the classics were both commercial and avant-garde in their day, always respect an exciting idea even if it is not perfectly executed, and ever remember the five big "E's" of the theatre: Entertainment—Enlightenment—Exaltation—Expression—with a special emphasis on Enthusiasm, which, when translated from the Greek means "the presence of a God!"

Such sound advice from so prestigious a group of critics should be given serious consideration. We shall now mention three other outstanding critics, with further discussion of John Gassner. The reader should become familiar with the work of these four men. Although their work represents the very top of their profession, it was a rare occasion when any three or four arrived at the same conclusion about a production or a single artist.

Brooks Atkinson, who was for many years dramatic editor of *The New York Times* and whose work is still esteemed, was always known for his fairness, his integrity, and his insight and understanding of the theatre's conventions. He demanded the very best of all those who would work in the theatre, placing great stress on substance and idea. A cornerstone of his critical standard was that the play should be optimistic in tone and should show a genuine faith or respect for mankind with love for one's fellow men. He could find greatness in the play that professed such a faith, even though he might be critical of the playwright's form and technique. He could praise the plot and characterization as well as the theatrical effectiveness of a play, but criticize the fact that it left the audience at a dead end—frustrated and in a dilemma. Brooks Atkinson praised the inconsequential *Blithe Spirit* (he once called Noel Coward "the master of the inconsequential"), or *The Man Who Came to Dinner* as fine pieces of theatre, but regretted that they lacked substance. Atkinson, who seemed always to be looking for the best that he could find, would consider a second-rate piece of art with something to say preferable to a first-rate play of diversion.

Walter Kerr, drama critic for *The New York Times*, has been a playwright and a director as well as an actor and a college professor of theatre. All this has given him a grasp and knowledge of what the drama can be in the theatre. Few critics understand the art of acting and directing as well as he. It is this background, coupled with his flair for expression and his high standards in all phases of production, that makes his writing so interesting and so challenging. As a man of the theatre he understands and recognizes the audience as the real master. He has faith in that audience and places great stress on the importance of the play's popularity. He has respect for Broadway and its ability to do great things. When it fails in this respect, Kerr can be very acid in his remarks, which are frequently both pithy and witty. His "theatre sense" is highly developed, and he sees the drama as a work of art that has not realized itself until it has been successfully done in the theatre. He measures greatness by audience appeal, although he demands integrity, proportion, and clarity in every production. He is convinced that the minority theatre has never produced an important work and that every great play has come out of a popular playhouse.

A critic who must always be given serious consideration is Eric Bentley, the youngest of the group. He is more a literary man and scholar than a man of the theatre, but his contributions have been enormous since he published a provocative work, *The Playwright as Thinker*. A more recent book, *The Life of the Drama*, indicates that in the intervening years he has not only altered his premise but mellowed a bit toward the theatre as an institution. He is still opposed to the so-called popular theatre—Broadway as we know it. In this respect he and Kerr are still poles apart. Eric Bentley follows the Mandarin point of view insisting, too, on the necessity of government subsidy, the importance of the intellectual. He would have the audience raise its own standards rather than theatre artists aiming to please that audience.

For our fourth critic we return to John Gassner, who was, perhaps, the most prolific writer on the theatre in modern times. He was known for his brilliant mind, his apparent knowledge of all subjects and their history, and the constant challenge he demanded of theatre, whose inherent values and weaknesses he understood so well. He was a liberal in that he seemed to be ever searching for a new way of approaching or interpreting theatre values. More than any other critic he was able to go to the very heart of a play and find its value as literature or as theatre. His vast knowledge of both makes for exciting reading. In his book *The Theatre in Our Times*, Gassner stated his demands of the theatre so well that the passage is quoted here in full:

> I believe that the American stage is most vital when closest to American sensibility and interest, whatever their shortcomings, but that the European enterprise in theatre provides a necessary perspective and corrective. I also believe that realism and contemporary interest alone can give us a living theatre, but that realism should not limit us to realistic technique or style while contemporary interest should not limit us to commonplace or topical matter and attitudes. I grant the importance of *re-theatricalizing* the modern drama that realism *de-theatricalized*, but do not believe that theatricalism can be the sole end of an art, that attained cultural stature in modern times with Ibsen, Strindberg, Chekhov, and Shaw. We must develop or

re-define dramatic and theatrical forms, but these should not be regarded as absolutes rather than as a means for making drama a more intense or revealing experience. I believe in stylization, but suspect a tendency among stylizing modernists to "style" humanity right out of the theatre in the name of art. I do not expect all good drama to be "literature," but am gratified when it is that, too; I favor literary drama, but require it to be theatre as well. I like to be entertained as much as anybody else, but prefer to be stimulated. I favor excitement, but prefer to be excited into some recognition or to some purpose. My quarrel with many of our effective plays is that they are excitative without being formative. I also favor a critical spirit in the drama, but like the theatre to be intelligent rather than intellectual.[11]

There are common pitfalls in analyzing dramatic productions, and one of the great dangers in drama reviewing or criticism involves a desire to be clever, to say the smart thing or to play with words. The annals of critical writing are filled with devastating comments by sharp-witted critics who may have found the event less than satisfying.

A series of such comments is given below for your entertainment rather than for their instructive value. Clever as these remarks may seem, and justified as they may have been, they do *not* constitute dramatic criticism. Even though they come from the pens of some of our most noted critics, they may be classified pejoratively, as attempts to be clever. *The Reader's Digest Reader* lists them under the title, "When the Critics Crack the Quip."

> When Mr. Wilbur calls his play *Halfway to Hell*, he under-estimates the distance.
>
> . . . Brooks Atkinson
>
> Katherine Hepburn [in *The Lake*] runs the gamut of emotions from A to B.
>
> . . . Dorothy Parker
>
> [Tank-town performance of *Uncle Tom's Cabin*] The dogs were poorly supported by the cast.
>
> . . . Don Herold
>
> The locale [of *The Liar*] is seventh- century Venice and as any student of painting knows, the dames then had high rounded bust lines. In her first act costume, which had a V-shaped bodice, Miss Lawrence was quite interesting because she looked like an ingeniously arranged double-scoop ice cream cone. (Vanilla)
>
> . . . John Chapman
>
> He played the King [Lear] as though someone led the ace.
>
> . . . Eugene Field
>
> *If Booth Had Missed* missed so completely that even the ushers failed to show up on the third night.
>
> . . . George Jean Nathan

[11]From THE THEATER IN OUR TIMES by John Gassner. © 1954 by John Gassner. Used by permission of Crown Publishers, Inc.

Perfectly Scandalous was one of those plays in which all of the actors, unfortunately, enunciated very clearly.

... Robert Benchley

(Entire review of *Tonight or Never*) Very well, then, I say never."

... George Jean Nathan

Excuse me for mentioning it, but a play called *Are You Decent?* opened last night.

... John Mason Brown

As dangerous as the temptation to be clever is the tendency of the writer to cite picayune details or minor accidents in performance rather than to search for the real dramatic values. If ever the old expression about not seeing the forest for the trees is applicable, it is here. The untrained critic pounces on a fluffed line, a delayed light cue, a property not wholly authentic, some light discrepancy in make-up, a ravelling on a costume, or some similar detail not worthy of mention. Sometimes, however, a total production features faults like these so numerous or so blatant as to denote carelessness on the part of the artists, or to take precedence over major elements of the production. That is another story, and adverse criticism is justified, although the details themselves need not be mentioned individually.

First nights in any theatre are often chaotic affairs. The nervousness of the entire company and the importance of the event often produce unforeseen accidents, but the discerning critic never allows them to sway his opinion of the production as a whole.

This second danger may easily lead into a third. It is especially typical of the novice, although certain seasoned playgoers and professional critics seem never to enjoy a dramatic event because they have become so involved in looking for something wrong that they miss the valuable points of the art itself.

The intelligent playgoer soon finds that such pettiness is only an early phase of his development. Soon he ceases to think of details and begins to study the production as a whole. When he arrives at this point, criticism will take its logical place and become a factor in greater theatre enjoyment. He likewise soon becomes aware that the word *criticism* need not imply the adverse qualification, for the honest critic may also praise.

The cardinal rule for the beginner in dramatic criticism should be: Have some good reason for whatever opinion is expressed.

In presenting a written criticism, one should never tell the story. It is permissible to tell the theme and maybe what the play is about. Information should never be revealed if it will mar the enjoyment for one who reads the criticism before seeing the event. This means that the critic should assume that the reader has not seen the performance.

A critic should always be as objective as possible in his reporting. Where emotion is involved, objectivity is very difficult, but the critic should report the reaction of the audience—especially if it has differed from his own. He should then analyze either reaction and strive to find a reason for it. Of course it is not an easy matter to place the blame when a production does not seem quite right. There are so many elements involved, and their interworkings are similar to the cogs of a huge machine. One cannot locate the source of the problem by casually examining either the machine or a production. Even artists of the theatre with their professional knowledge may differ in just which "cog" needs adjustment. Thus experienced playwrights are often reluctant to allow nonprofessional groups to try out their new scripts. Only through an audience reaction can a playwright find a weakness or rectify his errors. But, as Marston Balch has written:

> The colleges and universities are in a uniquely advantageous position to be able to nurture and assist new playwrights to present, if only experimentally, new dramatic work—not only plays by their own students, but worthy scripts received from writers already at grips with the formidable obstacles of the professional and producing theatre.

Dr. Balch continues by quoting a well-known and successful playwright who, when asked whether he would be inclined to submit a new script for a campus premiere, replied:

> "I don't know. I certainly wouldn't jump at it unless I had no faith in the script at all—if so, why inflict it on a college group? I am not being snobbish. I have nothing to be snobbish about. What would bother me is that semitrained actors can raise hell with parts. How would I know whether I was wrong or the actor was wrong? Would it be right to make a line simpler because the actor couldn't do it? Since a show is completely re-written during rehearsals, what would the end result be if each part was tailored to the ability of each actor —to say nothing of the director?"[12]

The problem of recognizing where a fault lies was brought home vividly as this book was being written. The New York production of *Philadelphia, Here I Come!* generated much enthusiasm for the sensitivity, universality, quiet humor, and characterizations; the fine balance of realism, expressionism, and theatricalism; and the generally imaginative quality in writing and production. A careful reading of the text gave assurance that this would be an ideal modern script to use in Chapter Two.

When the road company was scheduled to appear in a nearby city, we attended the performance eagerly. A more than mild disappointment

[12]Marston Balch, "Prologue," *The Tufts University Theater*, xxii, No. 2, December, 1966.

followed when the whole production seemed to lack all the qualities so evident in New York. The story, the stage movement, the lines spoken, even five members of the original cast—including the two leads—were there. Nevertheless, the production lacked the sensitivity, feeling, truth, and excitement so evident in the earlier experience. The audience did not respond to the humor, and the actors reacted with the same indifference. They seemed to be "walking through" the play.

An audience vote would undoubtedly have blamed the play; but it was the same script that had delighted audiences in New York for a long run, received almost unanimous critical acclaim, and barely missed winning the Critics' Award as the best play of the year. Only a discerning member of the audience would have placed the blame on the actors, where, in our opinion, it belonged. Because the material, the humor, the dialect, and the setting were unfamiliar to this Midwest audience, the actors had an additional job to do. However, they did not sense this need, did not care, or were weary from having played the roles for over a year. When the audience did not immediately catch the spirit of the play, the actors responded with the same coolness. They failed to follow the advice of Howard Lindsay, who played so successfully the role of Clarence Day in *Life With Father*. He said: "If you can't amuse them, convince them." If this cast had brought back to their performances the same spirit and feeling they had displayed in New York, the audience would have soon become involved.

It is not necessarily the critic's duty to say what should have been done, for he is not a creative artist. He is a reporter who also includes his opinions on the artistic merits of the occasion. He need not mention everyone concerned, but should single out outstanding individual efforts. Fundamentally, a critic judges the play *and* the production on the basis of his own response or reactions to it. It is his duty to be didactic—to make up his mind, to speak his feelings—whatever they may be—honestly, forthrightly, sincerely. "The best dramatic criticism," Burns Mantle once said, "is like writing a letter home."

Although a dramatic evaluation may carry more weight because it appears in the morning paper and may seem more authentic because the writer has prestige, it is not necessarily more honest or of greater value than the opinion the average theatregoer with some real theatre knowledge, who has conscientiously followed an honest set of principles of dramatic criticism.

In conclusion, we present ten items we believe should be incorporated in any theatre criticism. The first five are concerned with the critic himself and involve both the obligations of an audience and the requisites of a dramatic critic as they have been previously discussed. The second five are concerned with the work of the artists involved in the production.

All ten draw upon the facts, principles, and opinions that have been or will be discussed in this book in an effort to explain the substance, form, and technique of those who make up the theatre—playwright, actors, technicians, director, and audience. The application of these ten statements should bring forth an intelligent and honest evaluation of a dramatic production.

Ten Commandments of Dramatic Criticism

1. *I must* constantly—in all my theatre experience—use imaginary puissance.

2. *I must* know, understand, evaluate, and discount my own prejudices.

3. *I must* evaluate each of the theatre's five areas and the work of all artists involved in the production.

4. *I must* measure the entire production in terms of life and understand what each artist has personally contributed through and of himself to make or mar the production.

5. *I must* arrive at every decision only after using Goethe's three principles of artistic criticism.

6. *Each and every artist* must make crystal clear what he is trying to say through proper emphasis, sincerity, and technique.

7. *Each and every artist* must work within the medium at hand or successfully adapt any elements borrowed from another medium.

8. *Each and every artist* must cooperate and coordinate his work toward a single goal which is, in turn, the theme or the purpose of the production.

9. *Each and every artist* must seem real and be wholly believable in his contribution to the production, which is a work of art; in short, each must give a picture of life interpreted through his personality.

10. *In the final analysis* the production may move me, stir me, excite me, amuse me, teach me, or transform me, but the one thing it *dare not do* is to bore me. The one thing it *must do* is send me on my way somehow better equipped to face life.

All the verbs used in Commandment Ten have been carefully chosen, for it is a basic tenet to our theory of dramatic criticism that the theatre exists on several planes and can be many things to many people. There is ample room in our world of theatre for *The Odd Couple* and *Waiting for Godot*, for *Auntie Mame* and *Long Day's Journey Into Night*, for *Charley's Aunt* and *Mother Courage*, for *Three Men on a Horse* and *Hamlet*, for *Blithe Spirit* and *Oedipus Rex*, for *Who's Afraid of Virginia Woolf* and *Bus Stop*, and for all the levels that lie in between.

As individuals we might prefer the theatre that gives us more than mere escape, but at times we might also profit from purely escapist dramatic fare. We might favor the theatre that is a teacher and an art, but we would not dismiss that which only attempts to amuse or to excite. The release of these emotions can also send us on our way better equipped to face life.

We would now suggest that all this background and what will be said throughout these pages be permitted to sink into the substrata of your being to be used only in general terms rather than specific, for nothing is so annoying as the bandying about of technical terms in general conversation or discussions. We do suggest that the wise theatregoer open his mind when he opens his programs; try to see not only those dramatic events that promise to be good, but also those that are prospectively bad. A poor production sometimes has more to teach than a great one. (Indisputably, bad art is helpful in recognizing the good.) It is well, furthermore, to see the plays one has sworn never to see; to think again about the performance approved so highly a few nights ago, and forget what the professional critics have said. In the theatre one should always be prepared for a surprise—many times it may be a very happy one!

Achieving the balanced attitude described above constitutes the chief difference between the educated and the cultured man. The educated man knows the facts, but the cultured man, although he may have stored away fewer facts, is able to assimilate those he knows, apply them to the world about him, fit them to his own needs, and arrive at a personally meaningful appreciation. In short, the artist and the cultured spectator can speak one language.

Questions for Discussion

1. Show how your experience with any dramatic event—stage, motion picture, or television—was marred because some individual in the audience did not observe the obligations of an audience member.

2. Name a television program that you would rather observe with a group than alone and explain why. Name one that you would prefer to see alone.

3. Can you remember a time when an audience either made a poor play seem successful or a generally good play seem less so?

4. Give an example of a person wholly unqualified with respect to knowledge of the subject, who tried to criticize a dramatic production.

5. Choose any one of the opinions expressed on pages 11–12 and present arguments for or against it.

6. Choose any of the seven basic principles presented in this chapter and present arguments for or against it.

7. List three or four of your opinions so far as the theatre, motion pictures, or television are concerned. Try to find some dramatic principle out of which this opinion has grown.

8. Make up your own list of five facts, five opinions, and five dramatic principles you now accept as valid. Try not to use any that have been discussed in this chapter.

9. Name a character in a play whom you have found most pleasant or delightful. Would you like to have this character as a neighbor or a personal friend?

10. Apply Goethe's three questions to the total effect of any recent effort—stage, screen, or television.

11. Choose any well-known television program and break its script down into the elements of art—substance, form, and technique.

12. Contrast the Mandarin theory with the current rating systems so powerful in television.

13. Give some examples of occasions when you or others have acted or reacted differently because you were members of a crowd.

14. Can you name among your acquaintances an escapist—a moralist—an artsakist—so far as the theatre is concerned? How do they, or you, justify each stand?

15. Have you as a participant or as a member of a theatre audience witnessed two performances of the same production? How did they vary? What was the reason for the change?

16. Read the report of a reviewer or critic. Has he written a review or a criticism? How closely has he answered the questions raised in this chapter?

Bibliography

For Supplementary Reading or Special Projects

Albright, H. D., William P. Halstead and Lee Mitchell, *Principles of Theatre Art*. New York: Houghton Mifflin Company, 1955.

Altshuler, Thelma and Richard Paul Janaro, *Responses to Drama*. Boston: Houghton Mifflin Company, 1967.

Barnet, Sylvan, Morton Berman, and William Burto, *Aspects of the Drama, A Handbook*. Boston: Little, Brown and Company, 1962.

Bentley, Eric, *In Search of Theatre*. New York: Alfred A. Knopf, Inc., 1953.

————, *The Life of the Drama*. New York: Atheneum Publishers, 1964.

————, *What is Theatre?*, Boston, Mass.: Beacon Press, 1956.

Brown, John Mason, *The Art of Playgoing*. New York: W. W. Norton & Company, Inc., 1936.

Clurman, Harold, *Lies Like Truth*. New York: Grove Press, Inc., 1958.

Dolman, John, Jr., *The Art of Play Production*, (rev. ed.). New York: Harper & Row Publishers, 1948.

Gassner, John, *Directions in Modern Theatre and Drama*. New York: Holt, Rinehart and Winston, Inc., 1965.

————, *The Theatre in Our Times*. New York: Crown Publishers, 1954.

————, *Theatre at the Crossroads: Plays and Playwrights of the Mid-Century*. New York: Holt, Rinehart and Winston, Inc., 1960.

Gorelik, Mordecai, *New Theatres for Old*. New York: Samuel French, Inc., 1940.

Guthrie, Sir Tyrone, *A Life in the Theatre*. New York: McGraw-Hill Book Company, Inc., 1959.

Hamilton, Clayton, *The Theory of the Theatre*. New York: Henry Holt and Company, 1939.

Hatlen, Theodore W., *Orientation to the Theater*. New York: Appleton-Century-Crofts, 1962.

Hollingworth, H. L., *Psychology of the Audience*. New York: American Book Company, 1935.

Kernodle, George, *From Art to Theatre*. Chicago: University of Chicago Press, 1944.

MacGowan, Kenneth and William Melnitz, *Golden Ages of the Theater*. Englewood Cliffs, N.J.: Prentice-Hall, Inc., 1959.

Marx, Milton, *The Enjoyment of Drama*, 2nd ed. New York: Appleton-Century-Crofts, Inc., 1961.

Rowe, Kenneth Thorpe, *A Theater in Your Head*. New York: Funk & Wagnalls Company, 1960.

Seltzer, Daniel, *The Modern Theatre Readings and Documents*. Boston: Little, Brown and Company, 1967.

Whitman, Robert F., *The Playreader's Handbook*. Indianapolis: The Bobbs-Merrill Company, Inc., 1966.

II

The

Script

2

The Play

and the

Playwright

As we begin a consideration of dramatic literature, the playwright as he has appeared in time, and the plays he has written, it seems logical to read widely in the world literature of drama. However, there are always the questions: Why read a play? Why not simply experience the play in the theatre? There are at least three good answers, two of which have been given force by John Gassner in his introduction to the *Selected Plays of Sean O'Casey*:

> It is customary, of course, to maintain that a playwright's place is on the stage, as indeed it is. But if he is not to be found on it, there is all the more reason for looking for him in the library ... and in a theatre poorly suited to the prime requirement of keeping masterpieces on display, productions have not exactly been lavished upon Ibsen, Strindberg, and Chekhov either. They, too, along with the great Greeks, have become largely books for us. For immortality, indeed, the great playwrights need to interest us as readers as well as playgoers. They are dependent upon the theatre of the mind as well as upon the theatre of the boards.[1]

First then, the important intermediary, the production, may be missing or inadequate. Often, too, its artistic integrity does not equal that of the original dramatic creation. Great performances of music can be recorded and almost the same artistic experience made available at any time

[1]John Gassner, Introduction to *Selected Plays of Sean O'Casey* (New York: George Braziller, Inc., 1956), p. vii.

anywhere. Leaving out for the moment the mass media—cinema, radio, and television, which have special limitations of their own—we realize that the great stage production is likely to be limited to live performances in New York or London or Paris or Berlin or Moscow, once in a decade. Once it is finished, "untaped," it is lost except in memory. For great drama to be available as we need it, we are sometimes forced to rely upon reading.

Second, as Gassner points out, the greatest plays must serve in dual capacities—"the theatre of the mind as well as the theatre of the boards." We may find that a charming play "on the boards" loses its charm in the book, and its interest is ephemeral. Some plays, of course, read well but are impossible to produce. These are likely to be found in a category called closet drama, to which we shall return. They may be legitimate literature, but are not likely to be legitimate drama until such time as production catches up with them, if this ever happens. The greatest drama can be given exciting performance either in the theatre or in the imagination. And the greatest drama acquires new dimensions for the sensitive receptor when he both reads and sees, rereads and views again, the same play. Certainly *Hamlet* grows in meaning during one's experiences from sixteen to sixty, in the book and on the stage—Walter Hampden to Sir John Gielgud to Sir Laurence Olivier, to Richard Burton—and the possibilities for growth seem unlimited.

The third reason for reading plays is a reciprocal one—you can see and hear more when you subsequently go to the theatre. You should, of course, go to the theatre as training for reading plays. From such experience you can extract a guide to the production of a play in the mind. You can assemble all the star performers, make the settings as lavish or as austere as you wish, and repeat the scenes you wish to view again. The intermediary production retains its significance, but it is the receptor who produces. Such practice makes for a better critical receptiveness in the theatre itself.

The section at the end of this chapter, Tests of a Play's Greatness, may be needed as a basis for analytic discussion of individual plays; but the section itself grew out of analysis and discussion. The problem is something like that of the chicken and the egg. Perhaps the best plan is to read through and return. Simultaneity simply cannot be achieved.

Toward a Definition

In most theatre and theatrical experiences the playwright and the play, or the dramatist and his drama, come first in time. Then the performance is put together, then the play goes before the audience.

There are exceptions. Sometimes, for example, the "playwright" is hardly identifiable. In the case of improvisations or pantomimes the playmaker's functions may be taken over by the actor. The *commedia dell' arte* in Italy worked from an outline of action and without a dialogued script. And sometimes, for one reason or another, the form of a play has been imitated by a writer who has no intention of staging a performance before an audience in the theatre. This is called closet drama and bears the same relationship to legitimate drama as does the artistic epic to the folk epic or the artistic ballad to the popular or folk ballad. Of course, closet drama—Milton's *Samson Agonistes*, for example—may at some later time be given production. (Milton was too much the Puritan to visualize his "drama" on the boards of a Restoration theatre.) But these exceptions do not affect our basic assumption that a writer makes a play, the writer's play is remade in a theatre, and the theatre's play is then performed before an audience.

This cannot be overemphasized: The written manuscript of a play is a drama, referred to in the theatre as the script. It does not actually become a play until it is brought to life by actors, before an audience. As a play the written script becomes a new work of art involving the interpretation of the playwright's creation on the part of the actors, the scene designer, the costumer, and other technicians. All these artists are more than mere interpreters. They too are creating as the written drama becomes something new, the play as performed—a sort of fusion of the arts, as Richard Wagner viewed it. It is the director (the French call him the *metteur en scène*, the "putter on the stage") who, in our modern theatre, unifies and pulls together everyone's efforts and so translates the drama into a play. That organism will vary from performance to performance, and the reaction of the audience contributes to this variation. This is one reason that drama, of all the forms of literature, is most like music among the fine arts in its dependence upon performance. (The dramatist is analogous to the composer; the director, to the conductor; the actors, to the musicians.) Conversely, it is why theatre has to depend on the dramatist, just as music requires a composer. This helps to explain why the greatest playwrights have almost always had broad experience of the theatre, often as actor and/or director —Molière, Shakespeare, probably the Greeks, and to some extent Ibsen. Molière was, perhaps, the most fortunate in that he wrote his plays, directed them, and usually acted a major role.

The word *drama* comes from the Greek verb for *to do* or *to act*. Aristotle, in the *Poetics*, makes drama a form of poetry and by extension treats it as one of the arts that "are all in their general conception modes of imitation." He then points out that the objects of imitation are persons acting, and later that tragedy is "the imitation of an action." He distinguishes between narration, in which the poet can either take another personality or speak unchanged in his own persona, and drama, in which the poet imitates "by making all his actors live and move before us." The dramatist does not tell his story, he shows it. Clayton Hamilton's definition has the virtue of simplicity: *A play is a story devised to be presented by actors on a stage before an audience.*

Unlike the novelist or the essayist, the playwright must constantly think in terms of how the words will sound to the ear rather than how they read on the printed page. He must omit descriptions and speak in terms of action and movement. He must be constantly aware of the pictorial effect, the rhythm of speech, the setting, the properties, and the acting. He must know the limitations of the physical theatre for which he is writing and realize that the theatregoer cannot go back and re-read a speech to make sure he has got the full meaning. Furthermore, his characters must be vital and interesting individuals with dynamic personalities. (Not many of our acquaintances would fit, as-is, into a play.) Every individual in a play must be distinctive, possessing both a will and a purpose. In real life we are often unsure of other peoples' motives, but in a play we must be sure or the characters become blurred.

A play must have conflict or at least some element of crisis. Something must constantly be happening, and this movement must be revealed through the acts or lines rather than by exposition on the part of the author or by the speeches of the other actors. A play must possess dramatic movement, which means that the characters are always reacting to stimuli. Growth or change of some kind—not necessarily physical —must always be present, reflected in a constant alteration of relationships.

The playwright must think in terms of the contemporary physical theatre, and remember that structure helps to determine both the form and the aesthetic style of his play. Historically, the physical theatre has been largely responsible for the sweep and grandeur of Greek drama, written as outdoor religious spectacle, the poetic power of the Elizabethans, the brilliant and often vulgar theatre of the Restoration, the artificial, extreme morality of the Victorians and, finally, the popular language spoken in the more realistic theatre that came into prominence soon after the middle of the last century.

A playwright frequently has specific actors in mind when he creates his roles. Our best evidence that Richard Burbage must have been a great actor is that William Shakespeare wrote for him such roles as Hamlet, Macbeth, and King Lear. More recently Robinson Jeffers did *Tower Beyond Tragedy* and *Medea* primarily as vehicles for Dame Judith Anderson. Some plays have appeared great in the hands of the actor for whom they were written, losing that prestige when the star was no longer able to play the role.

More than any other man in literature, the playwright must write with an audience rather than an individual in mind. He knows the variety of his society and his potential audience. Other literary men may create for a small group or class or even the individual. They may choose their clientele—but the writer of a play cannot. He is, or is not, chosen by his public. He must appeal to the widest possible audience, from the youngest and most uneducated to the oldest citizen or deepest thinker of his day. A full appreciation of any play is dependent upon a knowledge of the relation of the subject to the time and society for which it was written.

The tools of the playwright are the very elements of drama. They include the story or plot (the specific incidents that make up the story), the theme or idea (which is the truth or generalization concerning life that the play is trying to make), the characters involved, their language or dialogue, and the mood or atmosphere that the play seeks to create. A sixth element, spectacle, sometimes calls attention to itself when the work is not sufficiently endowed with the five major elements to hold an audience. Spectacle rarely possesses real literary value. It may consist of the use of mob scenes, beautiful costumes, musical backgrounds, dance extravaganzas—sequences that present elaborate stage pictures but make little contribution to the ultimate goal. Aristotle, in the *Poetics*, arranged the six elements of drama in what he conceived to be their order of importance: plot, character, thought, diction, song or melody, spectacle. Different ages produce different designations and arrangements, but the continuity is more vital and remarkable than the changes.

These historical considerations—the physical theatre, the occasion or individual prompting the choice of particular material, the audience, the society of the period, and the emphasis upon certain elements of drama in certain periods—suggest a closer look at the development of drama. We should consider its history from its beginnings, stressing eras that have given us our theatrical literature and that may contribute significantly to the latest play. There is nothing absolutely new in the area of human and dramatic experiences, only infinite recombinations and sharpened relevance to the present.

Drama in Ancient Greece

Although the beginnings of drama are hidden in antiquity, most scholars agree that drama developed more or less independently among the ancient Greeks in the seventh and sixth centuries B.C., the Hindus of the first century A.D., and the Chinese, lost in time, probably from primitive religious festivals and imitative dances and, especially in the East, from shadow plays, puppet shows, and pantomimes. Oriental drama, however, developed and was arrested in development almost without European contact and exerted negligible influence upon European drama until very recent times. (The Japanese Noh play, for example, helps to explain some of the drama of William Butler Yeats.) The greatest influence in the theatre of the Western world remains the Classic Greek play.

As we look back at the rise and fall of the greatest periods of dramatic art, three periods (two without dispute) seem to stand out preeminently: the fifth and fourth centuries B.C. in Athens; the (Renaissance) sixteenth and seventeenth centuries in England, France, Spain, and Italy; and the modern period, we add with perhaps too much pride, beginning with Ibsen in the second half of the nineteenth century and manifesting itself continuously in almost all the countries of Europe, in Britain, and in the United States.

Three other periods of real creativity and interest—but not quite equal to the greatest—may be seen in Roman comedy of the second century B.C.; medieval drama of the fourteenth and fifteenth centuries, particularly in England and France; and the brief flashes of Restoration England following the 1640–1660 curtain on the English Renaissance. Except for a very occasional isolated dramatist of interest (Goldoni in eighteenth-century Italy, for instance), the stretches between are relatively arid. Our historic sketch will comprise main periods and will, in general, remain silent in the desert places.

The origins of Greek drama were cloudy even to Aristotle, and the conjectures of scholars are more numerous than they are certain. Among the more enlightening theories are those relating Greek drama to religious festivals in honor of Dionysus and Demeter and to the Pindaric ode. One significant fact about the beginnings of drama anywhere is its relation to public worship and religious rites. This connection gives drama a certain high seriousness and central place in human experience.

Dionysus, or Bacchus, was the Greek god of wine and fertility, a young deity in the Olympian hierarchy whose worship spread with frenzy. Demeter, an older goddess, was patroness of the grains and harvest; crop fertility depended upon her favor. In any country where bread and wine were necessities of life, the importance of Dionysus and Demeter to the public welfare was self-evident.

The Greeks' pagan worship sprang up not from a sense of sin but for propitiation of and gratitude to these nature divinities. There was, therefore, the seriousness of conventional religiosity but also a gaiety in celebration that we of a more ascetic Judaeo-Christian culture do not usually associate with worship. Mystery religions, like the cult of Eleusis, flourished in pre-Periclean Greece. Priests, their assistants, and the initiates developed increasingly elaborate ceremonies of worship, including the dance, singing, and incantations before an altar. At the Dionysia in Attica—the rural autumn festival for the harvest and the greater or city festival in the spring for the sowing—drama is said to have developed in the twin channels of tragedy and comedy. Certainly both were established, if still relatively primitive, by the time Aeschylus appeared as a dramatist, about 500 B.C.

The ode, a form of lyric poetry, was probably older than drama and thus ready for adaptation to dramatic uses. Both the earliest forms of Greek literature, the epic and the lyric having attained maximum development in Homer, Pindar, and Sappho, were at hand for and contributed to the dramatic artist. The first gave him subject matter, the second, technique and form.

Let us glance at the Pindaric ode, a highly formal, public, ceremonial lyric poem, divided into strophe (or stanza), antistrophe (which had to match in rhythm and structure the strophe), and epode (a stand, or afterpiece). Normally, an ode was composed to honor an event of public importance—an Olympic contest or a military victory—and presumably was given public performance. Elaborate compliments to the gods and goddesses were included.

We can say, if only by analogy, that the earliest Greek dramas were highly lyrical, not far removed from the ode. It has been supposed that the priest and his assistants in a chorus chanted to a processional dance from the altar of the amphitheatre the strophe, returned to their initial position chanting the antistrophe, and in fixed position chanted the epode or stand whenever one occurred. Gradually there developed solo lines for the priest and the beginning of dialogue between priest or leader and the chorus. Narrative elements began to assume importance in the lyrical, emotional praise of the god—a story connected with the legendary life of Dionysus would be acted out, still in highly formalized fashion.

This account, however conjectural, prepares us for the innovations of Aeschylus and for his lyrical dramas, in which drama can be seen to emerge, freeing itself from the parent forms. Aristotle says, in the *Poetics*, that "Aeschylus first introduced a second actor; he diminished the importance of the Chorus and assigned the leading part to the dialogue." Although *Agamemnon* (and the whole *Oresteia*, of which trilogy it is the first play) is the best known of the works of Aeschylus, it represents a more advanced development of drama, by including the Sophoclean third actor, than certain earlier plays. In the *Prometheus* and *The Suppliants*, for instance, one can almost see what pre-Aeschylean drama could have been like at its best. The Suppliants are the fifty daughters of Danäus, fleeing from the fifty sons of Aegyptus in pursuit of matrimony. Led by their father, Danäus, they are the chorus and principal actors in the drama. Pelasgus, King of Argos, and the Herald, are the actors separated from the chorus. The Argive ancestor of the Danaides (who were born in Egypt) was Io, who has an important role in *Prometheus Bound*. Aeschylus was committed, in the earlier plays, to turning "a series of events into drama almost without the help of action." In the lyrical tragedy of the single actor like Prometheus, such a drama, says H. D. F. Kitto, "cannot and need not move, but nothing is more foolish than to assume that on this account it is undramatic. The drama lies in the lyrical plane, and consists of an increasing tension." It is, then, the growth of emotional impact in an essentially static, although dramatic, situation. (After all, Prometheus bound to the rock is about as static as you can get.) It is good to remember this possibility for drama when we come to the modern period, although between Aeschylus and Chekhov European drama followed a somewhat different course. Although for Aristotle, in the century following Aeschylus, Sophocles seemed to be the superior tragedian, and for many moderns the more psychological Euripides has greater appeal, it would be a mistake to consider Aeschylus primitive and a lesser figure than his successors.

The *Oresteia* has the highest claim to a permanence of interest. The sheer theatricality of the brooding opening scene of the watchman and the signal fires from Troy, the confrontation of Agamemnon and Clytemnestra in the struggle over the purple carpet, the chorus of old Argive men arguing with a frenzied Cassandra, the pursuit of Orestes by the Furies (and earlier by his sister, Electra) is still highly effective, even in fairly close translation of the original Greek. And when you look at the large number of step-children of this trilogy, beginning with adaptations by Sophocles and Euripides down through Eugene O'Neill's *Mourning Becomes Electra*, Jeffers's *Tower Beyond Tragedy*, and T. S. Eliot's *Family Reunion*, to mention only a few, you have some idea of the achievement of Aeschylus. In many ways he seems comparable to the writers of Old Testament literature, particularly in his concern with religious, moral, and ethical problems. The theme of Agamemnon's story might be paraphrased in the biblical warning: "The sins of the fathers are visited upon their children, even to the third and fourth generations." Aeschylus saw his drama in the situation of man in the universe.

Oedipus the King

Sophocles had a different concept of drama; the tragedy was in man, the real conflict in himself. Oedipus the King is the model Aristotelian tragic hero, a good man with a tragic flaw or error in judgment who brings upon himself catastrophe out of proportion to the fault. Events are ironical; good intentions are not sufficient for salvation. Sophocles added a third actor (a technical innovation amounting to a breakthrough rationale for any number of players subsequently necessary) and further diminished the role of the chorus, often treating the chorus as an actor in the drama. *Oedipus Rex* is probably the most typical Sophoclean play, certainly the one Aristotle refers to most often in the *Poetics* as the best of its kind. He makes at least ten specific references to this play as admirably fulfilling the functions of a tragedy.

The action of *Oedipus Rex* is unified and compact. In the beginning, Oedipus is approached by a priest and a chorus of Theban suppliants and begged to relieve the distress of his city caught in a plague of sterility. There is no harvest. Flocks and herds and women produce no young. Civil panic has reached a state of emergency. The king, concerned by the problem, has sent Creon, a kind of prime minister and his wife's brother, to the oracle at Delphi for advice. Creon enters with the news that the murderer of the former king, Laius, must be apprehended and punished; this is the pollution that infests the land. Oedipus questions, "Where in the world to find the far, faint traces of a bygone crime?" and is answered, "Who seeks shall find; who sits with folded hands or sleeps is blind." From this point on, we have a detective-story investigation in addition to the tragic development. Oedipus, who had once saved Thebes by guessing the riddle of the Sphinx, responds in pride, "I will once again make dark things clear." He then pronounces sentence on the murderer: banishment and utter rejection. Tiresias, the blind old Theban soothsayer; Jocasta, the queen; the messenger from Corinth; and finally the herdsman of Laius all contribute to the progressive revelation that Oedipus himself is the criminal he seeks. The king's initial reaction is disbelief—it must be a plot by Creon and Tiresias to gain the throne—and anger. After a doggedly stubborn search for the truth, Oedipus experiences catastrophe: his mother-wife Jocasta commits suicide, and he mutilates himself, blinding the eyes that saw not. But, although blind, he has gained self-knowledge and understanding, and the audience is left at his self-banishment "with calm of mind, all passion spent." The action of the play has been continuous, with no intermission, and contained well within the single revolution of the sun that Aristotle recommended. The unities of action and time even pulled along with them the post-Aristotelian (Neoclassic) unity of place. Setting: Thebes. Before the Palace of Oedipus.

The character of Oedipus fulfills equally well Aristotle's requirements for the tragic hero. He is essentially a good man, larger and nobler than the average, born into a royal family although ignorant of his true parents. He has impulses to serve others and to control his own fate;

Stratford Shakespearean Festival, Ontario, Canada. Scene from *Oedipus Rex*, 1955; directed by Tyrone Guthrie. Center: Douglas Campbell as King Oedipus surrounded by the old men of the chorus.

his faults are human faults, not mean or degrading ones. Pride and impetuosity bordering on impatient anger are part of his nature; they serve him well in the pursuit of truth, yet ultimately contribute to his downfall. He makes errors in judgment, but acts with the best information he possesses; unfortunately it is not enough. Who among men is not faced with making decisions under similar circumstances? This permits, even makes necessary, our feeling of fear for ourselves as well as our pity for Oedipus. Our experience of emotional catharsis or cleansing is as close to inevitable in our involvement with this drama as in any other. To match the experience we must come to Shakespeare.

The character of Oedipus has been established by the time the play opens, but it is revealed progressively in the course of the play's action and in frequent references to his actions in earlier times. The catastrophe brings Oedipus to intense suffering, worse than death, out of proportion to assignable guilt, but his acceptance of responsibility in his hard-won knowledge increases the stature of his nobility. Additionally, there remains a dimension of mystery in the character of Oedipus that makes him human beyond analysis. The play also presents us with finely realized characters in Jocasta, Creon, and Tiresias, all dramatically effective in their own rights and in confrontation with Oedipus.

The theme of *Oedipus Rex* is larger and more significant than any statement of it. It has to do with the human condition: Let no man consider himself happy until he has come to the full course of his life. The chorus expresses the thought most succinctly: "For he who most doth know of bliss hath but the show." Suffering and disaster are the common lot of man, even of kings. But it takes an Oedipus to say, "So be it."

The dialogue and diction in this play are brilliant (even in inadequate translation of the Sophoclean original) in variety, scope, and rhythm. The measured and stately speeches of the characters are relieved at appropriate intervals by what the Greeks called *stichomythia* or dialogue in single alternate lines, often a question and answer fencing pattern between two opponents.

The changes of pace are always in keeping with the action. Here, for example, is a part of Oedipus's confrontation with the herdsman, leading to the ultimate revelation of the truth:

> OEDIPUS: Arrest the villain, seize and pinion him!
> HERDSMAN: Alack, alack! What have I done? What wouldst thou
> further learn?
> OEDIPUS: Didst give this man the child of whom he asks?
> HERDSMAN: I did; and would that I had died that day!
> OEDIPUS: And die thou shalt unless thou tell the truth.
> HERDSMAN: But if I tell it, I am doubly lost.
> OEDIPUS: The knave methinks will still prevaricate.
> HERDSMAN: Nay, I confessed I gave it long ago.
> OEDIPUS: Whence came it? Was it thine, or given to thee?
> HERDSMAN: I had it from another, 'twas not mine.
> OEDIPUS: From whom of these our townsmen, and what house?
> HERDSMAN: Forbear for God's sake, master, ask no more.
> OEDIPUS: If I must question thee again, thou'rt lost.
> HERDSMAN: Well then—it was a child of Laius' house.
> OEDIPUS: Slave-born or one of Laius' own race?
> HERDSMAN: Ah me! I stand upon the perilous edge of speech.
> OEDIPUS: And I of hearing, but I still must hear.
> HERDSMAN: Know then the child was by repute his own.
> But she within, thy consort best could tell.
> OEDIPUS: What! She, she gave it thee?
> HERDSMAN: 'Tis so, my king.
> OEDIPUS: With what intent?
> HERDSMAN: To make away with it.
> OEDIPUS: What, she its mother?

HERDSMAN: Fearing a dread weird.

OEDIPUS: What weird?

HERDSMAN: 'Twas told that he should slay his sire.

OEDIPUS: Why didst thou give it then to this old man?

HERDSMAN: Through pity, master, for the babe. I thought
    He'd take it to the country whence he came;
    But he preserved it for the worst of woes.
    For if thou art in sooth what this man saith,
    God pity thee! Thou wast to misery born.

OEDIPUS: Ah me! Ah me! All brought to pass, all true!
    O light, may I behold thee nevermore!
    I stand a wretch, in birth, in wedlock cursed,
    A parricide, incestuous, triply cursed.

(Exit Oedipus)

Song and spectacle in *Oedipus Rex* are mostly reserved to the chorus of Theban suppliants or elders. Their major role, perhaps, is to stand between the audience and the action, to interpret and state ideas. Dramatically they create movement.

Euripides, the most modern of the ancient Greek tragedians, has often been called romantic and might be called naturalistic. He saw man, and especially woman (witness the shift of interest from Agamemnon and Oedipus to Medea, Iphigenia, the Women of Troy), in the trammels of a nonrational universe, and he made protest against things as they are. He achieved penetrating psychological analysis of human character. He further reduced the importance of the chorus so that it might in the future be adjunct to the action, like the gossiping women in *Medea*, or eliminated. The dramatic conflict in his works is most often between man and man or between man and woman. His play *Hippolytus* might more accurately have been called *Phèdra*, as it was when redone by Racine in the France of Louis XIV.

Tragic drama achieved its greatest expression, exploring vast possibilities of dramatic concept concurrently with the development of comedy. However only the eleven comic plays of Aristophanes remain today of an extensive Greek comedic literature. Here is the gaiety of a Bacchic festival, or orgy, if you prefer. Even the gods may be tipsy, as Bacchus is in *The Frogs* and sex (fertility) is exploited for its full comic worth. Aristophanic humor is bawdy but not obscene, as many Victorian readers assumed. It helps, perhaps, to remember that huge phallic symbols were part of the stage props for old Greek comedy. Sex was not then associated with the idea of sin; the subject was treated openly, honestly if enormously; and there was not yet what D. H. Lawrence calls the rubbing of the "dirty little secret," or innuendo. Like Rabelais,

Aristophanes is as "healthy as a barnyard," unrepressed and uninhibited. Since Aristophanes, sex and drink have been staples in comedy. Politics, too—no public figure in free Greece was safe from attack. "Monkeys and nightingales in the treetops" remains perhaps the best summary of the Aristophanic comic approach.

The Birds

It is difficult to select the one play by Aristophanes that best represents his unique contribution to the world of comedy. It could be *Lysistrata*, that wonderfully ribald peace play where the women win the battle between the sexes in order to stop the battle between Sparta and Athens. Complete with the phallic props we have just referred to, the kind of lusty dialogue that probably only Rabelais has since approached, and choruses of old men and old women in fantastic antic conflict, *Lysistrata* represents one side of Aristophanes very well. The best of another side might be *The Frogs*, which makes good fun of Dionysus or Bacchus himself along with Aeschylus and Euripides. The play, although somewhat literary and disjunctive, has the wonderful device of a chorus of frogs chanting along the River Styx, an Ur-Bronx cheer to punctuate pomposity and profundity alike. But put to the final hard choice, probably *The Birds* best shows the complex of what Aristophanic comedy has so richly to offer.

The Birds by Aristophanes, directed by Walter Kerr. Courtesy The Catholic University of America.

The action that sets up the comic situation can be told briefly. Peisthetaerus and Euelpides, two Athenian citizens, fed up with law suits and taxes and the public banalities of that most enlightened and self-satisfied of democracies, decide to seek another homeland where presumably they will find some tax advantages. They decide to go to the birds. A whole aviary provides a noisy and colorful chorus. The leader of the birds, the hoopoe, who is really Tereus (man turned bird in the rather infamous Procne-Philomela story), is intermediary for the political entrepreneurs from Athens. The plan is to build a wall separating men and gods and bring both to recognize the sovereignty of the birds. In a remarkably short time this is accomplished, and Cloudcuckooland is named and founded.

The satire is then directed against new Athenian visitors to Cloudcuckooland, opportunists who want to get in on the deal: a priest, a poet, an oracle-monger, a land surveyor, a commissioner, and a statute-seller. Iris, the goddess, flies by, blusters, threatens, is terrified, and flies back to Zeus. Soon arrives a peace-seeking deputation from the Olympian gods—Poseidon, Heracles, and the uncivilized Triballian—and the birds get all their demands, including the goddess Sovereignty as a wife for Peisthetaerus. A wedding with the birds singing praise to Hymen appropriately closes the comedy in as you like it fashion.

Comic themes are interwoven in *The Birds*:[2] politics, money, pretensions, prattfalls, and sex (which rears its beautiful head only occasionally, with the appearance, for example, of Procne).

> PEISTHETAERUS: Zeus be praised, what a pretty little bird! So
> delicate and fair.
> EUELPIDES: I'll tell you what, I'd kiss her without any hesitation . . .
> PEISTHETAERUS: You fool! She's got a beak like a pair of scissors.
> EUELPIDES: By Zeus, I'll have to shell her like an egg, Take off
> the covering and kiss what's underneath.

At this point the chorus breaks into highly lyrical and lovely praise of Procne, going on to speculate on differences between men and birds:

> Lovely bird of tawny throat
> Precious partner of my song,
> You have brought your silver note
> Here to where your arts belong . . .
> We address mankind, who are naturally blind,
> and decline with the fall of the leaf.

[2]Aristophanes, *The Birds*, trans. Peter D. Arnott. Copyright 1958, by Appleton-Century-Crofts, Inc. Reprinted by permission of the publishers.

Frail creatures of clay that endure for a day,
　　whose estate is compounded of grief.
In the shadows you grope, without wings,
　　without hope, like dream-stuff and
　　destined to die.
So give heed to our words, the Immortals,
　　the Birds, who endure for an age in the
　　sky . . .

The Gilbert-and-Sullivan effect of the choral ode is not at all inappropriate. Men have often dreamed of being birds, of escape, and now the skies are full.

Between the years 499 B.C., when Aeschylus first competed in dramatic contests, and 387 B.C., a probable date for the death of Aristophanes, the greatest drama the world has ever known (save that of Shakespeare, who is their equal) was conceived, written, and produced as plays in Athens. In spite of what separates us from this drama—chiefly stage conventions, verse, and the Greek language—the three dozen or so plays that remain to us from the several hundred of the period have a constant and impressive fascination for us. Why? The perception with which the Greek dramatist probed human nature and experience, and the absolute intellectual, rational integrity with which he stated what he saw plus, of course, the imponderable elements of creative genius supply a partial answer.

Some of the above difficulties that separate the modern reader or theatregoer from Greek drama have occasionally inspired modern "innovations" in the theatre. They have even given the modern audience the impact of the new and different. Thus they should be examined a little more fully.

It cannot be said too often, that every dramatist is bound by (limited or freed by) the stage conventions of his time and place. In ancient Greece plays were produced in the brilliant Mediterranean sunlight, in a large amphitheatre, for which our closest analogy, architecturally speaking, is probably the football stadium. Immediately some of the problems are revealed. Obviously the dance, group chanting, and exaggerated, formalized gestures would be good ways of "reaching" the audience (think of half-time entertainment on the football field). The tragic and comic, masks that were worn by Greek actors would be a good indication of the kind of play being performed. The subtleties of facial expression would be lost by distance anyway. The masks also served as megaphonic devices in the absence of electronic public address systems (and they were more reliable than some of our equipment). The mask must have produced an additional effect, a distancing—an effective, if not deliberate, barrier to realism; a solemnifying effect for tragedy, a Joe E. Brown-Jimmy Durante hyperbolic effect for comedy. Reintroduced into the theatre at intervals since the period of Greek drama, use of the mask can be startling and exciting (as, for instance, in Eugene O'Neill's *The Great God Brown*).

Besides the differentiation between tragedy and comedy by means of masks, the use of the buskin (*cothurni*, or elevated shoes) for tragedy elevated characters literally as well as figuratively, and the use of the sock (no shoes at all) diminished the stature of comic types. The chorus, however lessened its importance in the hands of Euripides, remained an integral stage convention for both tragedy and comedy and gave a solid, formal, massive, public core to Greek drama. The focal center of the theatre itself remained the altar to the god placed in the middle of the orchestra (a dance area in its original meaning) before a formal scene building that might represent either temple or palace. Obviously action, to be logical, had to be confined largely to one place—there was no curtain, and the columned portico was too solid to move. This limited action to the orchestra and the portico. Action off stage could be reported, however, which may account for the numerous messengers in Greek drama (not any more numerous, it must be confessed, than the maids and butlers of the past hundred years). Violence normally occurred within or at a distance. The cries of Agamemnon or Medea's children could be heard, and the chorus might pantomime the action. Machines were employed for special effects, sometimes very spectacular. The *deus ex machina* came from above, and the *eccyclema* was wheeled on to display an interior scene. One stage direction, for example, in *The Birds* reads, "A turn of the eccyclema brings out the Hoopoe, together with a portion of his dwelling, a little copse." An effect of this sort might be a riot for comedy but not appropriate for the tragic intensity of *Oedipus Rex*.

Perhaps an even greater impediment to direct modern experience of Greek theatre is the use of verse. Actually, the use of prose for drama is the real break in tradition and an almost modern innovation. The most accurate translations of the Greek plays are in prose, but the effect of the plays themselves is lost. Poetic translations may approach the original effect, but even the best is crabbed and diffuse compared with the Greek. Today we have almost, if not quite, lost the habit of poetry, the spontaneous emotional response to the music of words arranged in rhythmic pattern. Happily some Shakespearean passages still evoke this reaction. And in the modern theatre there have been repeated attempts to return poetry to the stage—by T. S. Eliot and Christopher Fry, for instance. Some of the efforts have been fairly successful. The arguments for and against verse drama make a large chapter in modern dramatic criticism. The proponents have at least a firm ground in history.

Difficult though the study of the drama of the ancient Greeks may be, it remains absolutely necessary for twentieth-century man if he is to understand his own theatre and his own world. All in all, *Oedipus Rex* is the almost perfect tragedy for the ancient Greek theatre as we have reconstructed it. It was made to fit contemporary stage conventions with an accurate conception of maximum effects—action, masks, chorus, *cothurni*, gesture, poetry, and significance. A state university theatre production in 1967 announced *Oedipus Rex* as "the towering summit of world theatre." If *The Birds* does not equal in comedy the position of *Oedipus* in tragedy, perhaps it is because comedy itself is more diffuse in its effects. Old comedy (the Aristophanic) can not pretend to speak fully for new comedy that comes after.

Roman Drama

Following Aristophanes, there developed in Greece "new comedy," chiefly associated with the name of Menander. But none of his plays is left in the repertory of the theatre. Fortunately, it appears that the best of Menander was appropriated or plagiarized by the Roman writers of comedy, Plautus and Terence in the second century B.C. New comedy, as opposed to old, was decidedly more sophisticated. It has been supposed that there was a shift from rural to urban life reflected in subject matter and in audience composition. Wealth brought refinement. The phallic symbol disappeared or at least diminished to a gesture, and the comic use of sex followed somewhat subtler channels. Comic types were established that are recognizable in the modern theatre: the miser, the braggart soldier, the duped husband, to mention a few. The figure of the mother-in-law gives us a good idea of the immediate comic effects of the introduction of a stock character with the weight of a tradition of laughter behind it.

The Roman theatre produced some technical innovations that moved drama a little closer to the modern. Scenic design brought the play somewhat nearer the pictorial effect; the city street with rows of houses down either side apparently the equivalent of painted flats (very much like our old vaudeville curtains) permitted action closer to the houses of people less removed from the audience than princes or priests. The chambermaid could (and did) throw a pot out a second-story window, and "policemen" could pursue a second-story man down the street.

Further innovations and peculiarities in Roman drama led to excesses and eventual disintegration. Theatre in Rome was not so much associated with religion and worship as with spectacle, in its later manifestations completely reversing Aristotle's order of importance for the elements of a play. Games or *ludi*, the circus, chariot races, and even naval battles staged in a water-filled orchestra were typical of the time. (Perhaps our ice shows and aquacades are modern developments of the same kind of spectacle.) If the people have no bread, let them be entertained into forgetting their political and economic miseries. As the Roman Empire deteriorated after Augustus, sensational, indecent, exotic, and spectacular elements increased in the Roman theatre. As the Christian era began in Rome after Constantine, who died in 337 A.D., the immorality and decadence of the theatre and the theatre itself were suppressed. This was probably the beginning of a long antagonism. But the best of Roman drama, the work of the comic playwrights Plautus and Terence, belonged to the much earlier period of the Roman Republic.

Almost two hundred years before the birth of Christ, Plautus and Terence were writing comedies (or rewriting those of Menander) that have remained good theatre to the present day. These in turn have received frequent rewritings. *Amphytrion 38* by Jean Giraudoux is an excellent example of this tendency to reuse a good plot. It is the thirty-eighth dramatization, supposedly, of the story that Plautus used in *Amphytrion*. Lunt and Fontanne made this play as fresh on the modern stage as it must have been in antiquity. Another example of the longevity of good comedy is the Plautus *Menaechmi*, which became successively Shakespeare's *Comedy of Errors* and Broadway's *The Boys from Syracuse*.

Note that the new comedy of Plautus and Terence presents us with the tightly knit plot, an often incredibly intricate intrigue with discoveries, mistaken identities, long-lost twins, and all's well that ends well endings. Artificiality is recognized for what it is, and made to serve comic purpose.

Roman tragedy, as represented by Seneca during the first century of the Christian era, was certainly not great drama of permanent interest in the way that Roman comedy is. However, it did exert considerable influence on Renaissance tragedy. For Seneca, subject matter remained the material of the older Greek tragedies, with the one important addition of a tragedy based on relatively recent Roman history. Seneca's treatment of his material was bombastic, heavily oratorical; he emphasized violence and blood (if one killing is good, six are better—a touch of the modern in Imperial Rome) and employed stage machinery such as the trap door. He also used a five-act division that was to be copied by the Elizabethans.

With the collapse of the Roman Empire, Classical drama—Greek and Roman tragedy and comedy—disappeared down its own trapdoor for hundreds of years. Fortunately monks preserved for a later age manuscripts of a large and brilliant repertory. Drama, however, had one thread of continuity from Classical antiquity down to its rediscovery in the Renaissance—the popular, improvisational theatre of the Italian common people, which developed into the *commedia dell' arte* and which has exerted a great influence on more sophisticated dramatists from Molière to Samuel Beckett. The *commedia*, without written script, maintained, modified, and introduced new stock characters in the manner of new comedy and carried over the Greek tradition of masks. Polichinelle, Dottore, and Harlequin, among others, became sign and symbol for laughter. [The thread was undoubtedly pulled thin in the so-called Dark Ages, but it seems doubtful if it broke, so persistent are folk traditions.]

Opinion concerning the values of *commedia dell' arte*, at least as it emerged with the Italian professionals after 1550, has been rather divided in recent times. The beginnings had been Roman Atellan farce, mime and pantomime. Edwin Duerr, in his history of acting, flatly condemns the actors of the *commedia* as having failed in their revolt from the dramatists, and states that they did not see the light until after 1750 when Goldoni told them that actors and playwrights "require the assistance of one another, and we ought to entertain for one another reciprocal love and esteem." When speech became a weak accompaniment to gesture and movement and "stage business," actors turned in desperation to pantomime, to anything that would substitute for words. But the impact of *commedia* performances, however inadequate in themselves, certainly contributed to the dramaturgy of men such as Molière and Beckett, and probably, via whatever means, of Shakespeare as well. It seems best neither to overestimate nor to underestimate the importance of *commedia dell' arte*.

The Medieval Period

In the Middle Ages drama had a new birth in Europe. Consideration of this phenomenon provides interesting parallels with the origins of Greek drama and points to a strong if narrow influence into the modern theatre. The mystery, miracle, and morality plays were born in the Christian church. It seems logical to suppose that the mystery play, a dramatization of the life of Christ or some portion thereof, came first. Visual aids are not a modern discovery. What could be more effective than the Christmas pantomime of the Virgin at the manger, with shepherds, Wise Men, and sheep? The Easter story likewise lends itself to dramatic uses. The miracle play, which differed slightly in Europe and England, extended the lesson to include material from the lives of the saints. The morality play dramatized abstract lessons: Virtues and vices were personified, characterized, flesh and blood before your eyes.

There was soon grafted upon this new born and indigenously Christian drama the folk impulse for comedy. Perhaps tragedy and comedy first became mixed at this time, although the *commedia dell' arte* contained the elements of both. The people acting the church play would improvise and insert comic relief (perhaps at first inadvertently). Tolerant priests smiled: The attention of the audience was assured. Soon, however, the comic tail began to wag the serious dog. The English *Second Shepherd's Play* (circa 1400) is a fine example—and a superior play. Here the story of the nativity is used, however innocently—if indeed innocently—for a major work of comic realism and farce. Drama, however regretfully, was expelled from the chancel to the cathedral porch, then to the streets. But the people thought it too good to lose. Guilds were formed. The plays were put on wagons and drawn through the streets, and if church attendance did not fall off, neither did public enthusiasm for theatre.

Everyman

The medieval play that best stands on its own dramatic merits even in the modern theatre is undoubtedly the fifteenth-century English work, *Everyman*. As a morality play it has, of course, a lesson to teach. Most simply stated this lesson is: In the midst of life remember death, and so live that you are prepared to render a final account at any time. The characters of a morality play are abstractions and generalizations, but the unknown author of *Everyman* managed to particularize and humanize enough of these abstractions to make them dramatically interesting. Death, Fellowship, Goods, and Knowledge, are given the dialogue of people reacting to the person of Everyman. The action of the play is apparently simple. God tells Death to go to Everyman and call him "to a sure reckoning/Without delay or any tarrying," although this is also put in terms of a pilgrimage that "he must on him take." The simple action is thus complicated by the fact that it must take place simultaneously, or alternately, in two time sequences.

Everyman, still young and thinking on fleshly lusts and his treasure, and close companion to Fellowship (who is rather like a college senior), is called in haste. "Now, gentle Death, spare me till tomorrow." And Death answers, "Nay, thereto I will not consent, . . . For thou mayst say this is the day . . ." This gives the impression of a compact unity of time for the action. But the summoning is to a journey, to a pilgrimage, and Everyman tries to engage friends to keep him company on the trip. Fellowship, Kindred, Cousin, and Goods leave him somewhat unceremoniously; Knowledge, Beauty, Strength, Discretion, Five Wits and Good Deeds, after the visit to Confession, go along with him, with some dropping off. With this cast we are led by the beautifully implied but unstated analogy to the end of *Ecclesiastes* (the grinders cease, the

The *Salzburg Everyman* by Hugo von Hofmannsthal. Translated and directed by John Reich, starring Donald Buka, Goodman Theatre, November, 1957.

windows be darkened, the silver cord loosed, the golden bowl broken) to the realization that Everyman as he descends into the Grave with Good Deeds is an old man. The simultaneously projected single day and lifetime are two lenses that give a stereopticon view. The initial reaction is a pleased surprise, then perhaps an amused smile at medieval naïveté. But then should come the understanding that this is right, that in the sight of God these two time sequences are precisely the same and philosophically justified. The morning, noon, and evening of the Sphinx's riddle to Oedipus is simply taken literally.

The scene of the final abandonment of Everyman by his faculties, physical and mental, rather like man at the end of *Ecclesiastes*, is worth a closer look.

> EVERYMAN: What, Beauty, whither will ye?
> BEAUTY: Peace! I am deaf. I look not behind me,
>   Not and thou would give all the gold in thy chest.
> *(Exit Beauty)*
> EVERYMAN: Alas, whereto may I trust?
>   Beauty goeth fast away from me:
>   She promised with me to live and die.
> STRENGTH: Everyman, I will thee also forsake and deny.
>   Thy game liketh me not at all.

EVERYMAN: Why, then ye will forsake me all?
　　　　　Sweet Strength, tarry a little space.
STRENGTH: Nay, sir, by the rood of grace,
　　　　　I will hie me from thee fast,
　　　　　Though thou weep till thy heart to-brast.
EVERYMAN: Ye would ever bide by me, ye said.
STRENGTH: Yea, I have you far enough conveyed.
　　　　　Ye be old enough, I understand,
　　　　　Your pilgrimage to take on hand.
　　　　　I repent me that I hither came.
EVERYMAN: Strength, you to displease I am to blame;
　　　　　Yet promise is debt, this ye well wot.
STRENGTH: In faith, I care not!
　　　　　Thou art but a fool to complain.
　　　　　You spend your speech and waste your brain;
　　　　　Go, thrust thee into the ground. 　　(*Exit Strength*)
EVERYMAN: I had weened surer I should you have found.
　　　　　He that trusteth in his Strength
　　　　　She him deceiveth at the length.
　　　　　Both Strength and Beauty forsaketh me,
　　　　　Yet they promised me fair and lovingly.
DISCRETION: Everyman, I will after Strength be gone;
　　　　　As for me, I will leave you alone.
EVERYMAN: Why, Discretion, will ye forsake me?
DISCRETION: Yea, in faith, I will go from thee;
　　　　　For when Strength goeth before
　　　　　I follow after evermore.
EVERYMAN: Yet, I pray thee, for the love of the Trinity,
　　　　　Look in my grave once piteously.
DISCRETION: Nay, so nigh will I not come.
　　　　　Farewell, every one! 　　　(*Exit Discretion*)
EVERYMAN: O all things faileth, save God alone—
　　　　　Beauty, Strength, and Discretion;
　　　　　For when Death bloweth his blast,
　　　　　They all run from me full fast.
FIVE WITS: Everyman, my leave now of thee I take;
　　　　　I will follow the others, for here I thee forsake.
EVERYMAN: Alas; then may I wail and weep,
　　　　　For I took you for my best friend.
FIVE WITS: I will no longer thee keep;
　　　　　Now farewell, and there an end. 　　(*Exit Five Wits*)
EVERYMAN: O Jesu, help! All hath forsaken me!
GOOD DEEDS: Nay, Everyman; I will bide with thee,

I will not forsake thee indeed;
Thou shall find me a good friend at need.
EVERYMAN: Gramercy, Good Deeds! Now may I true friends see.
They have forsaken me, every one;
I loved them better than my Good Deeds alone.
Knowledge, will ye forsake me also?
KNOWLEDGE: Yea, Everyman, when ye to death shall go;
But not yet, for no manner of danger.
EVERYMAN: Gramercy, Knowledge, with all my heart.
KNOWLEDGE: Nay, yet I will not from hence depart
Till I see where ye shall be come.
EVERYMAN: Methink, alas, that I must be gone
To make my reckoning and my debts pay,
For I see my time is nigh spent away.
Take example, all ye that this do hear or see,
How they that I loved best do forsake me,
Except my Good Deeds that bideth truly.
GOOD DEEDS: All earthly things is but vanity.
Beauty, Strength, and Discretion do man forsake,
Foolish friends and kinsmen, that fair spake,
All fleeth save Good Deeds, and that am I.
EVERYMAN: Have mercy on me, God most mighty;
And stand by me, thou Mother and Maid, holy Mary!
GOOD DEEDS: Fear not, I will speak for thee.
EVERYMAN: Here I cry God Mercy!
GOOD DEEDS: Short our end and 'minish our pain.
Let us go and never come again.
EVERYMAN: Into thy hands, Lord, my soul I commend.
Receive it, Lord, that it be not lost.
As thou me boughtest, so me defend,
And save me from the fiend's boast,
That I may appear with that blessed host
That shall be saved at the day of doom.
In manus tuas—of might's most
For ever—*commendo spiritum meum.*
(*Everyman and Good Deeds descend into the grave*)
KNOWLEDGE: Now hath he suffered that we all shall endure;
The Good Deeds shall make all sure.
Now hath he made ending.
Methinketh that I hear angels sing
And make great joy and melody
Where Everyman's soul received shall be.
ANGEL (*within*): Come, excellent elect spouse to Jesu!

Everyman has been brilliantly adapted to the modern theatre in the German version of the same name, *Jedermann*, by Hugo von Hofmannsthal. Whether staged in the open air, on carts, on a stage, or on a cathedral porch, the voice of God from above is upper right, and the grave is a trapdoor, lower left—a medieval theatre convention with symbolic force and meaning. The medieval drama has made a new and recent impact on modern drama, particularly in the work of Michel de Ghelderode.

Elizabethan Drama and the Renaissance

This is roughly the state of affairs at the advent of the Renaissance which rediscovered with excitement, among other things, the theatre of the old Greeks and Romans. The Renaissance, beginning in Italy in the fourteenth century, spreading to Spain and France by the end of the fifteenth, and reaching England in the sixteenth, did not produce its first effects upon theatrical performances of the times. It was not until Machiavelli (*The Mandrake*) in the early sixteenth century; the Elizabethans from 1570 to 1620; the Spaniards Lope de Vega, Tirso de Molina, Calderón of a similar, slightly longer period, that Renaissance drama really yielded its own fruits. The French Renaissance in the theatre, occurring somewhat later than its manifestations elsewhere, is almost exactly concurrent with the seventeenth century.

What we find at first is the excitement of bringing together two relatively independent dramatic traditions, the medieval and the classical. Christopher Marlowe's *The Tragical History of Dr. Faustus* is one of the best examples of what came of this most productive marriage—not yet fully consummated perhaps, but resulting in a drama great in spite of weaknesses. The morality (*Everyman*) base is perceptible in the presence of the seven deadly sins, the good and evil angels, and the moral tone of the piece. There is a struggle for a man's soul. A tragic hero, almost Greek in stature and somewhat Promethean; movement through fourteen scenes, later to lead to a Senecan five-act division; remnants of a chorus; and the most important effect of a catharsis give evidence of Classical influence. There is also the mixing of comic and tragic sequences as in the late medieval mystery play.

During the Renaissance the theatre moved indoors—more or less, remembering the unroofed Elizabethan theatres—and stage conventions were thereby considerably modified. Actors were still men in England, and female impersonators usually had to do one of two roles—the man-souled, masculine woman (Lady Macbeth), or the boy-girl ingenue (Ophelia or Viola). However, the continent used women on the stage.

Stage properties were few, lighting restricted mainly to candles or day-light through the roof. Scenes could be changed with great rapidity—as long as a potted bush and a placard could produce the Forest of Arden. Of course, dialogue frequently included descriptive details of the setting and, as in Shakespeare's *Henry V*, a prologue might ask the audience to use their "imaginary forces" to create the scene. The audience, however, by the facts of walls and limited seating or standing room, was brought into more intimate contact with the players; asides became popular, and the wink became a possible dramatic gesture.

There is no one Elizabethan theatre, of course, and the Swan differed from the Fortune and from the Globe probably as much as any two or three theatres in any of our cities. They shared some features, however, in addition to the semi-open enclosed structure. A proscenium or open stage with standing room for audience on three sides, backed by an inner stage with curtains and/or doors above which an upper stage or roofed balcony appeared, provided several distinct acting areas. These areas might be used singly or in combination to give exceptional flexibility and rapidity of movement from one scene to another. (It is interesting to note that the architects of many theatres being built in the second half of the twentieth century are reaching for the flexibility of the Renaissance by constructing a thrust stage, which is closer to the Elizabethan than to the picture-frame stage of the nineteenth and early twentieth centuries.) Galleries ran around three sides and provided seats and roofed protection for those who could afford to pay more than the cost of standing room in the pit. Mr. Harley Granville-Barker has done much to interpret Shakespeare's drama in the light of the way it was probably acted on the Elizabethan stage.

To summarize the effects of the Renaissance theatre briefly is almost impossible, but we must point out at least the breakdown of categories—tragedy, comedy, mystery, miracle, morality—into the famous Hamlet classification: "tragedy, comedy, history, pastoral, pastoral-comical, historical-pastoral, tragical-historical, tragical-comical-historical-pastoral."

We must also note two opposing tendencies. First, there was a fairly strict regard, particularly in France, for Classical unities including those of place and time. This attitude was based on the period's respect for the classics and its compounding of Horace's misunderstanding of Aristotle's *Poetics*—a certain rigidity of formula. Second, a breaking loose occurred, a romantic movement from place to place and across time—*Antony and Cleopatra*, for instance—a delight in experimentation, in coining words, an extravagant love of words for their own sake. Typifying this breaking loose was an exploration and exploitation of innumerable sources for dramatic material (Shakespeare with Plutarch and Holinshed; Molière with Plautus and Lucretius and *commedia dell' arte*). Certainly general interest shifted from the action, as emphasized by the Greek play, to character. Most of all, Renaissance theatre was alive, and, like the Greek theatre, remains alive.

Hamlet

Shakespeare devoted his creative life to the theatre. One tradition has it that he started to work by holding horses outside the theatre door, and he certainly became part owner of the small company-owned Globe Theatre before he ended his career. His major work was as actor and dramatist. He was equally successful in creating comedies, histories, and tragedies. Probably the best-known and perhaps the best of his plays is *Hamlet*. One reason may be a certain ambiguity that has permitted a multitude of interpretations, some of them almost contradictory, from 1600, the approximate date of the play's first production, to the present. Not only does every age have its own *Hamlet*, play and character, but that generation is poor which does not come up with three or four. Why? It is by no means because of any lack of clarity in the action or plot. What happens, what does not happen, and what finally happens are clear enough.

Hamlet by William Shakespeare. The Gielgud Production. Photo by Vandamm, courtesy of the Theatre Collection the New York Public Library at Lincoln Center, Astor, Lenox, and Tilden Foundations.

The tragedy opens with a gloomy scene in Denmark outside the castle at Elsinore. The soldiers on watch are uneasy. It is cold and dark and midnight. Preparations for war are going on in some secrecy. And there has appeared a ghost. Something is rotten in the state of Denmark. Skeptic Horatio, Hamlet's friend, verifies the ghost as the form of the recently deceased king, Hamlet's father. Hamlet must be told.

The next scene is within the castle. Laertes, son of Lord Chamberlain Polonius, obtains King Claudius' permission to return to Paris. The king then turns to Hamlet, his nephew and the son of his newly acquired queen, Gertrude:

> KING: Take thy fair hour, Laertes. Time be thine,
>   And thy best graces spend it at thy will!
>   But now, my cousin Hamlet, and my son,—
> HAMLET: (*Aside*) A little more than kin, and less than kind.
> KING: How is it that the clouds still hang on you?
> HAMLET: Not so, my lord; I am too much i' th' sun.
> QUEEN: Good Hamlet, cast thy nighted colour off,
>   And let thine eye look like a friend on Denmark.
>   Do not forever with thy vailed lids
>   Seek for thy noble father in the dust.
>   Thou know'st 'tis common; all that lives must die,
>   Passing through nature to eternity.
> HAMLET: Aye, madam, it is common.
> QUEEN: If it be,
>   Why seems it so particular with thee?
> HAMLET: Seems, madam! Nay, it is; I know not "seems."
>   'Tis not alone my inky cloak, good mother,
>   Nor customary suits of solemn black,
>   Nor windy suspiration of forc'd breath,
>   No, nor the fruitful river in the eye,
>   Nor the dejected haviour of the visage,
>   Together with all forms, moods, shows of grief,
>   That can denote me truly.   These indeed seem,
>   For they are actions that a man might play;
>   But I have that within which passeth show,
>   These but the trappings and the suits of woe.

Hamlet is not granted leave to return to the university of Wittenberg, whence he had come for his father's funeral. Alone on the stage he voices to himself—and to the audience—his first of seven great soliloquies:

> O, that this too, too solid flesh would melt,
> Thaw, and resolve itself into a dew!

Or that the Everlasting had not fix'd
His canon 'gainst self-slaughter! O God! God!
How weary, stale, flat, and unprofitable,
Seems to me all the uses of this world!
Fie on't! oh fie, fie! 'Tis an unweeded garden,
That grows to seed; things rank and gross in nature
Possess it merely. That it should come to this!
But two months dead! Nay, not so much, not two.
So excellent a king; that was, to this,
Hyperion to a satyr; so loving to my mother
That he might not beteem the winds of heaven
Visit her face too roughly. Heaven and earth!
Must I remember? Why, she would hang on him
As if increase of appetite had grown
By what it fed on; and yet, within a month,—
Let me not think on't!—Frailty, thy name is woman!—
A little month, or e'er those shoes were old
With which she followed my poor father's body,
Like Niobe, all tears,—why, she, even she—
O God! A beast, that wants discourse of reason,
Would have mourn'd longer—married with mine uncle,
My father's brother, but no more like my father
Than I to Hercules; within a month,
Ere yet the salt of most unrighteous tears
Had left the flushing of her galled eyes,
She married. O, most wicked speed, to post
With such dexterity to incestuous sheets!
It is not, nor it cannot come to good.—
But break, my heart, for I must hold my tongue.

Then Hamlet meets the ghost, who informs him of two crimes and urges two diverse courses of action. First, Hamlet's father had been murdered by his own brother,

Sleeping within mine orchard,
My custom always in the afternoon,
Upon my secure hour thy uncle stole,
With juice of cursed hebenon in a vial,
And in the porches of mine ears did pour
The leperous distilment . . .
Cut off even in the blossoms of my sin, . . .

For this, revenge. The second but earlier crime was the adulterous seduction of the queen by Claudius, but, says the ghost, as if to prevent an Oresteian dilemma,

> Taint not thy mind, nor let thy soul contrive
> Against thy mother aught. Leave her to heaven...

And so Hamlet's dilemma becomes clear, as a fixed decision for revenge in a world of murky uncertainties. It may be necessary to "put an antic disposition on."

> The time is out of joint;—O cursed spite,
> That ever I was born to set it right!

Hamlet's nature was meant for other things: for art, philosophy, for rule, for love. But it must be subverted. Did the ghost speak truly? Or was it a spirit from hell to ensnare the soul? Hamlet pretends madness, but his feigned distraction is often close to the real thing. Spies are set against him. Polonius and Claudius decide to use Rosencrantz and Guildenstern, old school friends of Hamlet—and even Ophelia, the girl who might have brought him happiness—to ferret out the truth of Hamlet's posture. And Hamlet will use the traveling players to ferret out the truth of Claudius' crime. The present duty of the prince forces the rejection of Ophelia:

HAMLET: Ha, Ha! are you honest?

OPHELIA: My lord!

HAMLET: Are you fair?

OPHELIA: What means your lordship?

HAMLET: That if you should be honest and fair, your honesty should admit no discourse to your beauty.

OPHELIA: Could beauty, my lord, have better commerce than with honesty?

HAMLET: Ay, truly; for the power of beauty will sooner transform honesty from what it is to a bawd than the force of honesty can translate beauty into his likeness. This was sometime a paradox, but now the time gives it proof. I did love you once.

OPHELIA: Indeed, my lord, you made me believe so.

HAMLET: You should not have believed me, for virtue cannot so inoculate our old stock but we shall relish of it. I loved you not.

OPHELIA: I was the more deceived.

HAMLET: Get thee to a nunnery: why wouldst thou be a breeder of sinners? I am myself indifferent honest, but yet I could accuse me of such things that it were better my mother had not borne me. I am very proud, revengeful, ambitious, with more offences at my beck than I have thoughts to put them in, imagination to give them shape, or time to act them in. What should such fellows as I do

crawling between heaven and earth? We are arrant knaves
all; believe none of us. Go thy ways to a nunnery. . . .

OPHELIA (alone): O, what a noble mind is here o'erthrown!
The courtier's, soldier's, scholar's, eye, tongue, sword;
The expectancy and rose of the fair state,
The glass of fashion and the mould of form,
The observ'd of all observers, quite, quite, down!
And I, of ladies most deject and wretched,
That suck'd the honey of his music vows,
Now see that noble and most sovereign reason,
Like sweet bells jangled, out of tune and harsh;
That unmatch'd form and feature of blown youth
Blasted with ecstasy. O, woe is me,
T'have seen what I have seen, see what I see!

Hamlet proves to his own satisfaction the guilt of the king with the
play within a play which he calls "The Mouse-trap." But at his first opportunity to kill Claudius, he finds him praying. This is not the time
to do it. His soul must go not to heaven but to hell. Then the characters
begin to die. Polonius is stabbed behind the arras where he was spying
on Hamlet in his mother's room; the truly mad Ophelia drowns; Rosencrantz and Guildenstern are killed in England (Hamlet escaping from
this destiny, devised by the king for the prince). Finally, by poisoned
drink and poisoned rapier Gertrude, Claudius, Laertes, and Hamlet
perish. Revenge has been taken, Denmark purged, but at what a cost!
Hamlet begs:

O good Horatio, . . .
If thou didst ever hold me in thy heart,
Absent thee from felicity awhile
And in this harsh world draw thy breath in pain
To tell my story . . .
But I do prophesy th' election lights
On Fortinbras; he has my dying voice.
So tell him, with the occurrents, more or less,
Which have solicited—The rest is silence.

Order is restored in Denmark; all the principals are dead; the action
is over. But the main interest is in the character of Hamlet, and here
lies the potential ambiguity. Hamlet is sensitive, an artist, a scholar, a
philosopher, a courtier, a soldier, a prince. Which do you emphasize? In
the course of the play he is disillusioned in every principal character
except Horatio. It depends on which relationship you focus on, where
you put your spotlight, what manner of Hamlet you get.

The play is a long one and can be cut to any of a number of patterns. If the focus is on the sensitive, artistic young man, you have a dreamy, romantic Hamlet incapable of action by nature. If the focus is on Hamlet's disillusionment in his mother, you may get, as in the Olivier film, a Freudian interpretation of an Oedipus complex—Hamlet becomes a psychiatric case. If the focus is on a disappointed prince seeking rule in a chaotic political situation, you get a study of the police state and the political incapacities of an idealistic young man. If you concentrate on belief in and doubt of the ghost, you get a Hamlet wrestling with metaphysical and religious problems.

No one of these Hamlets is necessarily the wrong Hamlet, but he may be a partial Hamlet. We are always interested in his psychology, in what makes his motivation. And Hamlet, "sicklied o'er with the pale cast of thought," seems to represent a particular pattern of modern man's dilemma—too evolved in culture and civilization to act without thinking, too thoughtful to be willing to act when the consequences seem wrong, too pressed by contemporary political and moral evils not to act. Hamlet would have had a rough time with his draft card in the twentieth century.

The thought and theme of *Hamlet*, however slanted the view taken of the prince's character, have to do with private feelings and responsibilities in a family and public world. The conflict varies in its manifestations but remains constant in itself. There is no chorus in Hamlet, but the seven spaced soliloquies perform a similar bridging function, connecting audience and Hamlet. Ophelia's songs of isolation are particularly touching. Of intrinsic spectacle there is a good deal—the ghost, the play within the play, and the struggle in the grave and the duel at the end. *Hamlet* is a good example of Renaissance tragedy. One can relatively easily identify with the protagonist, and the cathartic experience of pity and fear is readily accessible to the sensitive modern mind. Some surprisingly good critical perceptions of the play are embodied in Tom Stoppard's *Rosencrantz and Guildenstern Are Dead*, which ties *Hamlet*, Jan Kott fashion, to the modern theatre of the absurd.

Tartuffe

What Shakespeare and *Hamlet* are for Renaissance tragedy, Molière and *Tartuffe* are for Renaissance comedy. Molière uniquely combines with his own ingredients the best of Shakespeare's romantic comedy and Ben Jonson's satiric comedy to produce the best and most comprehensive comedy for theatre since Aristophanes, Plautus, and Terence. Certainly it is the best in a modern idiom. *Tartuffe*,[3] first presented in

[3]Excerpts from EIGHT PLAYS BY MOLIÈRE, translated by Morris Bishop. © Copyright 1957 by Morris Bishop. Reprinted by permission of Random House, Inc.

1664 at Versailles, was reworked and revised for five years before its first public performance in 1669, since which time it has been presented more often than any other play by Molière. Its subject is a new comic type, the religious hypocrite—difficult, dangerous, and delicate to handle, potentially offensive to religious groups and censors. But equally important and satirized as thoroughly as Tartuffe, the religious hypocrite and confidence man, are those members of society who are gulled by him—Orgon, the dupe, and Orgon's mother Madame Pernelle, the fool. As is customary in Molière's comedy, we find the voice of reason, the spokesman for the dramatist, who represents the Aristotelian "nothing too much" and guides the thinking of the audience. In *Tartuffe*, however, we have in unusual fashion two such characters: Cléante, brother-in-law of Orgon, and Dorine, companion of Orgon's daughter Mariane.

Tartuffe by Moliére. Courtesy American Conservatory Theatre, San Francisco, California.

The action of the play involves comedy of situation, comedy of character, comedy of manners, and farce. Madame Pernelle is very happy that her son has taken Tartuffe into his household, and she scolds everybody else there because, not recognizing his seeming piety and direction, they offer objections to Tartuffe's growing domination of the family. Madame Pernelle's servant Flipote is a farcical character, a dunce with round red rouge patches and a stupid expression, who does little more than get her ears boxed. Orgon's children, Damis and Mariane, and their stepmother, Elmire, take the brunt of Madame's wrath. Dorine and Cléante try to hold out against the flood.

DORINE: It seems to me perfectly scandalous
That this outsider should take over things.
He came to us a beggar, with no shoes,
And all his clothes were worth about a dollar.
But that's forgotten, now he's found his place;
He has the final veto; he's the boss.

And then

CLÉANTE: You want to put a stop to conversation?
Wouldn't it be somewhat regrettable
If we should have to give up our best friends,
Just because fools may say some foolish things?
Even supposing we should bar the door,
Do you think people then would cease to talk?
There is no wall so high it shuts out slander.
So let's not give a thought to silly gossip,
And let us try to live in innocence,
And let the talkers talk just as they please.

But Madame Pernelle is concerned with reputation and leaves in a huff. When Orgon arrives home we have a scene of interrogation with Dorine that is justly famous as an example of what Bergson meant in his theory of the mechanical, the inelastic, as the source of comedy:

ORGON: Everything's been all right the past few days?
How's everyone? What's been going on?
DORINE: Two days ago, your lady had a fever,
And a bad headache, really terrible.
ORGON: And Tartuffe?
DORINE: Tartuffe? Oh, he's doing fine,
So fat and red-faced, such a healthy color.
ORGON: Poor fellow!
DORINE: She had some nausea in the evening,
And couldn't touch a single thing at supper.
Her headache still was a real torture to her.
ORGON: And Tartuffe?
DORINE: Ate his supper in her presence,
And piously devoured two partridges,
Also a hash of half a leg of mutton.
ORGON: Poor fellow.
DORINE: During all the following night
She did not shut her eyes a single moment.
It was so warm she could not sleep;
We had to sit beside her until morning.

ORGON: And Tartuffe?
DORINE: Oh, Tartuffe was sleepy enough.
          He went right after dinner to his room,
          Immediately he got in his warm bed,
          And peacefully slept until the following day.
ORGON: Poor fellow!
DORINE: She listened to our arguments,
          And had the doctor give her a good bleeding,
          And after that she felt a great deal better.
ORGON: And Tartuffe?
DORINE: Why, he cheered up very nicely.
          To fortify his spirit against trouble
          And to make up for Madame's loss of blood,
          He took at lunch four glasses full of wine.
ORGON: Poor fellow!
DORINE: Now both are doing very well.
          I'll tell Madame the sympathetic interest
          You've taken in the news of her recovery.

The romantic interest in the comedy, Mariane and her fiancé, Valère, is in for trouble, as Orgon has decided to offer his daughter's hand to Tartuffe. And he has also decided to disinherit Damis in favor of Tartuffe. In Act II Mariane and Valère are manipulated by Dorine into and out of a lover's quarrel on the subject of Tartuffe. Tartuffe himself enters in Act III. Molière's detractors have stupidly criticized the delayed appearance of the central character, but it is a brilliant, original, appropriate entrance of one who has been so much there before his appearance.
          (Enter Tartuffe. He observes Dorine and calls offstage.)

TARTUFFE: Put my hair shirt away and my flagellator,
          Laurent; and pray for heaven's continual grace.
          If anyone wants me, say I'm off to the prison
          To give away the charity given me . . .
                              Oh, dear heaven!
          Before you speak, please take this handkerchief.
DORINE: What?
TARTUFFE: Cover that bosom which I must not see.
          Such sights as that are hurtful to the spirit,
          And they may well awaken guilty thoughts.
DORINE: You must be very sensitive to temptation.
          Flesh makes a great impression on your senses!
          Of course, I don't know how you're stimulated,
          But I am not so readily aroused.
          If I should see you naked from head to foot,
          I wouldn't be tempted by all the skin you've got.

TARTUFFE: Please be a little modest in your speech,
　　　Or I must leave the room immediately.

As a matter of fact, it is precisely Tartuffe's weakness of the flesh for
woman (Elmire, in particular) that finally unmasks him to Orgon in a
wonderfully comic scene with Orgon hiding under a table. The conquest
is well advanced when Elmire coughs to bring her husband out. Finally
she says,

ELMIRE: But first, open the door a little, please;
　　　See if my husband isn't in the hall.
TARTUFFE: What sense is there in worrying about him?
　　　He is the type that you can lead by the nose,
　　　The type to glory in our intimacies.
　　　He can see anything now and not believe it.

That does it. Orgon emerges, enraged. But it is too late to order Tartuffe
from the house—it is already signed over to him by deed of gift. And
Orgon is yet more worried because of some confidential papers that may
be in Tartuffe's possession. We are almost ready for the fifth act resolution and dénouement. But first there are two brief scenes of importance.
In the first Cléante makes clear how much of the satire is directed against
Orgon.

ORGON: What! Under all his outward show of fervor,
　　　To hide a treacherous heart, an evil soul!
　　　To think I picked him up, a penniless beggar!
　　　All right, I now renounce all worthy men,
　　　Henceforth I'll have a terrible horror of them;
　　　I'm going to be a devil to them all!
CLÉANTE: Now there you go again, getting excited!
　　　You can't be moderate in anything ...
　　　Because a blackguard boldly takes you in,
　　　Impersonating an austere believer,
　　　You would conclude that everyone's like him,
　　　And that no true believer now exists? ...
　　　Distinguish virtue from its outward seeming.
　　　Never give your esteem too hastily,
　　　Keep to the reasonable middle way.
　　　Try not to give your honor to imposters,
　　　But don't insult genuine piety.
　　　And if you must choose one extreme or the other,
　　　Let your fault be excessive leniency.

This is as close to a stated theme as can be found.

The second, very comic, scene occurs when Orgon can't convince his mother of Tartuffe's hypocrisy. The dénouement, with the artificial intervention of the king's officer, who unexpectedly arrests Tartuffe, is a gracious tribute to Louis XIV. Also, it is an admirable all's well that ends well climax, with a two-line reference to the coming marriage of Mariane and Valère.

Although Tartuffe, Orgon, and Madame Pernelle are the primary comic butts, they are essentially caricatures. The real interest in comic character is directed toward Dorine, who has a place beside Shakespeare's Beatrice and Rosalind, beside Molière's own Agnès and Célimène, and beside Congreve's Millament. If you follow Bergson, the "jack-in-the-box" comic technique and the satiric purpose of social corrective are well illustrated in *Tartuffe*. If you follow Henry Fielding—that the only source of the true ridiculous is affectation arising either from vanity or hypocrisy—*Tartuffe* is an equally good illustration. George Meredith has insisted that there can be true comedy only in a culture where there is a true equality of the sexes. And Dorine is certainly the equal of any man in the play. Molière had toured the provinces for years before returning to Paris, and he had learned the lessons of stagecraft well, as actor, manager, director, dramatist. He incorporated the best of *commedia dell' arte*, Classical comedy, French peasant farce, and the Rabelaisian tradition into a new whole. He is reported to have said, "I take my good where I find it."

Restoration Comedy

In France the seventeenth century was a relatively stable one, the Age of Gold of Louis XIV. There are in the contemporary tragedies of Corneille and Racine and in the comedies of Molière a poise and serenity and polish that bespeak the Versailles touch. Theatre was popular and royally sponsored. In seventeenth-century England, however, Puritan elements gained strength politically and morally. They brought the Renaissance theatre to a full stop by closing the playhouses in 1640. The plays of the great Elizabethans and Jacobeans—Marlowe, Shakespeare, Jonson, Webster, Beaumont-Fletcher—remained in manuscript, or print, during the midcentury years. With the Restoration of King Charles II *and* the theatre in 1660, there was an almost total loss of continuity between the drama of before and after the closing. To look at the late seventeenth- and eighteenth-century rewriting of Shakespeare is to become aware of the gap.

Charles and his court, who had been exiled in France, brought to England tastes modified by the French theatre. Restoration comedy and tragedy (although less effectively) show the stronger influences of French drama. There is greater care for the unities, a higher polish, more sophistication and urbanity. In the plays of Wycherly and Congreve (*The Way of the World*), for example, we have what was, for England, a new comedy of manners and wit. Classical new comedy, which also represented a shift toward urban and sophisticated manners, gave much to the comedy of Restoration England. The years following, particularly during the reigns of William and Anne, moved toward the intricacy of intrigue, comic artificiality, and brilliance of dialogue typical of Plautus or Molière. Women were now acting women's roles, and Molièresque satire was directed against foibles and frailties peculiarly British in expression. Thus the late seventeenth-century English theatre achieved a genuine éclat, and a lasting interest, to which the revivals of *The Country Wife* attest. Attempts to achieve these qualities were made by Goldsmith and Sheridan in the eighteenth century in *She Stoops to Conquer, The Rivals,* and *The School for Scandal;* but not until Oscar Wilde in the 1890's were they found again in the English theatre.

The major changes in the European and English theatre, between 1700 and 1850 were probably architectural, although there were fads and fashions, including the rage for Italian opera. The theatre building as we generally know it today, with proscenium arch somewhat like a picture frame; orchestra for seating instead of pit; loges and balconies; curtains, scenery with moveable flats, gradually evolved. Plays were written, but the greatest productions depended on manuscripts of the past. To this generalization perhaps an exception could be made of Carlo Goldoni, the Molière of Italy, in and around 1750. In the theatrical darkness of the mid-nineteenth century—in spite of the new gas lamps—with the well-made, but on the whole, dull plays of Eugène Scribe and others, the backdrop for the advent of modern drama was being prepared.

Ibsen and the Beginnings of the Modern Play

Ibsen raised the curtain. We might as well say categorically that modern drama begins with his shift from the manner of his early poetic and romantic plays *Peer Gynt* and *Brand* to prose and the problems of his contemporary society. This is true whether you begin with *A Doll's House* (1879) or *Ghosts* (1881) or wait until *Hedda Gabler* (1890). Why? There are many reasons to see the approach of a different era, a new way of looking at life, toward the end of the nineteenth century. Some of them must be mentioned because of their special implications for the dramatist.

Charles Darwin's *Origin of Species* (1859) had the effect of bringing certain philosophical and religious assumptions concerning man's place in the universe, and the universe itself, into an agitated questioning. This intellectual cataclysm probably caused as much rumbling as the fall of the Roman Empire, if not more; it was almost a Greek questioning, without the calm. Karl Marx, a contemporary of Darwin, provided the challenge and disturbance for the political and economic world. Nobody, certainly, denies that this struggle is an integral part of modern times, or pretends that it has been settled. In roughly the same period, 1860–1890, psychology became vocal if not vociferous as a science or pseudo-science. Sigmund Freud did not discover sex and inhibitions, but he certainly gave to the discussion of them an impetus that knocked Victorian inhibitions right out of the room. Add Einstein and atomic fission, and in many respects the upset of the modern world becomes simply an extension of Darwin, Marx, and Freud rather than a new beginning. These events are, in a way, dramatic but non-theatre.

Like the theories, the technological aspects of new science were soon to give the modern touch to the modern stage. Machinery was built to make all sorts of effects, or spectacle, possible. The turning on of electric lights in the theatre was probably one of the most revolutionary things ever to happen to drama.

In any event, the modern era evolved out of and in many ways represented a reaction against nineteenth-century Victorianism. In the course of his work as a playwright, Henrik Ibsen (1828–1906) was successively romanticist, realist, psychologist, symbolist. It is not the romantic Ibsen who is modern, although seeds of his later development can be seen in *Brand* and *Peer Gynt*. But in bringing realism and prose and the social problem of venereal disease together in the one play, *Ghosts*, he certainly dealt a body blow to Victorianism in his day. In later plays, emphasizing symbolism, Ibsen pointed the second direction for the new drama—antirealism.

Ghosts

Ghosts is realism at its best and, because of what it says, remains more modern than *A Doll's House*, where the issue of the emancipation of women is not quite as pressing as it was around 1880.[4] Ibsen's friend and fellow writer, Björnson in an interview right after Ibsen's death, chose *Ghosts* as his colleague's greatest work. Although the point is

[4] Extracts from "A Doll's House" and "Ghosts" are reprinted with the permission of Charles Scribner's Sons from Volume VII, THE COLLECTED WORKS OF HENRIK IBSEN, translated by William Archer, and with the permission of William Heinemann Ltd.

debatable, the play itself is the first work in which Ibsen applies "his new technical method," says William Archer. "He is under the sway of a prosaic ideal—confessed in the phrase, 'My object was to make the reader feel that he was going through a piece of real experience.'" And Georg Brandes has pointed to this play as marking Ibsen's final break with his early, almost hereditary, romanticism.

Ghosts by Henrik Ibsen. Photo by Vandamm, courtesy of the Theatre Collection the New York Public Library at Lincoln Center, Astor, Lenox, and Tilden Foundations.

The play is in three acts, a more characteristically modern and realistic structure than the Elizabethan five-act division. They are tightly knit, following each other so closely in time, and in the same setting, as to give the effect of unity and continuity. We are in Mrs. Alving's upper middle class country home in western Norway, and there are only five characters: Mrs. Alving; her son Oswald, who suffers from hereditary syphilis of the kind that attacks the brain; Pastor Manders, who represents conventional society and its nineteenth-century Christian ethics; Jacob Engstrand, a carpenter, common and often drunk; and Regina Engstrand, Mrs. Alving's maid but also the natural daughter of that lady's deceased husband and therefore Oswald's half sister. The revelation of these relationships is gradual and natural. The occasion for the appearance of Pastor Manders and Jacob is the completion of an orphanage that has been built in memory of Captain Alving and with his money.

Manders, an old friend of the family, has come from the city for the dedication the next day. He is a literalistic, conservative, unimaginative type of minister, who is greatly shocked in Act I by evidence of intellectual and moral liberalism on the parts of Mrs. Alving and her son. Manders insists on speaking to Mrs. Alving in his role as clergyman. It was he to whom Mrs. Alving had fled when, after less than a year of married life, she had left her husband and refused to return to him. Manders had performed the ceremony of the family-arranged marriage, and he sent her back to her duty to the dissolute man to whom she was "bound by the holiest ties." After this event, Manders had ceased to call on the unhappy couple, feeling that his reputation had been compromised by Mrs. Alving's coming to him, with the hint of a romantic attachment between them. The curtain comes down on a ghostlike repetition of an incident in the dining room—Oswald grappling with Regina just as Captain Alving had done with Regina's mother. The pastor who learns of the latter occurrence from Mrs. Alving, now knows the truth about Regina's parentage. We discover, however, that Manders is chiefly bothered by the lies that Engstrand had told on the occasion of marriage to Regina's mother, implying that he himself had slipped before seeking benefit of clergy. The pastor is wounded by the idea of having been deceived.

In the second act he speaks of this to Mrs. Alving:

> MANDERS: But such a piece of duplicity on his part! And towards me, too! I never could have believed it of Jacob Engstrand. I shall not fail to take him seriously to task; he may be sure of that.—And then the immorality of such a connection! For money—! How much did the girl receive?
>
> MRS. ALVING: Three hundred dollars.
>
> MANDERS: Just think of it—for a miserable three hundred dollars, to go and marry a fallen woman!
>
> MRS. ALVING: Then what have you to say of me? I went and married a fallen man.
>
> MANDERS: Why—good heavens!—what are you talking about! A fallen man!
>
> MRS. ALVING: Do you think Alving was any purer when I went with him to the altar than Johanna was when Engstrand married her?

MANDERS: Well, but there is a world of difference between the two cases—

MRS. ALVING: Not so much difference after all—except in the price:—a miserable three hundred dollars and a whole fortune.

This is a searing, if quiet, indictment of the double standard; it was very disturbing to the society of Ibsen's time. Manders reminds Mrs. Alving that her marriage was in full accordance with law and order, and Mrs. Alving answers, "Oh, that perpetual law and order! I often think that is what does all the mischief in this world of ours." The key speech for the title of this play is given to Mrs. Alving.

MRS. ALVING: Ghosts! When I heard Regina and Oswald in there, it was as though ghosts rose up before me. But I almost think we are all of us ghosts, Pastor Manders. It is not only what we have inherited from our father and mother that "walks" in us. It is all sorts of dead ideas, and lifeless old beliefs, and so forth. They have no vitality, but they cling to us all the same, and we cannot shake them off. Whenever I take up a newspaper, I seem to see ghosts gliding between the lines. There must be ghosts all the country over, as thick as the sands of the sea. And then we are, one and all, so pitifully afraid of the light.

Manders is taken off by Engstrand to the orphanage for a prayer meeting for the workmen who have completed their job. Oswald, who has been kept away for most of his youth, then tells his mother about his illness.

OSWALD: He was one of the first doctors in Paris. I told him my symptoms; and then he set to work asking me a string of questions which I thought had nothing to do with the matter. I couldn't imagine what the man was after—

MRS. ALVING: Well?

OSWALD: At last he said: "There has been something worm-eaten in you from your birth." He used that very word— *vermoulu.*

MRS. ALVING: (*Breathlessly*) What did he mean by that?

OSWALD: I didn't understand either, and begged him to explain himself more clearly. And then the old cynic said— (*Clenching his fist*) Oh—!

MRS. ALVING: What did he say?

OSWALD: He said, "The sins of the fathers are visited upon the children."

But Oswald cannot believe in his father's guilt because Mrs. Alving, in her letters, had always presented him as virtuous. So Oswald blames his own, relatively mild, dissipations. "If only it had been something inherited—something one wasn't responsible for! But this!" Then, interrupting Mrs. Alving's intended revelation of the whole truth to Oswald and Regina, comes the news that the orphanage is on fire. (The orphanage had not been insured because Pastor Manders felt that it would imply a lack of complete trust in Divine Providence.) This is the second act curtain.

The revelation does come in Act III, as Mrs. Alving picks up a phrase used by Oswald, "the joy of life," to discuss her former husband.

> MRS. ALVING: Well then, child of joy as he was—for he was like a child in those days—he had to live at home here in a half-grown town, which had no joys to offer him—only dissipations. . . . Your poor father found no outlet for the overpowering joy of life that was in him. And I brought no brightness into his home.
>
> OSWALD: Not even you?
>
> MRS. ALVING: They had taught me a great deal about duties and so forth, which I went on obstinately believing in. Everything was marked out into duties—into my duties, and his duties, and—I am afraid I made his home intolerable for your poor father, Oswald.
>
> OSWALD: Why have you never spoken of this in writing to me?
>
> MRS. ALVING: I have never before seen it in such a light that I could speak of it to you, his son.
>
> OSWALD: In what light did you see it, then?
>
> MRS. ALVING: (Slowly) I saw only this one thing: that your father was a broken-down man before you were born.
>
> OSWALD: (Softly) Ah—!

When Mrs. Alving explains to Regina who she is, Regina leaves to look for her "career" in town, for "the joy of life." Mrs. Alving is left alone with her son, who extorts a promise from her that when the final attack comes and he is "lying there helpless, like a little new-born baby, impotent, lost, hopeless—past all saving—" that she will help him out of life with the twelve pills he has collected. As the sun rises, Oswald goes to pieces; and Mrs. Alving is left with a decision to make: "No; no; no!— Yes!—No; no!"

That the issues and ideas of *Ghosts* are still valid and still dramatic may be seen in the use made of this play in Lionel Trilling's short story, or novella, called "Of This Time, Of That Place." Another Oswald, Ferdinand Tertan, contributes to a discussion of *Ghosts* in an American college. The question is, who's to blame for what happens? The obvious suggestions are made: Captain Alving and heredity, Pastor Manders, the society of the time and place. But Tertan points to Mrs. Alving and her confession, "I brought no brightness into his home." If this is a valid accusation, and it is certainly a possible one, Mrs. Alving with her enlightenment and catastrophe is a good example of a modern tragic figure.

Realism and Naturalism

Modern drama is characterized by a diversity and experimentation that go beyond the Renaissance, and yet partake of some of its excitement and enthusiasm. It has produced a variety of schools or forms or modes of expression. Its weakness may be that it rides in all directions, but that is a source of its strength as well. No subject is unsuitable for dramatic uses. *Ghosts* itself opened the field. Where dramatic tension or conflict exists—that is, almost everywhere—there is a play. Contemporary play production and, consequently, contemporary dramatists, have moved in two main and opposite directions (although sometimes in both at once): realism and nonrealism. Realism includes by extension naturalism. In spite of some confusion of terms in twentieth-century criticism, let us look at the former first.

In some ways the entire evolution of drama from the Greeks to the present has been a movement toward greater realism or verisimilitude or representationalism. In whatever way you may consider it, it is the attempt to convince the audience that it is watching life rather than a play. Artifices such as the chorus and the mask have been dropped along the way, in the interests, one assumes, of greater realism. The use of women to play the roles of women was another move in this direction. The stage itself evolved from amphitheatre to proscenium arch built toward the ideal illusion of a room with the fourth wall removed. The audience supposedly watches and hears men and women who are unaware of their presence—a most unrealistic idea, but the core of theatrical realism. Actors eat real food, behave in an entirely unwatched manner. Out go the asides and any direct address to the audience.

The writing of plays in the realistic and naturalistic schools followed and paralleled realism and naturalism in the other genres, particularly the novel (although perhaps its turning was more abrupt). Note, for example, that tragedies from the Greeks through the Elizabethans took for their heroes men or women of noble birth or position, aristocrats to whom great misfortune came. The fall from a height is the greater fall. Mrs. Alving is at least middle class, perhaps upper middle. Now it is the comman man—Willy Loman the salesman, or even an anonymous man in the street—who is most often the tragic hero: greater realism, greater pathos, a shorter fall. One should recall as well that the comic figures of the Greeks and Elizabethans were for the most part peasant or servant, men and women "worse than we are," shorter in stature at any rate. Restoration comedy moved toward making fun of a mannered aristocracy; modern comedy, bourgeois to be sure, has exploited a disappearing aristocracy in, for example, the passing off of a flower girl as a duchess in *Pygmalion*—or its adaptation, *My Fair Lady*. All characters are now stage-worthy and democratically mixed.

Realism achieved perhaps its best effects in the theatre when closely related to the psychology of human behavior, and when dealing with the manners and speech of particular classes. It easily took the form of the problem play, and it was easy for the problem to become a social problem—venereal disease in *Ghosts*, court proceedings and the penal system in Galsworthy's *Justice*. Social problems, particularly when economic and political in origin, fed into naturalism as in Hauptmann's *The Weavers* or in Galsworthy's *Strife*.

Naturalism—in the theatre as in the novel largely the work of Émile Zola—has a narrower basis in focus, technique, and philosophy than realism. It tends to stress the sordid photographic view of the sores of society. It is deterministic, the twin fates of naturalism being heredity and environment. Its tone is a tone of protest. Besides Zola and Hauptmann we have Gorki and *The Lower Depths*, and in America, Caldwell's *Tobacco Road*.

The greatest masters of realism in the theatre were probably Ibsen and Chekhov. These men represent rather divergent realistic approaches, although both tend toward some poetic use of symbolism as seen in their metaphorical uses of a wild duck and a sea gull. Chekhov's dramatic realism is not unrelated to his use of realism in the short story. Here were the beginnings of that "slice of life" technique in which stories do not begin, come to a climax, and end in the old sense but rather start and stop, cut off, leaving a feeling of continuation. In Chekhov you often find the "realism of the irrelevant," or more precisely in Chekhov, the realism of the apparently irrelevant.

The Cherry Orchard

An initial difficulty for Americans in a Chekhov play is likely to be the cast of characters. Russian names sometimes with multiple diminutives, can be hard to hold on to, but it is worth trying. Another problem is that not much seems to happen, yet all the characters talk a great deal, often without response from persons addressed. Yet that is a fairly realistic picture of life. One more difficulty, for critics as well as for audience or reader, is trying to decide whether a Chekhov play is a comedy or a tragedy. *The Cherry Orchard*,[5] *The Sea Gull*, and *The Sisters* are often played as one or the other, but that does violence to Chekhov's realism. Stark Young says a Chekhov play "can fall only within some softer, less sharply defined mood," and calls attention to his lyricism—"the music of his profound and gentle humanity." The dramatic tone actually is strikingly original and is closest to that form of poetry called *vers de société*, a light, sophisticated verse that ideally produces a simultaneous smile and tear. As in Oliver Wendell Holmes's "The Last Leaf" or "My Maiden Aunt," there is humor, and tragic implication also, but the two are carefully mixed.

The Cherry Orchard by Anton Chekov. Photo by Vandamm, courtesy of the Theatre Collection the New York Public Library at Lincoln Center, Astor, Lenox, and Tilden Foundations.

The Cherry Orchard was adapted to the American scene in *The Wisteria Tree,* using the parallel between the roughly concurrent situations of post-Civil War Southern aristocracy and Northern carpet baggers and the Russian aristocracy after the freeing of the Russian serfs and the emancipation of slaves in America. The old order changes, and the play captures a moment of change. The Russian aristocracy, thoroughly charming and incompetent, gracious and foolish, generous and irresponsi-

[5]Extracts from "The Cherry Orchard" are reprinted with permission from The Modern Library and the translator, Stark Young, from the volume BEST PLAYS BY CHEKOV. Copyright 1956 by Stark Young.

ble, is represented by Madame Ranevskaya, an impoverished estate owner, who is returning from Paris with her younger daughter, Anya, and the governess, Charlotta; by her brother, Leonid Gayeff, a useless man of about fifty whose only interest is shooting pool; and another penniless landowner Boris Borisovitch Semyonoff-Pishtchik, whom it might be just as well to forget because of his name. The rising middle class with money is represented by the merchant, Yermolay Lopahin, whose father and grandfather were serfs of the Ranevsky family. Fiers, an old serf who would have nothing to do with emancipation has stayed on as servant; he is now eighty-seven. It is May, the cherry trees are in bloom, but there are three degrees of frost when the play opens with the expected arrival of the travelers from Paris. Lopahin is talking with Dunyasha, the maid.

> LOPAHIN: Lyuboff Andreevna [Madame Ranevskaya], I can see
> her now, still so young, so slim, led me to the washbasin
> here in this very room, in the nursery. "Don't cry," she
> says, "little peasant, it will be well in time for your wed-
> ding." Yes, little peasant—My father was a peasant truly,
> and here I am in a white waistcoat and yellow shoes.
> Like a pig rooting in a pastry shop—I've got this rich, lots
> of money, but if you really stop and think of it, I'm
> just a peasant—"

The arrival presents a lot of action, at least bustle. Varya is Madame Ranevsky's adopted daughter, some seven years older than Anya and left on the family estate. Dunyasha is a maid in the house.

> LYUBOFF ANDREEVNA: The nursery, my dear beautiful room—I
> slept here when I was little—(*Crying*) And now I am
> like a child—(*Kisses her brother and Varya, then her
> brother again*) And Varya is just the same as ever, looks
> like a nun. And I knew Dunyasha—.(*Kisses Dunyasha*)
> GAYEFF: The train was two hours late. How's that? How's that
> for good management?
> CHARLOTTA (*To Pishtchik*): My dog he eats nuts, too.
> PISHTCHIK (*Astonished*): Think of that!
> DUNYASHA: We waited so long—
> ANYA: I didn't sleep all four nights on the way. And now I feel
> so chilly.

Charlotta's speech, sometimes translated, "My little dog eats nuts," is the most famous example of Chekhov's irrelevancies. It's not prepared for; the others pay no attention. Another example follows shortly after:

ANYA: Well, how are things? Has the interest on the mortgage been paid?

VARYA: How could we?

ANYA: Oh, my God, my God—!

VARYA: In August the estate is to be sold—

ANYA: My God—!

LOPAHIN: (*Looking in through the door and mooing like a cow*) Moo-o-o—. (*Goes away*)

VARYA: (*Tearfully*) I'd land him one like that—(*Shaking her fist*)

ANYA: (*Embracing Varya gently*) Varya, has he proposed?

No, and he never does; all potential love affairs in this play are talked about, but never get anywhere. Lopahin tries to get Madame Ranevskaya to do something.

LOPAHIN: Merciful God! My father was a serf; belonged to your grandfather and your father; but you, your own self, you did so much for me once that I've forgotten all that and love you like my own kin—more than my kin. . . . I want to tell you something very pleasant, cheerful. I'm going right away. There's no time for talking. Well, I'll make it two or three words. As you know, your cherry orchard is to be sold for your debts; the auction is set for August 22nd, but don't you worry, my dear, you just sleep in peace, there's a way out of it. Here's my plan. Please listen to me. Your estate is only thirteen miles from town. They've run the railroad by it. Now if the cherry orchard and the land along the river were cut up into building lots and leased for summer cottages, you'd have at the very lowest twenty-five thousand rubles per year income.

But of course Madame Ranevskaya can come to no such decision, to no decision at all. She is completely improvident.

LYUBOFF ANDREEVNA: Oh, my sins—I've always thrown money around like mad, recklessly, and I married a man who accumulated nothing but debts. My husband died from champagne—he drank fearfully—and to my misfortune I fell in love with another man. I lived with him, and just at that time—it was my first punishment—a blow over the head: right here in the river my boy was drowned and I went abroad—went away for good, never to return. . . . I shut my eyes, ran away, beside myself, and he after me—mercilessly, brutally. I bought a villa near Mentone, because he fell ill there, and for three years I knew no rest day or night, the sick man exhausted me, my soul dried up. And last year when the villa was sold for debts, I went to Paris and there he robbed me of everything, threw me over, took up with another woman; I tried to poison myself—so stupid, so shameful—And suddenly I was seized with longing for Russia, for my own country, for my little girl. . . .

On the day of the auction, the Ranevsky's give a ball, orchestra and all, with no money. The estate is sold to Lopahin. In the last act everybody leaves the house, which is to be torn down, except old Fiers, who has been forgotten there. He's locked in and lies down on the sofa; in the distance, the sound of an axe chopping down the cherry trees.

No character in *The Cherry Orchard* undergoes a reversal of fortune. They all remain at the end what they were in the beginning, only more so. It is not a tragedy. But it is not a comedy, either. There is no re-establishment of order at the end, no marriages, no all's well that ends well feeling. Life goes on, in "slice of life" fashion or, more accurately, life slips away. There is an impression of formlessness within a tight "musical" form: overture or arrival, lento (slow), scherzo (lively), and departure or coda "movements." None of the people is heroic, nor is there a single protagonist. It is rather a way of life, a social group, that acts as protagonist and falls or changes. The drama, lyrical in ways that remind one of Aeschylus, absorbs the audience in its enclosed world, and the tensions are cumulative until one is overwhelmed by the blows of the axe.

Drama of Ideas

With *The Cherry Orchard* in 1904 Chekhov had achieved what he had been working toward, an utterly realistic drama independent of artificially introduced violence for its dramatic effect. There are no shootings, no murder, no suicide. In England George Bernard Shaw was working out his own dramaturgy, those plays in which the conflict, the chief "action," was to be ideas clashing with ideas. Shaw's approach to theatre was unique; he was a drama critic, an early defender of Ibsen in England, turned playwright. His first play, *Widowers' Houses* (1892), although far from his best, shows the kind of drama to come. It was attacked as "a rather silly play by a rather clever man," "a revolting picture of middle class life" showing "with Zolaesque exactitude that the middle class even to its womanhood is brutal at heart," "a discussion with open doors of the pros and cons of slum landlordism." The key word is *discussion*, although we can see a connection with the problem play, and with the naturalists, from whom Shaw differed greatly in one important respect. The naturalists were deadly serious and wrote tragedies about the lower classes; Shaw was witty and wrote his own kind of play which can only be called Shavian comedy.

Allan Lewis has said of Shaw's first play, "It was gay, full of laughter and irrepressible wit. The author was a potent combination of Ibsen, Molière, and Henry George; the three factors of wit, socialism, and discussion he was to develop to the point where they became a meaningful extension of the modern theatre."[6] Probably Shaw's drama of ideas achieved its special character most completely in *Man and Superman, Major Barbara*, and *Saint Joan*, three of the best plays of a surprisingly large output. In the Don Juan in Hell scene of *Man and Superman*, four characters (the Devil, Don Juan or John Tanner, Ana de Ulloa or Ann Whiteside, and the Statue or her father) discuss good and evil, punishment, love, and happiness in what has been called the "talkiest piece in all dramatic literature." It has been given with some success by itself in the theatre, with three actors and an actress sitting at a table.

Added to Shaw's method of dramatic discussion is his device of using inversion as wit, which is reminiscent of his countryman, Oscar Wilde. But what in Wilde comes out froth, in Shaw has a serious core. Wilde wrote: The only way to get rid of a temptation is to yield to it. And Shaw: Hell is the home of honor, duty, justice, and the rest of the seven deadly virtues. Wilde: The truth is rarely pure and never simple. Modern life would be very tedious if it were either, and modern literature a complete impossibility! Shaw: Unless you state a thing irritatingly you might as well not state it at all.

Similar "sentences" could be placed side by side almost indefinitely. But Shaw's wit goes beyond the sentence, beyond standing an idea on its head, then putting it back on its feet in a different setting, so that one is shocked into fresh thought and observation. It extends to plot and character. Don Juan is not really the great lover; his success is due to his rejection of female pursuers. Andrew Undershaft, the munitions manufacturer, is the most religious of men because he is honest and in tune with the modern world.

Shaw's plays are more than mere debate, although there is more talk than what we usually think of as action. You find characters—Eliza, Henry, Major Barbara, Saint Joan, Cleopatra, Candida—situation, conflict of aims, crises, resolutions. But Shaw used the theatre to present a

[6]Allan Lewis, *The Contemporary Theatre* (New York: Crown Publishers, Inc., 1962), p. 83.

philosophy, to evoke opposing values in a many-sided discussion, thereby challenging in the audience a special level of response. There is no point in saying that discussion cannot be drama when Shaw proves otherwise.

Sean O'Casey called Shaw "the greatest British playwright of his age; none equalled him then, none equal him now. None of those who learned from him have yet thrown a wider chest than his own." Lewis summarizes Shaw's frame of reference, which gave him the basis for brilliant comedy.

> You have to believe in a set of values before you can ridicule what has gone before or what is in effect today. Complete cynicism is never comedy. Shaw, like Molière and Aristophanes, was able to laugh at what was because he had a sense of what ought to be. And in advancing beyond Ibsen, he created a wider range for the unfolding of the modern theatre.[7]

Shaw, like Chekhov, had no real imitators; nobody else had quite the same combination of dramatic ingredients. But both have added to the world's dramatic literature and both exert far-reaching influences on the drama of the mid-twentieth century.

Major Barbara

Major Barbara was published in 1905 by Shaw. One of his interminable prefaces, forty-three pages called "First Aid to Critics," preceded one hundred ten pages of play. Perhaps the best remark in this preface is the cynical, "Well, it cannot be denied that the English are only too anxious to recognize a man of genius if somebody will kindly point him out to them. Having pointed myself out in this manner with some success, I now point out Samuel Butler ... " Shaw's descriptions of his settings and characters are equally lengthy, but not without point. There are three sets in *Major Barbara*. Let us begin with part of the opening stage directions:

> It is after dinner on a January night, in the library of Lady Britomart Undershaft's house in Wilton Crescent. A large and comfortable settee is in the middle of the room, upholstered in dark leather. A person sitting on it (it is vacant at present) would have, on his right, Lady Britomart's writing-table, with the lady herself busy at it; a smaller writing-table behind him on his left; the door behind him on Lady Britomart's side; and a window with a window-seat directly on his left. Near the window is an armchair.

[7]Lewis, *The Contemporary Theatre*, p. 111.

Lady Britomart is a woman of fifty or thereabouts, well dressed and yet careless of her dress, well bred and quite reckless of her breeding, well mannered and yet appallingly outspoken and indifferent to the opinions of her interlocutors, amiable and yet peremptory, arbitrary, and high-tempered to the last bearable degree, and withal a very typical managing matron of the upper class, treated as a naughty child until she grew into a scolding mother, and finally settling down with plenty of practical ability and worldly experience, limited in the oddest way with domestic and class limitations, conceiving the universe exactly as if it were a large house in Wilton Crescent, though handling her corner of it very effectively on that assumption, and being quite enlightened and liberal as to the books in the library, the pictures on the walls, the music in the portfolios, and the articles in the papers.

Major Barbara by George Bernard Shaw. Photo by Vandamm, courtesy of the Theatre Collection the New York Public Library at Lincoln Center, Astor, Lenox, and Tilden Foundations.

One almost thinks, what need is there of dialogue? But dialogue there is, and it conveys precisely and on its own Shaw's description of things as they are. The family situation is somewhat irregular, although settled. Mr. Undershaft doesn't live here any more, and presumably hasn't for some fifteen years. The separation reflects a husband-and-wife difference of opinion. Undershaft is looking for an adoptable foundling, to be named Andrew Undershaft, to whom he can leave the Undershaft cannon business; this has been the traditional succession since the reign of James the First. Legitimate children just won't do, although Lady Brit has different ideas about her son Stephen. Of Stephen's two sisters, Sarah is to be married but will need financial help, and Barbara, a Major in the Salvation Army, has a sort of fiancé, too—Adolphus Cusins, a professor of Greek who has followed her into the Army. For these reasons the father, Andrew, has been invited to the house. The two fiancés, "Cholly" and "Dolly," are also present. Enter the munitions king.

LADY B.: Good evening, Andrew.

UNDERSHAFT: How d'ye do, my dear.

LADY B.: You look a good deal older.

UNDERSHAFT (*apologetically*): I *am* somewhat older. (*with a touch of courtship*) Time has stood still with you.

LADY B. (*promptly*): Rubbish! This is your family.

UNDERSHAFT (*surprised*): Is it so large? I am sorry to say my memory is failing very badly in some things. (*He offers his hand with paternal kindness to Lomax.*)

LOMAX (*jerkily shaking his hand*): Ahdedoo.

UNDERSHAFT: I can see you are my eldest. I am very glad to meet you again, my boy.

LOMAX (*remonstrating*): No, but look here, don't you know—. (*overcome*) Oh, I say!

LADY B. (*recovering from momentary speechlessness*): Andrew: do you mean to say that you don't remember how many children you have?

UNDERSHAFT: Well, I am afraid I—. They have grown so much —er. Am I making any ridiculous mistake? I may as well confess: I recollect only one son. But so many things have happened since, of course—er—.

LADY B. (*decisively*): Andrew: you are talking nonsense. Of course you have only one son.

UNDERSHAFT: Perhaps you will be good enough to introduce me, my dear.

LADY B.: That is Charles Lomax, who is engaged to Sarah.

UNDERSHAFT: My dear sir, I beg your pardon.

LOMAX: Notatall. Delighted, I assure you.

LADY B.: This is Stephen.

UNDERSHAFT (*bowing*): Happy to make your acquaintance, Mr. Stephen. Then (*going to Cusins*) you must be my son (*taking Cusins' hands in his*). How are you, my young friend? (*To Lady Britomart*) He is very like you, my love.

CUSINS: You flatter me, Mr. Undershaft. My name is Cusins: engaged to Barbara. (*Very explicitly*) That is Major Barbara Undershaft, of the Salvation Army. That is Sarah, your second daughter. This is Stephen Undershaft, your son.

UNDERSHAFT: My dear Stephen, I beg your pardon.

STEPHEN: Not at all.

UNDERSHAFT: Mr. Cusins: I am much indebted to you for explaining so precisely. (*Turning to Sarah*) Barbara, my dear—

SARAH (*prompting him*): Sarah.

UNDERSHAFT: Sarah, of course. (*They shake hands. He goes over to Barbara.*) Barbara—I am right this time, I hope.

BARBARA: Quite right. (*They shake hands.*)

UNDERSHAFT: My difficulty is that if I play the part of a father, I shall produce the effect of an intrusive stranger; and if I play the part of a discreet stranger, I may appear a callous father.

A little later the discussion points to future developments in Act II at the Salvation Army Shelter and in Act III at Undershaft's munition works.

UNDERSHAFT: Not at all. The more destructive war becomes the more fascinating we find it. No, Mr. Lomax: I am obliged to you for making the usual excuse for my trade; but I am not ashamed of it. I am not one of those men who keep their morals and their business in watertight compartments. All the spare money my trade rivals spend on hospitals, cathedrals and other receptacles for conscience money, I devote to experiments and researches in improved methods of destroying life and property. I have always done so; and I always shall. Therefore your Christmas card moralities of peace on earth and good will among men are of no use to me. Your Christianity, which enjoins you to resist not evil, and to turn the other cheek, would make me a bankrupt. My morality—my religion—must have a place for cannons and torpedoes in it.

STEPHEN (*coldly—almost sullenly*): You speak as if there were half a dozen moralities and religions to choose from, instead of one true morality and one true religion.

UNDERSHAFT: For me there is only one true morality; but it might not fit you, as you do not manufacture aerial battleships. There is only one true morality for every man; but every man has not the same true morality.

LOMAX (*overtaxed*): Would you mind saying that again? I didn't quite follow it.

CUSINS: It's quite simple. As Euripides says, one man's meat is another man's poison morally as well as physically.

UNDERSHAFT: Precisely.

LOMAX: Oh, that. Yes, yes, yes. True. True.

STEPHEN: In other words, some men are honest and some are scoundrels.

BARBARA: Bosh. There are no scoundrels.

UNDERSHAFT: Indeed? Are there any good men?

BARBARA: No. Not one. There are neither good men nor scoundrels: there are just children of one Father; and the sooner they stop calling one another names the better. You needn't talk to me: I know them. I've had scores of them through my hands: scoundrels, criminals, infidels, philanthropists, missionaries, county councillors, all sorts. They're all just the same sort of sinner; and there's the same salvation ready for them all.

UNDERSHAFT: May I ask have you ever saved a maker of cannons?

BARBARA: No. Will you let me try?

UNDERSHAFT: Well, I will make a bargain with you. If I go to see you tomorrow in your Salvation Shelter, will you come the day after to see me in my cannon works?

BARBARA: Take care. It may end in your giving up the cannons for the sake of the Salvation Army.

UNDERSHAFT: Are you sure it will not end in your giving up the Salvation Army for the sake of the cannons?

BARBARA: I will take my chance of that.

UNDERSHAFT: And I will take my chance of the other. (*They shake hands on it.*) Where is your shelter?

BARBARA: In West Ham. At the sign of the cross. Ask anybody in Canning Town. Where are your works?

UNDERSHAFT: In Perivale St. Andrews. At the sign of the sword. Ask anybody in Europe.

The way the play ends holds hardly any surprises. At the Salvation Army Shelter the souls that Barbara saves are sad representatives of the working class; poverty (the only sin according to Undershaft) drives them to accept religion and coffee. Undershaft wins Barbara quite easily by buying out the Salvation Army. They need funds. They can carry on only with the money they get from Bodger, the maker of bad whiskey, and from Undershaft, the maker of cannon. Barbara and Cusins are the only people the industrialist has met "at home" who interest him. On a technical point they are able to prove Cusins's illegitimacy, which makes him a candidate for succession. Barbara agrees to marry him when he accepts, and she will thereafter devote herself to saving the souls of the well cared for workmen living in neat, clean homes near the Undershaft plant.

One is bound to experience increasing frustration on coming to the drama of the last fifty years, in deciding in what category to place which work. A play by Luigi Pirandello is particularly difficult to categorize. One must remember that the work of any playwright of real stature and originality is uniquely itself. There is really as much difference between Aeschylus and Euripides as between Oscar Wilde and Samuel Beckett. But distance tends to blur distinctions and bring out similarities.

There is some justification for trying to fix a label *if* it reveals something of the nature of what it labels, and if we affix it modestly and tentatively. Pirandello's drama seems to belong to the drama of ideas, although of course his ideas are not Shaw's ideas, and his technique is quite divergent. But he has been classified with almost equal validity as the most violent of antirealists, as an expressionist, as a symbolist, as an existentialist, even as a writer of the Theatre of the Absurd, along with Beckett, Ionesco, and Jean Gênet. This latter grouping seems a little absurd itself, although one channel of Pirandello's influence may flow in that direction.

One thing now seems certain. Pirandello is the greatest dramatist Italy has produced. During the season of 1965–66 the most exciting theatre in Italy was the revival of the minor plays of Pirandello. In Paris, where one has a wider choice, two of the memorable productions since 1950 have been *Right You Are* (*Chacun sa vérité* in French, for the title is tricky) at the Comédie Francaise and Jean Vilar's production of *Henry IV*. The placing of Pirandello as antirealist is certainly correct in one respect. He was always conscious of the play as play, and its particular artificialities as an art form. Allan Lewis says:

> Ibsen and those who fought at his side stormed the citadel of ro-
> mantic intrigue and vacuous formula plays, to establish the theatre
> of psychological insight and integrity in human relations. No sooner
> was realism triumphant than it was attacked from all quarters as
> limiting the vision of man to the earthly and confining it to the
> middle-class living room. If Ibsen is realism's affirmation, Pirandello
> is its negation.[8]

At the center of Pirandello's ideas, of his philosophy, is the relativity of truth. Ibsen had found truth perishable, good for perhaps twenty years. Pirandello says it is impossible to find and fix. Theories of relativity have upset not only modern mathematics and physics but modern philosophy and metaphysics as well.

[8]Lewis, *The Contemporary Theatre*, pp. 127–28.

Right You Are (If You Think So)

Right You are (If You Think So) is sometimes called It Is So (If You Think So),[9] which may be closer to the Italian Così è, (se vi pare!) but not quite as close to the play's meaning. It was written in 1917 and is generally considered the most famous statement of Pirandello's relativism. However, it is not a bald statement. It is a devastating satire of idle curiosity and gossip, and the damage they can do. There is, as in the typical mature Pirandello, a character who speaks for the author— the honest man of reason used much as Molière had used him. Here it is Lamberto Laudisi, the brother of one of the curious matrons. The struggle is caused by the desire of other people to know the truth about a certain family, the Ponzas, newly moved to "a small Italian town, the capital of a province," which is therefore full of bureaucrats.

Right You Are If You Think You Are by Luigi Pirandello. Photo by Vandamm, courtesy of the Theatre Collection the New York Public Library at Lincoln Center, Astor, Lenox, and Tilden Foundations.

There is one setting, the parlor in the house of Commendatore Agazzi, Laudisi's brother-in-law and an official under whom Signor Ponza has come to work. "A door, the general entrance, at the back; doors leading to the wings, left and right." At the Comédie Française a raked stage

[9]Excerpts from the book NAKED MASKS: FIVE PLAYS by Luigi Pirandello. Edited by Eric Bentley. Copyright, 1922, by E. P. Dutton & Co., Inc. Renewal, 1950, in the names of Stefano, Fausto, and Lietta Pirandello. Dutton Paperback Edition. Reprinted by permission of the publishers.

was used and the floor was covered with large square tiles in yellow and black, giving a chess-board effect and concentrating vision on the entrance center backstage. The curious are chiefly Agazzi and his wife Amalia, their daughter Dina, and Sirelli and his wife, who bring along Signora Cini and Signora Nenni to find out what the others know.

> SIGNORA SIRELLI: Amalia dearest, we have come here as to the fountain of knowledge. We are two pilgrims athirst for the truth!
>
> AMALIA: The truth? Truth about what?
>
> SIGNORA SIRELLI: Why . . . about this blessed Mr. Ponza of ours, the new secretary at the prefecture. He is the talk of the town, take my word for it, Amalia.
>
> SIGNORA CINI: And we are all just dying to find out!
>
> AMALIA: But we are as much in the dark as the rest of you, I assure you, madam.
>
> SIRELLI (to his wife): What did I tell you? They know no more about it than I do. In fact, I think they know less about it than I do. Why is it this poor woman is not allowed to see her daughter? Do you know the reason, you people, the real reason?
>
> AMALIA: Why, I was just discussing the matter with my brother.
>
> LAUDISI: And my view of it is that you're all a pack of gossips!

Agazzi has been to the prefect (police) because his wife and daughter have been refused entrance twice when they "called on" Signora Frola, Ponza's mother-in-law.

> AGAZZI: You see, some of the talk had reached his ears already. And he agrees that it is better, as a matter of his own official prestige, for all this mystery in connection with one of his assistants to be cleared up, so that once and for all we shall know the truth.

Laudisi bursts out laughing, because, as is reported, he says that no one can ever know the truth. We slowly find out that Signor Ponza and his wife live on the fifth floor of a tenement apartment building at the edge of town. She never goes out. Signora Frola is established in an apartment in the same building as the Agazzis. She goes to see her daughter but talks up to her from the courtyard only; they pass messages by means of a rope and basket. There *must* be some reason. Signor Ponza, under duress, explains that his wife is not the daughter of Signora Frola, but a second wife. His first wife, who was her daughter, is dead, but the Signora is mad in this one respect and refuses to believe it. She explains that Ponza is mad in one respect. He has never recovered from the delusion that his first wife died while she was away in a hospital, and the marriage ceremony was performed a second time to humor Ponza. Relations between mother and son-in-law are very good, each doing his best to preserve the other's illusion.

Agazzi tries to obtain official documents, to question people in the community from which the Ponzas came. That's the way to get at the truth. But they came from a village in Marsica, recently destroyed by earthquake. There are no documents to be had. And families and friends all died at the same time. The frustration of the truth seekers mounts, goaded by Laudisi's sneers and laughter, until at the end of the play they have arranged to interview Signora Ponza herself.

> (The Company divides to either hand. A lady has appeared at the door in back. She is dressed in deep mourning and her face is concealed with a thick, black, impenetrable veil.)

> SIGNORA FROLA (*uttering a piercing shriek of joy*): Oh, Lena! Lena! Lena! Lena!

> (She dashes forward and throws her arms about the veiled woman with the passionate hysteria of a mother who has not embraced her daughter for years and years. But at the same time from beyond the door in the rear another piercing cry comes. Ponza dashes into the room.)

> PONZA: No! Julia! Julia! Julia!

> (At his voice Signora Ponza draws up stiffly in the arms of Signora Frola who is clasping her tightly. Ponza notices that his mother-in-law is thus desperately entwined about his wife and he shrieks desperately.)

> PONZA: Cowards! Liars! I knew you would! I knew you would! It is just like the lot of you!

> SIGNORA PONZA (*turning her veiled head with a certain austere solemnity toward her husband*): Don't be afraid! Just take her away! Go!

> (Signora Frola, at these words, turns to her son-in-law and humbly, tremblingly, goes over and embraces him.)

> SIGNORA FROLA: Yes, yes, you poor boy, come with me, come with me.

> (Their arms about each other's waists, and holding each other up affectionately, Ponza and his mother-in-law withdraw through the rear door. They are both weeping. Profound silence in the company. All those present stand there with their eyes fixed upon the departing couple. As Signora Frola and Ponza are lost from view, all eyes turn expectantly upon the veiled lady. Some of the women are weeping.)

SIGNORA PONZA (*having looked at them through her veil, speaking with dark solemnity*): What else do you want of me, after this, ladies and gentlemen? There is a misfortune here, as you see, which must stay hidden: otherwise the remedy which our compassion has found cannot avail.

THE PREFECT (*moved*): We want to respect your compassion, madam. It's only that we'd like you to tell us...

SIGNORA PONZA (*slowly, and with clear articulation*): Tell you what? The truth? Simply this: I am the daughter of Signora Frola...

ALL (*with a happy intake of breath*): Ah!

SIGNORA PONZA: ... and the second wife of Signor Ponza....

ALL (*amazed and disenchanted, quietly*): ... What!

SIGNORA PONZA (*continuing*): ... and, for myself, I am nobody!

THE PREFECT: No, no, madam, for yourself you must be either one or the other!

SIGNORA PONZA: No! I am she whom you believe me to be. (*She looks at them all through her veil for a moment, then leaves. Silence.*)

LAUDISI: And there, my friends, you have the truth! (*With a look of derisive defiance at them all*) Are you satisfied? (*He bursts out laughing.*)

At the end Laudisi is more clearly Pirandello than anywhere else. There is a bitterness, almost a malice, underlying this comedy, which is as much philosophical and metaphysical as satiric. But it leaves the shock of heightened awareness that Eliot calls for in a work of art.

Expressionism and Antirealism

Realistic drama has continued without significant changes to produce theatre since Ibsen (and some of its best and most artistic uses have been in the film documentaries). However, the modern pressures that brought it about—Darwin, Marx, Freud and others—have also impelled dramatists to find other forms and modes of expression. Symbolism, not always divorced from realism as we have seen in examining Ibsen and Chekhov, was probably an attempt to say more in condensed space, to point dramatic interest, and to express the inexpressible. It moved briefly toward an impressionistic, neoromantic theatre in Maeterlinck and some of Rostand before developing into expressionism. One of the notable schools of modern drama and one of the most vital of the antirealistic movements, expressionism is often unacknowledged by its practitioners. From August Strindberg through Frank Wedekind and Karel Capek and others, this form found its reason for being: the expression of an inner reality or psychological state not subject to realism or photographic naturalism. Dreams, for instance, most of them Freudian, are sufficiently real human experience; but they must be shown by symbolism and exaggeration and an underlining of irrationality. Expressionistic theatre can be as exciting as plays by O'Neill, Wilder, and Tennessee Williams.

A great disservice has been done to expressionism by marking its end with Ernst Toller and Georg Kaiser. They were, of course, expressionists, but really a little channel by themselves that soon dried out—perhaps they were too extreme. In any event, almost everyone agrees that the movement was begun by Strindberg. In his preface to *The Dream Play* (1902) Strindberg, who had already written plays in the realistic and naturalistic modes, indicated an expressionistic approach to drama, "Anything may happen; everything is possible and probable. Time and space do not exist. On an insignificant background of reality, imagination designs and embroiders novel patterns; a medley of memories, experiences, free fantasies, absurdities, and improvisations." There is for drama, as for literature in general, an important analogy here with expressionism in painting, where the artist attempts to externalize an inward vision by the use of nonrepresentational symbols, by the juxtaposition of objects whose relationship sets up tensions, or simply by outlining a figure in black.

To those who think that the best of the theatre of the mid-twentieth century is "modified realism," it is time to suggest that it would be equally proper, perhaps more proper, to call the genre modified expressionism. We shall return to this problem later.

Dynamo

Eugene O'Neill openly acknowledged his deep indebtedness to August Strindberg by calling him "the precursor of all modernity in our present theatre . . . the greatest interpreter of spiritual conflicts which constitute the drama—the blood—of our lives today." *The Emperor Jones* and *The Hairy Ape* have often been analyzed as examples of O'Neill's expressionism and, more particularly, of the influence of Strindberg. Of equal interest, perhaps, although less often played, is *Dynamo*,[10] a three-

[10]Excerpts from PLAYS OF EUGENE O'NEILL. Copyright 1929 and renewed 1957 by Carlotta Monterey O'Neill. Reprinted from PLAYS OF EUGENE O'NEILL by permission of Random House, Inc.

act play dated 1929. Allan Lewis very properly relates this work to Strindberg in discussing the earliest of the Swedish playwright's expressionistic dramas, *To Damascus.*

> The protagonist seeks peace and order and redemption as he senses, somewhat reluctantly, the deeper meaning of God's enduring grace. The mystery of life on earth is paralleled by the mystery of God's way with man. It is not the God of institutionalized religion. The dogma of all faiths, dutifully interpreted, is of no avail. Strindberg tried to hammer out a personal religion, as O'Neill much later, under the influence of Strindberg, attempted to do in *Dynamo.* The concept is Promethean; the realization, a combination of Dürer and Kandinsky.[11]

O'Neill employs several expressionistic techniques in *Dynamo* to externalize the inner conflict. First, there is an underlining by simplification of the two most extreme religious positions in the modern world: The conservative, orthodox, literalistic fundamentalism of the Reverend Hutchins Light is opposed to the atheism of his next-door neighbor Ramsey Fife. Fife works at the electric plant in the small Connecticut town and carries atheism to the point of religious bigotry. The staging is non-realistic, much like that in O'Neill's otherwise naturalistic play, *Desire Under the Elms.* "Only the half sections of the two houses are visible which are nearest to each other, the one containing the Fife sitting room, with Ramsay's and May's bedroom directly above it, and the section of the Light's home in which are their sitting room and Reuben's bedroom on the floor above. As the separate scenes require, the front walls of these rooms are removed to show the different interiors." Interspersed with the dialogue are the spoken inner thoughts of the characters—not, presumably, in the "freeze" fashion of *Strange Interlude,* but in a cross between the old aside and soliloquy of Renaissance theatre that would never be found in a realistic play. And finally, there is the central symbol of the dynamo itself, with a suggested distortion in the direction of an idol.

We first see the Lights on a May evening with a thunderstorm coming. Reuben, the seventeen-year-old son, is in his bedroom looking out the window and dreaming of Ada, the girl next door. The house is small and miserably furnished, although clean, with only kerosene lamps for lighting. The minister tells Mrs. Light that he has decided on Reuben's future—he will be a minister like his father and grandfather. But the antagonism between the Lights and the Fifes becomes clear when Reuben sneaks out to see Ada. Mr. Fife arranges with Ada to lure the boy into their house.

[11]Lewis, *The Contemporary Theatre,* p. 50.

Dynamo by Eugene O'Neill. Photo by Vandamm, courtesy of the Theatre Collection the New York Public Library at Lincoln Center, Astor, Lenox, and Tilden Foundations.

FIFE: I want a serious talk with you, young man! That's why I had Ada invite you in! (*Reuben stares at him bewilderdly*) But before we start that, let me ask you, is your reverend father ever going to take up my challenge to debate with me!

REUBEN (*shamefacedly*): I—I don't think so.

FIFE (*jeeringly*): He's afraid I'd beat him!

REUBEN (*defensively*): No, he isn't! He can answer all your arguments easy—with things right out of the Bible! He's only scared that folks'd think he was wrong to argue with you! (*Then raising his voice defiantly*) But I'd argue if I was in his place!

MRS. LIGHT (*from her hiding place by the hedge has caught Reuben's raised voice—with horrified stupefaction*): That was Reuben's voice! ... he's actually in there talking to that atheist! ... oh, I wish I could get closer to the window! ... but she'd see me! ... (*But she comes around the end of the hedge as far as she can and strains her ears*).

FIFE (*smiling mockingly at Reuben*): Well, maybe after you're a minister you and me'll argue it out sometime.

REUBEN (*glad to make a show of independence before Fife*): I'm not going to be a minister! Father wants me to, but Mother doesn't—and I don't want to be. Besides, I've never felt the call. You have to feel God calling you to His service.

FIFE (*with a leer*): And how does God call you, tell me? I'm thinkin' He wouldn't use the telegraph or telephone or radio for they're contraptions that belong to His arch-enemy Lucifer, the God of Electricity.

Fife asks Reuben his intentions toward Ada, and the boy says he wants to marry her. He then plays a somewhat elaborate trick on Reuben, based on a newspaper story he has just read. Swearing him to secrecy, he confesses that his real name is Clark, that he is guilty of murder, that his life is in Reuben's hands. Back home, however, Mrs. Light worms the story out of her son while the minister hides in the boy's closet. There is a beating scene as the storm grows worse. Mr. Light leaves to go to the police; jeers between Fife and Light, then Ada explains the "joke." All the Lights are in the street, the Fifes in their house, as we approach the first-act curtain.

LIGHT (*points a shaking finger at Reuben*): This dunce—this stupid dolt—now I shall be the butt of all their sneers! And to think I stayed my hand—! But wait! I'll show him what a real whipping is!

REUBEN (*fiercely*): You'll never dare touch me again, you old fool! I'm not scared of you or your God any more! (*There is a blinding flash of lightning. Light, his nerves already at the breaking point, gives a gasp of superstitious fright.*)

LIGHT: God have mercy!

REUBEN (*with a sneer*): What God? Fife's God! Electricity? Are you praying to It for mercy? It can't hear you! It doesn't give a damn about you! (*There is a tremendous crash of thunder. Reuben looks up and gives a wild laugh as though the thunder elated him. His mother and father shrink back from him as he shouts up at the sky*) Shoot away, Old Bozo! I'm not scared of You!

MRS. LIGHT: Reuben! You don't know what you're saying!

REUBEN (*with a hard, mocking laugh—to his mother*): What's the matter? Do you still believe in his fool God? I'll show you! (*He jumps to his father's side and grabs his raincoat by the lapel—addressing the sky with insulting insolence*) If there is his God let Him strike me dead this second! I dare Him; (*His father squeals with terror and tries to break away from his hold. His mother screams. He laughs triumphantly*) There! Didn't I tell you! (*Light finally tears his coat from Reuben's grip and runs panic-stricken off right, dragging his moaning wife by the arm. Reuben turns his back on his home determinedly and starts walking off left—with bitter defiance*) There is no God! No God but Electricity! I'll never be scared again! I'm through with the lot of you!

Fifteen months pass. Reuben returns home on a hot August day and finds that his mother is dead. The boy has become a man physically, and he gives Ada what he now knows she wants. Their positions have changed, as Reuben says to Ada:

REUBEN: Cut out that talk of being scared! What are you scared about? Scared what we did was a sin? You're the hell of an atheist! And you're the one that used to be always kidding me about being a goody boy! There's nothing to be scared about or sorry for. What we did was just plain sex—an act of nature—and that's all there is to it!

Which does not, of course, satisfy Ada. Reuben gets a job at the electrical plant where Fife works and turns with increasing sympathy to Ada's mother, a big, indolent, earth-mother type, who, like Reuben, admires the dynamo and its song. In the last scene of the second act we come for the first time to the dynamo.

Exterior of the Light and Power Company's hydro-electric plant about two miles from town. . . . Through the window and the open door of the dynamo room, which is brilliantly lighted by a row of powerful bulbs in white globes . . . , there is a clear view of a dynamo, huge and black, with something of a massive female idol about it, the exciter set on the main structure like a head with blank, oblong eyes above a gross, rounded torso. . . . The air is full of sound, a soft overtone of rushing water from the dam and the river bed below, penetrated dominatingly by the harsh, throaty, metallic purr of the dynamo.

Reuben enters and worships, alone.

> REUBEN: ... It's like a great dark idol ... like the old stone
> statues of gods people prayed to ... only it's living and
> they were dead ... that part on top is like a head ...
> with eyes that see you without seeing you ... and below
> it is like a body ... not a man's ... round like a woman's
> ... as if it had breasts ... but not like a girl ... not like
> Ada ... no, like a woman ... like her mother ... or mine
> ... a great dark mother! ... that's what the dynamo is!
> ... that's what life is! ...

By the third act, which takes place four months later, Reuben has
become an ascetic, fanatic worshipper of the dynamo, in which he has
amalgamated the spirit of his dead mother and the image of Mrs. Fife.
His new god demands sexual abstinence, and he rejects the persistent
advances of Ada, finally killing her in the dynamo room with two shots
from a revolver. Only Mrs. Fife observes the last scene, which brings a
feeling of inevitability—Reuben's self-immolation on the dynamo itself.
The stage directions tell us.

> (He throws his arms out over the exciter, his hands grasp the carbon
> brushes. There is a flash of bluish light about him and all the lights
> in the plant dim down until they are almost out and the noise of the
> dynamo dies until it is the faintest purring hum. Simultaneously
> Reuben's voice rises in a moan that is a mingling of pain and loving
> consummation, and this cry dies into a sound that is like the crooning
> of a baby. ... There is a startled cry from Mrs. Fife as she runs to
> the body. The dynamo's throaty metallic purr rises slowly in volume
> and the lights begin to come up again in the plant.)

The characters in *Dynamo* are not well developed and the plot is rather
thin; but this has to be the case if such a dynamic theme or idea is to
be supported. Power there is. And a problem put in specifically modern
terms. This is what Darwinism, the "mystic wound," the nineteenth-
century split between religion and science, has led to. This play as
drama is the equivalent of the distressed search described in *The Education
of Henry Adams*, where the author philosophically worries the concepts
of Venus, the Virgin, and the Dynamo. Venus was a force in the Classical
world, and Adams quotes Lucretius. The Virgin was a force in the
Middle Ages and built cathedrals; Chartres is her work. But "in America
neither Venus nor Virgin ever had value as force—at most as sentiment."

> Then he showed his scholar the great hall of dynamos, and explained
> how little he knew about electricity or force of any kind, even of his
> own special sun, which spouted heat in inconceivable volume, but
> which, as far as he knew, might spout less or more, at any time,
> for all the certainty he felt in it. To him, the dynamo itself was but

an ingenious channel for conveying somewhere the heat latent in a few tons of poor coal hidden in a dirty engine-house carefully kept out of sight; but to Adams the dynamo became a symbol of infinity. As he grew accustomed to the great gallery of machines, he began to feel the forty-foot dynamos as a moral force, much as the early Christians felt the Cross. The planet itself seemed less impressive, in its old-fashioned, deliberate, annual or daily revolution, than this huge wheel, revolving within arm's-length at some vertiginous speed, and barely murmuring—scarcely humming an audible warning to stand a hair's breadth farther for respect of power—while it would not wake the baby lying close against its frame. Before the end, one began to pray to it; inherited instinct taught the natural expression of man before silent and infinite force. Among the thousand symbols of ultimate energy, the dynamo was not so human as some, but it was the most expressive.... Langley seemed prepared for anything, even for an indeterminable number of universes interfused—physics stark mad in metaphysics.[12]

If God is dead, the dynamo isn't. And man must learn the proper relations with this manifestation of force, or risk being destroyed.

That O'Neill was the first giant among American dramatists is usually recognized. He emerged alone in the 1920's, held his place in the 1930's with some competition; and his posthumous plays have added to his stature. By the 1940's, however, three other American dramatists had achieved a similar significance: Thornton Wilder, Tennessee Williams, and Arthur Miller. All three employed a great many expressionistic and "epic" techniques and were certainly more theatrical than "realistic." The confusion that arises when they are classified as realists, however this term is modified, may be the result of confusing reality with realism. All artists are seriously concerned with presenting what is "real" to them. Realism has been concentrating on surfaces, on verisimilitude, on those things capable of verification by the senses. There are, however, many things real enough, that cannot be so verified. Memory, for instance; and Williams' *The Glass Menagerie* is the first of many plays to objectify the gauzy, fleeting, free-associational quality of this reality. Miller's *Death of a Salesman* carries this essentially expressionistic technique into a new complex.

Death of a Salesman

Place and time are normal and specific in the realistic play, and movement is straightforward. In *Death of a Salesman*[13] the action takes place in Willy Loman's house and yard and various places he visits

[12]Henry Adams, *The Education of Henry Adams* (Boston: Houghton Mifflin Company, 1918), pp. 380–82.

[13]Excerpts from DEATH OF A SALESMAN by Arthur Miller. Copyright 1949 by Arthur Miller. Reprinted by permission of The Viking Press, Inc.

in New York and Boston, moving with the greatest of ease through an unfixed and scaffolded setting whose spatial reality is in flux. We move very freely in time back and forth in Willy's mind, which toward the end of his life is more subject than ever to instability. Uncle Ben is particularly hallucinatory and an effective symbol for a central part of Willy's American dream—the rags to riches, get rich quick scheme. Probably no more expressionistic character has ever appeared on the American stage. The use of musical themes to indicate the movement of Willy's mind is an excellent objectification of an interior state. Color symbolism reinforces idea. Here is a part of Miller's own description of his scene.

> Before us is the Salesman's house. We are aware of towering, angular shapes behind it, surrounding it on all sides. Only the blue light of the sky falls upon the house and forestage; the surrounding area shows an angry glow of orange. As more light appears, we see a solid vault of apartment houses around the small, fragile-seeming home. An air of the dream clings to the place, a dream rising out of reality. The kitchen at center seems actual enough, for there is a kitchen table with three chairs and a refrigerator. But no other fixtures are seen.

There are two bedrooms at split-level raised heights.

> The entire setting is wholly or, in some places, partially transparent. The roof-line of the house is one-dimensional; under and over it we see the apartment buildings. . . . Whenever the action is in the present the actors observe the imaginary wall-lines, entering the house only through its door on the left. But in the scenes of the past these boundaries are broken, and characters enter or leave a room by stepping "through" a wall. . . .

This is an expressionistic painting, even to the angry orange glow.

There seems little point in further argument about whether the play is or is not a tragedy. Perhaps Miller wished to sidestep the issue when he called it "certain private conversations in two acts and a requiem." Willy Loman is not a prince, except perhaps in the American slang use of the word; he is common, undistinguished, often vulgar. But he does bring upon himself a catastrophe that appears out of proportion to his flaws of character and errors of judgment. And he represents *us*; he is definitely American, definitely twentieth-century man. In a way, too, he is Kafka's Gregor Samsa, commercial traveler, the difference being that Loman is a salesman. In the business world of today, anybody who doesn't try to succeed in business is aberrant. But the universality of this play can be further delineated—it forces us to participate, whether we're in business or not, whether we like it or not. This is our life. You build a house in the country and what happens? It becomes suburbia and then city.

Death of a Salesman by Arthur Miller. Photo by Graphic House, Inc.

WILLY: The way they boxed us in here. Bricks and windows. Windows and bricks.

LINDA: We should've bought the land next door.

WILLY: The street is lined with cars. There's not a breath of fresh air in the neighborhood. The grass don't grow any more, you can't raise a carrot in the back yard. They should've had a law against apartment houses. Remember those two beautiful elm trees out there? When I and Biff hung the swing between them?

LINDA: Yeah, like a million miles from the city.

WILLY: They should've arrested the builder for cutting those down. They massacred the neighborhood. . . .

WILLY: There's more people! That's what's ruining this country! Population is getting out of control. The competition is maddening! Smell that stink from that apartment house!

And we all have to buy refrigerators, whether we're salesmen or teachers or lawyers. And cars. And houses.

WILLY: Whoever heard of a Hastings refrigerator? Once in my life I would like to own something outright before it's broken! I'm always in a race with the junk-yard! I just finished paying for the car and it's on its last legs. The refrigerator consumes belts like a goddam maniac. They time those things. They time them so when you finally paid for them, they're used up.

LINDA (*buttoning up his jacket as he unbuttons it*): All told, about two hundred dollars would carry us, dear. But that includes the last payment on the mortgage. After this payment, Willy, the house belongs to us.

WILLY: It's twenty-five years!

There are lots of contradictions in Willy's life, and ours: pride in the automobile—Chevrolet or Studebaker—and cursing the machine when it needs repairs—"that goddam car." There is Willy's need to praise himself, and underneath it his feeling of inferiority. Many Americans exhibit a bluster over emptiness that may be quite touching.

WILLY: Oh, I'll knock 'em dead next week. I'll go to Hartford. I'm very well liked in Hartford. You know, the trouble is, Linda, people don't seem to take to me.

Sex is no answer to the loneliness and frustration, as even Willy's sons find out.

HAPPY: I get that any time I want, Biff. Whenever I feel disgusted. The only trouble is, it gets like bowling or something. I just keep knocking them over, and it doesn't mean anything. You still run around a lot?

Willy's American dream is more complicated than the simple idea of getting rich quick some day. It centers most significantly on his sons and his hopes for them. They were fine athletes and very well liked. But they weren't much as students—Biff, a potential Red Grange, didn't graduate from high school. The boys' morality is weak, too. When they were young, Willy alternated between excessive pride and a deep worry. Now in their thirties they have not realized the potential Willy thought they had. He alternately blames himself and them. As he is fired by the company for which he had worked for thirty-six years, and in the period of grace on his life insurance policy, Willy realizes that he is worth more dead than alive. There is a final family confrontation before the catastrophe.

BIFF: No, you're going to hear the truth—what you are and what I am!

LINDA: Stop it!

WILLY: Spite!

HAPPY (*coming down toward Biff*): You cut it now!

BIFF (*to Happy*): The man don't know who we are! The man is gonna know! (*To Willy*) We never told the truth for ten minutes in this house!

HAPPY: We always told the truth!

BIFF (*turning on him*): You big blow, are you the assistant buyer? You're one of the two assistants to the assistant, aren't you?

HAPPY: Well, I'm practically—

BIFF: You're practically full of it! We all are! And I'm through with it. (*To Willy*) Now hear this, Willy, this is me.

WILLY: I know you!

BIFF: You know why I had no address for three months? I stole a suit in Kansas City and I was in jail. (*To Linda, who is sobbing*) Stop crying. I'm through with it. . . .

WILLY: I suppose that's my fault!

BIFF: And I never got anywhere because you blew me so full of hot air I could never stand taking orders from anybody! That's whose fault it is!

WILLY: I hear that! . . .

BIFF: Pop, I'm a dime a dozen, and so are you!

WILLY (*turning on him now in an uncontrolled outburst*): I am not a dime a dozen! I am Willy Loman, and you are Biff Loman! (*Biff starts for Willy, but is blocked by Happy. In his fury, Biff seems on the verge of attacking his father.*)

BIFF: I am not a leader of men, Willy, and neither are you. You were never anything but a hard-working drummer who landed in the ash can like all the rest of them! I'm one dollar an hour, Willy! I tried seven states and couldn't raise it. A buck an hour! Do you gather my meaning? I'm not bringing home any prizes any more, and you're going to stop waiting for me to bring them home!

WILLY (*directly to Biff*): You vengeful, spiteful mutt! . . .

BIFF (*at the peak of his fury*): Pop, I'm nothing! I'm nothing, Pop. Can't you understand that? There's no spite in it any more. I'm just what I am, that's all.

(*Biff's fury has spent itself, and he breaks down, sobbing, holding on to Willy, who dumbly fumbles for Biff's face.*)

LINDA: He loves you, Willy!

There is nothing left but the suicide in the car and the funeral to which almost nobody comes. The best defense of Willy, and of our concern for the play, came earlier, from the salesman's wife:

LINDA: . . . I don't say he's a great man. Willy Loman never made a lot of money. His name was never in the paper. He's not the finest character that ever lived. But he's a human being, and a terrible thing is happening to him. So attention must be paid. He's not to be allowed to fall into his grave like an old dog. Attention, attention must be finally paid to such a person. You called him crazy—

BIFF: I didn't mean—

LINDA: No, a lot of people think he's lost his—balance. But you don't have to be very smart to know what his trouble is. The man is exhausted.

HAPPY: Sure!

LINDA: A small man can be just as exhausted as a great man. He works for a company thirty-six years this March, opens up unheard-of territories to their trademark, and now in his old age they take his salary away.

Arthur Miller wrote later of Willy Loman, "He gave his life, or sold it, in order to justify the waste of it." The argument over Willy Loman (low-man) goes on. I, for one, can identify with Willy sufficiently to experience a catharsis not unlike that produced by the Greeks and Shakespeare.

Epic Theatre

One offshoot of expressionism has developed into a school of its own, the epic theatre of Bertolt Brecht. This is an intellectual theatre, avowedly designed to make the audience think rather than feel, deliberately antagonistic to realism, and including every possible device for promoting recognition of the artifice and artificiality of a play. Its impact may be emotional, although marshalled against emotional involvement, in plays like *Our Town* and *Skin of Our Teeth* by Thornton Wilder, who has more successfully made use of some of Brecht's innovations than other of our playwrights. Many "epic" effects have been borrowed for plays which are not primarily epic theatre, such as Williams' *Camino Real*.

Epic theatre, as has been often pointed out, is rather injudiciously named. Brecht himself finally thought that theatre whose purpose was to present historical fact in such a way that the audience would be compelled to think and to judge, should be called dialectic theatre. It was to be theatre as education and, by extension, theatre as propaganda. When it is more propaganda than play, it fails. Its best effects have been a forthright theatricality, unhesitating use of any technique to shake up and hold an audience until the time comes to shake it up again.

Brecht's work has been re-evaluated of late. It seems that such works as *Three-Penny Opera* and *Galileo* and perhaps *The Rise and Fall of the City of Mahagonny* will retain importance in the future. Two of these, of course, have the added advantage of music by Kurt Weill.

Drama of Cruelty

The drama of cruelty is hardly a school of theatre or a movement, but the term is used, and it has a limited applicability to some stage effects. In our time it is most often associated with Antonin Artaud who, in his book *The Theatre and Its Double*, advocates a theatrical return to the intensity of primitive rites, to cruelty, incantation, and dream. The dramatic values of cruelty can certainly be traced back to Seneca, and can be seen in the Elizabethan theatre in Shakespeare's *Titus Andronicus* and in plays by Kyd, Webster, and others.

In France the Grand Guignol played for horror, and of course we have a tradition of horror movies. Occasionally this approach can be used in conjunction with material of some significance to make an interesting play. The *Marat/Sade* success of 1965–66 would fall in this category. Often cruelty is found in violent expressionism, and sometimes in combination with the theatre of the absurd—the work of Jean Gênet would be a case in point.

The Visit

A good example of such an amalgam—expressionism, the absurd, the epic, and the cruel—might be Friedrich Dürrenmatt's *The Visit*[14] or, translating the German title fully, *The Visit of the Old Lady*. This play was great theatre as performed by Alfred Lunt and Lynn Fontanne. It is, of course, at the farthest possible remove from realism. Dürrenmatt calls his play a tragi-comedy, but it is perhaps better described as a macabre parable. It was first published in 1956.

The setting is the town of Guellen, a small town somewhere in central Europe, just as universal as the American *Our Town*. The people are different from Wilder's characters, however—more like the residents of Mark Twain's Hadleyburg. And the time is now. Guellen is completely

[14]Excerpts from THE VISIT by Friedrich Dürrenmatt, Grove Press edition. Copyright 1956 by Peter Schifferli Verlag AG. Copyright 1962 by Jonathan Cape Limited. Reprinted by permission of the publishers.

The Visit by Friedrich Dürrenmatt. Photo by Vandamm, courtesy New York Public Library at Lincoln Center.

run down and impoverished. This is made very clear when the play opens at the railway station, as the expresses go roaring through—Venice-Stockholm, Hamburg-Naples. They used to stop, but now all the factories are shut down and there is no economic life in the community at all. In the past Goethe spent the night in Guellen and Brahms composed a quartet there. Now the town is sorely in need of renewal, and everyone is waiting for the announced visit of Claire Zachanassian, multimillionairess, who once lived in Guellen as Claire or Clara Wascher. Her old boy friend, Alfred Ill, is still there as shopkeeper. As in a number of expressionistic plays, many other nameless characters appear: Mayor, Priest, Schoolmaster, Doctor, Man One, and Men Two through Four. Claire arrives, pulling the emergency brake on the Racing Roland Express. She is sixty-three—red hair, pearl necklace, enormous gold bangles —unbelievably overdressed and yet a Society Lady with a rare grace, in spite of all the grotesquerie. She is followed by her entourage: Boby, Toby, Roby, Koby, Loby, and Husband VII. There is an argument with the ticket inspector, until he finds out who she is. "It is Guellen, Moby," she says to Husband VII, "I recognize the wretched dump." Then there is a touching reunion with her former lover, Ill.

> CLAIRE: Call me what you always used to call me.
> ILL: My little wildcat.
> CLAIRE (*purrs like an old cat*): And what else?
> ILL: My little sorceress.
> CLAIRE: I used to call you my black panther.
> ILL: I still am.
> CLAIRE: Rubbish. You've grown fat. And grey. And drink-sodden.

ILL: But *you're* still the same, my little sorceress.

CLAIRE: Don't be daft. I've grown old and fat as well. And lost my left leg. An automobile accident. Now I only travel in express trains. But they made a splendid job of the artificial one, don't you think? (*She pulls up her skirt, displays left leg*) It bends very well.

Claire asks a series of peculiar questions. She asks the priest if he comforts the dying, and people condemned to death. He answers that the death sentence has been abolished in this country. Claire responds that it may be reintroduced. She has a coffin sent to her rooms at The Golden Apostle.

There is an open scene change, façade of station and little adjacent building soar into the flies, the hotel sign of The Golden Apostle is let down. The next scene is Konrad's Village Wood. The Hotel Apostle flies away, four citizens enter with a simple bench, then take their places, holding twigs at arm's length to designate trees. This is one of the places where Alfred and Clara used to make love. Ill kisses her right hand with the words, "The same cool white hand." Claire answers, "No, you're wrong. It's artificial, too. Ivory." When Ill wants to know if she is all artificial, she tells him.

CLAIRE: Practically. My plane crashed in Afghanistan. I was the only one who crawled out of the wreckage. Even the crew died. I'm unkillable.

They return to the inn. Claire asks the doctor if he makes out death certificates and tells him:

Next time, diagnose heart attack.

ILL (*laughing*): Clara has such a golden sense of humour! I could die laughing at one of her jokes!

This remark has a kind of double irony. Claire offers the assembled community one million marks on one condition.

CLAIRE: I'm buying myself justice.

MAYOR: Justice can't be bought.

CLAIRE: Everything can be bought.

She introduces her butler, Boby, formerly Chief Justice Courtly of Guellen. He explains for her.

BUTLER: Madame Zachanassian will give you all a million if you right the wrong she was done in Guellen. . . . The year was nineteen ten . . . I had a paternity claim to arbitrate.

Claire Zachanassian, at the time Clara Wascher, claimed that you, Mr. Ill, were her child's father. At that time, Mr. Ill, you denied paternity. You called two witnesses.

ILL: Oh, it's an old story. I was young, thoughtless.

CLAIRE: Toby and Roby, bring in Koby and Loby. (*The two gum-chewing giants lead pair of blind eunuchs on to centre of stage, blind pair gaily holding hands.*)

They had been the witnesses, who swore a false oath that they had slept with Clara, bribed with a pint of brandy by Ill. Claire had tracked them down, one in Canada, the other in Australia. Thereupon she had turned them over to Toby and Roby, two Manhattan gangsters bought out of Sing Sing, who castrated and blinded the false witnesses. The child of the paternity suit had died after one year; Claire had become a prostitute; old Zachanassian, with his Armenian millions, had found her in a brothel and married her because he fancied her red hair. Now a million for Guellen if someone kills Alfred Ill. Act I ends with Guellen calm and upright.

MAYOR: Madame Zachanassian: you forget, this is Europe. You forget, we are not savages. In the name of all citizens of Guellen, I reject your offer; and I reject it in the name of humanity. We would rather have poverty than blood on our hands. (*Huge applause*)

CLAIRE: I'll wait.

In Act II, Alfred experiences fear. Claire divorces Husband VII and marries VIII. The Guelleners begin to buy lots of things on credit, most conspicuously new yellow shoes. They carry guns because Madame Zachanassian's pet black leopard has escaped from its cage. Ill tries to take his suitcase and escape by train, but he is surrounded by Guelleners who bear him down. At the beginning of Act III the schoolmaster and the doctor appeal to Claire to extend credit to make a business investment in Guellen. But Claire already owns everything in town.

CLAIRE: I had my agents buy the whole ramshackle lot and shut every business down.

SCHOOLMASTER: Madame Zachanassian! You're a woman whose love has been wounded. You make me think of a heroine from antiquity: of Medea. We feel for you, deeply; we understand; but because we do, we are inspired to prove you further: cast away those evil thoughts of revenge, don't try us till we break. Help these poor, weak yet worthy people lead a slightly more dignified life. Let your feeling for humanity prevail!

CLAIRE: Feeling for humanity, gentlemen, is cut for the purse of an ordinary millionaire; with financial resources like mine you can afford a new world order. The world turned me into a whore. I shall turn the world into a brothel. If you can't fork out when you want to dance, you have to put off dancing. You want to dance. They alone are eligible who pay. And I'm paying. Guellen for a murder, a boom for a body.

The schoolmaster then goes to Ill, who has grown to a new way of thinking.

ILL: I've realized I haven't the least right on my side.
SCHOOLMASTER: No right? No right compared to that damned old woman, that brazen arch-whore changing husbands while we watch, and making a collection of our souls?
ILL: That's all my fault, really.
SCHOOLMASTER: Your fault?
ILL: I made Clara what she is, and I made myself what I am, a failing shopkeeper with a bad name. What shall I do, Schoolmaster? Play innocent? It's all my own work, the Eunuchs, the Butler, the coffin, the million. I can't help myself and I can't help any of you, any more. . . .
SCHOOLMASTER: They will kill you. I've known it from the beginning, and you've known it, too, for a long time, even if no one else in Guellen wants to admit it. The temptation is too great and our poverty is too wretched. But I know something else. I shall take part in it. I can feel myself slowly becoming a murderer. My faith in humanity is powerless to stop it. And because I know all this, I have also become a sot. I, too, am scared, Ill, just as you have been scared. And finally I know that one day an old lady will come for us, too, and then what happened to you will also happen to us. . . .

A community murder is arranged, and Guellen has gone the way of Hadleyburg, a town that prided itself on its incorruptibility—it is thoroughly corrupted by money, lots of money. But Guellen fools the assembled press into protecting its public image, with the aid of the Schoolmaster:

SCHOOLMASTER: O people of Guellen! Such is the bitter truth! We have connived at injustice! I am of course fully aware of the material possibilities inherent for all of us in a million. Nor am I blind to the fact that poverty is the root of much evil, nay, of great hardship. And yet, and yet: we are not moved by the money (*huge applause*): we are not moved by ambitious thoughts of prosperity and good living, and luxury: we are moved by this matter of justice, and the problem of how to apply it. Not yet by justice alone, but also by all those ideals, for which our forbears lived and fought, and for which they died; and which constitute the values of our Western World. . . .

There is then a chorus, with the recurring line: "Let us then root out the wrongdoer," which reminds one of Oedipus and the figure of the scapegoat. Alfred is killed; the doctor diagnoses heart attack; the mayor says, "Died of joy." Claire carries off the body in the coffin. In a final formal chorus, all the prosperous Guelleners sing:

> Our suppers now are simmering at home
> And Everyman, contented and well-shod,
> Buys cigarettes of quality at last,

which seems a rather bitter echo, in reverse of an earlier Everyman.

Friedrich Dürrenmatt wrote a postscript for the published version of his play in which there are some illuminating comments.

> To play his character, the actor needs little: only the very outer skin, the text, which of course accords with it. That is to say, just as any creature is sealed off inside its skin, so the play is sealed off inside speech. For speech is all the dramatist provides. It is his end product. And it is consequently impossible to work on the element of speech alone, but only on that which gives rise to speech, namely thought and action; only dilettantes work on speech alone.

The dramatist provides three other things in *The Visit*: the conception of the characters themselves, the songs of the choral movements and the extensive refrains or repetitions, and the spectacle—particularly as indicated in stage directions and set changes. The playwright suggests the "style of folk-plays."

Dürrenmatt also says this about the characters:

> Claire Zachannassian doesn't represent Justice or the Marshall Plan or even the Apocalypse [interesting demurrers], she's purely and simply what she is, namely the richest woman in the world and, thanks to her finances, in a position to act as the Greek tragic heroines acted, absolutely terribly, something like Medea. She can afford to. This lady has a sense of humor. . . . While Claire Zachanassian, fixed and unmoving, is a heroine from the very beginning, her one-time sweetheart still has to develop into a hero . . . who in death, achieves greatness. . . . That death is both meaningful and meaningless. It

would only have been entirely meaningful in the mythological king-dom of some ancient *polis*. But the action of this story unfolds in Guellen.

We suspect the town's name has some unpleasant connotations. (For example, the French expletive, *"ta gueule,"* is perhaps most politely rendered, "your gullet.") The real fall in this play is the fall of the Guelleners, with their representative, the enlightened schoolmaster, whose fall is neither easy nor quick. The playwright's last words are:

> The old lady is a wicked creature, and for precisely that reason mustn't be played wicked. She has to be rendered as human as pos-sible, not with anger but with sorrow and humour, for nothing could harm this comedy with a tragic end more than heavy seriousness.

This play is as didactic and thought-provoking as any epic theatre production.

Theatre of the Absurd

The theatre of the absurd has been receiving more than its share of attention in the beginning of the second half of the twentieth century; there is something faddistic about it—it makes the press. Perhaps the term is well chosen for our times. If realism is clearly a revolt against romanticism, and expressionism a revolt against realism—which is the case—the absurd may be seen as a revolt against epic theatre. Epic theatre has a message, something to communicate to the audience; the theatre of the absurd says that communication is impossible in all cir-cumstances. No two people can communicate with each other in the modern world. The absurdists celebrate the breakdown of language and the absence of values and deliberately baffle the audience. As George Kernodle says so well, "If confusion and chaos are the human condition, then the form of the play itself must make use of interruption, discon-tinuity, incongruity, senseless logic, and senseless repetition."[15] This is the true theatre of disruption.

Eugene Ionesco, in 1950, called his first play an "anti-play." Besides Ionesco, a Roumanian in Paris, the nucleus of the best absurdist drama-tists includes Jean Gênet, a Frenchman; Samuel Beckett, an Irishman; and Arthur Adamov, an Armenian-Russian—all living and working in Paris. Many feel that the best of their plays are those that are least absurd, those that are most theatrical, those that have some frame of reference—in the traditional theatre of the past. *Waiting for Godot*

[15]George Kernodle, *Invitation to the Theatre* (New York: Harcourt, Brace & World, Inc., 1967), p. 310.

has echoes of the *commedia dell' arte* and medieval drama all through it. *Rhinoceros* has echoes of Molière and symbolism. *The Blacks* combines the theatre of cruelty and the propaganda of a social problem with the absurd. In America the best work in this "genre" has come from Edward Albee, who has written *The Sandbox, The American Dream, Tiny Alice*. Albee's best play, with the most story and least absurdity, is *Who's Afraid of Virginia Woolf?* In England, we find the dramatist of the absurd most likely to achieve a lasting place in theatre repertory, Harold Pinter.

It is Ionesco, however, who shows the widest range of absurdist principles and practices. In *The Bald Soprano* (1950) the dialogue is nearly devoid of meaning—and this allows him to make his point: that the empty phrases we habitually use destroy not only communication, but the sense of identity as well. Characters are interchangeable, life is inane. But there is a purpose in the ways of the dramatist if not in the universe. Ionesco wrote (in *Notes and Counternotes*, as cited by George Kernodle in *Invitation to the Theatre*):

> To feel the absurdity of the commonplace, and of language—its false-ness—is already to have gone beyond it. To go beyond it we must first of all bury ourselves in it. What is comical is the unusual in its pure state: nothing seems more surprising to me than that which is banal: the surreal is here, within the grasp of our hands, in our every-day conversation.

Things are as meaningless as words, and as numerous and as cluttered. In *The Chairs* and in *The New Tenant* things crowd out people and, given some of the problems of waste disposal in our cities of the 1960's, this may be as "real" a truth as can be found in the drama of the realists. If life is meaningless, so is death; both *The Chairs* and *Amédée* show this. The idea that God is dead entered (or re-entered) the theatre with the existentialists, and remained with the absurdists.

William Packard in an August, 1966 article entitled "The Theatre: Stress on Soul-Searching in Plays Reflects the Eras," in *The Wall Street Journal* (p. 2) justifies some of the absurdist depression as a necessary soul-searching:

> Occasionally one hears the question: Why do so many contemporary plays seem to be preoccupied with soul-searching, pessimism, and the experience of alienation? And there really is no adequate answer, any more than there is an answer to the question of why Jacob had to go through the terrible ordeal of wrestling with the dark angel in order to get a blessing—it was simply something that had to be done.
>
> And the fact that so many of our leading playwrights feel com-pelled to confront the so-called darker side of life—the anguish of their own estrangement, the disintegration of the psyche, the break-

down of communication in personal relationships—this is also something which cannot really be accounted for. It is simply something that has to be done in our time, because it is a large part of the world we live in . . . the only honest exercise of faith, when all our other faiths have failed.

Realistically, we know that everything in the outside world is in an ethical shambles—over one hundred million human beings have been killed in military action alone in this century, and the killing is still going on. . . . And now our leading theologians are telling us that "God is dead," which is to say, we must face the chaos we have made, without the assurance of our traditional convictions.

And that is why we wrestle with our dark angel on the stages of our theatres. It is at least traditional for drama to speak to the people of their present needs, whether they see them or not, whether they like it or not.

The Homecoming

Harold Pinter may be on his way to becoming a modified absurdist (he certainly has an excellent sense of the theatrical). His earliest plays in 1957 (*The Room, The Dumb Waiter,* and *The Birthday Party*) might be called five-finger exercises in the kind of theatre made known if not popular by Ionesco and Beckett. Pinter moved toward a more personal statement in *The Caretaker* and, more recently, to an art apparently both mature and all his own: *The Homecoming.*[16] In the 1966–67 season New York witnessed the same kind of ruffled excitement and flurry that greeted T. S. Eliot's *The Cocktail Party* (1949). That play put the dramatist on the cover of *Time* magazine during its first season, and the ensuing stir was so brilliantly recorded by James Thurber in his *New Yorker* piece, "What Cocktail Party?" A parallel event occurred in February 1967, when *The New York Times* printed an article called "What's Pinter Up To?" in which seven prominent persons attempted to answer this question.

Is there more to the plot of *The Homecoming*—some larger significance —than appears on the surface? Indeed, the most interesting change in Pinter is that one can more clearly see a plot emerging. There is a story line.

The setting is a large, sparsely furnished drawing room in an old house in North London. This is the "middle-class drawing room" of innumerable Ibsen and Shaw plays, with a devastating difference— realistic details, comfort, wall-to-wall carpeting have been ruthlessly

[16]Excerpts from THE HOMECOMING by Harold Pinter. Reprinted by permission of Grove Press, Inc. Copyright © 1965 and 1966 by H. Pinter Ltd.

peeled away. Characters are angry, self-centered, and talk past each other, with pseudorealistic cutting remarks that are designed to kill but never do. The dialogue is closer to that of novelist Ivy Compton-Burnett than to anything that has yet appeared in the theatre; it attains the polished venom that one would like to have spoken but usually thinks of too late.

The Homecoming—The Royal Shakespeare Repertory Company, New York Production. Photo by Friedman-Abeles, Inc.

This is an odd household: Max, the seventy-year-old patriarch, had assumed many "maternal" roles even before the death of his wife, Jessie; the two sons at home, Lenny, the witty and cunning pimp, and Joey, the rather stupid but sentimental would-be boxer; and Max's brother, Uncle Sam, the chauffeur. The opening father-son conversation is a typical one:

> MAX: . . . He was very fond of your mother, Mac was. Very fond.
> He always had a good word for her. (*Pause*) Mind you,

she wasn't such a bad woman. Even though it made me
sick just to look at her rotten stinking face, she wasn't
such a bad bitch. I gave her the best bleeding years of
my life, anyway.

LENNY: Plug it, will you, you stupid sod, I'm trying to read
the paper.

MAX: Listen! I'll chop your spine off, you talk to me like that!
You understand? Talking to your lousy filthy father like
that!

LENNY: You know what, you're getting demented.

After six years absence, the oldest son Teddy, professor of philosophy
in an American university, returns with his wife Ruth, whom he had
married just before leaving England. They have left their three sons
behind, and the "homecoming" is intended to introduce Ruth to the
family. Teddy and Uncle Sam (whose names may reinforce the American implications) consider themselves successes but are in reality more
dead than alive. The three other men—Max, Lenny, and Joey—failures
in some respects, are very much alive. But most vital of all is Ruth, the
woman who soon becomes the force around whom the others gravitate.
Ruth is very much like the Lulu of Frank Wedekind's *Earthspirit* and
Pandora's Box, a woman who controls the men around her through the
power of sex. Ruth establishes her superiority over Lenny initially in a
grotesque little scene centering on a glass of water:

LENNY: And now perhaps I'll relieve you of your glass.

RUTH: I haven't quite finished.

LENNY: You've consumed quite enough, in my opinion.

RUTH: No, I haven't.

LENNY: Quite sufficient, in my own opinion.

RUTH: Not in mine, Leonard. (*Pause*)

LENNY: Don't call me that, please.

RUTH: Why not?

LENNY: That's the name my mother gave me. (*Pause*) Just give
me the glass.

RUTH: No. (*Pause*)

LENNY: I'll take it, then.

RUTH: If you take the glass . . . I'll take you. (*Pause*)

LENNY: How about me taking the glass without you taking me?

RUTH: Why don't I just take you? (*Pause*)

LENNY: You're joking. (*Pause*) You're in love, anyway, with another man. You've had a secret liaison with another man.
His family didn't even know. Then you come here without a word of warning and start to make trouble. (*She
picks up the glass and lifts it toward him.*)

RUTH: Have a sip. Go on. Have a sip from my glass. (*He is still.*) Sit on my lap. Take a long cool sip. (*She pats her lap. Pause. She stands, moves to him with the glass*) Put your head back, and open your mouth.

LENNY: Take that glass away from me.

RUTH: Lie on the floor. Go on. I'll pour it down your throat.

LENNY: What are you doing, making me some kind of proposal? (*She laughs shortly, drains the glass.*)

RUTH: Oh, I was thirsty.

Ruth puts down the glass, having won the battle of wills. Later, as Teddy prepares to return to America and their three sons and his seminar, Ruth accepts the proposition of the father and two brothers that she stay with them, earning her keep as a part-time prostitute managed by Lenny, and ministering to the needs of the Family.

TEDDY: What have you been saying to her? (*He goes to Ruth*) Here's your coat. (*Lenny goes to the radiogram and puts on a record of slow jazz*) Ruth. Come on. Put it on.

LENNY (*to Ruth*): What about one dance before you go?

TEDDY: We're going.

LENNY: Just one.

TEDDY: No. We're going.

LENNY: Just one dance, with her brother-in-law, before she goes. (*Lenny bends to her*) Madam? (*Ruth stands. They dance, slowly.*) (*Teddy stands, with Ruth's coat.*) (*Max and Joey come in the front door and into the room. They stand.*) (*Lenny kisses Ruth. They stand, kissing.*)

JOEY: Christ, she's wide open. Dad, look at that. (*Pause*) She's a tart. (*Pause*) Old Lenny's got a tart in here. (*Joey goes to them. He takes Ruth's arm. He smiles at Lenny. He sits with Ruth on the sofa, embraces and kisses her. He looks up at Lenny*) Just up my street. (*He leans her back until she lies beneath him. He kisses her. He looks up at Teddy and Max*) It's better than a rubdown, this. . . .

MAX: You going, Teddy? Already?

The woman Ruth is more than real, the only realist; her being a wife and mother makes her nonetheless a whore, and there is no implication that anything is wrong with that. But there is the implication that the Family is a "ghastly institution." Brendan Gill, reviewing the English film *Accident*, praised the screenplay by Harold Pinter, saying:

Mr. Pinter is fantastically clever at presenting family scenes that, under a smooth surface, are so charged with the ability to ravage and destroy that even Count Dracula might hesitate to pull up a chair and join the group. . . . Mr. Pinter appears to believe . . . we are fallen creatures who slowly bleed ourselves to death by the infliction upon each other of innumerable small spiritual injuries.[17]

Donald Harrington, Senior Minister of New York's Community Church, gave one of the most thoughtful answers to *The New York Times* question:

> What Pinter has cooked up here is a preview of what modern man is coming to—back home to the brute. Motherhood is dead. Father (God?) is not even decently dead, but a vestigial, malevolent brute. Women are things, objects of sexual interest only, to be used, and to be watched for their wiles. Caring is passé. Even jealousy has been "outgrown." Commercialization of all human relationships is "a workable arrangement." . . . Intellectual equilibrium, meaning to be unfeeling, capable of standing apart, "not lost in it" like the primitives, is the goal, and it produces the uninvolved, "adaptable," "broad-minded" college professor son.
>
> Here are human beings from whom all the human qualities have been washed out by a civilization with other concerns, concerns like "success," "promotion," to be "head of the department." They are people who have forgotten the past, letting "bygones be bygones," only to find they have returned to the most distant past—the real brutes of their own origins. What a "homecoming" is this! . . .
>
> Typically, the professor of philosophy has no faith, and no affirmations beyond the success banalities of contemporary American civilization. When Lenny, the pimp, asks his philosopher elder brother the question, "Have you noticed the logical incoherence of the affirmations of Christian theism? How can the Unknown merit reverence, and who in his right mind would reverence the known?" we have the bald statement of the hell of alienation in which modern atheistic, relativistic man finds himself caught. . . .
>
> Here are humanlike creatures from which all love, all graciousness, all caring, all morality, all pity, all consideration, all communication have disappeared. . . .[18]

Here, at least, is an initial vantage point from which to look at the play. It is still absurd, it is still vulgar, it is still depressing; but it is not completely absurd. And in the vitality of a handful of characters there is promise of something to come. They are honest with each other at a very basic level, and there are even brief gestures of tenderness in the stroking of hair. At one point Joey is jealous of others' attentions to Ruth: "Eh, wait a minute. I don't want to share her." That's something to build on.

It has been said that Pinter's language is "outwardly lucid and inwardly impenetrable." He makes much use of conversational banalities, realistic

[17]*The New Yorker*, April 22, 1967, pp. 150, 151.
[18]*The New York Times*, February 5, 1967, Section 2, pp. 1, 3.

vulgarities that are distorted by repetition and individualized rhythms to the point of nonrealistic originality and incantation.

Eclecticism and the Traditional—"Vitalism"

The more modern half of modern drama, whether you begin that half with Pirandello or with Bertolt Brecht and his epic theatre and including the absurdists, has been recently characterized as a serious dialogue that is:

> ... difficult, oblique and garbled. It sometimes seems like a bad 'phone connection—full of static, elusive, abrupt, frustrating and almost hostile. United States playwrights have even cut the wire—for the moment they have nothing to say about either humanity or the human predicament.

So says *Time* magazine [July 8, 1966], and takes to task Tennessee Williams, Arthur Miller, and Edward Albee for their work in the middle sixties. By implication, however, *The Glass Menagerie, A Streetcar Named Desire, All My Sons, Death of a Salesman,* and *The Crucible* are accepted as significant and worth saving. The article goes on:

> Thus, at the center of the contemporary stage remains the European drama represented by Beckett, Ionesco, Gênet, Pinter and Osborne. None are alike; yet all raise a hemlock toast to the twentieth century. Theirs is a drama of metaphysical anguish, rigorous negation, asocial stance, skin-pricking guilt and anxiety, and abidingly absurd humor. In their plays, the situation of man is horrible and funny at the same time. Ionesco says that man laughs so as not to cry. The problem these playwrights pose is man's oldest and newest—the existence problem.

That critic is referred to who called a Beckett hero a perverse Cartesian: I stink, therefore I am.

But there are other manifestations of modern theatre, and even the "oldest-newest" existence problem implies the traditional. It is only natural to want to call the most recent theatre an exercise in eclecticism, and indeed this name is often given to what is supposed to be a "movement." But everyone knows that eclecticism is hardly new. Shakespeare pieced his plays together from many different elements. This may have been true also of Sophocles, although we cannot clearly identify the sources of the elements. We seem to be thrashing around in a box, in dire need of a new term; perhaps we have run out of "isms".

In our experience, the best drama of the past forty years has had a vital excitement and a theatrical thrust, making a demand on the imagination for participation. If a word is needed here, it could well be "vitalism," which is elastic enough to include playwrights with violently different goals and personal style or technique. The term can describe with equal accuracy the experience in the theatre of *The Cocktail Party* and *Who's Afraid of Virginia Woolf*, of *The Homecoming* and *Murder in the Cathedral*, of *Waiting for Godot* and *The House of Bernarda Alba* or *The Iceman Cometh* or *Our Town*.

The *Time* article referred to above included some summary, if sweeping statements on the modern theatre.

> Indeed, in the two and a half milleniums [sic] since Aeschylus, the number of dramatic geniuses could be counted on one and a half hands. The theatre does not live on its masterpieces but between them. Man created the theatre in his own image, and it wears two masks and a thousand faces. The mask of tragedy says weep—and bear it. The mask of comedy says grin—and bear it. The theatre is witness and partner to man's endurance.

Since Shakespeare, of course, the masks are more likely to be interchangeable in the same play; and since Chekhov the one mask may say smile *and* weep. *Time* concludes:

> The need to measure chaos with chaos pits the serious modern playmaker against the traditional function of Western art, which T. S. Eliot defined as "imposing a credible order on ordinary reality, and thereby eliciting some perception of an order *in* reality."

But this forces a dichotomy that may be more apparent than real.

In most discussions of modern theatre such dramatists as J. M. Synge, W. B. Yeats, Garcia Lorca, Christopher Fry, and T. S. Eliot, are placed a bit to one side of the main stream and put into the category of the traditional, or poetic drama (in an age of prose), or even the theatre of exaltation (when everyone knows we are in an extended age of depression). However, there are two possible errors here. First, the number of dramatists capable of poetic vision and exalted language even if they have not always chosen to write in verse, with exaltation, is much larger than the usual listing implies—add Giraudoux, Anouilh, W. H. Auden, Archibald MacLeish, Ghelderode, and many others. Second, the distinctions between this group and the relativist-absurdists have been, perhaps, exaggerated. All these dramatists are too vitally conditioned by and concerned with the problems of twentieth-century man not to write about the same depression and the same disruption. The fact that some work through to a kind of exaltation and others do not is not necessarily the most important distinction to be made among them.

Traditionalism is not the thinned-out stream it is sometimes pictured to be. Romantic and lyrical plays continue to be written; so too, religious drama of an older tradition. The kind of morality play represented by W. H. Auden's *The Age of Anxiety* faces up to the world as a metaphor of dread just as well as Ionesco or Beckett.

Philadelphia, Here I Come!

Let us look at one more play of 1965, not a great play, probably, but one that almost surely can be considered a good play—and modern, traditional, eclectic, vital: Brian Friel's *Philadelphia, Here I Come!*[19] Swift, Sheridan, Wilde, Yeats, Shaw, Joyce—the Irish have long contributed the most important single impetus to English literature. Borrowed is the device of the "memory play" which had been used in *The Glass Menagerie*, in *Death of a Salesman*, and yet more recently in Hugh Leonard's dramatic adaptation of Joyce (*Portrait* and *Hero*, in *Stephen D.*) for the Irish Theatre Festival in 1962.

Philadelphia, Here I Come! Photo by William Warncke.

Philadelphia, Here I Come! was written for the Irish Theatre Festival of 1965. Its most original device is a variation on the old problem represented by the soliloquy—how to convey the thoughts of the character without violating the realism of the flow of spoken, articulated language. The main character, a not completely unheroic hero, Gar O'Donnell, is simply divided into Public and Private, and played by two actors. Thirty-six years after *Dynamo* a dreamy interlude of characters during which time other characters pay no attention was no longer needed. Here nobody pays any attention to Private Gar at any time. The dramatist explains:

> The two Gars, Public Gar and Private Gar, are two views of the one man. Public Gar is the Gar that people see, talk to, talk about. Private Gar is the unseen man, the man within, the conscience, the alter ego, the secret thoughts, the id. Private Gar, the spirit, is

[19]Reprinted by permission of the publishers, Farrar, Straus and Giroux, Inc. from *Philadelphia, Here I Come!* by Brian Friel. Copyright © 1965 by B. Friel.

invisible to everybody, always. Nobody except Public Gar hears him talk. But even Public Gar, although he talks to Private Gar occasionally, never sees him and never looks at him. One cannot look at one's alter ego.

There are three episodes, set in the present in the small village of Ballybeg in County Donegal, Ireland. The action is simple, taking place on the night before, and on the morning of, Gar's departure for Philadelphia. Gar, at twenty-five, is one more emigrant to the land of opportunity; and the conflict is between his ambitions and his emotional ties to his home and past. These ties are few, equivocal, and seen with great clarity. First, there is the girl he had been in love with, now married to another:

> PUBLIC (*softly*): Kate . . . sweet Katie Doogan . . . my darling Kathy Doogan. . . .
>
> PRIVATE (*in the same soft tone*): Aul bitch. (*Loudly*) Rotten aul nobby bitch! Just like her stinking father and mother—a bugger and a buggeress—a buggeroo and a buggerette!
>
> PUBLIC: No, no; my fault—all my fault—
>
> PRIVATE (*remembering and recalling tauntingly*): By God, that was a night, boy, eh? By God, you made a right bloody cow's ass of yourself. (*Public goes off right.*) Remember —when was it?—ten months ago?—you had just come back from a walk out the Mill Road, and the pair of you had the whole thing planned: engaged at Christmas, married at Easter, and fourteen of a family, seven boys and seven girls. Cripes, you make me laugh! You bloody well make me die laughing. You were going to "develop" the hardware lines and she was going to take charge of the "drapery"! The drapery! The fishy socks and the shoebox of cotton spools and rusted needles! And you—you were to ask Screwballs for a rise in pay— "in view of your increased responsibilities"! And you were so far gone that night, Laddybuck,—(*Public and Kate enter from the left, and walk very slowly across the front of the stage. They stop and kiss. Then they move on again.*) So bloody-well astray in the head with "love" that you went and blabbed about your secret egg deals that nobody knew anything about—not even Madge! Stupid bloody get! O my God, how you stick yourself I'll never know!
>
> PUBLIC: Kate—Kathy—I'm mad about you: I'll never last till Easter! I'll—I'll—I'll bloody-well burst! (*He catches her again and kisses her.*)

PRIVATE: Steady, boy, steady. You know what the Canon says: long, passionate kisses in lonely places. . . .

PUBLIC: Our daughters'll all be gentle and frail and silly, like you; and our sons—they'll be thick bloody louts, sexy goats, like me, and by God I'll beat the tar out of them!

KATE: But 3 pounds 15 shillings, Gar! We could never live on that.

PUBLIC (*kissing her*): Mmmmm.

KATE: Gar! Listen! Be sensible.

PUBLIC: Mmm?

KATE: How will we *live*?

PRIVATE (*imitating*): 'How will we *live*?'

PUBLIC: Like lords—free house, free light, free fuel, free groceries! And every night at seven when we close—except Saturday; he stays open till damn near midnight on Saturdays, making out bloody bills; and sure God and the world knows that sending out bills here is as hopeless as peeing against the wind . . .

KATE: Gar! No matter what you say, we just couldn't live on that much money. It—it's not possible. We'll need to have more security than that.

The second "memory" scene is Gar's reliving the visit of his Aunt Lizzy (his late mother's sister) and Uncle Con Sweeney from Philadelphia, and their wanting to virtually "adopt" him. He finally agrees, but not without reservations:

PRIVATE: September 8th, the sun shining, not a breath of wind— and this was your mother's sister—remember. And that's how you were got! Right, honey? Silly and impetuous like a Gallagher! Regrets?

PUBLIC: None.

PRIVATE: Uncertainties?

PUBLIC: None.

PRIVATE: Little tiny niggling reservations?

PUBLIC: None.

PRIVATE: Her grammar?

PUBLIC: Shut up!

PRIVATE: But, honey, wasn't it something?

PUBLIC: Go to hell.

PRIVATE: Her vulgarity?

PUBLIC: Bugger off.

PRIVATE: She'll tuck you into your air-conditioned cot every night. (*Public, so that he won't hear, begins to whistle 'Philadelphia, Here I Come!'*)

PRIVATE: And croon, 'Sleep well, my li'l honey child.' (*Public whistles determinedly*) She got you soft on account of the day it was, didn't she?

It was the day of Kate Doogan's marriage.

But most of all Gar waits for some word, for some sign, of affection on the part of his father, old S. B. O'Donnell. But it never comes. The men cannot communicate with each other; and each one's memory plays him false. At the end Gar tries to break down the wall.

PUBLIC: The fishing we used to do on Lough na Cloc Cor.
S. B. (*confused, on guard*): Oh, ay, Lough na Cloc Cor—aye, aye—
PUBLIC: We had a throw on it every Sunday during the season.
S. B.: That's not the day nor yesterday.
PUBLIC (*more quickly*): There used to be a blue boat on it—d'you remember it?
S. B.: Many's the fish we took off that same lake.
PUBLIC: D'you remember the blue boat?
S. B.: A blue one, eh?
PUBLIC: I don't know who owned it. But it was blue. And the paint was peeling.
S. B. (*remembering*): I mind a brown one the doctor brought from somewhere up in the—
PUBLIC (*quickly*): It doesn't matter who owned it. It doesn't even matter that it was blue. But d'you remember one afternoon in May—we were up there—the two of us—and it must have rained because you put your jacket round my shoulders and gave me your hat—
S. B.: Aye?
PUBLIC:—and it wasn't that we were talking or anything—but suddenly—suddenly you sang "All Round My Hat I'll Wear a Green Coloured Ribbono'—
S. B.: Me?
PUBLIC:—for no reason at all except that we—that you were happy. D'you remember? D'you remember? (*There is a pause while S. B. tries to recall.*)
S. B.: No...no, then, I don't...(*Private claps his hands in nervous mockery.*)
PRIVATE (*quickly*): There! There! There!
S.B.: 'All Round My Hat'? No, I don't think I ever knew that one...
S. B.: And you say the boat was blue?
PUBLIC: It doesn't matter. Forget it.

This is a very moving scene, as Gar tries to find something in his past to hold on to. There is nothing, as he prepares to leave for Philadelphia, but Gar is revealed as a man you can build on—he has a desire for human relationship, even with the inadequate father.

As we look back over the work of the dramatists from Aeschylus and Sophocles down to Pinter and Friel, we should be able to make some working generalizations about the nature of drama. However, we need the constant reminder of the artificiality of categories, for the understanding of a play depends not upon a Procrustean cutting to fit so much as seeing in what ways it is like and unlike the idea of a particular form. The dramatic elements that dominate a play may serve to identify it as a certain type of play, and this broad classification may help one to arrive at the most fruitful understanding of it. If the material is of a serious nature according to conventional classification, the play is likely to be either a tragedy or a melodrama. If the treatment is in a lighter vein, even though the subject itself is a serious one, the play may be a comedy or a farce. Various names have been suggested to designate a hopper for plays that do not rest comfortably in one of the four classic pigeonholes. The least difficult, if the least distinctive, is the term *drama*. The major groupings can be useful, however, and one should always "try out" the first four categories before resorting to miscellany.

Tragedy

Tragedy is the oldest written drama. It has always been of a very serious nature and is ranked as one of the most artistic works of civilized man. It offers the spectacle of a great or noble human being, or one who bears the seeds of greatness in him, shattering himself against insuperable obstacles rather than compromising with circumstances or conditions as they exist. The Greek tragic heroes were usually in conflict with the gods or with fate, the Elizabethans' conflicts stemmed from inner faults, and the moderns struggle with their immediate surroundings, their total environment, their society; but always the force is greater than the individual, who must go down in defeat. The leading character, or protagonist, was until recent times a person of high station or an individual with some nobility. In more modern plays he has been a representative of a class or a social group, a common man or woman who speaks and acts for others caught in a similar dilemma; his larger-than-life size is in breadth rather than in height.

Two specific emotions experienced by an audience in great tragedy are pity and fear. Pity for the hero who seems to be suffering unjustly is sometimes called empathy, a term implying identification with the hero more than sympathy. Fear that we ourselves might become involved in comparable circumstances is also felt. It is not necessary, in experiencing *Oedipus Rex*, that we fear killing our father and marrying our mother, only that we realize the basic human condition of having to act on the best knowledge that we possess—and that such data may not be complete or true. This experience of pity and fear is the most essential factor in great tragedy; Aristotle called it *catharsis*, often translated as emotional cleansing or, alternately, a purification or purgation of the emotions or passions.

The leading figure on the stage passes through a great crisis and in that crisis comes to realize a personal weakness or fault within himself (Aristotle's *hamartia*). He may have lost the battle and his life—but he dies a happier and better man for having recognized that error. John Gassner called this recognition *enlightenment*, by which he meant more than the gaining of knowledge through the lines of the play or the coming of information to alter the course of the plot (that is, via dialogue or action)—although Aristotle places what he calls recognition or discovery ideally *with* the peripety or change of fortune. Gassner said that pity, fear, and enlightenment become a "marriage of emotion and understanding," as something felt or achieved by the leading character and through him transferred to the audience. Aristotle had said, "Such a recognition and peripety will produce pity and fear, and tragedy is an imitation of actions producing these feelings." Aristotle and Gassner are thus dealing with the same concept in slightly different ways.

In discussing the tragic vision George Kernodle notes Francis Fergusson's reference in *The Idea of a Theatre*, to Kenneth Burke as the namer of three movements in tragedy: Purpose, Passion (or Suffering), and Perception.[20] These are useful terms. Under "purpose" Mr. Kernodle then places Hamlet's taking on of the terrible burden of action to set right his time out of joint. Oedipus similarly has the civic purpose of cleansing his land of a blight, no matter what the cost. Willy Loman, indignant and displaced from his rightful place in the world, facing a terrifying failure he cannot understand, "demands justice—of his sons, of the past, of his long-lost brother, of the night." "Isolation is the immediate price the hero pays for taking up his burden, but it is an isolation, a rebellion, that gives him identity." The passion is the suffering, the catastrophe, that engages the pity of the audience. And the perception is the enlightenment that we have just discussed.

When we in the audience, with full knowledge of our own frustrations, inhibitions, personal faults and weaknesses, see those human errors brought out into the open on the stage, we, too, are spiritually cleansed.

---

[20]Kernodle, *Invitation to the Theatre*, pp. 153–54.

Tragedy serves as a sort of public confession, but this is not enough in itself. We must put our own houses in order, resolving to go out of the theatre better men or women for the experience of purgation and the new insights acquired. It is this enlightenment or perception—this "calm of mind, all passion spent"—that permits us to say we have 'enjoyed' a tragedy. There is, as George Steiner has said, "a fusion of grief and joy, of lament over the fall of man and of rejoicing in the resurrection of his spirit. No other poetic form achieves this mysterious effect: it makes of *Oedipus, King Lear,* and *Phèdre* the noblest yet wrought by the mind."

Sometimes perception occurs in the audience and sometimes it is only sensed or recognized by the audience as it happens within the leading character in the play. It is their varying degrees of recognition of this enlightenment—or failure to recognize it—that cause so much debate over whether many modern serious dramas are tragedy or melodrama. So much depends on the individual's background, knowledge, and sensitivity.

In modern literature we have very few tragedies. There are some, but few that can stand beside *Oedipus Rex, Electra, Hamlet, Macbeth, King Lear, Phèdre,* and other undisputed masterpieces. Among the best candidates for the position of tragedy during the past hundred years (granting the adequacy of our own "background, knowledge, and sensitivity") are *Ghosts, Death of a Salesman, Long Day's Journey Into Night, Winterset, Desire Under the Elms, Blood Wedding,* and *The House of Bernarda Alba.* There is, it seems, a new reach of criticism to include some of these plays and a few others within the larger experience of tragedy.

If we study tragedies from all periods, we find at least five basic principles. And we may risk the charge of oversimplification to say that when a playwright fails to meet any one of these demands, his drama is pushed outside the realm of pure tragedy.

Requirements of Tragedy

1. The play must concern a serious subject and be treated seriously.
2. The leading character must be a great figure or one who is representative of a class. He must represent more than himself.
3. The actions of the protagonist must be absolutely honest and without the element of coincidence or chance. What should happen must happen.
4. The basic emotions are those of pity and fear, the *catharsis* of Aristotle—pity for the protagonist in his suffering, and fear that the same fate might befall the audience.

5. In the final analysis the protagonist must meet defeat, but before this defeat must come enlightenment or perception.

Melodrama

Melodrama as a term has not the antiquity nor the dignity nor the exaltation of the term tragedy. It seems to have its origin as a word descriptive of a nineteenth-century genre, although the concept has been extended backward to explain its beginnings and sometimes to explain what have appeared to be failures of tragedy.

Where the tragic writer says, What is the one thing these people would do under these circumstances? the writer of melodrama says, What is the most thrilling action I can devise here? and then, How can I make it seem logical that the characters would do this? This approach often brings about inconsistent characterizations. One plot escapade rapidly follows another, and the excitement that ensues makes melodrama one of the most entertaining and popular types of drama.

Webster defines melodrama as "a kind of drama, commonly romantic and sensational, with both songs and instrumental music interspersed; hence, any romantic and sensational drama, typically with a happy ending." The name derives from the expression, *drama with music*, for melodrama had its origin under those circumstances. It may well have grown out of the popularity of opera in the eighteenth century.

Mr. Kernodle summarizes the form in this way:

> The melodrama was the poor man's romantic play. It simplified the complex hero by dividing him into two characters—a spotless hero and a deep-dyed villain. It kept the guilty hero but made the guilt false, a lie invented by the villain. Sometimes the hero himself thought he was guilty, but always at the end he was cleared by the proper papers or confession.... As the heroine fled from danger and the villain pursued her, the greatest excitement was the chase—out windows, over roofs, off bridges into the water, through fires, floods, earthquakes, explosions, train wrecks....
>
> The appeal of melodrama has remained the same on the movie or television screen as it was on the nineteenth-century stage. By setting a good hero against a wicked villain, it captures the most elemental sympathies. Whether the villain is a ... banker threatening to foreclose the mortgage in order to get the heroine in his power, ... a Western cattle rustler, a city gangster, or a Nazi or Communist spy plotting to blow up the capital, we know that the hero must come to the rescue and come fast.[21]

Perhaps a word of defense would not be out of place. The term melodrama has been used disparagingly because of its background of late

[21]Kernodle, *Invitation to the Theatre*, pp. 74–75.

nineteenth-century melodramas such as *Uncle Tom's Cabin, Ten Nights in a Barroom, East Lynne*, and hundreds of others that often seem to parody themselves. In these plays black was black and white was white. The playwright pitted good against evil. Excitement was the key word and coincidence a commonplace. However, many serious plays written since 1900 modify the same basic pattern and still make good and exciting theatre. Both tragedy and melodrama are legitimate methods for planning a serious play and for saying something truthful about life. Life itself is divided between chance and character. Melodrama would make more of the chance; tragedy would place emphasis upon character. Melodrama would show what might happen; tragedy would show what must happen. If tragedy must *tell the truth*, melodrama *must not lie* (at least in action—characters are sometimes so one-sided as to be clearly fictive); and the world knows full well that there is a vast difference between those two injunctions! Arthur Miller has said, "When I show you why a man does what he does, I may do it melodramatically; but when I show you why he almost did not do it, I am making drama."

In melodrama there is a chance of victory, for the protagonist is the victim of external circumstances over which he may win; tragedy exists when the protagonist *has within him the power to win*, but is, nevertheless, doomed to failure. Of course in melodrama the hero almost always *does* win, which is like eating your cake and having it too, and it can become the greatest artificiality.

In recent melodramas the characters are involved in the most exciting events that can be conceived, and the leading character may emerge from one situation only to be plunged immediately into another. The whole play is episodic. The basic emotion may be pity, but the element of sentimentality is always present.

Sentimentality is said to exist when we are so anxious to experience an emotion vicariously that, as long as we get the thrill, we do not pause to discriminate. We sympathize with a child because he is a child, or with a troubled pretty girl just because she is pretty and in distress, without analyzing the causes. In reality, neither may deserve our sympathy. Sentimentality exists, according to this definition, when we are permitted to experience an emotion without paying for it; for the sentimentalist lives on wishful thinking, on emotion rather than reason. He sees just what he wants to see. To him life is a conflict between good and bad—with no in-between. He refuses to apply intelligence and fact to a situation or to think it through. Instead he relies solely on human feeling. Favorite stories show the young man struggling to be honest against the commercial-minded world; the innocence of childhood; downtrodden minority groups; the successful struggles of poor but honest persons; motherhood; the rehabilitation of gamblers, gangsters, women of the streets, and drunkards; and the complete revival of the hard-hearted and stingy old man whose soul is saved through the love of a little child.

Sentimentality is an important segment of melodrama. There may also be fear, but it is of a temporary or surface variety. We are more interested in the situation and the circumstances than we are in the intricacies of characters involved. Sentimentality, under control, and not as one's exclusive diet, can possess great emotional power—a good cry can be temporarily therapeutic. Out of control, it only lies.

The characters in melodrama being as unauthentic as they are, the members of the audience are able to fit themselves into any role and thus receive a greater vicarious enjoyment. Of course, the role chosen is almost always that of the hero or heroine; the melodramatic villain must lead an essentially lonely life. In the plays we have analyzed—not one a true melodrama—Madame Claire Zachanassian, "The Woman Who Corrupted Guellen," is probably closest to being such a character.

The story seems to deal with charmed lives, for the ending is nearly always a happy one. Herein lies the greatest appeal of melodrama to the average audience. It furnishes an excitement and a happiness often denied in their everyday lives, for more often than not the protagonist wins his struggle. In melodrama there is never the enlightenment of a tragedy. As in tragedy, five comparable principles can be considered basic in the study of any melodrama:

Requirements of Melodrama

1. It treats of a serious subject, but the manipulation of the action may not be well concealed.

2. The characters are more loosely drawn than in tragedy. This makes it easier for the audience to identify with the characters, thus creating a more immediate empathic response.

3. Whereas tragedy must be absolutely honest, the element of chance enters into melodrama. It is episodic and the most exciting incidents possible, often improbable, are brought into the play.

4. There may be pity, but it borders on sentimentality. Fear may be evident, but of a temporary or surface type.

5. There is no real enlightenment even in defeat, and in most instances the protagonist does win his battle.

One can always justify a good melodrama, both as escape and as an artistic theatrical experience. As escape it receives its greatest popularity with the masses, because it permits them to forget their own troubles; although they may view the troubles of someone else, the experience is a vicarious one and essentially temporary. There is no lasting strain or suffering on their part. As critics we should evaluate each type in its own realm of theatrical entertainment, for either tragedy or melodrama should be accepted as a legitimate means of relating a serious story.

Comedy

Man is the only animal capable of realizing the miseries of life, and he is the only one that has been given the privilege of knowing how to laugh at those miseries. He likes to make the most of that opportunity, and psychologists have tried to find the reason for his laughter since psychology became a science. George Meredith and Henri Bergson have addressed themselves to the nature of comedy and laughter with great insight. Both insist on the social nature of comedy, Bergson seeing as its basic principle the "mechanical encrusted on the living." Certain elements or areas of comedy have been suggested by Alan Reynolds Thompson.[22] His "ladder of comedy," if studied carefully—particularly with the addition of a rung or two—can be helpful in differentiating between two general types of humor: comedy and farce. The reader must never forget, however, that the artist's treatment or presentation of the material will determine whether it is high farce that borders on comedy or low comedy that borders on farce. Nor must he forget that comedy may incorporate any of the elements of farce into its broader and higher vision. This does not imply that one is better than the other. Each is a legitimate method of presenting a lighter story.

FARCE   HIGH COMEDY
                                      6. Comedy of ideas and satire
                                   5. Inconsistencies of character
                          4. Verbal wit
                     3. Plot device
                2. Physical mishaps
          1. Obscenity

Obscenity is considered the lowest form of comedy. It needs little explanation and is rather scarce in our modern theatre, except where combined with one of the higher forms of humor as a necessary part of a specific character or situation. There have been times in dramatic literature when references to the digestive processes or the most animalistic elements of love-making were wholly acceptable on the stage. The

[22]Alan Reynolds Thompson, *The Anatomy of the Drama* (Berkeley: University of California Press, 1946).

audience expected and accepted these as a logical part of a play. The essentially comic aspects of sex, which are not necessarily describable as obscene, are still good theatre and inherent in all great comedy.

The repartee of the upper classes during the Restoration may be shocking even to relatively sophisticated audiences of the twentieth century. Restoration comedies used to be so heavily edited in American productions that it is little wonder they lost much of the humor we know they had in their day. But times are constantly changing. With the appearance and acceptance of plays like Pinter's *The Homecoming* we are almost back to Renaissance and seventeenth-century looseness, or freedom, depending on your point of view.

Moving up the ladder of comedy, we come to *physical mishap*. This, too, means exactly what it says. The most obvious mishap is the common "prattfall"—a chair jerked from under an unsuspecting character, or a banana peel that sends someone sprawling across the stage. Much of what is called slapstick comedy is comprised of such elements. These physical eventualities are found today only in the broadest of comedy, or in an occasional motion picture or television farce. When they do appear, some critics cannot refrain from exclaiming, "Oh, no, no, not that, please!" for the distinction is so fine between farce which we must believe and burlesque which we need not believe that only a real artist can know and keep within the boundaries. On the other hand, physical action that is comic, patterned, rigid in Bergson's jack-in-the-box sense, can be very effective and can puncture social pomposity and pretension better than more subtle wit. The drunk on the edge of mishap in a dignified social ritual is an example of this.

The third step is *plot device*. Shakespeare, whose comedies until recently were considered less effective than his tragedies, often turned to this type of comedy, and most effectively. It involves misunderstandings, cross purposes, inopportune or embarrassing occurrences, mistaken identity, and often mistaken sex. In this area of comedy the author manipulates his material so as to arrive at hilarious combinations and ludicrous situations.

The next step is *verbal wit*. Even in reading, this dialogue seems humorous and sends an audience into gales of laughter the first time it is heard as a play. In the English language few playwrights have surpassed Oscar Wilde's great gift for this sort of comedy. He is known for such epigrams as: "To love oneself is the beginning of a lifelong romance"; "Wicked women bother one. Good women bore one. That is the only difference between them"; "There is nothing in the world like the devotion of a married woman. It's a thing no married man knows anything about"; "Experience is the name everybody gives to their mistakes"; and one as modern as "Spies are of no use nowadays. The newspapers do their work instead." His *The Importance of Being Earnest* is considered our most nearly perfect example of verbal wit. In the English language, verbal wit, or linguistic comedy, as it is sometimes called, goes back to Shakespeare, with characters like Dogberry and Bottom who are mastered by the language—and amuse with what has become known as malapropisms—and characters like Beatrice and Benedick who master the language. George Bernard Shaw and Noel Coward carry it into the twentieth century. Linguistic comedy includes punning, which in the hands of a Shakespeare or James Joyce can be masterful.

In America George Kaufman, Moss Hart, and S. N. Behrman are known for their wit in such plays as *The Man Who Came To Dinner, You Can't Take It With You, First Lady*, and others. Like Wilde, they too occasionally give treatment to the characters who will speak the lines so that the distinction between farce and comedy is difficult to make. The more recent *Barefoot in the Park* and *The Odd Couple* might similarly be cited.

Obscenity, physical mishap, plot device (or situation), and verbal wit (or linguistic comedy)—these four elements of comedy are considered the basic materials of farce. The fact that they are ranked low on the ladder of comedy does not mean that they should be considered any the less artistic. A study of most of the examples would reveal that the authors were able *by their treatment* to lift the farcical material to as high a degree of artistry as farce, which can always be a legitimate part of comedy. (We could point out many plays that failed because the same material received inadequate treatment, and the plays were for that reason undistinguished.) It is very important that we be able to recognize the material itself and also the nature of the treatment it has received by the artist. These may be separate entities.

Character is the foundation of comedy, and *inconsistency* of character is our next step in the ladder of comedy. Here the unexpected on the part of an individual is found in the surprise action or speech so contrary to his appearance or nature and yet believable as a characteristic rather than simply as a humorous touch. Inconsistency may also be found in a discrepancy between professed and real qualities in a character—Tartuffe, for example. As Henry Fielding said in his brilliant preface to *Joseph Andrews*, the only source of the true ridiculous is affectation, which proceeds from one of two causes, vanity or hypocrisy; and this accounts for the majority of comic characters.

In the theatre as in life, man has attained a higher rung of comedy when he reaches what Alan Thompson called a *comedy of ideas* or *satire*. These qualities of humor are found in man's ability to laugh at that which is closest to his heart—his family, his friends, his religion, his politics, his country, himself. It is a gift of irreverence, an ability to kid the things we take seriously. One is said to have a real sense of humor when he can appreciate the humor of his own pretensions and shortcomings. This may be called high comedy and may be defined as a criticism of life, although we must point out that farce too, is often raised by its treatment to the level of satire. Sometimes the laughter may be violent and angry, and again delightful, tongue-in-cheek, accompanied by an intensity of response because the characters involved, then we as an audience, realize the seriousness of their acts and thoughts as well as the humor involved in them.

Possibly there is a comic character rarer and more difficult to describe than the inconsistent characters who form the working ground of comedy. His is the highest type of all, for he can see and understand, yet sympathize with, the comic situation of man in the universe. Chaucer achieves it in a nondramatic mode with Troilus at the end of his story. Shakespeare's Rosalind in *As You Like It* is certainly another example. Molière usually saves this role for his "man of reason," whether Dorine, Cléante, or Philinte in *The Misanthrope*, or Chrysalde in *The School for Wives*. This quieter kind of character, less spectacular than a Tartuffe, represents both the author and a sensitive audience in the attitudes expressed. Closely related is the ultimate comic vision which is only a hair's breadth from the tragic vision, although it suggests renewal rather than finality. From the highest perspective, life is both tragic *and* comic. And from this point, if we are lucky, we may hear the laughter of the gods.

One of the most interesting recent interpretations of comedy leans rather heavily toward the mythic; it is that of Northrop Frye, in *Anatomy of Criticism* and elsewhere. The movement of comedy is cyclical, individual characters tending to be submerged in a social group. The comedy itself proceeds toward a triumph of mankind, a second chance, renewal, continuity, moving through disruption and the seasons toward spring and marriage and beginning again. The movement of tragedy, by contrast, is linear; the drama, the suffering of a single character isolated from the group. The tragedy moves toward the defeat of one human being cut off, usually by death, passing through the seasons toward fall. Comedy reveals man in a context of society and nature: One among Many rather than One against Many.

> At the beginning of the play the obstructing characters are in charge of the play's society, and the audience recognizes that they are usurpers. At the end of the play the device in the plot that brings hero and heroine together causes a new society to crystallize around the hero, and the moment when this crystallization occurs is the point of resolution in the action, the comic discovery. . . .[23]

[23]Northrop Frye, *Anatomy of Criticism* (Princeton, N.J.: Princeton University Press, 1957), p. 163.

The very proximity of farce to comedy in the realm of humor is exemplified by the common denominator of the highest comedy and the lowest farcical material, namely, that they both demand a sense of detachment on the part of the audience. Both frown upon sentiment or sentimentality, and neither will permit the audience to identify itself with what it sees on the stage. Both high comedy and farce regard life objectively, and either can be a strong agent toward the elimination of social injustice or the individual's defections, in his personal habits, from social norms. As Molière wisely said, "People do not mind being wicked, but they object to being made ridiculous." Herein lies comedy's force as a "social corrective," to use Bergson's phrase.

Comedy is one of the most miscellaneous of all the dramatic forms and therefore one of the most difficult to define. We assume that it must present believable and understandable characters; that the situations should be both possible and probable; that it treat of the individual and his personal problems in a social context; and that it take an attitude toward life on its lighter side. Although a comedy may often have a serious subject—infidelity, war, communism, tolerance, religion, marriage, or divorce—as its substance, it treats that subject more lightly than would tragedy or melodrama. In comedy, as in tragedy, the protagonist has within him the power to alter the immediate obstacle facing him.

Much of comedy is based on incidents that occurring in the lives of others provoke laughter in us, but if they happened to us would be found unpleasant. In this special brand of comedy, the element of perspective gives us the detachment we need. The seriousness with which the characters attack the problem provokes us to laughter. Perspective is a vital factor in comedy.

All comedy is but a point of view; the very seed of comedy lies in the intellect, in an ability to think rather than to feel, to place one's self outside a situation or a character and to see it in perspective. Detachment is the key. Hugh Walpole once said, "Life is a comedy to those who think and a tragedy to those who feel"; and Max Beerbohm always contended that only the emotion of love was on a higher level than the emotion of laughter.

In comedy the protagonist usually overcomes his obstacles, but the means of his success should be consistent with the laws of life. We may, as an audience, laugh at the situations even while we sympathize with the characters. Northrop Frye comments that:

> Comedy usually moves toward a happy ending, and the normal response of the audience to a happy ending is "this should be," which sounds like a moral judgment. So it is, except that it is not moral in the restricted sense, but social. Its opposite is not the villainous but the absurd....[24]

[24]Frye, *Anatomy of Criticism*, p. 167.

Historically, the Greeks revelled in a rollicking sort of humor with much biting satire, and everything else on the ladder from obscenity up. *The Birds, Lysistrata,* and *The Frogs* hold up surprisingly well as great comedy, which is probably more subject to the erosions of time and translation than tragedy. The Romans leaned toward buffoonery and ingenious plots, *The Menaechmi* and *Amphytrion* being among the best. The Elizabethans gave us the romantic comedy of Shakespeare with its lyrical poetry—light-hearted stories of love and adventure, some of them shadowed by tragic possibilities and despair held at arm's length. There was also the comedy of Ben Jonson with bitter satire and ridicule, as in *Volpone.*

Molière is considered to be the greatest writer of comedy that ever lived. *Tartuffe, The Misanthrope, The School for Wives,* and *The Imaginary Invalid,* are among the best of the twenty-three comedies that make up his work. His was the most skillful satire, and his plays are said to have evoked the "thoughtful laughter" whose presence marks the final true test of comedy. (This is in contrast with the "thoughtless laughter" brought forth by farce as such.) Various names have been given this phase of comedy, including comedy of manners, high comedy, artificial comedy, and intellectual comedy; but the purpose is to satirize man in society, concentrating on either man or society, often the social customs of the upper classes. It creates thoughtful laughter, although it may not stir our emotions very deeply.

> True comedy arises rather out of character, usually the clash of foibles in character against common-sense truth; out of the vices and weaknesses of human nature held up to ridicule. If at the same time sympathy is aroused, the play borders on sentimental comedy. What is generally accepted as essential comedy—"high" comedy—is the satiric sort, untinged with sympathetic appeal.[25]

This is a debatable position. Northrop Frye, for example, says:

> In tragedy, pity and fear, the emotions of moral attraction and repulsion, are raised and cast out. Comedy seems to make a more functional use of the social, even the moral judgment, than tragedy, yet comedy seems to raise the corresponding emotions, which are sympathy and ridicule, and cast them out in the same way.[26]

Perhaps the clue to real distinction here is the difference between the necessary *empathy* in tragedy and the possible *sympathy,* a much more detached feeling for others, in comedy.

No one would question that comedy is one of the most popular of all types, challenged only by farce. If man wants escape he can usually find it through laughter. Fortunately, modern drama has continued to

[25]Sheldon Chaney, *The Theatre* (New York: Longmans, Green & Co.), 1930.
[26]Frye, *Anatomy of Criticism,* p. 177.

produce comedy at a very high level—witness most of the works of, for example, Shaw, Giraudoux, Anouilh, and Pirandello. For comedy, as for tragedy and melodrama, we suggest five principles that tend to define the form:

Requirements of Comedy

1. It treats its subject in a lighter vein even though the subject may be serious in itself.
2. It provokes what can be defined as "thoughtful laughter."
3. The action is both possible and probable, although the appropriate artificiality and manipulation of endings may strain probability.
4. It grows out of character rather than situation.
5. It is honest in its portrayal of life.

Farce

A common error is to use the word *comedy* when thinking in terms of *farce*. As we have pointed out, farcical elements often appear in comedy, and *Tartuffe* is such a comedy; but Molière's *Physician in Spite of Himself* is a farce. Farce is to comedy what melodrama is to tragedy. Its exaggerated incidents and characters are dominated by plot, and there is only a pretense of reality. More often than not farce develops on a series of misunderstandings between the characters. If comedy is both possible and probable, farce is possible, but not very probable. Farce has been called a purely mathematical sequence of laughs. The object of the author is to make the audience believe only for the moment. The incidents come rapidly, and the whole play is episodic. The audience has little time to think because farce portrays the strictly ludicrous in life; if spectators were to analyze the action, believability would be sacrificed.

Farce depends upon extreme improbability that usually grows out of someone's mental or physical distress. Paradoxically this type of humor has always flourished most in ages of great cultural activity and refinement. The reason lies in the fact that farce, although improbable, is usually based on logic and objectivity, qualities that are an integral part of education and culture.

The author of a farce usually asks the audience to grant him a few improbabilities at the very beginning, thereafter proceeding in a world of reality. It is often true that farce exists when a story would evaporate entirely and the play be concluded if at any time each character were to tell the whole truth. However, it is our acceptance of an initial improbability, or a lack of knowledge common to all the characters, that makes the series of events so highly enjoyable.

While observing a farce in production we should, with a modicum of imaginary puissance, believe what we are watching. We may not believe the story or the characters once out of the theatre, and perhaps not even during the intermissions, but during the actual performance, there must be a sense—however detached—of believability.

One of our most famous farces is *Charley's Aunt*, which Ray Bolger made into a very popular musical comedy, *Where's Charley?* As a popular stage piece it has had a most amazing career. Ludicrous as it is in content, it is so theatrically effective that an audience is ready to accept the improbabilities and howl with laughter, with temporary belief—*if* the players attack these improbable situations with sincerity. Measured by the tests that follow, this play becomes an almost perfect example of farce.

The dialogue of farce may run from the epigram of Oscar Wilde to the "gag" in the most recent radio or television script. In either instance any speech could be given to almost any character in the play. The lines have no special relation to character but exist for whatever laugh value they may possess. On the other hand, the lines in good comedy help to define the character and belong specifically to him. We can see the logic of farce dialogue when we realize that the term farce comes to us from the Latin word meaning "to stuff."

Like melodrama, farce is most delightful when done well; both are more likely to delight than to teach. The motion pictures lean heavily to this type of theatre and have done with it some of their best work, as with the Marx brothers. Some years ago there was an influx of English farces, notably those of Alec Guinness, which added much to our appreciation of the value of the genre. Certain qualities of farce have been constant since Aristophanes.

Requirements of Farce

1. It has as its object riotous laughter and escape.

2. It asks the audience to accept certain improbabilities, but from that point proceeds in a lifelike manner.

3. Its story is possible, but not very probable.

4. Farce is dominated by situation rather than character, and calls for little or no thought.

5. It must move very rapidly in an episodic manner, and is believable only for the moment.

Drama

Our miscellaneous class will list no requirements, for this is only a convenient resting place for that play which is not primarily a tragedy, a melodrama, a comedy, or a farce. Some critics have preferred the French word, *drame*, perhaps to avoid confusion with the larger meaning of drama to cover all writing for the theatre. But confusion is relatively inevitable and might as well be faced. In his *Invitation to the Theatre*, George Kernodle tried to solve the problem partly by straddling it and partly by ignoring it. He mixed genres and movements and came out with a nine-fold division, which from one point of view is too many (three kinds of tragedies) and from another is too few (since realism is given children it never fathered, perhaps on the principle that "the children of my wife are mine"). As we have frequently insisted, every play in one sense is unique and follows its own laws of being, particularly if it is not just an imitation. The conventional categories, however, have uses for the critic and the playgoer, if the right spirit of use prevails. Here are handles to hold lightly, to pick up the pot and pour out its contents; one must not confuse handle or pot with the food or its nourishment.

Obviously, some plays are not close enough to one of the four preceding categories to be explained thereby. But such plays may still be drama, and even good theatre—*Everyman*, for instance. The morality play, serious for the most part, but not tragic and not melodramatic, presents a moral drama. The history play, from the isolated *Persians* of Aeschylus through Shakespeare and into the present theatre, may be a tragedy (as Shakespeare specifically labeled *Richard II* and *Richard III*). Or it may be almost a comedy; and *Henry IV, Part I, Part II*, and *Henry V* begin to so emerge in the view of modern critics. But there is also the history play that is neither—*Martin Luther, Elizabeth the Queen, Victoria Regina.*

The whole area of the tragi-comedy has to find rest somewhere. If the play is more comedy than "tragi" it can, of course, be considered a comedy. But Dürrenmatt's *The Visit*, which is specifically called a tragi-comedy, has a rather even balance between tragedy and comedy. The fall of Ill, the Schoolmaster, and all the Guelleners is a tragic movement. Perhaps the play should be called a comi-tragedy. *The Homecoming* presents much the same problem as *The Visit*, and so do other absurdist plays. They are, it seems convenient to say, drama, and not so mellow as sharp.

An even more serious problem comes with the attempt to classify the Chekhov plays. Although Chekhov himself regarded them as comedies, it is doubtful if we can let the matter rest there. A curious kind of comedy indeed! Certainly there are not the extremes of tragic vision and the comic-satiric modes of *The Visit* and *The Homecoming*. The line between the tragic and the comic is much more muted in *The Cherry Orchard*. That blow of the axe, heard in the distance, is both the symbol of the tragic fall of an old and delightful way of life and of the social, comic renewal of a pattern too much in the future to be celebrated by any ritual, certainly not by marriage. This is genuine realism, life both comic and tragic, but gently and quietly so. *The Cherry Orchard* is a lyrical drama.

What about O'Neill's *Dynamo*? It is basically a serious play, but enlightenment seems too much to ascribe to it. It is an idea dramatized, almost to out-Shaw Shaw, but it is hardly comic. Perhaps *Dynamo* is really an inverted morality play in modern dress. We can see the convenience, if not the logic, of using a relatively formless form not merely to pick up modern plays, but to accommodate certain much older ones as well.

Structure

In addition to choosing the kind of play he will write, the playwright must structure or build his play. Every play must possess certain specific materials: These are generally called the exposition, the inciting moment, the rising action, the turning point, the falling action, the climax, and the conclusion. Often they are called by corresponding Greek, Latin, or French names which usually do little to clarify structure for any but the initiated. Each has its place in the structure of a play.

The exposition usually is found in the first few minutes of the play, for this is where we learn who the characters are, what has happened before we met them, what they plan to do, their relationships with or feelings toward each other—in short, the *status quo* of their world. Suddenly something occurs that disturbs the picture of their world as we have found it. This point is called the inciting moment, and when it occurs we know at once what the play is going to be about. We know what the conflict is—what the characters are trying to get out of— what the actors want to bring into reality. The rising action is the phase of the play in which we see the various forces in conflict, each striving for its own end. This continues until one force suddenly seems to acquire the advantage over the other, and that moment or situation is called the turning point. The falling action—which is a misnomer, for the interest of the audience must not fall—continues to build the intensity as some new factor enters the picture, and this added element brings about the climax which is the final culmination of everything said or done by the characters thus far. The climax pulls all the threads together; the whole play ought to have built toward this, the solution of whatever conflict may have existed. Finally, the conclusion establishes once more, at least for the moment, a *status quo* that permits us to leave the theatre feeling that this situation, at least, has run its course or been resolved.

A *well-made play* (this is now generally a derogatory term) follows the above strategy exactly. In such a play we are able to foresee the whole story very soon after it has started. If this is possible the playwright has fallen down in his form, as well as in his technique, and the effort is frequently called *hack writing*. Sometimes exposition is stretched through the entire play, and it is possible for the turning point and climax to be almost the same. Soon after the curtain goes up, however, something must always occur to set the dramatic action in motion; the inciting moment is just as necessary as that single most exciting and tense moment which is the climax.

More must be said about the "well-made play," if only to underscore the indebtedness of those who have made departures from it. The first seventy years of the nineteenth century saw the development of this kind of drama in the hands of Eugène Scribe and Victorien Sardou, to name its most particular exponents. Its basically materialistic philosophy involved the preservation of ethical, social, and political *status quo*, the so-called bourgeois middle-class morality. Ibsen and Shaw above all others attacked this attitude. It was Shaw who knocked down what may have been already a straw man with his term "Sardoodledom." But the typical "well-made play" structure was less obviously open to criticism and lingered on, even when modified.

The British playwright Clifford Bax has been credited with these words: "We ought to admire the well-made play as we admire a well-made man, and if we were to elaborate this analogy we should find that many modern plays are skinny creatures or cripples or over-large in the head." American playwright John Van Druten has commented that we have all met well-made men with symmetrical but empty heads. Here are the arguments for and against the well-made play as it was written in the mid-nineteenth century. (Van Druten also acknowledges that an "acquaintance with the older rules of the well-made play is still a good basis for learning how to break them.")

The structural form of the well-made play demanded unity of style and a progressive development of plot, which itself had to consist of solid and dramatic story-telling—a "good story line." The end of the play concluded the story, although not necessarily resolving a particular social problem that the play had presented. As a matter of fact, the drama of social thesis usually followed the Scribean structure. Such plays were realistically presented, most often set in a living room, office, or court of law. Stage directions were detailed, and craftsmanship was often skillful. Ibsen and Shaw particularly carried on, even improved on, this tradition. Craftsmanship, of course, still makes for good theatre, even if the idea of a carefully planned "well-made" play no longer adequately represents modern life, which often seems to be without plan and not really well-made.

It is often said that in a three-act play the first act is given to establishing a situation, the second to complicating it, and the third to resolving it. Few plays are that simple, but it is a fairly good over-all rule. A common criticism of television writers is that they leave out the third act because of their time limit. It is easiest for the writer to set up a situation and its complications. Resolving a story takes more time, more thought, and greater artistry.

Technique in Playwriting, Theme, and Plot

The plot has been called the body of a play and the theme has been called its soul. Most plays have a conflict of some kind between individuals, between man and society, man and some superior force, or man and himself. The events that this conflict provokes make up the plot. One of the first items of interest is the playwright's treatment of the plot and what theme he would draw from it. The same plots have been and will be used many times; it is the treatment that supplies each effort with originality or artistic worth. Shakespeare is said to have borrowed all but one of his stories, but he presented them so much better than any of the previous authors that he is not seriously criticized for the borrowing. The treatment of theme is equally varied.

The same theme or story may be given a very serious or a very light touch. It may be a severe indictment or a tongue-in-cheek attack. It could point up a great lesson or show the same situation as a handicap to progress. The personality, background, and social or artistic temperament of the playwright are responsible for the treatment that he gives to his story or theme. We must, therefore, both understand and evaluate these factors.

If the dramatist is attempting to tell us something and that something is not clear, his play lacks communication and is open to criticism on that count. If life is complicated further rather than clarified, the play has fallen down as a work of art. This does not necessarily mean that everyone extracts the same theme from a given play. Individual backgrounds or ability to understand may be responsible for differences of opinion on a play's meaning. We may dislike the way the playwright has presented his substance, or question its truth, but we should never leave the theatre without knowing what he was trying to say. It is the duty of the playwright, as an artist, to make clear to his audience what he thinks and feels and what he is trying to say or do. A great play such as *Hamlet* or *The Homecoming*, however, may contain a measure of ambiguity.

If an author chooses to write fluff and smart repartee, he should be given that privilege. If he chooses to write poetic drama, we should accept the resulting play on its own terms. We need not prefer it or praise it or go to see it, but we should not try to compare the work of the poetic playwright to that of the escapist or to the discussion plays of those who use the theatre to teach or uplift. Bernard Shaw once answered a critic who complained that a certain play was not great, "Its author never meant it to be a great play. The question is how does it rank with the type of play it is trying to be?"

To endure, a play should have a theme. It is sometimes suggested in the title as in *Loyalties, Justice,* or *Strife, You Can't Take It With You,* or *The Physician in Spite of Himself.* At other times it is found in the play itself, as in *Craig's Wife* when the aunt says to Mrs. Craig, "People who live to themselves are often left to themselves." Sometimes theme is less obvious, necessitating closer study.

If a play has a theme, we should be able to state it in general terms and in a single sentence, even at the risk of oversimplification. The theme of *Hamlet* is usually stated as the failure of a youth of poetic temperament to cope with circumstances that demand action. The theme of *Macbeth* is that too much ambition leads to destruction; of *A Streetcar Named Desire,* that he who strives hardest to find happiness oftentimes finds the least; and of *Green Pastures,* that even God must change with the universe.

Of course the theme, no matter how fully stated, is not the equivalent of the play. The play is a complex experience, and one must remain open to its manifold suggestions.

As indicated above, the statement of the play in specific terms is the plot presented. Plot and theme should go hand in hand. If the theme is one of nobility or dignity, the plot must concern events and characters that measure up to that theme. As we analyze many plays, we find that some possess an excellent theme, but are supported by an inconsequential plot. One famous play of this nature, *Abie's Irish Rose,* held the stage for many years. The theme said: Difference of religion need not hinder a happy marriage. The plot was so thin, and both characters and situation so stereotyped, that justice was not done to the theme. This weakness was most obvious in the play's revival after twenty years.

Examples of the frequent fault of superior plot and little or no theme come to us in much of the work of our current playwrights. Known for their cleverness in phrasing and timing, and their original, extremely witty conceptions, these plays are often very successful. More often than not, however, they are utterly lacking in a theme or truth that will withstand more than momentary analysis. They are delightful but ephemeral. An audience believes them only while watching in the theatre. Consequently, the authors, although now among our most popular, will not endure as artists, nor are their plays likely to be revived a hundred years hence. They but emphasize more strongly the axiom that a good plot or conflict is needed for transitory success, but a great theme is more likely to assure a play a long life.

The greatest single criticism of our theatre today is that playwrights speak but far too often have nothing to say. They lack purpose, skimming over the surface and not really probing the reason for the characters' acts.

Strategy and Tactics

Strategy is the over-all plan of the story as the playwright conceives it. The manner of carrying out this strategy can be considered his tactics. It is the artful weaving in of the exposition so that it seems a logical part of the story. Details concerning the background and history of the characters are introduced so naturally as to form a logical and believable part of the conversation.

Tactics are also evident in the playwright's ability to create suspense or to bring in the element of surprise. Suspense is the most important single ingredient in any dramatic work and has been defined as that space of time which elapses between an action and the consequences of that act. Expectation is increased and emotion becomes more intense. The ability to hold us off for the very maximum of time without straining our credulity is a very important part of an artist's technique. Surprise has dramatic worth equal almost to that of suspense, but surprise is not really dramatic unless it fits naturally and logically into the dramatic action of the play. Surprise for the sake of the sudden and unexpected is never truly dramatic. It must be relevant to the action; it must have a reason for being.

Further evidence of tactics is the manner of getting characters on and off the stage, then of giving them sufficient time to accomplish the acts that are necessary to the dramatic action. Every action must be motivated and made logical, meaningful, and consistent with character.

If the great playwrights of the past were masters in strategy, some of them fell down on their tactics. On the other hand, our modern playwrights—especially those who have written for the motion pictures and television—have shown great adroitness in their tactics but frequently have been less successful in their over-all strategy.

The observation of the playwright's success in this role is no small part in our evaluation of his technique.

Moral or Immoral

Some people might object to a discussion of morality in terms of the play and the playwright. They might consider the subject a matter of taste rather than morality, or point out that one of the world's eternally unanswered questions, what is moral? is influenced by many diverse factors.

This lack of an absolute standard only makes the playwright's task more complex. The community or educational theatre frequently finds its selection of plays greatly limited on this account. Even the professional field is often threatened with censorship. The motion pictures and television are constantly faced with the facts of what they can do and say and what they dare not. It is most important that artistically honest criteria be found for determining the morality of a play. Otherwise, how shall we answer intelligently the more vocal segment of the audience, whose moral code may not permit them to accept what the playwright has written.

Long dissertations on artistic freedom, or pleas for broadmindedness on the part of the audience would not help to answer the fundamental criticism that a given play, or some part of it, is immoral. What we must establish is a basic and honest measuring stick, to enable the intelligent theatregoer to evaluate what he sees and hears and thus decide for himself. Few would deny our premise that the theatre is a reflection of life. It follows logically that its duty is to picture life truthfully as well as artistically. It must not show just one phase of life or the little segment of which an individual approves, but *all* life of *all* classes and *all* groups and *all* personalities and *all* ages. We do not necessarily agree with the man who said, "Good plays are only written about bad people." We do contend that if some evil does not appear to conflict and contrast with the good, we do not have a very satisfactory play. It is *only* when the supposed evil succeeds, or is praised as such, that the play can justly be called immoral by any honest standard.

Today the items most often condemned as immoral are the elements of swearing, drinking, and any suggestion of sex deviation or promiscuity. Yet like the proverbial ostrich, a small segment of the audience would bury their heads in the sand or close their eyes to the things they do not want to see. Judging the world by their personal codes of morality, on that basis they would rate themselves above reproach. By that same code they would devaluate any differing moral standards.

No so-called sins need be endorsed, but all such types of behavior should be recognized as existing in life, and if the artist is to portray life, he may need to include them. If the character is a swearing man or a drinking man, it is more moral and honest to picture him thus than to falsely alter his character. The audience need only remember that the playwright is describing a particular character, not all men; they should see and understand that character as an individual. In short, it is the obligation of the audience *to judge the characters of a play in terms of life, rather than to judge life in terms of a particular play or character.*

Ibsen does not say that all women should leave their husbands, but that Nora—one woman who is not permitted to be an adult, to have a personality, or live a life of her own—does have the right to walk out of her home and leave her family.

Ibsen wrote in a day when the double standard was generally accepted. He challenged that belief, along with many other conventional ideas of his period. As Bernard Shaw pointed out, Ibsen was protesting "against the ordinary assumption that there are certain moral institutions which justify all means used to maintain them." He insisted that "the supreme end shall be the inspired, eternal, ever-growing one, not the external, unchanging artificial one; not the abstract law, but the living will." It is only natural that Ibsen's plays disturbed both the typical audience member and the typical dramatic critic of the nineties. Drama should, in fact, be regularly disturbing. Shaw concluded with words equally true today, "The plain working truth is that it is not only good for people to be shocked occasionally, but absolutely necessary to the progress of society that they should be shocked pretty often."

Just so long as the author has a true insight into the lives of his characters and pictures them as they are, the play is moral. If he makes his audience admire a vile character or invents excuses for situations that have no valid excuses, lauds the villainy within the characters, allows weakness to be rewarded, or lies in any way about his characters, then we may say the play is immoral.

Chicago banned *Tobacco Road*, with Henry Hull in the leading role, as an immoral play. Any intelligent and honest person who saw Mr. Hull in the play must have felt that a prohibition on the grounds of immorality was unjust. The entire company made of that play a truthful, and for that reason a moral, picture of life along Tobacco Road. After the language of the first few minutes had come to be associated with the characters as they were, one was not conscious of the profanity as profanity. The play was honestly conceived, the characters played with sincerity. It was far more moral for the author to employ the language he did than the substitution of less fitting dialogue would have been. It should be emphasized, however, that the discussion here concerns the production starring Henry Hull. Had the Chicago authorities banned the same play as performed by some later companies, the ruling could have been more easily understood. Later companies attempted to attract a less discerning audience by capitalizing on the publicity given the Chicago ban. They reduced the play to uninhibited farce, playing it solely for laughs rather than the near-tragedy intended. They made the most of all profanity and unsavory situations. All the criticized aspects of the play were emphasized as such rather than as inherent in the characters of the unfortunate class of humanity portrayed by the playwright. The dramatist had not been immoral, but the debased productions had been.

The whole question of morality is as involved as human nature itself, but the basis for determining morality in the theatre should be one of honest and objective analysis. Such an approach would demand that, since a play proposes to give a picture of life, we must always measure the play *in terms of life* and never life in terms of the play. With this fundamental principle in mind we may then ask specific questions:

> 1. Has the playwright lied about his characters? If, at any point he has, the play, by our standard, is immoral.
>
> 2. Has the author permitted any evil or wrong to be rewarded? Have the wicked achieved their goal because of or through their wickedness? If so, the play may be left open to the charge of being an immoral play.

If we have been completely honest in judging the plays in terms of life rather than according to our own conception of what life should be, and may still answer either of these questions in the affirmative, then we have the personal right to classify the play as immoral.

We would further emphasize that the artistic merits of a play are not necessarily affected by a decision as to its morality or immorality. Morality is no guarantee of greatness. We have merely presented what we considered basically honest criteria for evaluating the work of a playwright whose effort may be at odds with the moral or religious beliefs of some of his audience.

Journalistic—Literary—Theatrical

One further question should be given consideration in the playwright's technique. Is the play primarily journalistic, theatrical, or literary? Some may ask if these factors might not be inherent in the substance itself. We, however, are suggesting that the same material might possess any one of these qualities—or even all three at the same time. Once more, it is the treatment the dramatist has given the subject that, in the final analysis, makes it fit any or all three terms: journalistic —theatrical—literary.

A play that can be called journalistic is one written for a given time and a given audience, largely because that particular type of play or that subject seems to be popular and timely. The vast majority of scripts seen on television conform to one of several given patterns in any season —crime, particular kinds of comedy, detective stories, westerns, mystery plays, historical pieces, foreign intrigue, or those featuring some aspect of science fiction. There is a demand, and the playwright rushes to his typewriter and tries to satisfy that demand. Externally motivated, these "plays" serve the same purpose as the field of journalism. The audience is waiting for a particular program much as they await the daily newspaper. They choose the programs that fit their demands of the moment just as they choose the newspapers that reflect their views on civic, religious, or political questions. The playwright writes because the public wants him to speak, and his work is as dated tomorrow as yesterday's headlines.

The purely theatrical play, on the other hand, may last for several years, will bear seeing a number of times, and may even be revived as a period piece by another generation. It may not read as well as one would like, but it does play well in the theatre. It has suspense, characterization, excitement, and some truth or theme to give it stability and meaning in the theatre. In fact, such a play is often called "good theatre."

The literary piece always has some inkling of eternity. It belongs not to a particular day or period, although its plot may stem from an incident of a specific date. The literary play achieves originality without attempting to be novel or unusual. Its goal is not so much to shock its audience (although, as with Ibsen, it frequently does) as to reveal some truth that the author must share. Journalism seeks to be timely; the theatrical to be exciting. Both approaches are interested in facts, often box office facts. The literary man is interested not in the facts as facts, but only insofar as they represent recurrent truths of human existence. The literary playwright writes from an inward impulse. He has something to say, and he must say it. Tennessee Williams summarized it very well: "To snatch the eternal from the desperately fleeting is the great magical trick of human existence."

Playwrights have different goals. Occasionally a drama may possess two or even all these characteristics—sometimes the journalist writes better than he knows. But the one that is envisioned in an "out of time— out of place" atmosphere belongs to the description of "literary," and is likelier to live than one specifically dated by events or characters, or one devised for the abilities of a given actor or for a particular theatre's equipment.

Tests of a Play's Greatness

We would not say that every play must be great. Not every play can be great. Dramatists do not always attempt to write great plays. Few works could meet the tests that one could logically set up for a really great play, for greatness makes many demands. Nevertheless, we must try to find a working formula that will help the beginner to determine whether a drama could stand alone or whether its success is dependent on the work of the actors, the technicians, the director, or on the over-all production.

Every play must please its audience *now*, or it has failed *as theatre*, great as its other values may be. In the theatre, this *of-the-moment* response is of prime importance, for the theatre must capture and hold the immediate interest of its audience and give that audience the maximum of pleasure *at that instant*.

Harold Hobson has stated this very well by saying that "greatness comes to a play when (1) an intense experience in a fine mind is (2) translated with ecstasy into (3) effective theatrical terms." Mr. Hobson goes on to emphasize that by all odds the most important of these three elements is "theatrical effectiveness," without which there is no play. Theatrical effectiveness, however, is the least "literary" of the three ingredients. We must add that with it alone we are right back where we were, without "greatness." Hobson further points out that with all three we may have an *Othello*, with just the last two we have *The Importance of Being Earnest*, and with the third alone we have a *Charley's Aunt*. For any degree of greatness we must have at least two, the third being essential in the pair.

Frequently a drama that has great literary worth—or the first two of Hobson's elements—is revived on the basis of these values, or because it has lived as literature for many years. In its day it may have been "theatrically effective," but owing to the nature of our times and the demands of present audiences, this important element may not seem to be present. Fortunately, there is always a small audience of theatre enthusiasts who will find real enjoyment in a fine production of such a drama. Yet because it may leave much to be desired by the majority of its potential audience such a production has fallen down as theatre, great literature though it may remain. It must be noted that succeeding generations may rediscover as good theatre a play we have rejected. Then the fault is ours. If the play passes permanently out of the theatre, we may say that it does not have what it takes for the first rank. As critics we should be able to recognize these different values and appraise them. We should not flatly condemn a play, or derogate an audience for lack of enthusiasm, or place primary blame on a production for not doing justice to a piece of literature that has withstood the tests of time. The blame may be distributable, and the critic should try to put it in the right place or places.

Theatrical effectiveness has many degrees. Some plays may send an audience on its way ecstatic with the most enthusiastic approval; others may please in a quieter manner; some may hold the attention in performance, becoming the source of thoughtful deliberation in the days to follow. Still others may hold the attention for the moment but, outside the theatre, lose much of their luster. These varying attitudes must be considered in evaluating any play's true worth.

In addition to Harold Hobson's definition of greatness, we have a set of valid tests given by Albright, Halstead, and Mitchell in *Principles of Theatre Art*.[27]

> ... The intensity of pleasure at the moment of perception
> ... The duration of that pleasure in retrospect
> ... The quality of the after-impression
> ... The quality of pleasure upon witnessing a second performance
> ... Comparison of the pleasure with that caused by similar compositions

These tests are self-explanatory, and they can be very useful in our appraisal of a play's claim to greatness. A third excellent test is found in the five questions asked by Joseph Mersand.[28] Does the play:

> ... possess universality of appeal in time and space?
> ... create living characters in convincing situations?
> ... stir, move, enrich, or transform us?
> ... express its thought in beautiful or appropriate language?
> ... teach life's meaning and strengthen our own hand in facing life's problems?

Regardless of what yardstick we may choose to use, we know that a play worthy of the term "greatness" must do more than merely hold our interest or entertain us for the moment. It must be really effective in some very definite respect, such as moving us emotionally with its beauty or with its truth; and it must have sufficient strength to sway our thoughts.

[27] H. D. Albright, William F. Halstead, and Lee Mitchell, *Principles of Theatre Art* (Boston: Houghton Mifflin Company, 1955), pp. 74–76.
[28] Joseph Mersand, *The Play's the Thing* (New York: Modern Chapbooks, 1941–1948), pp. 32–39.

There are, of course, degrees of greatness in the work of dramatists. Let us make a tentative evaluation of the plays we have analyzed. They are all good plays; but the very highest places have generally been given to *Oedipus Rex, Hamlet, Tartuffe,* and *The Cherry Orchard.* (Some people might object to including Chekhov's play here, but as many would defend the choice.) Almost as great are *Ghosts, Death of a Salesman, The Birds,* and *Everyman.* Plain great plays are *Right You Are, The Visit, The Homecoming,* and *Major Barbara.* Good, but perhaps not great, are *Dynamo* and *Philadelphia, Here I Come!* Note two things: On recent plays we cannot yet be sure of the verdict of time. Second, this is not a rating of the dramatists—Shaw's *Saint Joan* would go higher than *Major Barbara,* as other O'Neill plays would outrank *Dynamo.* Difference of opinion can be expected, but more surprising, perhaps, is a general area of critical agreement.

Whatever system of evaluation you choose—and each must choose his own—in the interests of simplicity let us suggest, Pied-Piper fashion: Follow me, and I'll show you where it's at. . . . A great play should be honest. It imitates, to be sure, but it must honestly recognize what it is doing. It must not pretend to be something it is not. Great drama must be exciting. It must stir up, emotionally or intellectually, or both. What T. S. Eliot calls the "shock of heightened awareness" is perhaps what all great art must produce. If a drama does not deliver this kind of shock, it is not dramatic. Finally, the great play treats a significant subject significantly. The meaning of the play must make a difference to human beings as human beings.

The Goethean questions can always be asked:

> What did the playwright set out to do?
> How and how well did he do it?
> Was it worth the doing?

They lead to the heart of the matter. The heart of the manner, however, is to convey integrity and excitement.

Questions for Discussion

1. The script of a play, or the drama itself, can be "played" in as many different ways as a musical composition. Think of a play you have seen in two or more quite different interpretations, or imagine two quite opposed interpretations of a script you know well. (Often a parody, or comic use of a serious play, will suggest itself—for instance, Shakespeare parodies *Romeo and Juliet* in the Pyramus-Thisbe play within *A Midsummer-Night's Dream*). What elements make the essential difference between the effects? If the script remains constant, other theatrical elements must make the difference.

2. Is there any play that you would rather read than see? Why? Is this therefore a "closet drama"?

3. One favorite distinction since Nietzsche is the difference between the "Apollonian" approach to art—measured, quiet, rational, and dignified—and the "Dionysiac" approach—impassioned, wild, irrational, and moving. Why is it perfectly appropriate that the Greek theatre (and most of our theatre since the Greeks) be more closely centered on Dionysus than on Apollo? Is this true of comedy as well as of tragedy?

4. Consider the literary and satiric uses of having man view himself in transformation into animal, or vice versa, in such works as *The Birds*, Kafka's *Metamorphosis* or "A Report to an Academy," Swift's last voyage of Gulliver, Orwell's *Animal Farm*, Ionesco's *Rhinoceros*, and any others you can think of.

5. Think of *Everyman* as an allegory and place it beside another allegorical drama such as *Waiting for Godot* to point out similarities and differences.

6. Which of the many Hamlets do you find most convincing? Think of some performance of *Hamlet* you have seen—stage, screen, or television—and try to place it in some category, attacking or defending the characterization, with references to lines from the play.

7. In *Tartuffe* the satire is directed against religious hypocrisy and the gullibility of those who are taken in by it. What other "foibles and follies" of mankind are satirized in other plays? What is being

satirized in *Right You Are*? In *The Visit*? Do not be satisfied with just the easy or obvious answers.

8. What specifically are the "purpose, passion, and perception" in *Ghosts*? Who is the "tragic hero" in this play?

9. Can you find the same kind of balance, a trembling balance, between the tragic and comic visions in any play other than *The Cherry Orchard*? How well does *The Glass Menagerie* fit? Is the major difference between these plays that of realism and expressionism?

10. Two Cub Scouts once shocked their Den Mother when, asked what play they would most like to give in their puppet theatre, they responded, Chekhov's *The Cherry Orchard*. (They had recently seen a college theatre production of it with their father.) What things in this play would lend themselves very well to puppet theatre production?

11. What examples of shock and paradox do you find in *Major Barbara*? What significance do you see in the double military imagery, the Salvation *Army* and munitions for war?

12. How does Lamberto Laudisi in *Right You Are* speak for the dramatist? How is he like and unlike Cléante in Tartuffe?

13. If O'Neill's *Dynamo* were to be rewritten in the Post-World War II period, might an atomic reactor be substituted for the dynamo? Discuss the growth of the science-religion controversy.

14. The death of a salesman is only a terminal point. What are the major elements that go into the *"Life" of a Salesman*?

15. If *The Visit* is a combination of the theatre of the absurd, the theatre of cruelty, expressionism, and epic theatre, which elements in it belong most specifically to each of these theatrical movements? How does all this theatricality work against realism? How does the "suspension of disbelief" still operate?

16. How does the basic metaphor of *The Homecoming* compare with other "homecomings"—for instance, *The Family Reunion* of T. S. Eliot, the homecomings in Eugene O'Neill's *Mourning Becomes Electra* and Thomas Wolfe's *You Can't Go Home Again*? How does "homecoming" imply "home leaving?"

17. Discuss *Philadelphia, Here I Come!* as a memory play. How does this device in the theatre compare with the novelistic flashback? With the cinematic flashback?

18. The Spanish philosopher Ortega y Gasset, in *The Dehumanization of Art*, speaks of the relationships of art and life in terms of looking through an artistic windowpane set in a frame toward a real garden, noting that one concentrates his vision either at the pane or on the garden.

Similarly a work of art vanishes from sight for a beholder who seeks in it nothing but the moving fate of John and Mary or Tristan and Isolde and adjusts his vision to this. Tristan's sorrows are sorrows and can evoke compassion only in so far as they are taken as real. But an object of art is artistic only in so far as it is not real. . . .

During the nineteenth century artists proceeded in all too impure a fashion. They reduced the strictly aesthetic elements to a minimum and let the work consist almost entirely in a fiction of human realities. In this sense all normal art of the last century must be called realistic. . . . Seen from the vantage-point of our day, Romanticism and Naturalism draw closer together and reveal their common realistic root.

Works of this kind are only partially works of art, or artistic objects. Their enjoyment does not depend upon our power to focus on transparencies and images, a power characteristic of the artistic sensibility; all they require is human sensibility and willingness to sympathize with our neighbor's joys and worries . . . , inasmuch as it is not art but an extract from life.[29]

Defend the theatricalism of the twentieth century theatre, from expressionism to the present, as a return to art.

19. Try to pinpoint those elements in a play which make that play exciting. What causes the "shock of heightened awareness," or the "double-take?"

20. Use Harold Hobson's tests of a great play to make three lists of the plays you know.

21. Apply Joseph Mersand's tests of greatness to any play.

22. Do the same regarding (1) Type, (2) Style, (3) Structure, (4) Strategy, and (5) Tactics, and whether or not the play is basically literary, journalistic, or theatrical.

23. Give several examples of thoughtful laughter as contrasted with the mirth provoked by situation comedy so prevalent on the television screen.

24. Describe an incident in a play wherein an effort was made to portray reality by imitation. Cite another in which the artist has used suggestion.

25. Name several plays or instances where the element of sentimentality has been the source of the emotion. Where was it handled so well that you were fooled by it? Where was it so obvious that it was unpleasant? In any case, was this the fault of the script or of the production?

26. Choose a play or motion picture that has been termed immoral in some quarters and either justify or refute the criticism.

[29]José Ortega y Gasset, *The Dehumanization of Art* (Garden City, N.Y.: Doubleday & Company, Inc., 1956), pp. 10–11.

Bibliography

For Supplementary Reading or Special Projects

Barber, C. L., *Shakespeare's Festive Comedy*. New York: Meridian Books, 1963.

Bentley, Eric, *The Playwright as Thinker*. New York: Reynal & Hitchcock, 1946.

Bergson, Meredith, *Laughter; An Essay on Comedy*. Garden City, N.Y.: Doubleday & Company, Inc., 1956.

Bradley, A. C., *Shakespearean Tragedy*. Greenwich, Conn.: Fawcett Publications, Inc., 1965.

Brockett, Oscar G., *The Theatre—An Introduction*. New York: Holt, Rinehart and Winston, 1964.

Cooper, Lane, *Aristotle on the Art of Poetry*. New York: Ginn and Company, 1913.

Corrigan, Robert W. and James L. Rosenberg, *The Context and Craft of Drama*. San Francisco: Chandler Publishing Co., 1964.

Esslin, Martin, *The Theatre of the Absurd*. Garden City, N.Y.: Doubleday & Company, Inc., 1961.

Fergusson, Francis, *The Idea of a Theatre*. Garden City, N.Y.: Doubleday & Company, Inc., 1955.

Frye, Northrop, *Anatomy of Criticism*. Princeton, N.J.: Princeton University Press, 1957.

Kernodle, George R., *Invitation to the Theatre*. New York: Harcourt, Brace & World, Inc., 1967.

Kerr, Walter, *How Not to Write a Play*. New York: Simon and Schuster, 1955.

Kitto, H. D. F., *Greek Tragedy*. Garden City, N.Y.: Doubleday & Company, Inc., 1954.

Knight, G. Wilson, *The Wheel of Fire*. New York: Meridian Books, 1957.

Kott, Jan, *Shakespeare Our Contemporary*, Garden City, N.Y.: Doubleday & Company, Inc., 1966.

Krutch, Joseph Wood, *"Modernism" in Modern Drama*. Ithaca, N.Y.: Cornell University Press, 1953.

Lewis, Allan, *The Contemporary Theatre*. New York: Crown Publishers, Inc., 1962.

Marek, Hannelore, *The History of the Theatre*. New York: The Odyssey Press, Inc., 1964.

Meserve, Walter, *Discussions of Modern American Drama*. Boston: D. C. Heath & Company, 1965.

Nicoll, Allardyce, *The Development of the Theatre*. New York: Harcourt, Brace and Company, Inc., 1947.

Pronko, Leonard Cabell, *Avant Garde*. Berkeley: University of California Press, 1964.

Shaw, George Bernard, *The Quintessence of Ibsenism*. New York: Hill & Wang, Inc., 1963.

Sievers, W. David, *Freud on Broadway: A History of Psychoanalysis and the American Drama*. New York: Hermitage House, 1955.

Young, Stark, *The Theatre*. New York: Hill & Wang, Inc., 1927.

III

The

Production

3

The Director

and the

Direction

During its long history the theatre has belonged to each of its many artists. The playwright, actor, scenic artist, electrician, costumer, and director—each has had his "hour upon the stage." At present that pre-eminence belongs to the director. It is he who is responsible for the selection, the organization, and the design of the over-all production. He is the leader, the coordinator, the guide, the unifier of all the diverse elements that make up the production. Any play that passes through his imagination will have about it something of him, for no longer does a director just put on a play. In the modern theatre, and most especially in the United States, the theatre production itself has come to be an artistic work. The dominance of one individual who creates and organizes or coordinates as well as interprets became a reality between 1895 and 1915 through the work and writings of Gordon Craig, and to a lesser extent, Adolphe Appia. Their insistence on the artistic harmony of all elements—setting, lighting, costume, movement, music—was responsible for the emergence of the German *regisseur*, the French *metteur en scène*, the English "producer," the American "artistic director" of the twentieth century.

Little was definite about the work of the director until comparatively recent times. We are led to believe that Aeschylus played some part in the staging of his productions, for critics hailed the "brilliant mounting" of his plays. Shakespeare's advice to the players in *Hamlet* assures us that he had firm ideas regarding the acting of his own works. We know

173

that Molière directed the young actors in his comedies. A contemporary noted that "a glance of the eye, a step, a gesture, were observed with an exactitude that was unknown until then in the theatre of Paris."

Theatre for the Greeks was a part of their religious ceremony. Everyone knew the stories that were enacted, and belief in the gods combined with civic pride made for a common attitude. Audiences of thousands came to the great outdoor theatres to honor Dionysus. It was a common emotion, and the re-enactment of a legend affected the audiences as if the event were actually occurring before their eyes. Something of the same religious fervor was evident in medieval times when the Christian Church revived the theatre and enacted biblical stories in the various stations about the church. Performances were motivated by a basic faith. Of course there was supervision or direction, but the story was paramount.

Shakespeare and Molière found audiences similarly unified. These theatregoers were protected by a ruling monarch who had permitted and endorsed the performances they watched. They came for sheer enjoyment—for pleasure—for escape. None were confounded by (or aware of) the many aesthetic aspects that we consider a part of the theatre today.

The first great change came with the painted scenic background introduced during the Renaissance. Both the playwright and the play lost some importance with this innovation. As background in the theatre developed from mood evoked to a suggestion of place, then to a portrayal of locale, and finally to an almost complete replica of place, the visual element took over. Subsequently, during the eighteenth and nineteenth centuries, we had the great performances of individual actors. These "stars" sometimes called "actor-managers" took over. In Germany we know that Ekhof demanded rehearsals and the use of such items as were needed in the play. The Great Schroeder told his actors exactly what he wanted them to do. In his famous Weimar Court Theatre, Goethe held many long rehearsals, was most careful in his casting, and even devised a long list of stage rules. His cry was for a "beautiful reality" which came only from planning and careful rehearsal.

In England it was David Garrick in the mid-eighteenth century who first began to think of the production as a whole. In the Drury Lane he drove the gallants from the stage, installed footlights, took great care in casting the minor roles, gave orders regarding properties, costumes, and scenic backgrounds. The picture frame stage behind the proscenium arch was further enhanced by Garrick, although most acting still took place on a stage apron that extended thirteen feet in front.

The real era of the director, however, began in 1874 when the Duke of Saxe-Meiningen introduced his company to Berlin. He demanded of his actors great discipline, coordinated acting, accuracy in all technical details, and minute attention to small roles, stage movement, and gestures. He thought in terms of unity and gave the greatest care to all the technical aspects. Each part was thoroughly integrated, assuring that the total production would take precedence over any single element. The duke became the first regisseur, the first designer or creator of an entire production. His work inspired André Antoine and later the great Russian director, Constantin Stanislavsky. Lee Simonson summarized Saxe-Meiningen's contribution to modern theatre by saying he furnished us "the necessity for a commanding director who could visualize an entire performance and give it unity as an interpretation by complete control of every moment of it; the interpretative value of the smallest details of lighting, costuming, make-up, stage setting; the immense discipline and the degree of organization needed before the performance was capable of expressing the soul of the play!"

It is difficult to overstress the power of the director in today's theatre. Kenneth Tynan of London and Harold Clurman of New York have agreed that this individual is more powerful in the United States than abroad. It has been said that Paris is the playwright's city; London is the actor's city; and New York is the director's city. A knowledge of recent activity in these areas would readily bear out this assumption. Albert Bermel, in a facetious vein, composed the following "Director Wanted" ad for a trade paper:

> Man needed to assume control of a stage. Must have intimate knowledge of acting, scene design, costumes, costs and casts, and know how to give an audience what it wants. Must be prepared to audition hundreds of men and women; tell the playwright how to fix the slippery spots in the script; make sure that the scenery doesn't get under the actor's feet and that the incidental music doesn't swamp their voices; give the performers plausible motives so that they have some idea of what they're talking about; provide a shoulder for the actresses to cry on when they get confused and kind words for the actors when they muff their lines during rehearsals. Working conditions: frantic. Hours: all day and night. Salary: above average. Duration of employment: uncertain. Applicants need not produce references, but they will be expected to prove (and improve on) previous successes. . . .[1]

On a more serious note, Harold Clurman, one of our most capable directors, has said that the director might be called the author of the stage production. He further noted:

> Though the director does not act, he is, or should be responsible for the kind of acting we see on the stage; though he does not usually design the sets, he is, or should be, responsible for the kind of impression the sets make; and this applies to everything else on the stage.[2]

[1]Albert Bermel, "The Director's Signature," reprinted by courtesy of *Playbill* magazine.
[2]John Gassner, *Producing the Play* (New York: The Dryden Press, 1953).

In one sense the director is comparable to the conductor of a symphony orchestra who plays no instrument in a performance but unifies the work of many individuals into an artistic whole. He regulates tempo, commands every variation in emphasis, and creates an interpretation. He must constantly think of the total effect, for he is the representative of the composer [author]. It is the director's responsibility to see that each artist suggests a creditable reality so far as the play, his character, and the period represented are concerned. Furthermore, the director must see that together they *translate, interpret, and express the illusion that best conveys the playwright's attitude.*

The theatre has frequently been called a kind of "organized chaos," but cannot the same be said of life itself? The theatre has always been a confrontation of life—a picture of the times. Perhaps no other medium can so clearly mirror the mystery, the magic, the purpose, the pattern, the hopes, dreams, ambitions, and fears of man. With imagination as one parent and reason as the other, theatre becomes essentially a dialogue between the audience and the actor. Man's character is a combination of all his basic animal instincts and the raw emotions that have been called the "pathetic," and the "ethical" elements of learning, thought, or reason. Likewise, according to Nietzsche, Greek tragedy was born of the light, beauty, reason, moderation, and order of Apollo and the frenzied, ecstatic, self-assertion of Dionysus. The modern director soon realizes these as the ingredients that he must bring into a harmony that will be the "organized chaos" of his production.

The director's work begins with his choice of script. If one of his major obligations is to interpret the work of the playwright, this obligation obviously extends to the playwright whose script was chosen. The director's obligations include these considerations. He should: ... thoroughly understand the script and be capable of directing it, ... be able to hire a wholly adequate cast, ... ascertain the availability of (at least) the minimum physical equipment necessary for production ... assure himself of an ample budget, ... be confident that an audience will be ready for this particular play. As a very important adjunct, if the organization and the theatre itself is to grow, the script must be a challenge to those who will work in it and to the audience that will attend.

In view of these obligations and of our basic fidelity to Goethe's three questions, it would seem necessary to mention here a very important condition that exists in the American theatre, namely, that our theatre falls into two general classifications: the commercial and the noncommercial. Each possesses different reasons for existence; and each has its own special goals, all of which tend to affect the director's choice of script.

We have chosen to use the terms commercial and noncommercial in preference to professional and amateur because of the unfortunately derogatory connotation that has come to be associated with the latter term. In the theatre the actual distinction is many times a matter of attitude, and the so-called amateur performance, with its high purpose and sincerity, often matches and sometimes excels the work of many professional groups. A majority of our summer theatres, a few of our road companies, and an occasional New York production would suffer greatly by any artistic standards when compared with the best work of these noncommercial organizations.

The commercial theatre includes motion pictures and television as well as those living theatres centered on Broadway and off-Broadway, and the touring organizations emanating from there. During the summer there are approximately four to six hundred "straw-hat" theatres, many of which are commercial. During the remainder of the year regular stock companies reside in various areas. One of the most encouraging notes in recent years has been the establishment of repertory theatres in some thirty-five cities across the country, including Minneapolis, Detroit, Washington, D.C., Seattle, Los Angeles, and San Francisco, to name a few of the more prominent locations. The majority of these groups are recognized and operate under the rules of Actors' Equity Association, the union of professional actors. There are in addition some non-Equity companies whose personnel receive regular salaries. Since the companies are maintained solely through the box office, however, they are classified as commercial companies.

The noncommercial theatre falls roughly into two classifications: the community theatre and the educational theatre. The first category includes such well-established groups as the Cleveland Playhouse, and prominent theatres in Houston, Dallas, Kalamazoo, Midland (Texas), Buffalo, Des Moines, Omaha, Charleston (South Carolina), New Orleans, Rochester (New York), and many others too numerous to be listed here. Thousands of church, fraternal, civic, and other drama groups also exist as art theatres, community enterprises, service organizations, and so on.

The educational theatre comprises, as the term implies, high school, college, and university dramatic endeavors, all of which are related to and usually underwritten by the institutions of which they are a part. Many college theatres can boast of well-paid and dedicated staffs of teacher-directors, designers, managers, and technicians. Some possess well-equipped auditoriums, as well as stages, scenery, and costume shops that surpass those of all but a few professional theatres. They have a constant flow of student actors, stage crews, and other—unsalaried—help. Some schools have recently begun to bring professionals to the campus as technicians, as actors, and as directors. Several universities have brought in an entire resident company to work with the students. The goal is to teach by observation and association with trained artists whose standards and experience are on a higher level than those often found among nonprofessionals. We would emphasize that each situation has different needs with different goals and problems. One of the director's first obligations is that of an administrator and a leader who must recognize all these entities and fit into them.

The director in the professional theatre is hired to direct a particular play and can be held responsible for its selection only in that he accepted the assignment. If the play is wholly unworthy, then he as well as the producer may be justly criticized.

On the other hand, every civic or educational organization in each theatrical community is a case in itself, calling for a different program of plays. The fact that a play was successful in New York does not mean that it is a great play. By the same token, a play that failed in New York, or never played there, is not necessarily a poor play. The great hit of a few years ago may or may not be right for a given theatre today. The types of theatre demanded by audiences in a metropolitan center, on a Midwestern college campus, or at a Texas community theatre are not at all the same. Locale and time are both involved in choosing plays for the noncommercial theatre, for a certain audience may not be ready for a particular play. To misjudge the temperament, desire, or understanding of the theatre workers or potential audience in any locality can only yield empty seats or an unenthusiastic house. Both, of course, are equally harmful to the theatre and to the producing group.

Allied with choice of play is casting, which poses a special problem for most directors in the noncommercial theatre. Their choice of program is frequently circumscribed by a limited number of actors suitable with respect to experience and age. Shaw, Chekhov, Pirandello, Shakespeare, Sophocles, Molière, Corneille, and even many present-day writers make some rather extravagant demands of the actor.

As noted above, it is unwise to choose a play—great though it may be —for which an adequate cast cannot be found. Directors often err in this respect. Bernard Shaw's admonition was, as usual, sage: "You must not keep on confusing the appreciation and understanding of parts and plays with the ability to act them." We would emphasize that good theatre can be exciting regardless of the period it represents. But the play must be well done if it is to excite the audience. The television and motion picture fields have been so very careful in this respect, and they have the distinct advantages of unlimited talent and apparently unlimited funds. If the stage is to attract an audience now accustomed only to the motion picture and television, its productions must be equally exciting, although perhaps in a very different way. The director who constantly strives to uplift the stage in the face of such competition is to be commended, but as a wise theatre man once said, "We are all for elevating the stage, but those of us who love the legitimate theatre would not suggest doing it by depressing the audience."

The director on the commercial stage must attract to the box office a sufficient audience to pay all production costs and running expenses with some margin of profit for producers who have underwritten the production. He hopes, also, to win the approval of a large portion of playgoers and the commendation of professional dramatic critics.

Although many of us feel that the commercial theatre often falls short in its obligations as an art form, we should remember that it is also a profession and a business—meaning that the economic element is inextricably interwoven with the artistic. Realizing this, we may be a little less prone to dismiss a production as mere "show business." Theatre workers must eat and theatre producers must live, and the commercial theatre is not to be overly censored for giving the audience what it will buy.

In contrast to this commercialized approach to art, the community theatres are usually organized, not for the purpose of making money, but to satisfy the creative desires of their members, to answer the frequent question of what to do with leisure time, and to bring together people in a community or group who have the same artistic interests. The community theatre, interested as it is in the artistic success of its productions and in balancing its budget, exists also as a creative and social organization for the benefit of its members and its audience.

Any director who serves such a theatre is responsible to his organization for fulfilling these additional goals. They are not only justified, but form a vital part of the organization itself. Each member of the audience has a right to demand as fine an example of theatre as the group can give. When he criticizes, however, he must not forget that the community theatre has obligations that are peculiarly its own. Neither must we forget that the community theatre and the educational theatre have yet a further obligation—that of bringing the living theatre to an audience which frequently has no other opportunity for such an experience. Furthermore, a director in an educational theatre should not be judged on the choice of a single play, or on a single season. The programs can be more fairly evaluated by considering three or four consecutive seasons, depending on what comprises the student generation.

The educational theatre must also serve as a teacher if it is to justify its existence as part of the institution it represents. Thus the educational theatre director must give the student body attending the performances an introduction to and eventually an appreciation of the best in dramatic literature, and of good theatre. In addition he must recognize individual students who wish to work in any phase of the dramatic program. The *desire* must, of course, be accompanied by sufficient *talent* and *ability*, but all students who possess these three important qualifications must be given equal opportunity to participate on a competitive basis. This can partially eliminate what is known as type-casting, thereby substituting a method far superior for actors being trained and the future of the theatre alike—a midpoint between type-casting and miscasting. This approach also puts emphasis on a greater number of participants, rather than promoting the use of the same actors over and over again. This holds true in all other areas of the theatre—carpentry, costuming, makeup, lighting, painting, designing, or writing. Truly, in the educational theatre lies a gigantic opportunity to teach cooperation, teamwork, loyalty, and responsibility. Nowhere is each quality better realized than in the well-rounded dramatic production. The educational theatre director holds in his hands the opportunity of helping his students to develop physically, vocally, intellectually, emotionally, culturally, and socially.

The director is also obliged as a representative of the educational system and to the theatre as an institution, to select plays from every period of dramatic literature that represent the best in type, style, and structure. His program should constitute a sort of living library. At the same time, he must not reach beyond the capacities of the students involved or the audience that he will attract. They must be challenged, but failure to meet the challenge can not only harm the participants but disappoint and lose the audience as well.

The choice of play, we must stress again, is of vital importance in every way. It must attract the audience initially as well as appeal to it once it is in the theatre. It has always been necessary for the theatre to build or create its audience, and today, if the stage is to survive, this must be accomplished by the directors in community and educational theatres. A balanced theatre program should not be too heavy or too avant-garde; it must begin with more popular dramatic material, for even if the director does personally prefer the classical, the experimental, the current, or the "way out" scripts, he must strive for a balance. Most of the potential audience is not familiar with live theatre, and their early experiences should be exciting ones. To start on a solid diet of the greatest literary masterpieces (or all avant-garde) can only mean playing to empty seats, creating dissatisfaction, and losing a potential audience.

Finally, there is the ever-important and not-to-be-forgotten obligation to the theatre director himself. He must satisfy his own artistic as well as educational standards. It can be done only after he has first considered positively the other demands, although at times it may be necessary to compromise here and there in order to give the most to the greatest number. Only in meeting the first four obligations can he as a director in the educational theatre meet the fifth, that of satisfying himself.

In summary, then, the director in the noncommercial theatre, community or educational, has at least four distinct obligations beyond bringing the best in live theatre to his audience and presenting artistic productions faithful in interpretation of the authors' scripts. These obligations are:

1. To entertain and educate the audience and also to build an audience for the theatre of the future.
2. To develop the talents and further the creativity of those actively involved in the production.
3. To further the aims or purpose of the organization he represents.
4. To contribute artistically to the theatre as an institution and an art.

Directors in countless noncommercial theatres throughout America are meeting these obligations most successfully. These organizations, and the recent development of the repertory theatre, are the living stage's greatest hope for the future. The creed of one university theatre summarizes so well what many educational and community theatres are trying to do that it is listed here in its entirety.

Our Theatre shall endeavor always:

... to develop its students as individuals—vocally, physically, emotionally and culturally—rather than for the commercial theatre;
... to train both audience and students to appreciate the living theatre;
... to present plays that picture all phases of life and dramatic literature;
... to approach perfection in its own realm without attempting to imitate any other dramatic production;
... to entertain but to contribute something more than mere entertainment;
... to encourage creative work in every phase of the dramatic arts;
... to add stature to the theatre in general, and to the college theatre in particular; and
... to be always *educational, challenging,* and *artistic!*

We must not dwell overlong on this subject, but if noncommercial theatres and their directors are to receive the honest critical evaluation we would ask for all artists, their particular problems and specific goals must be understood by the critic.

The director's substance is the script itself, and his interpretation of that script as it is brought to life in the theatre. This involves what *he wants* it to say to the audience as well as what he feels *the author meant* it to say. The director may change the period, the style, even the type.

There are many opinions as to the precise extent of the directorial license. Some contend that the moment the printed script becomes a living thing it has entered a new medium and that the director in creating the production is equally as creative as is the playwright who wrote it. There are others who feel that a script should not be altered but should be interpreted exactly as the author intended, or as nearly as it is possible to do. We would not enter into this controversy. We are now primarily interested in what the director has tried to do with the script, the actors, and the technicians; for it is through them, their artistry, and their cooperation that he will literally speak to the audience.

Once a script has been chosen, the artistic work of the director begins. During a period of study, he must discover the *exact* characters of the piece, searching out their motives and relationships to each other and to the story. He must understand just where the play begins, how it builds through a series of crises, what conflicts might exist, where the breaks will come. So doing, he should know what its strength and weaknesses are. Here, too, he must come to know and understand the playwright's form, for this he must project in such a way as to create suspense and hold the interest of the audience. This is what we call the structure or the building of the play. A belief has persisted from the days of the Greeks until the theatre of the absurd that every play must possess certain specific materials. They are generally called the *exposition*, the *inciting moment*, the *rising action*, the *turning point*, the *falling action*, the *climax*, and the *conclusion*. Each has its place in the structure of a play and all were discussed in Chapter 2, under *Structure*.

We would digress here to mention a frequent conflict between the literary analysis of a script and the theatrical analysis. The interest of the theatre audience must be held until the final curtain and the director must exhaust every means of doing this. Contrary to the literary view, which often uses the terms *turning point* and *climax* interchangeably, the director must project the full dramatic value of each, and the climax must grow out of the turning point. Milton Marx has made such a fine differentiation between the two that he is quoted here in full:

> An analogy [between turning point and climax] may help to make the distinction clear. The turning point in a man's career would be that action or event that ultimately leads to failure or success— winning the first big law case or successfully performing the first big surgical operation, deciding to become a criminal by an embezzlement or a forgery, choosing between retaining a throne or marrying for love. The *climax* to the lawyer's career might be his appointment to the bench of the Supreme Court; and the doctor, the saving of the life of some personage after everyone else had failed, or perhaps nationwide recognition at a celebration commemorating many years of service; the climax of the criminal's career

might be a life sentence to prison; that of a king who gave up his throne so that he could marry the woman on whom he had set his heart might be some subsequent achievement for his country that would list his name among its greatest heroes.[3]

The importance of the climax in a play can hardly be overemphasized. It is the very essence of the structure, for without a climax there is no play. Many playwrights have admitted writing the climax first and then the rest of the play—in other words, writing it backwards. The climax must be the culmination of everything that has been said or done by the characters, the solution of whatever conflict may have existed. It pulls all the threads together, for the whole play must have built to this moment.

One of the most common weaknesses in playwriting consists of the dramatist's permitting his characters to do something at this crucial moment that is not wholly consistent with the natures previously revealed to the audience. A strong character must not become suddenly weak, or a weak one show a totally unexpected strength. Any characteristic or action on the part of an individual during the climax must have been amply motivated—by the acting and by the directing—before that moment. The climax of necessity comes very close to the end of the play. On occasion two characters or two stories are almost equal in interest, in which case there may be an *anticlimax* when the second, usually the lesser of the two, is concluded.

The director must decide what predominant aesthetic style would be appropriate; for each production, in addition to the aesthetic style,will possess its own style—perhaps largely influenced by the director's personal style. It is his duty to discover what is in the words and beneath the words of the script; then he must find a means of putting across on stage subtleties and inner meanings only suggested by the words themselves. He must discover the mood or atmosphere, in short, determine exactly what the playwright has tried to say—his very reason for having written the script.

Next comes the choosing of his cast. Once the director has mastered the script's substance and form, he must think in terms of actors who will fit into the various roles. He must consider voices and personalities that will blend or contrast properly; movements and pictures; setting, stage décor, properties, lighting, sound, and many other details that will help to interpret and emphasize the "something" he believes the playwright was moving toward. Producers in the professional theatre do sometimes insist upon special friends for certain roles, and actors have been known to produce plays only so that they might play a coveted part, even though they were not equipped to do it well. Nevertheless, casting is normally

[3]Milton Marx, *The Enjoyment of Drama* (New York: Appleton-Century-Crofts, Division of Meredith Corporation, 1940), p. 79.

considered to be the province of the director. He may choose to type-cast, thus making his production easier to direct and more believable to the audience. On the other hand, he may choose to develop someone in a role by permitting the use of makeup to alter the actor's appearance and facilitate a change of personality.

There also enters the element of interpretation. The director must have decided on what each role demands. With thousands of good actors begging for parts, it is not unusual to read that the production of a play has been postponed because the director was unable to cast it. As an illustration, let us suppose that a playwright has pictured a specific character as shy, retiring, bashful, or reluctant to speak up and express himself. Such a character could be interpreted so as to arouse warm sympathy by his quaint, shy, and lovable quality; he might become a broad comedy character at whom the audience could laugh boisterously; or he could be a stupid individual whom the audience might prefer to boot right off the stage. Each interpretation could be logically justified.

Harold Clurman put it another way when he said that the whole meaning of the play, *Golden Boy* by Clifford Odets, depended on whether the director saw the leading character, Joe Bonaparte, as a fighter who had a gift for music, or as a musician who had a gift for fighting. Either choice is a matter of interpretation—the director's idea of the role and how he sees it in relation to the play and the other characters.

A director's success may be partially evaluated by observing any obvious miscastings, actors who do not give evidence of being what they would have us believe they are because of defects in their physical, their emotional, or their mental stamina.

When the cast is selected, the director turns to his work as creator. His several obligations, depending upon the theatre he represents, have been noted, and now he faces the most important obligation of all, for every good director realizes that there is only one standard of excellence in theatre art. He will not try to excuse the less-than-successful production by rationalizations of any kind. He knows that the inexperienced participants in an educational or community theatre may not come as close to scaling the artistic heights as do members of a professional group, but the chief goal of each and every dramatic production should be the same—*complete artistic success!*

To implement this all-important obligation, we would choose this definition of direction: *It is the duty of the director to create the complete and accurate theatrical effect demanded by the play's type, style, spirit, and purpose, and to project this creation through such visual and auditory stimuli as will produce in the audience a definite emotional and/or intelluctual impression.* As an adjunct to this definition of direction, it has been wisely said that the director decides *what is to be done*, and his fellow artists—the actors and technicians—are responsible for *how* the *what* is accomplished.

It is our conviction that director, actors, and technicians can find ample room for individual freedom of expression and interpretation within the confines of the "what" and "how." The work of the actors and technicians will be discussed in the chapters devoted to them. We now consider the director's contribution in fulfilling the intent of the above definition.

The living theatre, as must be perfectly clear by now, is in a constant state of change, and thus every term listed in this definition (theatrical, type, style, spirit, purpose, visual and auditory stimuli, intellectual and emotional meaning) can and does have a different connotation for each member of each audience in any given period. There is always present a new "avant-garde" that would alter the established conventions and set up new criteria. The most recent example is Bertolt Brecht's theory of "alienation" combined with the practice of "The Theatre of the Absurd."

Aristotle, as we have shown, placed great emphasis on illusion and empathic response on the part of the audience. These two new trends would greatly alter both. Aristotle emphasized the importance of plot, character, theme, and dialogue. He insisted that each drama should have a beginning, a middle, and an end. This new combination would discard plot, substitute symbols for character, noncommunication for theme, and dialogue that went in circles with its constant repetition. The total effect would be chaos or misunderstanding; in short, an absence of the orderliness or form associated with conventional theatre. Aesthetic distance (to be explained in detail later) with some additional connotations can be seen as the "alienation" and in a similar manner all the other terms can take on a varying degree of different interpretations. In the pages that follow, we propose to show how this definition can be implemented by the creative director, and we hope that the reader will give them sufficient elasticity to fit the period, the production and its goals, no matter what script may be involved.

A basic assumption and cornerstone of our approach to the theatre is that *theatricalism* is a part of any theatrical experience. The meaning of the term is at once obvious. It implies exaggeration, enhancement, life or nature *theatricalized*. As such, it many times carries a negative connotation. Some writers partially avoid this reaction by using the word *magnification*.

We would prefer to consider this essential factor in all theatre production in a thoroughly positive sense, defining theatricalism as *exaggeration under control*. When used with taste and discrimination, it supplies a spirit or quality that enhances every phase of a production. When misused or uncontrolled, it is a distraction, capable of destroying any admirable ideas, emotions, or qualities the production may wish to emphasize.

All theatre is exaggeration, for it must emphasize and project what it is trying to say. Theatre must be bigger than life if it is to reach an audience. Merely finding the truth is not enough. Reality must be interpreted and expressed in a distinctive way.

Once many of us believed that the theatre, with its great emphasis on realism, had lost much of its power because too many of its workers and some of its audiences held too great a fear of the theatrical. They looked upon theatricalism as a plague rather than as the very soul of the theatre, which of course it should be.

Walter Kerr very aptly expressed this theme in 1951:

> "Theatrical" has, in this day and age, very nearly become a dirty word. We have been obsessed with naturalistic stage deportment for so long that we have got ourselves into the paradoxical position of insisting that the theatre be as untheatrical as possible. We have become suspicious of any voice raised above a whisper, or any gesture more emphatic than that required to light a cigarette, of any facial display beyond the casually raised eyebrow. An overt performance seems to be a dishonest one, a mere ragbag of tricks employed by a calculating actor to conceal his interior poverty. In our enthusiasm for the "realistic" method, we have come to equate sincerity with low gear.[4]

In more recent times a kind of theatricality has gained more acceptance. Efforts to deter rampant realism that had so completely secured a foothold introduced many "isms," some of which will be discussed later. Dating from around 1900, and short-lived, none of these schools received lasting recognition or acceptance. The most successful one is the "epic"— or the work of Bertolt Brecht and his producer-director Erwin Piscator, which began in the mid-twenties. Their approach might be paraphrased thus: This is a theatre—you are witnessing the reenactment of a social injustice and a serious problem. Only you, the audience, can through your overt action correct the errors that are present. Epic Theatre will be further discussed under aesthetic styles, where we prefer to place it.

Thornton Wilder with *Our Town* in 1937 and *The Skin of Our Teeth* in 1942 drew strongly on theatricalism, and after the war this quality continued to creep back. We must mention especially, however, the influence of the absurdists in the late fifties and early sixties. In our own country, the work of Edward Albee, Jack Gelber, and Arthur Kopit was successful in combatting realism. The off-Broadway theatre in New York and certain noncommercial experimental theatres did much to add impetus to the movement. Theatricalism is most evident now in the works of Dürrenmatt, Frisch, and a number of other playwrights who make extensive use of it. Perhaps this return to the theatrical is only a natural

[4]Walter Kerr, "Don Juan in Hell," *The New York Herald Tribune*, November 4, 1951.

swing of the pendulum, for no art can consistently defy the very essence of its being. The Greeks displayed the theatrical in their dancing and changing choruses and the use of masks. It was a major influence in the *commedia dell' arte*, Shakespeare and Molière, for all art must use as its substance the unusual as opposed to the mundane—the abnormal to point up the normal or conventional. As Giuseppe Verdi once said: "It is better to invent reality than to copy it." If reality is only to be copied, what reason is there for art?

The goal of all theatre is to give what Aristotle called an imitation of an action. That very word "imitation" means that what the audience sees can never literally be the real thing; something must have effected an alteration. That something is the artist's personality, imagination, and creativeness. It is this addition that distinguishes theatre from life. *A Man for All Seasons, The Royal Hunt of the Sun, Philadelphia, Here I Come!* and most especially *Marat/Sade* have been greatly praised for their successful use of theatricalism. For the first time in almost one hundred years it would seem that the theatre is moving out of the firm grasp of realism.

Even in the most modern and realistic theatre, the language used by the playwright, the settings, the lighting, even the acting aimed at portraying emotions and movements in the most literal and lifelike manner— all must use artifice or techniques that can only give an *illusion* of life. The audience is always more or less conscious of being in a theatre, or at least of viewing an imagined situation rather than a real one. Both artist and audience are well aware that this theatre-audience-artist combination creates a relationship very different from the circumstances of real life. The result is an imitation of life and involves some degree of theatricalism.

The emotions experienced in life and those experienced in the theatre are essentially the same. The methods of *obtaining* and *expressing* those emotions, and the effects they have on both artist and audience, are vastly different. John Gassner defined these two elements as *life's reality* and *theatrical reality*. He saw the latter as making the most of all the theatre's elements rather than trying to hide or deny them, pointing out that in any theatre performance we are always witnessing some of both realities. By virtue of a kind of "double-vision," we go from what is "real" to what is "theatrical," and accept both as part of the theatre.

Vaudeville, musical comedy, the circus, the opera, and the works of Shakespeare, Molière, and the Greeks never abandoned their theatricality. The clown, Pierrot, Pierrette, Charles Chaplin's creations, Hamlet, Oedipus, and Tartuffe are supreme examples of theatricalism. Their emotions are just as real as are the emotions of Willy Loman or the protagonist in a melodrama. Each is theatrical in its own way, harmonizing with the dramatic event of which it is a part.

187 THE DIRECTOR AND THE DIRECTION

One can say things in a play that could not be said in any other way—because the hearers know it is "make-believe." Through the arts we can permeate iron or bamboo curtains, whether set up by politicians, by ignorance, or by provincialism. It is the very theatricality of the theatre that makes it so real. In the theatre we can get away with the truth because we do not mean it. Our guard is down. It is this essential theatricality that has made Mary Martin, Danny Kaye, and Bob Hope among the most influential ambassadors this country has ever had.

There are no rules to guide the director in his efforts to produce emotional truth or the illusions of reality through "theatrical reality." Neither are there any tests to measure the proper or most effective balance for a given characterization, scene, or production. We do know that everyone in the theatre is playing a kind of game, constantly alternating between reality and make-believe. The actor is both himself and the character he is playing; the audience wants to be moved emotionally, but only vicariously. Every intelligent director knows that too much reality and too little theatricality make for dullness or monotony. Similarly, too much theatricality is distracting and will make a production seem trivial. The challenge implied here demands experience, taste, knowledge of psychology, understanding, emotional sensitivity, and a keen sense of theatre.

The suggestion of reality must constantly serve as a check on theatricalism and vice versa. To know success is to bring together in harmony art, and the life that is being suggested in the production. Here lies the secret of greatness in playwriting, in acting, and most especially in the work of the director. How effectively has he balanced reality and theatricalism to give us the "illusion" that is right for a script? This is one of the first tests of the director's artistry.

Our recent move away from absolute realism has come from two sources—the epic theatre of Brecht and the theatre of the absurd. There are those today who would prefer to accept theatricalism as an additional aesthetic style. We would rather, however, consider it an influence *within* any given aesthetic style, although at times theatricality itself is so prominent that a whole production is accepted as one of pure theatricalism. This was most evident in the production of *Marat/Sade* in New York.

Before discussing type or aesthetic style it would seem wise to consider two items, both of which are closely allied if not part of any aesthetic style that may be present. The first is the production's individual style, for the director may have chosen to play the script "for real" with the utmost seriousness, or with a "tongue-in-cheek" approach. He may wish all his actors to play as actors who are merely telling a story, or he may want them to seem to actually represent the characters they are portraying. A farce may be played as a comedy or a melodrama as a farce; a fantasy as if it were actually occurring or a romantic play done realistically. Closely allied to the production style and always present whatever the aesthetic style is an actor and audience relationship. This is one of the earliest and most fundamental decisions the director must make for each production; whether the actor's performance will be *audience-centered* (presentational) or *stage-centered* (representational). Will it be *nonillusionistic* (no attempt to give the impression that these events are actually occurring) or *illusionistic* (these lines and these emotions are all very real, the characters mean what they say and do, the events are actually happening). Although the playwright's script and the direction may point out the proper approach, it is the actor's work and the spirit of his playing that makes it evident to the audience.

In the theatre of the Greeks, Shakespeare, Molière, the Restoration, of the eighteenth and nineteenth centuries, the form was essentially audience-centered. The large audience, outdoor performances, and the aesthetic styles of all these periods made it practically mandatory. The play was presented straight *to* the audience, almost as if it were another character in the drama—a character without lines to speak. The audience, in effect, was taken into the confidence of the actors. Such information, as it should have, was given out directly by the chorus, or through a soliloquy, and later by an aside. This form is common today in musical comedy, the variety act, or the television skit with two comedians engaged in a verbal feud but centering the whole of it directly to the audience. We call it presentational theatre. The old melodrama with the villain walking down to the footlights and confiding his thoughts to the audience was an exaggeration of this form.

Presentational drama can be either illusionistic or nonillusionistic. Certainly the actors in the roles of Oedipus, Electra, Agamemnon, Hamlet, Macbeth, King Lear, and even Tartuffe intended that the audience should believe what they saw and should receive the impression that this situation actually existed and that the emotions and incidents were all very real, though in a theatrical reality. They were, then, presentational and illusionistic. This same technique—presentational and illusionistic—is used by the monologist as exemplified by Hal Holbrook in *Mark Twain Tonight!* and by Cornelia Otis Skinner or the late Ruth Draper in their one-woman shows.

On the other hand, many comedies such as *The Rivals* and *She Stoops to Conquer* and much of the eighteenth- and nineteenth-century sentimental drama might easily have been meant to give the impression of only a group of actors—rather than characters—telling a story. Each actor takes on the vocal and physical characteristics of the character he portrays, but he, the actor, is always present. It is almost as if he is speaking in the third person. This treatment is called presentational and is nonillusionistic. In modern times, it is this relationship that Brecht requests in his epic theatre; the so-called "alienation" that he desires. He is reputed to have once told an actor that he should interpret each speech as if it had been prefaced with the words: "He said."

When the theatre moved indoors, the scenic background became more realistic, the lighting improved and with it the intimacy of the production, and there was greater emphasis on the effort to give the illusion of reality. The style leaned more and more toward realism or naturalism, and thus the stage-centered production came into existence. The audience no longer received the direct attention of the actors. The actors spoke only to each other. Lines were directed *at* the audience instead of *to* it. Eventually, an imaginary fourth wall was erected and the audience was, figuratively, looking through that wall at the actors. The actor's goal was to make the audience believe he was the character he pretended to be and that the story was actually occurring.

A play, then, can be audience-centered and nonillusionistic or audience-centered and illusionistic, or stage-centered and illusionistic. It is difficult to imagine a performance that was stage-centered and nonillusionistic, though that might sometimes occur. Occasionally, there may appear to be several different combinations of theatre form in the same production. In this instance it is the predominant over-all effect that should determine the classification.

Some plays can be nearly ruined because the actors have not understood, mastered or settled on a consistent approach as far as actor-audience relationship is concerned. An ultrarealistic modern play that depends upon the audience's belief and empathic response could have its very point shattered if one of the actors should suddenly step out of the illusionistic and stage-centered form and make a speech directly to the audience.

Two illustrations of where an accident caused such a break come to mind. The first was a performance of *Death of a Salesman* during the wrestling scene between the two brothers. The audience was completely involved with the scuffle as an illusion until Happy gave Biff a bit stronger push than usual and the latter, caught off balance, staggered beyond the proscenium arch and fell just at the edge of the stage. It was as if a huge plate glass window had been suddenly broken as Biff was hurled through it. The illusion suddenly became nonillusionistic. A similar incident is still related with horror concerning a New York production. A dueling scene was in progress when the sword was accidentally knocked from the hand of one of the duellers and went hurtling into the audience—with its point piercing the back of the only empty seat in the first row!

Interpretation, spirit, intent, director's or actor's goals, the playwright's purpose—all these help in dictating exactly how the actor will consider his role in respect to his audience. For our purpose it is necessary only that we understand the meaning of these terms so that we can judge more accurately what the director and actor are trying to do insofar as audience relationship is concerned.

When we consider the director's treatment of "type, style, spirit, and purpose" we find that, by definition, the first two terms possess greater limitation than do "spirit and purpose." All four terms must work together toward a single effect, yet the word "type" limits the over-all impression to being serious (tragedy or melodrama) or humorous (comedy or farce). The depth or treatment of any single type or the combination of two or more types will always vary widely with each director's interpretation. The same statement is true for a production's "style." Each script will manifest one dominant aesthetic style, suggested by the work of the playwright. Style, of course, is the most usual way of doing things at any given time, and the work of most playwrights falls into a specific aesthetic style, which we shall shortly define and explain. As we have previously noted, each production also has an individual style, which is even more determined by the director's personal style or technique.

It is highly doubtful if a playwright consciously chooses the aesthetic style in which he will speak. He writes as he feels or sees his substance, but he either *suggests* or *imitates* some aspect of reality as he transfers that reality into the written word, creating his own imagined world. Historically, the most common aesthetic styles are the classic, which grew out of the open-air Greek theatres; the romantic, of which Shakespeare is considered the greatest contributor, at least in the English-speaking world; the naturalistic of the late nineteenth century; and the realistic, which has dominated the past century. *Fantasy*, which belongs to no specific period, is also considered a style in itself, although it is frequently seen in combination with one of the others. Less common but important are the symbolic, expressionistic, and the most recent, the Brechtian epic. The last three represent efforts to break away from the realism of the more conventional modern theatre. Undoubtedly, many will want to include the absurd, although the absurdist drama has followed the realistic style in production more often than it has established one of its own. Also, at this writing, the theatre of the absurd or the anti-theatre of the late 1950's and early 1960's appears to have nearly run its course, allowing us to list it in this limited discussion with such other minor and transitory aesthetic styles as dadaism, surrealism, constructivism, and futurism.

We have already stated that we prefer to think of theatricalism as a part of another style rather than as an aesthetic style in itself. The director must find a suitable and appropriate manner of interpreting or projecting the playwright's style through the voices, movements, and gestures of his actors, as well as in the costumes and scenic background.

Here follows a brief survey of the chief characteristics of the eight aesthetic styles we have listed.

Classicism: The *classic* style comes to us from the Greeks. It suggests life through a certain worship of form and orderliness. Choruses were used in the early Greek plays to tell what had occurred before or to set the scene emotionally. Then, and often since, classical language has been in verses, a single mood predominates, and comedy is never found next to tragedy; there is loftiness, dignity, and distance on the part of the characters involved. *Oedipus Rex* and *The Birds* are classic plays.

Romanticism: The *romantic* style too suggests rather than imitates, yet it is more indifferent to form and order. It disregards tradition and scorns practical everyday life. The humdrum of daily existence is no longer present. Life is envisioned through the proverbial rose-colored glasses, without the mundane details of everyday living. Time may be telescoped; all is on a plane of imaginative grandeur, revealing the idealistic or imaginative side of man. The characters live what seem to be charmed lives in a world of theatre rather than a world of reality. Existence is filled with excitement, suspense, success. The locale is far away or fictitious; the playwright is unhampered in placing his action or in the choice of characters. He may choose prose or verse or silence, but he writes with freedom, beauty of language, and imagination, so permitting his characters to do and feel in ways we would like to think were possible. Characters are all bigger than life. Shakespeare is our greatest exponent of romanticism and *Macbeth, Hamlet, Romeo and Juliet, A Midsummer Night's Dream* are near-perfect examples.

Naturalism: The *naturalistic* style came as a revolt against the false romanticism of the French theatre during the last quarter of the nineteenth century. Émile Zola in particular fought for the naturalistic theatre and cried out for freedom, life, and naturalness in contrast to the artificiality that had grown out of so-called French romanticism. In 1873 in his preface to his *Thérèse Raquin* he wrote:

> There should no longer be any school, no more formulas, no standards of any sort; there is only life itself, an immense field where each may study and create as he likes.
>
> . . . I particularly insist—that the experimental and scientific spirit of the century will enter the domain of the drama, and that in it lies its only possible salvation. Let the critics look about them and tell me from what direction help is to be expected, or a breath of life, to rehabilitate the drama? Of course, the past is dead. We must look to the future, and the future will have to do with the human problem studied in the framework of reality. We must cast aside fables of every sort, and delve into the living drama of the two-fold life of the character and its environment, bereft of every nursery tale, historical trapping, and the usual conventional stupidities.

Zola's answer was naturalism, although its ascendancy proved to be the swinging of the pendulum to the opposite extreme. The theatre became more scientific than artistic in its effort to present life exactly as it was, with no attempt to theatricalize. Zola had called for "a slice of life," transferred to the stage, and pictured for an audience without thought of selection or even dramatic technique.

The Théâtre Libre in Paris with André Antoine as its leader became the center of this movement, naturalism. It had a greater grasp on France and Russia than on other countries, although to some extent Germany felt its impact. As a style it was short-lived, and by 1900 had completed its cycle for all practical purposes. In picturing life its followers chose as characters the lowest types of derelicts, prostitutes, outcasts, and with them all the ugliness of life. The settings were dirty, squalid, unpleasant. One of the more artistic works was Maxim Gorki's sordid and sombre *The Lower Depths*. Perhaps the main reason for the early demise, or at least alteration, of naturalism can be found in the basic principle that art is not representation but selection, further, that great art is a *conventionalized* representation of life rather than a photographic duplication.

Realism: Parallel with naturalism and growing from the same disenchantment with the artificiality of nineteenth-century romantic melodrama came the *realistic* style. An exact definition of realism is difficult. It is characterized by selection and modification of life, and emphasizes by presenting a point of view, all of which were frowned upon by naturalism. It tries to present an artistic, literal picture of life, an illusion of reality in character, in language, and in setting. "Life," however, is everyday life rather than imaginary life as depicted by the other styles we are discussing. Even *that* reality, however, varies in its interpretation by different artists, critics, or audiences, for all reality is relative and is seen differently by different people.

Nevertheless, realism to some degree has been dominant in our theatre for almost a hundred years. The word "motivation" came to have more significance than ever before. Neither the classic nor the romantic style had been concerned with what caused a character to act as he did. Man had simply reacted as he should in a given situation. The new scientific discoveries, the socialism of Marx, the evolutionary theories of Darwin, and the sex-psychology of Freud changed this attitude. There must be a scientific reason for every action, every speech. The playwright set a situation calling for a certain emotional reaction. The actor supplied it as best he could. Playwrights began to tell stories of common men, to discuss their problems and the effects of society on them. Heredity, environment, and even infancy now were recognized as affecting men and their behavior. Henrik Ibsen with his great social plays questioned all the accepted conventions of religion, marriage, private and social morality, ethics, indeed, any entity that might bring unhappiness to man. He shocked the world, although we realize today that in his plays he always left man a way out—all Ibsen's protagonists could have altered their courses and avoided discontent or destruction.

Critics of realism contend that poetry had been driven out of the theatre. There were also those who missed the tragic hero, the great personages, imaginative writing; but every age must find its own means of expression and, although the realistic theatre may have lost something, it also gained. Today we are able to discuss our own special problems and to see characters on the stage who might live next door. Without the realistic tradition we could not have had *Ghosts, The Cherry Orchard, Street Scene, Death of a Salesman, A Streetcar Named Desire, The Diary of Anne Frank*, or in a humorous vein, *Life With Father, Arsenic and Old Lace, The Odd Couple, Mister Roberts*, or *Auntie Mame*. For the opportunity to know these plays we have traded the dignity and power of the word as well as the exaltation of language and emotion that can be found in the earlier styles. The price we have paid for realism is an over-all littleness of conception, language, and character.

Fantasy: The *fantastic* chooses either to imitate or suggest and is frequently combined with another style. It is thoroughly imaginative and fairy tale-like, often embodying purely hypothetical situations. Fantasy is usually written in prose that may seem very much like everyday speech —at least natural and consistent with the imagined existence. *Alice in Wonderland* is one of our most delightful fantasies, and much of Walt Disney's work falls into this category. Its playing must go beyond realism on an imaginative plane that projects the mood both physically and vocally. Scenery and costumes, as in all styles, can be of great help.

Symbolism: The *symbolic*, too, frequently both imitates and suggests. It tells two stories at once in that one action is symbolic of another and calls to mind a second story. A very simple example would be a single man discovered on stage who merely raises a flag to half-mast, or quietly puts a bugle to his lips and plays "Taps." Far more is suggested than is shown or stated. This style is most evident in the script of *Our Town*, and many examples of it may be found among the more modern dramas listed in Chapter Two. Symbolism was highly developed at the beginning of the twentieth century as a method of moving away from the realistic theatre. Its projection requires a special attack that suggests much more than it appears to present on the surface.

Expressionism: *Expressionism*, like symbolism, represented an effort to move away from realism or the portrayal of surface meaning. It is considered to have begun in Germany shortly after World War I, although there are expressionist elements in the dream plays of Strindberg, which predate the German movement. Its purpose was to show man's inner self as well as his outer person, contending that the inner man is a truer "reality" than the outer one the world sees and knows. Expressionistic plays tried to find a means of exposing the inner man. In *Death of a Salesman* the protagonist talks to himself; in T. S. Eliot's *The Cocktail Party* he talks to a psychiatrist; Eugene O'Neill frequently used masks to depict the inner sides of man. In *Philadelphia, Here I Come!* by Bryan Friel, we saw two actors playing the roles of the public and the private Gar. Expressionism does not always put scenes in chronological order; the grotesque is often present; there is much emphasis on mood, distortion, and frustration. The work is highly imaginative, and the production must project the same spirit. Because its chief effort is to broaden the realistic theatre, expressionism always attempts to suggest far more of life than it portrays.

The Epic: The most recent and apparently lasting influence in the theatre derives from Bertolt Brecht, a Marxist who felt the theatre should not waste its time with make-believe, but rather had a duty to change the world. Some might not classify his efforts as an aesthetic style, but the *epic theatre* was so much influenced by the spirit of expressionism that, although it may be sufficiently different to stand alone, it seems to fit here more logically than anywhere else. Brecht chose the word *epic* to distinguish his work from the more conventional and dramatic theatre we have associated with the Greeks. He was always an anti-Aristotelian, revolting principally against the "illusion and the empathy that have been so great a part of the Western theatre." Although epic drama is imitative to a certain point, Brecht was violently opposed to an audience becoming too involved with what they witnessed to realize that the injustices portrayed existed all about them. As an advocate of social reform, Brecht wanted the audience to do something about these unsavory situations.

In seeking the effect he desired, of divorcing the audience from its becoming involved emotionally with the illusion on stage, he introduced the German word *verfremdung*, which has been translated as "alienation." We prefer the alternate translation "to make strange," for this comes far closer to what Brecht did in practice.

The goal of epic theatre is to break up the emotion and to make the audience always aware that they are in the theatre. For example, light or fantastic music is often used as a background for a very sombre scene. In theory, there is opposition to illusion or to an audience's becoming involved in the play. Brecht's ideal audience should be emotionally moved, but their experienced emotions should stimulate action when the play is ended. All this demands a special kind of treatment in production; and the director, again, must find the means that best accomplishes the goals of the epic style.

We now turn to those psychological concepts—empathy and aesthetic distance—which are in the hands of the director. This balance is determined by the extent to which he wants the audience to feel a part of the play, and how much he wants them to view it detachedly as an artistic work. Such involvement—a feeling of "into" or a feeling "apart from"—is a basic element in the director's form.

In the realistic theatre especially; this aspect has taken on great importance, and in recognizing their balance in plays of this style, we may sometimes find the explanation for our appreciation or lack of it. *Empathy*, the feeling "into," means the state of the spectator who both muscularly and emotionally experiences what he observes. Events happen in him, although he does not suffer the full physical or emotional strain that the characters on the stage would have him believe they are experiencing. He may to a small degree mimic the physical action of the actor, but the spectator's emotion is vicarious.

During a performance of a mystery-melodrama, a dignified and austere middle-aged man became so involved in the situation on stage that he unconsciously moved forward and raised his arm when the mysterious hand came out of the sliding panel. In doing so, he touched the shoulder of the young lady who sat directly in front of him and she, equally empathically moved, screamed uncontrollably. The whole impact of the scene was destroyed, for the distraction of her voice broke the illusion, reminding the audience that they were spectators observing a play.

In contrast to empathy is the feeling "apart," the detachment permitting the observer's attention to be held and his emotions to be touched, although he is conscious at all times that he is a spectator. Herbert S. Langfield[5] called the principle just described *aesthetic distance.*

Every theatre production has a planned proportion of these two qualities. We must emphasize that emotion and interest are involved in both empathy and aesthetic distance. In the latter, however, we are conscious of the fact that we are observing even while we are experiencing what we see. We may even be subconsciously evaluating the presentation as a work of art.

The motion pictures long ago sensed the values of empathy and aesthetic distance. Every means of playing upon them has been used. Film melodramas have shown as much surface realism, and as much of the physical reactions of actors as possible through the use of the close-up. Dramatic scenes are brought so close to reality that little is left to the imagination. A glance to right or left during a particularly strong sequence will show the contorted faces of the audience, the twisted handkerchiefs, and sometimes other overt physical responses. If one has

[5]Herbert S. Langfield, *The Aesthetic Attitude* (New York: Harcourt, Brace & World, Inc., 1920).

been too involved in the situation to make this observation, he need only recall the muscular tension felt when a given scene dissolved or faded into one that suddenly changed the emotion. The motion picture has likewise found great use for detachment in the musical extravaganzas, huge spectacles, and historical panoramas where it can excel so brilliantly.

Empathy does not always consist of the muscular reactions noted above. Women may empathize with the leading lady and men with the leading man. Likewise, each may subconsciously feel empathy in his or her attraction for the player of the opposite sex. For this reason, casting becomes a vital issue. Beauty, grace, stature, voice, personality, contrasts in coloring—all take on importance in eliciting the proper empathic response to each player.

In contrast, there is detrimental empathy, born of distraction or monotony—one's emotion is suddenly broken as he is snapped out of a situation he has come to accept or believe. This may be caused by a flickering lamp, a forgotten line or missed cue, a false cry or laugh, an extraneous sound, unstable furniture, or a characterization that the audience is unable to believe. Sometimes detrimental empathy comes through coughing in the audience, a contrary reaction to an emotion by an individual, an overheated auditorium, or some exterior element such as illustrated in the mystery-melodrama incident cited above. In this area, television dramas, played against a background of many home distractions, suffer more than stage or motion picture performances. It is this *effect* that Brecht desired in his "alienation," although he wanted to accomplish it deliberately and for a specific purpose.

Normally, melodrama requires a greater degree of empathy. Its loosely drawn characters permit the audience greater leeway in self-identification, and the very nature of the situations carries a greater emotional force. Of the four play types, the least empathy is found in a farce, for here the spectator rarely wishes to identify himself with the situation he observes. We have seen that actual involvement in such circumstances could be unpleasant; but observing them with other participants furnishes the audience a perspective, and this detachment, coupled with a feeling of superiority, brings about the unrestrained laughter associated with farce. The same may also be said for very high comedy. Empathy is found in varying degrees in comedy and tragedy. Both are built on character and when well written and performed, are so completely individual or removed from our experience that there is less opportunity for self-identification.

Aesthetic distance is not the exact opposite of empathy—it, too, involves emotional participation, but participation of a different nature. It comprises recognizing the work of an artist and still believing in and being a part of a play, yet always maintaining consciousness that it *is* a play.

In the theatre aesthetic distance is most evident when we suddenly applaud a splendid piece of acting, or a particular line.

Artists have always been aware of the importance of this detachment. A painter puts his picture in a frame; the sculptor places his statue on a pedestal; the architect sets off his work with surrounding space. The conventional theatre of today depends upon a brightly lighted elevated stage, a picture frame created by the proscenium arch, a curtain, and a darkened auditorium. It has not always been so. Aesthetic distance in the Greek and Shakespearean theatres was sustained by the language, the nobility of the characters, and the more formal presentation. During the Elizabethan and the Restoration periods in England, however, aesthetic distance and empathy were largely destroyed when spectators sat on the stage and oftentimes participated gratuitously in the action of the play. The same has been true of other countries in certain periods.

In the eighteenth and nineteenth centuries actors acted as actors and were appraised, with their art, as individuals. Aesthetic distance predominated in many performances, and audiences thought in terms of the individual actor's interpretation of a role, not that of the character he was portraying.

Today much criticism of the arena stage (theatre-in-the-round) comes from those who are distracted by the proximity of the actors or by spectators seen on the opposite side of the playing arena. In one sense this might be considered a loss of empathic response, but it also is destructive of aesthetic distance.

Some current productions in conventional theatres make use of entrances down the aisles, and even seat some of the actors among the audience. There are those who want to "put the play in the lap of the audience," and undoubtedly some theatre experiences could be enhanced by so doing. It is possible to use the entire auditorium as an acting area and still maintain aesthetic distance. To do this, however, the actor must remain a part of the play and never embarrass individuals in the audience by involving them in the action.

The type, style, spirit, and purpose of the play, as interpreted by the director, will determine how much empathy and how much aesthetic distance are to be sought by each artist involved. The twin balances of empathy and aesthetic distance and of reality and theatricalism, are two of the most important aspects of a theatre production. They involve not only the selection and arrangement, but the all-important problem of being just real enough to look *like* the imagined life and unreal enough not to *be* life. In short, the audience must share the emotions without actually experiencing their unpleasant aspects or becoming over-involved in the production.

Therein lies much of the theatre's and the director's art. The modern director, for example, is aware that it is difficult in our time for an audience to empathize in the Greek tragedies except as great literature or as poetry. When a really fine production does find its way into our theatre, we marvel at the spirit and beauty that pervade the scene; but even so our feelings are apart from rather than a part of the production. We are unable to sense the effects of majesty and nobility that the Greeks must have known, for our frame of reference is so different. We see the event more as a production than as a ritual; we appreciate it as art; we do not respond as to a communal religious event. Its beauty and its significance reach us more intellectually than emotionally. No doubt this has been brought about by our scientific approach to life. Joseph Wood Krutch has said that we have "lost our sense of man's dignity." Undoubtedly there are many reasons. John Mason Brown has expressed it so well:

> A period of realism and an age of prose are not the only hindrances. The lost or dwindling religious faith of many people; the encroachments of such a materialistic and earthbound theology as Marxism; an increasing uncertainty as to accepted or acceptable standards; our living with the threat of mass annihilation; great changes in the stresses and basic concepts of our economic and social life, the emergence of the "little man" as the new hero for hero worship; the shrinkage of the individual's importance under the pressures of superstates or ever-growing bureaucracies; indeed, not only the notion but the realization that the century belongs to the common rather than the exceptional man—all these factors, widening or limiting, which have altered tragedy along with everything else. Because of them, one wonders if the tragic blueprint, cherished for so long as an ideal, has not, at least in part, become a glorious anachronism.
>
> Not that tragedy is dead or will ever die. Or that Man has lost his touch with the heroic. No one who has watched men, women and children rise to the terrible trials of these past years can maintain that Man has become mean. The bigness of the so-called "little man" in the face of such trials and of daily living is one of the most hopeful facts of recent history. It is simply that the heroic has become different in scale and kind, and for this very reason tragedy needs to be rediscovered for our own time and in our own terms.[6]

It is *this* that the director must know and express!

There are further items for which the director is responsible. He must decide upon the furniture arrangement—the placing of entrances and exits. Such details are of major importance in visualizing the big moments and the movements of the characters about the stage; and this must be done because an audience is greatly affected by what it sees. The stage

[6]John Mason Brown, "American Tragedy," *Saturday Review*, August 6, 1949.

must always be pleasant to look at in an artistic sense; the sets should possess psychological meaning as well. Much is said through stage groupings and these are solely the director's work. Alexander Dean, the famous director and teacher, often said to his actors, "You are the hands of the clock up there on the stage, but I am out here where I can tell the time." Stage groupings must reflect consideration of the sight lines in the auditorium, so that every important phase of a play can be seen by the entire audience. They must emphasize the different physical and psychological relationships as the play progresses. The stage must always have the proper balance, emphasis, variety, and dramatic meaning to help carry the story, as well as present an agreeable picture. The stage is a continuously changing picture, never without a focal point.

The word *action* in the theatre denotes only the dramatic action of the play that is inherent in the lines and story. Change of position on the stage is called *movement. Business* includes bodily gesture and the handling of properties. Business and movement are executed by the actors and may be created by them. But every movement and every bit of business must have a reason and a specific purpose, and the director must decide whether or not to permit them to continue. Therefore, we may hold the actor responsible for ease and truth of execution, but appropriateness or lack of it, to a play, a scene, or a character is the responsibility of the director. Again we encounter the "what" of the director and the "how" of the actor.

We must always ask if every actor is playing in the same style or key. If not, the director is at fault. In one production of *Othello*, the play lost its meaning because Othello used all the gusto of the romantic style accompanied by the rant of declamation, and Iago was played in a most realistic manner. This error is more common in the noncommercial theatre than in more professional productions.

It is possible that a company of players too long away from a director may allow much to creep into the play that was not a part of the original direction. Some two weeks after *Death of a Salesman* had begun its Broadway run, it was completely redirected by Elia Kazan because, he said, the mother appeared to have lost her love for her sons. Mildred Dunnock, the actress playing that role, admitted that this was true, that she had become almost afraid of the boys who, in their fervor, had handled her roughly on the stage and hurt her physically. The recapturing of a subtle expression of maternal love was so important to Kazan that he ordered long rehearsals and complete reblocking of movement and business in order to restore this feeling.

Control of the elements of underacting or overacting may be considered largely the director's domain. Contrary to a commonly accepted belief, the noncommercial theatre is more likely to underact and the professional to overact. The director must tone up or tone down as the circumstances require. The director may sometimes be blamed for aspects of a performance for which he is not responsible.

Oftentimes after a production has been running for some time, an actor introduces bits of business that tend to attract attention to himself rather than to the play. There is an old story of a notice that appeared on a theatre callboard after several weeks of playing:

> Rehearsal Call—11:00 A.M. Monday.
> To take out the improvements.
> (signed) George M. Cohan

Everything that we see or hear on stage should have been the choice of the director, and each effect helps to determine the spirit and purpose of the production as he has conceived it. He has chosen to play a scene as farce, as high comedy, as melodrama, or as tragedy. He has chosen to play it up, throw it away, put it across. And these choices determine the style, the interpretation, and the very spirit that the director feels belong to the script. In short, it is the director's responsibility to see that the actors and all technicians not only play the characters they have been assigned and furnish the necessary background, but that they also *play the play* that has been written for them. The director endows the written script with the necessary dramatic action and dramatic sound required to project the intellectual and emotional meanings as he interprets them, for directing in the last analysis consists of the director's turning psychology and his own feelings about the script into behavior. He must make the audience feel and think in terms of the spirit and purpose he has found in the script and to have coordinated all its elements into a single unified impression. This is direction at its highest level. If he has made his intentions so clear that there is no doubt in our minds, he has been successful as an artist, even though we may not agree with his accomplishment.

As a final element in the director's form we turn to the seven pillars of the fine arts: emphasis, rhythm, balance, proportion, harmony, and grace. All seven are to be found in each of the arts involved in a theatre production; it is the duty of the director to strengthen them where they are weak and to coordinate the elements in the over-all production so that the final result has unity. It is in accomplishing this that he contributes his greatest service to the playwright and to the audience. In our explanations of these terms we would emphasize that although each possesses a special meaning of its own, there is inevitable overlapping.

Unity, as the name implies, is a oneness, a singleness of purpose. It would be absurd to place eighteenth-century costumes in front of a realistic setting. If a director proposes to do Shakespeare in modern dress, he must have sufficient imagination to convey the mood throughout the whole production. Costuming and scenery should suggest the same spirit. All acting should be in the same style, and that style should fit the spoken lines. Periods should not be mixed, nor should the voices or heights of actors be too divergent. A central idea or theme should be underlined in every way possible. Moods or emotions, although appropriately varied, should be in the same general key. The whole production should have what Plato called "unity in variety."

Emphasis is pointing up or stressing important points, singling out what is most vital or important. It may be accomplished by silence, lighting, movement, line, mass, color, force, or any other means the director or actor may wish to employ. At all times the audience must be able to perceive the goals of all the artists, and the theme or purpose of the play must be crystal clear. Unity and emphasis together afford the most effective means of eliminating distraction and monotony, the two enemies of attention. With proper emphasis we have no doubt unless doubt itself is what is being emphasized.

Three words have often proved to represent the greatest pitfall of the noncommercial theatre, the most difficult aspect of a play to explain, and perhaps the greatest single distinction between the experienced and inexperienced worker in the theatre. They are *rhythm*, *tempo*, and *pace* (under *acting* we call this *timing*). These elements, when they are handled with absolute precision can cover many faults and they are the director's responsibility.

Rhythm is the recurrence of an accented beat. Its place in music is easily established and understood. We are all creatures of rhythm in our breathing and heartbeats, in observing the days of the week and the seasons of the year. In the theatre, however, broken rhythm is employed, and the rhythm comes from many different sources. The emphasis of a word is, of course, significant but rhythmic emphasis may also come from the entrance or exit of a character, the use of a light, an offstage noise, a brightly colored costume, the gesture or movement of an actor, and many times—especially in comedy or farce—an audience reaction. We are often made suddenly conscious of rhythm when it is broken—by a fluffed line, an awkward pause, a break in the flow of the play. Too long a wait for an audience reaction also makes us aware that something has gone wrong. Detrimental empathy may be a cause.

The rhythm of a play is established very early and should remain basically the same throughout the performance. We must not confuse tempo with rhythm. It was Boleslavsky who said, "Rhythm is the prince of the arts; tempo is his bastard brother." The *tempo* alters, although the change may be ever so slight, with the entrance or exit of every character, or when a new thought or mood is injected. Thus tempo can change many times within a scene, and constantly during the evening.

The director who senses that a play is running slowly and calls out, "Speed it up!" is utterly lacking in knowledge of rhythm, tempo, pace, and their delicate balance. To speed a scene is merely to talk faster, to "railroad it," as we say in the theatre, and all that happens is that the scene is over more quickly. This, however, is the most frequent criticism of the untrained critic who proclaims, "The play was slow," or "It seemed to drag," or "The actors talked too fast," or "They didn't pick up their cues." All these are potentially valid criticisms, but the real fault has not been noted. The chances are much more likely that the director failed to point up a definite rhythm with the proper intensity.

As with all good things, there is danger in the other extreme. A director can become so involved in the rhythm of his performance that it stands out over the principal theme.

Pace is the relation between the over-all basic rhythm and the ever-changing tempo. Ideally these elements are so perfectly integrated, and all the speeches and movements of the actors so well coordinated with the audience reactions, that the production gives the impression of complete smoothness. Strangely enough, the director finds that success in this respect comes easier with serious plays. This is largely because he can more easily foresee the audience reaction to drama than to comedy or farce. At least, the former reaction is more constant. Comedy, and to an even greater extent farce, is most difficult to do successfully with an inexperienced cast. The comedy lines of the playwright, coupled with the actors' reading and interpreting of those lines, can provoke highly varied responses from the audience. Yet the actors must constantly cope with those changes, never losing the basic rhythm that the performance demands.

Actors in comedy or farce must alter their reading of lines or action within a single performance if they are to re-establish the rhythm as it was set by the director in rehearsals. When something unforeseen occurs on stage to alter that rhythm and pace, or when the audience contributes a new beat through an unscheduled laugh or other reaction (or fails to react as expected), only the actors can once more get the play back on the right track. It is this combination of audience reaction and actors' recognition of it that can make a comedy so much more satisfying on the stage than in either the motion picture or television.

Rouben Mamoulian, famous motion picture and New York theatre director, often establishes a rhythm through the use of a rocking chair, a metronome, or some similar device. He and others have been known to direct a play from out front with a baton. The pace of a performance and its integral parts are definitely in the province of the director, although his work is sometimes almost lost in the hands of an inept cast, because of an unexpected response from the audience. It is, nevertheless, part of the critic's task to ascertain what the director has tried to do with these intangibles of dramatic production.

Balance and *proportion* are so closely related that it is difficult to make a distinction between them. Both terms indicate an equalizing of forces, one against the other. Although it is not wholly true, we sometimes—at least in the theatre—think of balance as being visual, and proportion as implying a quantitative relationship. Using these connotations, we might consider balance as it relates to the stage setting and furniture arrangement, the symmetry and use of line, mass, and color in décor—all the components of the picture.

Proportion may then be considered the relation of theme to plot, music to story; the relation between the two contending forces in the play's conflict, and so forth. The old melodramas, for example, are poorly proportioned because they "stacked the cards" against the villain and in favor of the hero or heroine.

Plays have been thrown completely out of focus when a leading actor was far superior to the remainder of the cast. The wise director, therefore, may not permit an actor to give his most brilliant performance if the player opposite him is unable to rise to that height. The director must also balance the work of all the technicians. If the audience remembers setting, lights, or costumes at the expense of the play, the proportion has been faulty.

Harmony is a term with which we are all familiar. In the theatre it is the happy and smooth coordination of all phases of production so that nothing interferes with the basic meaning and purpose of the play. It is the ultimate objective of the artistic dramatic production.

Grace implies the minimum of effort on the part of each artist—work so smooth and so simple that it seems perfectly natural. Grace is the ease and facility with which the artist executes his work and masks his technique.

During this discussion of the director's form, the reader may have felt we were reaching into the area of technique. We would emphasize that we have been talking here only about the director's decisions, his plans, his goals, and the effects he wishes to attain—the "what" of the production.

We have tried to show that the actual *design* of a dramatic production is the director's form. In production, the effectiveness of that design—visually, vocally, emotionally—is the measure of the director's technique, his means of implementing or accomplishing his goals.

How a director has *managed to emphasize* the theme or style of his production should be observed and appreciated. Some directors' greatest ability lies in serious drama or tragedy, others find their strength in comedy or farce. Although it is generally agreed that few directors can make a poor play seem great, it has been proved over and over again that a good director can improve on a poor script. On the other hand, many a fine play has been ruined in the hands of an incompetent director.

No two directors could possibly produce the same over-all effect, even if they could use the same casts and staging. A director's particular style or treatment is always there, evident in shadings of meaning, a change in emphasis, interpretation, characterization, or movement.

Each director may place a slightly different emphasis on the theme as the author has expressed it, perhaps pointing up one of his own in order to make the play infinitely more timely and appropriate. This was done most effectively by Orson Welles in his New York production of *Julius Caesar* during the peak of Mussolini's power. Emphasizing the dangers inherent in dictatorships and staging the play in a modern style with the conspirators in black shirts gave the production an exciting, timely, new meaning. Mr. Welles is remembered for giving such original treatment to almost every script he has directed.

When a play's original emphasis is distinctly altered, the play may resemble the work of its director rather than that of its author. Max Reinhardt's *A Midsummer Night's Dream* was more Reinhardt than Shakespeare. Any production by David Belasco was obviously a Belasco product. Margaret Webster is always completely honest in her interpretations of Shakespeare, but they also carry the pictorial and colorful contributions that belong to Miss Webster.

Some directors, like Welles, prefer to do Shakespeare in modern dress. *Hamlet* has been seen with Ophelia drunk instead of insane, and Hamlet in a tuxedo smoking a cigarette. In *The Taming of the Shrew* Petruchio has arrived on donkey, on horseback, on a motorcycle, and in a battered old jalopy. Nineteenth-century melodramas have been burlesqued, and played perfectly "straight," as they were done in their respective periods. A script can be stylized in mood, the cast playing the parts as actors with tongue-in-cheek and reveling in the playwright's wit, or as a realistic comedy in which the audience is asked to believe the story. Many directors receive their most severe criticism in this area because they think of themselves as creators in their own right rather than as interpreters of the author's script. A director may have a special flair for creating stage business, for ingenious ideas of interpretation, or other embellishments through which he thrusts upon a play more of himself and his own techniques than are good for the production. Worthington Miner has said:

> If a director with a formula chooses a good play and attempts to apply the formula to it, he cheats the play and the author. The star director works for his star, the clever director and the director with a theory work for themselves, or sometimes ... for something extraneous to the play. A conscientious director in normal circumstances works and can work only for the play.[7]

[7]Gassner, *Producing the Play.*

The director should be primarily interested in the play rather than the separate parts, in scenes rather than particular lines, in the over-all stage picture rather than in individual actors. His job is to reveal the complete meaning and mood of the play, and the changing relations of each character to the play and to each other. Even though he may have to work with the individual, he thinks in terms of the whole as he strives for teamwork and unity in the over-all interpretation.

The alert theatregoer may come to recognize the technique of a given director, just as the connoisseur of art knows at a glance the work of a great painter, or the trained musician can recognize, after a few bars, the music of a well-known composer. The artists work alone, each striving for his own unity, emphasis, rhythm, balance, proportion, harmony, and grace. The director, too, seeks all these qualities, but he must achieve them by harmonizing the work of many artists.

In summary, we should look for the director's work or artistry in:

> ...his choice of script in accordance with the goals of the organization he represents, and in accordance with that group's potentialities as well as his own;
>
> ...his casting of the play, with some deference to the same limitations as above;
>
> ...his balance of theatricalism and reality with full recognition of the script's needs;
>
> ...his treatment of the play's type with the proper touch in breadth or subtlety;
>
> ...his choice and handling of the play's aesthetic style as well as its own particular style;
>
> ...his projection of the spirit and purpose of the play he feels is best suited to a particular time, a particular locale, and a particular audience;
>
> ...his own balancing of empathy and aesthetic distance and how it is projected through the audience-actor relationship, staging, groupings, picturization, décor, lighting, costuming—and all other visual or auditory stimuli;
>
> ...his coordination of these many elements and the combined work of all contributing artists to bring about a completely unified production with the proper emphasis, rhythm, balance, and proportion to project the maximum harmony with consummate grace.

Only through recognition of what the director tried to do and the extent to which he succeeded or failed in all these respects are we able to appreciate his form and his technique—his contributions and merit as an artist.

Questions for Discussion

1. Give several examples of theatricalism that you have found both pleasing and effective.

2. Give a personal experience with empathy and one with aesthetic distance in a stage, motion picture, or television production.

3. Consider the casting in a play you have seen. Were there any obvious miscastings? Type-castings? Try to imagine how one of the roles might have been interpreted in a very different manner. How could this new interpretation have been projected? Would it have helped or harmed the production?

4. Debate the two opposing theories of the noncommercial theatre: (1) To expose the actors and the audience to the very best in great drama even though their limited abilities to perform or understand them may cause the production to fall short in quality; and (2) to choose somewhat lesser dramas but to produce them in a more professional manner.

5. This book has emphasized the belief that there is only one standard of excellence in dramatic art. Many believe there should be various standards, depending on the producing group. Present arguments for both points of view.

6. Have you ever seen the same script in two different productions? How did they vary? What part of this variance can you say was attributed to the director's work?

7. Give some examples of one director's work in balancing reality with theatricalism. Have you ever known him to lean too far in one direction or another? Explain.

8. Choose a play and analyze it in regard to its structure. Show where and how each aspect is involved: exposition, inciting moment, rising action, turning point, falling action, climax, conclusion. State in its simplest terms the basic conflict in the script. What is the theme?

9. Develop the first part of the director's duty: "to create the complete and accurate theatrical effect" by applying it to a recent production.

10. What did the director do specifically to project the type, style, spirit, and purpose of some production?

11. Can you recall a noncommercial production that did or did not meet all the qualifications under the director's first obligation of selecting the proper script?

12. Prepare an ideal season of six plays for your own or a mythical college or university theatre. Try to meet all the needs of such a program. Do the same for a community theatre.

13. Give a specific example of a director's work in bringing about a satisfactory unity, emphasis, rhythm, balance, and proportion to a dramatic production. Can you cite an instance of one of these not being well handled?

14. Describe the form and the technique of any director by citing specific examples of his work.

Bibliography

For Supplementary Reading or Special Projects

Albright, H. D., William P. Halstead, and Lee Mitchell, *Principles of Theatre Art*. Boston: Houghton Mifflin Company, 1955.

Canfield, Curtis, *The Craft of Play Directing*. New York: Holt, Rinehart and Winston, Inc., 1963.

Cole, Toby, and Helen Krich Chinoy, *Directing the Play*. Indianapolis: The Bobbs-Merrill Company, Inc., 1953.

Dean, Alexander, *Fundamentals of Play Directing* (Revised by Lawrence Carra). New York: Holt, Rinehart, and Winston, Inc., 1965.

Hatlen, Theodore W., *Orientation to the Theater*. New York: Appleton-Century-Crofts, Division of Meredith Corporation, 1962.

Heffner, Hubert C., Samuel Selden, and Hunton D. Sellman, *Modern Theatre Practice*, rev. ed. New York: Appleton-Century-Crofts, Division of Meredith Corporation, 1959.

Hopkins, Arthur, *Reference Point*. New York: Samuel French, Inc., 1948.

Seltzer, Daniel, *The Modern Theatre: Readings and Documents*. Boston: Little, Brown and Company, 1967.

Sievers, W. David, *Directing for the Theatre*. Dubuque, Iowa: William C. Brown Company Publishers, 1965.

Whiting, Frank M., *An Introduction to the Theatre*, rev. ed. New York: Harper & Row, Publishers, 1961.

Young, Stark, *The Theatre*. New York: Hill & Wang, Inc., 1927.

4

The Actors

and the

Acting

Acting in all its many aspects is one of the most fascinating areas of human behavior. Everyone is to some degree an actor, in more than one sense. The very instant that we *consciously* endeavor to affect the thought or action of another, we are acting. The success we have in attaining our goal is the measure of our success as an actor—just as the measure of the performer's success on stage is equal to his effect on the emotions and the thinking of the audience. In this sense the most successful parent, teacher, minister, doctor, lawyer, salesman is also the most successful actor. It is not our province to consider further this type of acting, although we believe that there is art here, and that, no matter what profession one may plan to follow, valuable lessons may be learned in any well-organized course in the art of acting.

The universal instinct to "act" must be partially responsible for the fact that almost every individual feels, perhaps secretly, that he could be an actor. This is not true of the other arts. Ask someone to play the piano, paint a picture, design a costume, or build a set, and he will probably answer, "Oh, I couldn't. I have no training. I wouldn't know how to begin." But ask the same individual to take part in a play! There may be momentary hesitation, but there will also be a reaction of pleasure. If anyone declines, it will rarely be from a feeling of incompetence in handling a role. The principal reason for this situation is that good acting looks so easy and so natural. The finer the performance, the surer the

210

uninitiated are that "All one needs to do is learn the lines and be natural." George Kelly has expressed this universal phenomenon in a one-act comedy entitled *The Flattering Word*; the theme is that to make a friend one need only tell that person that he should have been an actor. George Jean Nathan once said, "Criticism of acting amounts to little more, save on its highest levels, than a reflection of the critic's notion of himself in the actor's role."

From earliest childhood we all find pleasure and escape in any game of "let's pretend." This experience has been a part of almost every individual's adult life as he has sought the opportunity of getting out of himself, being someone else, living in his imagination, and experiencing emotions and situations often removed from his everyday existence. This innate human instinct has been partially explained in Frederick Schyberg's essay "What Is An Actor?"

> At the bottom of the mystery of the art of acting lies something which is at the bottom of most of the mysteries of human behavior: egoism. Or let us use the more pleasant expression: self-assertion. He who play-acts asserts himself abruptly by talking and doing, by creating. He provokes laughter or admiration. He *is* somebody, and he rises above the others, both above those whom he imitates, and above those who are degraded into spectators: see what I can do? Man is vain, and he strives to be admired; man is lonely, and he seeks contact. Art is one of the means to these ends. In acting, man finds an outlet and an opportunity to reveal himself in play and in art, an opportunity of a more organic nature than any of the other art forms provide, because acting is created with the human body itself as the medium and the raw material. In its primitive phase, the art of acting is man giving vent in play to his inner vision, and in this way satisfying a deep need. The child plays a beautiful game, and the peacock spreads his gaudy tail feathers! At the bottom of the primitive acting temperament, we find three elements: loneliness, egoism, and eroticism.[1]

To those on the sidelines the life of the actor seems to be a round of interesting experiences, public acclaim, applause, curtain calls, easy living, and personal freedom. Actors are always in a position of prominence. They possess a beauty, a charm, and a personality not often found in the mundane lives of the general public. It is little wonder that the actor's life looks fascinating from afar. The truth, however, is quite contradictory, for the profession is far from an easy one. It involves hard work and serious vocal, physical, and mental training. It demands personal sacrifices, for the theatre is a jealous master. It requires God-given talent, and necessitates long hours of study and intense concentration, great imagination, persistence, determination and, above all, discipline. These requi-

[1]Robert W. Corrigan and James L. Rosenberg, *The Context and Craft of Drama.* (San Francisco: Chandler Publishing Co., 1964), pp. 340–41.

sites are not recognized by those who feel that anyone can act. Historically, acting is one of the most ephemeral aspects of the theatre, but at the moment of its existence it may be the most rewarding. Once concluded, the actor's performance lives only in memory. Thus when the last individual who witnessed the genius of Edwin Booth or Sarah Bernhardt is dead, the contributions made to man's aesthetic pleasure by these great artists will have gone out of the world forever.

During and immediately after a given performance it is often the work of the actor that commands the greatest attention. It is not unusual for the playwright, technicians, and director to be completely overshadowed by one actor's electrifying performance. History abounds in exciting stories about the great moments on the stage of Kean, Forrest, Booth, Cooke, Duse, Garrick, Jefferson, Burbage, Siddons, Matthews, the Barrymores, and many others. All these artists had triumphs, heard applause, took bows, read notices, and were heroes of the hour; but the future will find these moments recorded only in the books or in the memories of those who were privileged to witness the performance. We have photographs of the scenery and costumes, and we can read the script, but the work of the actor lives only for the moment. In the twentieth century we have perfected a method of recording the artists' voices and actions. For those who have seen the actual performance, these recordings or pictures can rekindle the flame; but those who have only the mechanical reproduction miss the all-important human quality.

Just as good acting is very difficult, so is its evaluation. Critics of the past were not able to agree upon the relative merits of our greatest actors. If experienced critics are divided in their opinions of the work of the giants, then conceivably lesser critics can find greater difficulty in agreeing on the art of lesser actors. One need only read the major New York critics the morning after an opening to understand that even the most experienced professionals may run the gamut in their evaluations of the actor's work. Every player may be mentioned in one or more reviews, but the work of each may be regarded with high praise, the cursory dismissal of "adequate in the role," or downright adverse criticism. There are many reasons for this, but one is that acting is based primarily on emotion, and emotions do obstruct the viewer's objectivity.

Perhaps nowhere in the theatre is the element of prejudice more apparent than in the analysis of acting. We like or dislike an actor, although it may be impossible to give any logical reason. These prejudices are often purely psychological in nature. Many of our most popular actors have attained their status not through talent or imaginative acting, but because their personality, physical appearance, or charm has caught the imagination of a large segment of the population, winning for them great reputations as actors. Although these individuals—and many could

John Barrymore as Hamlet. Courtesy of The
Walter Hampden Memorial Library at The
Players, New York.

Ethel Barrymore. Photo by Vandamm.

Sarah Bernhardt. Courtesy of the Walter
Hampden Memorial Library at The Players,
New York.

Leslie Howard as Hamlet, 1933. Photo by
Vandamm. Courtesy of the Theatre Collection,
the New York Public Library at Lincoln Center,
Astor, Lenox, and Tilden Foundations.

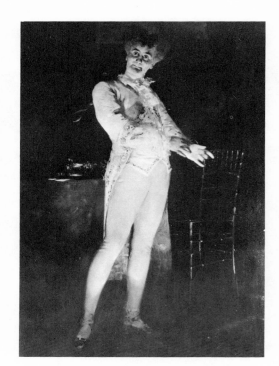

Joseph Jefferson as Bob Acres
in "The Rivals." Painting by
John W. Alexander. Courtesy of
the Walter Hampden Memorial
Library at The Players, New
York.

John Singer Sargent Portrait of
Edwin Booth. Courtesy of the
Walter Hampden Memorial Li-
brary at The Players, New York.

be named without difficulty—rank high in general esteem, they often lack dramatic talent and owe their success only to the public prejudices by virtue of which they were elevated to prominence.

We would not adversely criticize these individuals who have attained a certain success, but any evaluation of their work should include an understanding of why they became so popular. It was Henry Irving who said, "What makes a popular actor?—physique. What makes a great actor?—imagination and sensibility."

Another reason for the difficulties inherent in dramatic criticism is the rapid evolution of acting style. We need only observe a motion picture of a few years back to realize that acting changes almost as fast as style in dress. Undoubtedly the great actors we read of in history would not seem so magnificent to us today.

Furthermore, an actor's work with a role may change from performance to performance of the same play. Such an alteration may be due to physical or mental changes in an individual actor, or to the same variables in other members of the company. It can also stem from the reaction of the audience. Leading actors have stated that their acting varies considerably for matinees (which are attended largely by women), for the evening performances early in the week, and for the holiday crowds on weekends.

A featured player who has worked for years with one of our current stars has said that this actor's greatness is never fully realized except by opening night audiences, either in New York or on the road. The overall pattern is the same, and he may never give what could be called a bad performance; but that extra something that lifts and captivates an audience is certain to be present only on opening nights. This is not intentional on the part of the actor; it is just that the critics and first night audience bring to him an added stimulus. *Variety*, the theatre weekly, does a series of follow-up reviews, in which plays that have been running for several months or a year are re-reviewed. Often the acting is reported to be greatly altered from the opening performances—sometimes not as effective, sometimes much improved.

Such alterations in the playing of a role from performance to performance should further point up the futility of arguments about acting, even when the participants have observed the same performance; for in addition to the subjectivity involved, the actor's art may well be less generally understood than any other art of the theatre. Standards are confused, principles are misconceived, definitions are often unclear, and technical problems are unfamiliar to the vast majority of any audience. The fault lies in the fact that acting is too often judged according to personal whim rather than by well-defined artistic standards. It is frequently said that "the best acting is the least acting," which is to say that the best acting is so "right" that it seems not to be acting at all. The final answer may lie in the words of a fine old actor who concluded a lecture on the subject by saying, "Acting—after all is said and done—is only a matter of opinion."

It is the purpose of this chapter to formulate a set of definitions, classifications, and principles that will serve us not only in understanding the actor's form and technique, but in establishing a common ground on which to base that opinion. Our first task, then, is to agree on what acting really is.

Perhaps the most common simple definition is: Acting is make-believe; and there are few who would deny that the statement is true as far as it goes. Whether or not an actor really feels his role, both he and the audience are well aware that the experience is feigned, that the actor must consciously control his voice, body, mind, and emotions, and that he must always pretend to be something he is not. But acting is much more than this. If it were make-believe only, we could cite any group of children playing house, cops-and-robbers, or cowboys-and-Indians as perfect actors. The statement does not mention the craft or technique that must be combined with the make-believe. The actor, in addition to or along with his pretending, must memorize and rehearse his lines, in order to create a personage who says and does at a specific moment just what the character must do in cooperation with the other actors and in a manner that has been planned by a director. He must be conscious of an audience and its ever-changing and unpredictable reactions simultaneously, but he must not permit the audience to realize that he is aware of their presence or response.

This can lead to a second popular definition: Acting is doing consciously on the stage what people do without thinking in everyday life. On the surface, this statement too appears sound, for it tells exactly what the actor must *seem* to be doing; it fails because acting must go much farther than mere imitation. An actor, even in the most realistic or unrealistic theatre, must constantly select, enhance, exaggerate, conventionalize, and project just those aspects of the character and emotion that he wants the audience to grasp. Furthermore, such a definition would eliminate all past aesthetic styles, for the characters, language, and situations that have come to us from the Greeks, the Elizabethans, the neo-Classicists, the Restoration, or the eighteenth century do not picture the reality we know. Each of these periods and each of the playwrights of the period paints for us a particular kind of theatricalized reality. The actor must sense and project with truth that special world.

A third definition is: Acting is the art of abandoning one's own personality, taking on the personality and feelings of another character, and making these assumptions appear real to the audience. It is what some actors do. This statement may partially answer some of the questions we raised with regard to the previous definitions. Critics have praised performances by saying, "He *was* Hamlet (or King Lear or Willy Loman). The characterization was so complete that no evidence of the actor's voice, gestures, mannerisms, or personality was apparent. He seemed even to grow in stature!" This is high praise, and such an actor certainly must have been convincing. But what of the many stars of screen, television, and stage who always seem to be themselves? What of the actor-personality who draws millions to the box office?

Many further efforts to define acting could be discussed. There are certainly qualifications and questions on the statement we propose, but for our purposes, the most satisfactory definition is: *Acting is the art of creating the illusion of naturalness and reality in keeping with the type, style, spirit, and purpose of the script and with the period and the character being represented.* The word "art" implies recognition of form and technique; "illusion of naturalness and reality" indicates the all-important aspect of seeming to be rather than being; "in keeping with the type" defines the genre (serious or comic); "style" includes both the aesthetic and individual style of the artists involved; "spirit and purpose" involves playing the play and keeping within the confines of what the script is trying to say and do; "period and character being represented" can set the time and locale and define the limits of truth, consistency, and believability.

Although we have arrived at a definition that would seem satisfactory, some further classifications need to be clarified before we turn to the individual actor and his work.

Schools of Acting

One frequently becomes involved in discussing an aspect of the actor's work that has already been mentioned—whether he seems to be playing himself or appears to be a different individual in different roles. There is a tendency to judge an actor on these grounds. If we are to be consistent in our criticism, we must start with Goethe's first question, without considering which of the various schools is the more difficult or the more artistic.

The particular school the actor chooses to follow is determined by whether he *elects* to go to the role that the playwright has written and remake himself physically and vocally to fit that imagined character or whether he will bring the role to himself and remake it to fit his own vocal and physical characteristics. This is not an overt decision; it is determined by the actor's personal talent and by the demands of the role. It is easier or more natural for some actors to go to the role, thus becoming what we call *impersonators*. In the motion pictures, our best-known adherent to this school is Alec Guinness. Those who saw him play many different roles in *Kind Hearts and Coronets* will know at once what we mean by impersonation. Guinness has, likewise, shown his genius in this respect on the stage. In his portrayal of Dylan Thomas in the play *Dylan* he created a character that one believed to be Dylan Thomas himself, although in physical stature and temperament there was no similarity between the character in reality and the actor. Peter Sellers is a second example of this type of actor.

Such actors possess the peculiar talent of being able to step out of themselves and assume the personality of another person, making it appear completely believable to the audience, even fooling an audience about the real identity involved. Another perfect example of contemporary impersonator is found in Hal Holbrook's one-man show, *Mark Twain Tonight!* Holbrook, a comparatively young man, so completely lost himself and became the seventy-year-old Mark Twain that not a single gesture, movement, vocal quality, or nuance of Hal Holbrook himself was evident. Critics and audiences throughout the world have marveled at the complete and convincing transformation.

Hal Holbrook as Mark Twain in his one-man show, "Mark Twain, Tonight!"   Hal Holbrook

A second school, comprising those who bring the role to themselves, may be called the school of *interpreters and/or commenters*. The characters they play bear a close resemblance to themselves in age and appearance, and the actors interpret the parts without wholly losing their own identities. In our modern theatre, with its trend toward type-casting on both stage and screen, this school is much in prominence today. We would emphasize, however, that these actors are commenters on, as well as interpreters of, the roles they portray. This "comment" is of the utmost importance in good acting, and it involves the art of the actor subtly giving us his own thoughts and feelings concerning the character he is playing, and all that character is saying or doing. As an artist, he not only discovers, interprets, and projects the thoughts and emotions so that they are wholly clear to the audience, but he enhances that interpretation with his own particular talents, understanding, experience, personality, and charm. The character he plays takes on new dimensions as its passes through his mind and body to the audience. His voice may retain its natural quality, and he may use gestures that we have seen him use in other roles, but there will always be something new in the performance that makes a specific character an individual.

S. N. Behrman told of an actress who, by her reading of a line, made an indelible comment on the character she was playing:

> In London I saw Dame Edith Evans as Cleopatra in Shakespeare's play. She played it for high comedy. In an early scene Cleopatra is informed by Antony that his wife, Fulvia, is dead. Cleopatra's line is: "Can Fulvia die?" The Dame's reading of the line was delicious; it sent a ripple of laughter through the audience. She read it with a rising inflection of incredulity and pleasure, with a peculiar overtone of the last word which raced you through Cleopatra's mind. You heard her also saying: "Well! Evidently I have always underestimated Fulvia. I never suspected that she had the resource or the tact for a gesture like this!" Ever since then, when I see this play, I listen for the actress who plays Cleopatra to read this line; usually it comes out as a simple request for information, like: "Do you play canasta?"[2]

"Comment" has been made when the actor is able to say far more than the line itself; when he lets us know what he is thinking and how he feels about the character he is portraying, but does so as part of that character. Many critics believe that herein lies the greatest acting of all.

John Mason Brown has described this school of acting most effectively:

> Then there are the precious few, standing at the top of their profession, whose high gift it is to act themselves, to adapt their spirits to the spirits of the parts they are playing, to possess and then to be possessed, by the characters they project, and to give them the benefit of their beauty and their intelligence, their sympathy and their virtuosity, their poetry and their inner radiance, their imagination and their glamour.[3]

[2]S. N. Behrman, "Query: What Makes Comedy High?" *The New York Times*, March 30, 1952.

[3]John Mason Brown, *The Art of Playgoing* (New York: W. W. Norton & Company, Inc., 1936).

Owing largely to great deference to the box office, there is a third school of acting (often confused with the interpreter and commenter) which gives us what we choose to call the *personality actor*. He is common to all dramatic areas but is more frequently seen in the motion pictures and television. These actors have been defined by John Mason Brown as "the suave or tough, the charming or the brusque, the handsome or the portly 'straight' actors whose only, but whose quite considerable, talent is to be their off-stage selves on stage." Unfortunately, they are frequently the most popular and busiest actors of our day, for they have attained enviable reputations as personalities. Their great box-office appeal is owing to their appearance, sex appeal, a physical or vocal idiosyncrasy, or some special quality that has a strong mass appeal. They are what Brown further calls "the most delightful and serviceable contributors to our theatre of understatement."

In discussing an actor's work, we must determine which school he has chosen to follow. This may be difficult the first time we see him, for we may think that what he brings to us of himself is actually a part of the character. After John Kerr's third Broadway appearance, Eric Bentley wrote, "When I praised Mr. Kerr in two earlier plays, I thought I was praising acting. I now wonder if I was really praising a certain sort of personality—perhaps only a certain sort of sex appeal emanating from a pouting, indolent, insolent sort of face and a helpless, dead voice. In the next role he undertakes, let Mr. Kerr prove me wrong."

Regardless of which school of acting an actor may follow, there is a second frequently discussed aspect, one involving an actor's particular approach to a role.

The Actor's Approach to His Role

From the time of the very first appearance of an actor, there has been debate as to whether or not an actor really experienced or felt the emotion he portrayed while playing his role. Interesting as such a debate is, an answer one way or the other is really not pertinent to our discussion. We are interested primarily in whether or not the *audience* feels, for to move the audience emotionally and/or intellectually is the actor's ultimate goal. Consequently we shall do no more than mention the two most commonly accepted approaches to the art and craft of acting as it is practiced today.

One approach, often referred to as *the method*, springs from the writings of the great Russian actor and director, Constantin Stanislavski who, early in this century, recorded his theory of acting. Various translations and applications have given rise to considerable controversy over what he really practiced or meant. Basically he is believed to have endorsed the importance of actually feeling—at least, in having the emotion start within, and the importance of producing only outward gestures and movements or readings that grow out of that emotion. In short, the actor should work from the inside out and be possessed by the emotion of the role. The most publicized institutional follower of this acting theory has been The Actor's Studio in New York, under the direction of Mr. Lee Strasberg. Others of course, have interpreted the writings of Stanislavski in many different ways.

The opposition to "the method" includes those who would approach a role from a more objective point of view. They see acting as an art, but place at least equal emphasis on the craft. To simplify, we may say that they start from the outside and work in. After carefully studying the role to be played they may decide on the tone of the character's voice, the dialect or diction to be used, his manner of walking and gesture, his thoughts and his feelings, and certain physical or vocal incidentals that he may possess. They then consciously adopt these traits and, as one actor put it, "walk into the role." They may be said to follow the James-Lange theory of psychology which states that action precedes emotion— that we run and then become afraid, that we talk rapidly or loudly and thus develop an excitement or anger. In the modern theatre such actors are said to use the *technical approach.* They consciously do a specific thing for a specific effect. They do not disavow a certain amount of feeling, but they are primarily interested in control, both physical and emotional. They demand discipline and a technique that assures consistency for performance after performance.

Great acting can and does result from either approach, and prominent actors are strong advocates of each. Helen Hayes was once asked in a television interview what she thought of "method acting." Miss Hayes, who is generally considered to use the more technical approach, gave considerable praise to actors who follow the "feeling" method. However, she believed that they would all be fine actors no matter what approach they used, because all of those with whom she had worked possessed talent and all the other qualities that made for great acting. The interviewer pressed harder and said, "But Miss Hayes, you still have not said what you really think about the method. Does it help?" Miss Hayes answered him by saying that when she was a young girl in Washington, D.C., she attended performances of a stock company every week, and watched the work of an older actress whom she admired very much. Finally she managed to meet the stage manager and was permitted to observe from backstage. She was much interested to see that the actress always crossed herself before making an entrance. Miss Hayes, herself a good Catholic, finally mustered courage to approach the actress and say, "I notice that always, just before you go on stage you cross yourself—does that help?" Miss Hayes concluded with, "She answered me, just as I will answer you concerning the method. She said, 'Yes, it helps—*if* you can act!'"

Our conclusion is that either is acceptable, depending upon a given actor and how he works, with the truth, as usual, lying somewhere in between. If, however, the actor's approach detracts from his performance in any way—if it causes him to slight his obligation to playwright, director, or audience by losing control of his body, his voice, or his emotions, or if he permits his technique to show—then the actor has not been successful as an artist.

We now turn to the actor himself, who is unique in that he is ever three personalities: an individual personality, an artist, and the character he portrays. All three entities should be so deftly and completely blended that they appear united as the character of the play. The intelligent theatregoer, however, should recognize what the individual has accomplished in training himself as an artist and what the artist, in turn, has done to create the character. Not to do so is to deny the actor his art.

Let us first consider the individual or the actor himself, for he is his own instrument. Unlike most other creative artists he must work with his own body, voice, and emotions. He is judged by his native intelligence, his personal appearance, and his emotional limitations. Such physical attributes as height, build, coloring, weight, texture of skin, body and facial contour, stance, walk, speech, personal mannerisms will determine the roles he may be given. The degree of his success in the theatre will fall within his mental range; his ability to think or analyze, his emotional limits or temperament. The totality of these attributes comprises the psychological personality of the actor as an individual.

In addition to a controlled body, adequate vocal powers, and some mental acumen, actors must bring to the theatre an asset that we call dramatic talent. The first ingredient of dramatic talent is *imagination*, and without it one might as well give up the theatre at once, for acting is essentially the ability to respond to imaginary stimuli. An actor must be able to relive any situation, appreciate and understand the thinking and the emotions of another individual. He must also possess *sensitivity* —a consciousness of his own feelings and reactions to all stimuli, and *sensibility*—a consciousness of the emotions, feelings, and reactions of those around him. The two grow out of what we commonly call introspection and observation both of which are indispensable to the actor. However, he must go beyond merely sensing these qualities. He must record them in his memory and allow them to become part of himself. Introspection and observation are allied with the actor's love, respect, and understanding of his fellow men; together they constitute what Helen Hayes has called human warmth.

The next important item is *stamina* or courage. By this is meant health, physical strength, determination. The theatre demands all these in anyone brave enough to join its ranks. The would-be actor's talent should also include some *personal quality*. It may be symbolized by a physical characteristic, a mental agility, or an emotional response. It may be a strange combination of any and all; it means that the individual exists in terms of the theatre. His personality will project vividly over the footlights; he possesses some contagious quality of voice, or great beauty of presence noticeable, for example, in a fine theatre-mask. Perhaps he has a superb sense of timing, an infectious laugh, or other gift that is peculiarly theatrical and attractive to an audience. Some such quality must be present if one is to become a truly great artist in the sense that Duse, Bernhardt, Garrick, Barrymore, Booth, Gielgud, Lunt, Fontanne, Hayes, are so considered.

To imagination, sensitivity, sensibility, stamina, and a special quality we would add the "actor's five senses"—a *mimetic* sense, a *stage* sense, an *audience* sense, a sense of *rhythm* and *tone*, and a sense of *values, proportion,* or *taste*.

Mimicry is essential, for it is not enough just to imagine. The actor must implement imagination by creating, expressing, and projecting what he has imagined. Stage sense is a feeling for and an "at-homeness" on the stage, an understanding and feeling for its particular demands. Audience sense is an ability to feel the pulse of the audience—the possession of an inner voice that tells just how long a pause can be held, when a laugh will come, and the precise second when the laugh should be interrupted and the next line taken. Of equal importance is an innate sense of rhythm and tone—the ability to maintain the proper rhythm or to pick it up when the one established in rehearsal has been momentarily broken by an unexpected incident on stage or in the audience. An actor must have an ear for just the right spirit or mood to fit each scene, the ability to adjust rhythm and tone to the ever-differing reactions of an audience, or to his colleague's minute alterations of the established rehearsal pattern. He must at every moment be in tune with the whole production, and with the specific performance.

Finally, there is the actor's sense of proportion—his ability to put first things first, to understand values both in and out of the theatre, to exercise a sense of taste that keeps him always in harmony with and yet just a step ahead of his audience. We defined taste in Chapter One.

It is our belief that the dramatic talent of which we have been speaking is a God-given gift, in which the possessor should take great pride, but for which he deserves no credit. It is a mystic element, a priceless ingredient that by some peculiar twist of fate and nature comes with birth. When such talent is inherited, a potentially great actor is born; but good actors, reliable actors, and even successful actors are developed if individuals possess the desire, and drive to work harder and sacrifice more than in any other profession. The reader may immediately question the terms great, good, reliable, and successful. In our opinion, the difference between a great actor who is successful and a good reliable actor who is successful is in exact proportion to the presence or absence of talent *and the development of that talent.* It is in this sense that we would consider another attribute necessary to every actor: *ability.* This we define as the willingness to withstand hard study and dull exercises, the perserverance to develop voice and body, and a command of intellectual and emotional powers. An actor's training demands determination, drive, work, and the sacrifice of personal wishes, hopes, and ambitions outside the theatre.

It is by and through the individual's total personality that the artist speaks to us. As the artist he can and must alter, train, or learn to control the mind, the body, the voice, the speech, the talents, and the emotions; for the artist uses these aspects of the individual just as the painter uses paints or the composer, notes. It is an education that never ends, for the artist must always be studying, rehearsing, and learning more about himself as an artist and an individual—about life and about his fellow men.

This is the price of becoming an actor; the artist pays it as he develops whatever assets the individual may possess. The great, positive rewards that both individual and artist may finally acquire are *discipline* and *authority*, which must always be present in the third face of the actor— the character we see on stage. Discipline involves controlling, channeling, and directing all talents toward maximum effectiveness. Authority is the manner in which every word, action, or emotion is presented. Only through discipline and authority can the individual and artist achieve the mastery of mind, body, voice, speech, and emotions that leads to successful guidance or control of the character represented.

It is thus that the actor emerges, a composite of the individual, the artist, and the character he professes to be. Through that character he hopes to create an illusion that reveals reality, to give a reflection of human behavior that *seems* truer than life itself. In that creation the actor must have his freedom, but that freedom is no greater than his obligations to the playwright, the director, and the audience.

Every actor is guided by any description the playwright may have included concerning the role, by what the character himself says and does, and by what the other characters have said about him. When playing an historical figure, appropriate historical sources must be given consideration. An actor's imagination must work within the framework of the type, style, spirit, and purpose of the script as interpreted by the director. His responsibility to the audience is to make his creation constantly interesting, crystal clear, and to project it with vitality, variety, and validity.

In his very excellent work *All For Hecuba,* Micheál MacLiammoir has written:

> To be an actor demands a curious and complete surrender of the
> self and of many personal claims. More than any other art it is a
> rebellion against the mundanity of everyday existence. Far from being
> a copyist of life's surface tricks or a facile repeater of traditional
> antics, the actor should live with such delicacy, with such intensity,
> that he brings manner and style to all the unimportant trifles of ges-
> ture and speech, so that the eating of a fruit, the folding of a letter,
> the raising of the arm, the donning of a cap, all become, in his hands,
> images of significance, profound mirrors of character. To act is to
> live for a moment with an intenser life, to pass bodily into the
> sphere of sorrows and of joys greater than our own, to thrust the
> shoddy surface of what we call real life upwards to a transforming
> radiance; and while the painter must see and the poet and musician
> hear with passion before they hurry to canvas or to paper and ink,
> the actor must note all down with calmness and precision and must
> then give to the single moment everything he possesses, soul and
> voice and body, the inner and the outer selves.[4]

An actor's worth is measured by the total range and value of his mind
and spirit; by the depth of his feelings, and the breadth of his knowledge
of life and human nature; by his mastery of voice, body, mind, and emotions plus a personal quality that infuses his whole interpretation with
a fire that excites an audience.

Specific Tests of the Performance

In analyzing the work of an individual actor, or the over-all effect
of an entire cast, certain questions can be considered. The first deals with
the actor's personal qualifications, or what he brings to a role. The next
four concern the performance itself. They can be most helpful in pin-
pointing details that might otherwise evade us. The final question deals
with the actor's cooperative ability and unselfishness. This has taken on
greater importance since the theatre began to demand unified productions.

These six yardsticks for measuring an actor's work can be of assistance
in the discussion of any dramatic event. In the chapters dealing with the
playwright, the technicians, and the director, such questions come under
"Was it worth the doing?" or "Tests of Greatness." Since the actor is his
own instrument, they are part of his technique.

Six questions we would ask about every actor are:

1. What does the actor bring to a role in voice, body, personality,
   or as an individual?

[4]Micheál MacLiammoir, *All for Hecuba* (London: Methuen & Company, Ltd.,
1946).

2. Is his acting fresh?

3. Is his acting restrained?

4. Is his acting easy?

5. Is his acting convincing?

6. Does the actor fit into the production as an integral part of the whole?

1. What does the actor bring to the role in voice, body, personality, or as an individual? It may be imagination, a dynamic personality, temperament, a quality or style that is peculiarly his own, a voice or body that distinguishes him, or an authority that makes him master of all he does or is supposed to be. On the other hand, many of these factors may be negative. Above all else, each actor—on the stage—must be a distinct personality. Off the stage, he may be as ordinary as any citizen, but on the stage he must bring something definite to a role, and an audience must recognize and appreciate just what that something is. Particularly valid in the case of actors is the statement that personality is an aura that surrounds those individuals who are capable of doing some single thing extremely well and with consummate grace.

Let us first consider the actor's *authority.* Does he have complete command over his body, voice, and emotions? Is he above the role, or is he so involved in it that he lacks adequate control? The artist should ever be in the ascendancy, firmly guiding and controlling the character being presented. Control is evident in the way an actor handles emergencies such as a late entrance, a missed cue, an accident on stage, or an unnecessary disturbance in the audience. It is always evident in his command of what we have already called *stage* and *audience* sense.

How effective is the actor with the use of his voice and body? The voice must be pleasant in its pitch and quality, forceful enough to be heard throughout the auditorium. There is never an excuse for inaudibility. An actor must always speak without strain. Diction, which includes articulation, enunciation, and pronunciation, should be sharp and clear, but must never attract attention to itself. Unless unnatural diction is part of a characterization—a condition sometimes affecting any of the above requirements—there must be no evidence of regional dialect. Any false or artificial note instantly stamps an actor as insincere. He should have sufficient command of his vocal powers to impart the nuances that give originality to line readings—for unusual shadings that reveal hidden or new connotations in a line indicate not only brilliance of conception, but a voice highly trained in the art of expression.

An actor's body must be completely coordinated. His movements must be graceful, and his gestures used only to augment the voice. What he does physically must seem effortless, never attracting attention unless that is the specific demand of the play. Every movement and gesture on the stage must have a purpose and a meaning. The slightest twitch of a finger, or an unnecessary shift of the weight can become distracting elements.

Does an *individual style* or *quality* distinguish a person as an actor? Individual style does not mean the use of vocal or physical mannerisms as such. Rather, it implies the use of the actor's own body and voice *adapted* to the character he portrays, but adapted with intelligence, imagination, and originality. It is the lending of his own instruments of interpretation to the role (see John Mason Brown in his third classification of actors on page 219). It is very much more than an actor's just being himself, it is what he consciously does with himself. No wise actor ever attempts to copy any part of the style associated with another. No personal style is of any value unless it belongs solely to an actor as an individual. Imitation is the kiss of death to any artist, and above all to the actor.

Like all art, acting demands planning, precision, discipline. Experimentation is proper only in the rehearsal period. What the audience sees must not be haphazard or extemporaneous. Everything must be worked out in detail. Authority indicates control of the whole dramatic situation. That situation might vary slightly from performance to performance, but the over-all pattern should conform to plans worked out during the rehearsal period. An actor in a motion picture or a filmed or taped television performance has an advantage here, for another take is always possible. An actor's error or inspiration can be altered or used as the director and editor may choose.

What special characteristics make an actor excel? What does he do that is distinctive? Such a quality in an actor may be warmth or coldness, a dry sense of humor, winsomeness, or any other personal attribute that distinguishes him as an individual personality. It may be something we feel or hear or see. Whatever talent a particular actor possesses, it is worthy of recognition, for it is part of him and his art.

2. Is his acting fresh? Regardless of what the printed program may say, events on the stage or screen are supposed to be happening now. No matter what period in history is being presented, the audience has the right to demand that it give what William Gillette called "the illusion of the first time." Eva Le Gallienne has said that the actor's greatest problem is to re-create the original freshness, sincerity, and emotion of his character in every performance, regardless of how many times he has given it or what his own personal feelings may be. It is most important in the actor's work that each speech, each look, each action convey the impression of never having been said or done before.

On her five hundredth performance in *South Pacific*, Mary Martin appeared so fresh and so new that it seemed as if she experienced every emotion and spoke each line for the very first time. Another important member of the company read each comedy line almost as though making an official announcement: Here is a big laugh . . . get ready . . . it's coming . . . here it is! Then he settled back complacently and awaited the next response, which he knew so well would come. It was obvious to the least critical analyst that his inspiration was gone and that the task of performing the role had fallen into mere routine.

The "illusion of the first time" should be maintained when an actor comes into a room, locates an object, reacts to lines spoken by other members of the company; it should be carried by the tone of his voice. It can be especially evident in fleeting facial expressions just before he speaks a line. It is seen in the position of hands and feet, and in general posture. Not only is it of vital importance to the art of the actor, but also to sustaining the "half-faith" of the audience. It is the great test of an actor's thoroughness, his honesty, and his sincerity. Each audience has the right to demand this freshness, this illusion of the first time.

Another aspect of this illusion is the vocal communion between actors as they speak *to* rather than *at* each other. This involves using the nuance or tonal quality that is natural and right for each relationship represented. This communion goes beyond the emotion of the speech, or moment or the mood of the scene; it is the special vocal tone one recognizes as mother speaks to daughter, father to son, brother to brother, friend to friend, stranger to stranger.

Observe how an actor makes an entrance or an exit. How many times one has seen a character who has obviously been standing outside the door waiting for his cue, or who, since the author has not given him further lines, leaves because he might just as well leave. On the other hand, a truly meaningful entrance or exit can make a memorable moment in the theatre.

In addition, there are what might be called "proper transitions," involving a new attack, vocally and physically, as different items or situations are introduced. Stanislavsky discusses this under the category he names "Units and Objectives." A character in a play has an over-all objective, but he gains it bit by bit; he makes progress in some scenes and loses ground in others. Each new thought or move calls for a fresh approach. There is gradual growth or loss, a "funding" that alters the total picture and the character's reaction to that picture. A constantly new attack is necessary not only to development, and growth or change in the character, but to avoid monotony, one of the theatre's greatest enemies. A role is not just sustained, it must be clarified constantly, and made always interesting, with every evidence of spontaneity.

Many times an actor gives his all during the first act. This can only mean the arrival at a plateau, or monotony for the remainder of the play. He may also drop out of character when he has no lines to speak.

Nothing can destroy the spirit of a play or musical more quickly than catching disinterested expressions on the faces of the chorus or those in minor roles during moments when they have nothing to say.

Much as we have insisted upon technique, and important as it is to the actor, nothing is more dangerous than the acquisition of a little technique. A few successful productions sometimes give the nonprofessional confidence, convincing him that he knows exactly what to do on the stage at all times. Yet dependence on technique is also found in the work of the greatest stars of our stage, particularly after they have played a role for a great length of time. It is not difficult to detect that moment when the actor, as artist, walks off the stage both emotionally and mentally, leaving behind only the physical part of his character.

Again, the freshness of a performance tends to suffer more on the stage than in the motion picture, for the director may take and retake a scene until the actor has given just the performance desired. This is also true of the filmed or taped television program. Only the legitimate theatre, however, faces the problem of the long run.

3. Is the actor restrained? We have said that we go to the theatre to have our emotions touched, that whether a play is romantic or realistic, we want it to happen in us. The final test of an actor is, does he make *us* feel the part? The actor's greatest asset in the realization of this goal lies in the way he exercises restraint—how he avoids telling us all he is thinking or feeling, concealing something at the same time he is revealing. The power within him must be amply controlled. His job is to stir the imagination of his audience. Tears spilling down an actor's cheeks are usually less dramatic than an effort at control. The blubbering close-ups of the motion picture are highly inartistic, and far less effective than restraint would be.

The great actor hints at more than he declares. The real strength or power of any line lies in its tone. Watch how an actor builds within a speech or within a series of speeches—or even by pantomime—to a climax or crisis. Remember that sincerity or a crisis need not always be big. Sincere feeling is not necessarily big feeling, but rather depth and honesty of feeling. The word *ham* is greatly misused in the theatre, most frequently by those trying to describe something in acting that they do not quite know why they dislike. They often confuse broad and expressive acting with overacting. The first we need, the second is bad. We might say that the ham expresses small feelings in a big way. Any actor can be insincere, but only an actor with a big voice can be ham.

Great acting is suggestion more than actual doing. It has been said that a good actor never fully portrays the emotion he wants an audience to feel. He builds up to a particular moment, and when that moment arrives, the audience takes over, for the actor has set the tone. Brooks

Atkinson once pointed out that the real difference between a great performance and great acting is subtleness. This valuable quality of restraint is evident in the speaking of lines, in the handling of the body, in the grasp and expression of an emotion, in the smoothness and integration of all these elements. The restrained actor never overacts or overstates, but relies on suggestion plus imagination and the intelligence of an audience.

4. Is the actor easy? The audience must be totally unconscious of any effort on the part of the actor. So far as the audience is concerned, all hard work must have been done before opening night. As previously indicated, in performance the actor must be the master of himself, vocally, physically, and emotionally. He must seem relaxed—at home. His technique is there, but unnoticed. Whatever he does *seems* so natural that it is accepted without question. The perfect performance seems so easy and so right that the spectator is tempted to remark that he, without training, could do as well.

Observe the success of an actor in the "art of doing nothing," one of the most difficult phases of his work. It entails being on stage and a part of the scene, in full view of the audience, when the author has given him nothing to say and little to do. There is no better proof of the statement that acting is not so much acting as reacting than such moments of seeming to do nothing; they form another aspect of communion. It is then that the actor's integrity, sincerity, and imagination are challenged, with great personal control and restraint required. To be successful when speaking, stage center, is not nearly so great an achievement as being an important and necessary part of the picture without detracting from it and with, apparently, nothing to do.

Note an actor's sense of timing, how he uses the element of time through his mastery of pausing, phrasing, and holding. It has often been remarked that the actor's chief secret is his timing, an important facet of restraint. The term *time value* is sometimes applied to moments when words are not spoken, but the emotion and mood of the scene flow on. Anyone who has seen much theatre can remember particularly poignant moments when an actor played upon the imagination of the audience with a gesture, or some simple indication of his feelings, suggesting to the spectators a similar personal experience the evocation of which would not have occurred had the actor resorted to the limitation of words.

There is no more obvious single distinction between trained and untrained actors than their sense of timing. The inexperienced actor rushes forward, fearful that the audience will think he has forgotten his next line. The true artist makes the most of every time value, knowing that there is greater power in the suggestion of an emotion than in its actual delineation, that he can create more in the mind of the audience by the correct pause than by any words he could speak.

Timing is especially important in comedies. Watch how easily an actor plants a laugh, builds it, waits for it to reach a climactic peak, and stops it at just the right split second with his next line, so that the play can move on. Observe closely the actor's sense of rhythm in this respect. At its best, it resembles a tennis game in the give-and-take between actor and audience as the former varies his timing with the latter's response, never breaking the basic rhythm of the play.

Sense of timing is of no less importance in serious plays. The actor's command of the pause, his use of the time value, his feeling for the exact instant for speech or silence—these are his most precious tools for holding and moving the audience. The actor's training in this respect is one of his dearest possessions. It develops with the years and is the very core of his technique. For an audience not to recognize and judge an actor's facility in this area is to miss much of his art.

5. *Is the actor convincing?* Every item mentioned thus far on the subject of acting contributes in some way to this question. The ultimate goal of every actor is to make the audience *believe* him, and everything he says and does. His actions must at all times be rightly and fully motivated. His role must mesh with the whole production. There must be no inconsistency in his playing, or in the belief he wishes to create in the audience.

In theatre history we read of many an actor's great moments. Coleridge described witnessing the work of Edmund Kean as "like reading Shakespeare by flashes of lightning." We are also told that many actors had long and dull periods during a production when they seemed to be just saying the lines, saving themselves for the "high points" or dramatic scenes. Great as these moments may have been to audiences in the so-called good old days, it would seem that the players themselves lacked both the consistency and convincingness that we demand of actors today.

Sometimes an actor carries such conviction in his playing that audiences find it hard to accept him outside a certain part. Actors have been hissed on the street and refused service in public places while appearing in the role of a villain or obnoxious character. The fault here, of course, lies with audiences that failed in their obligation to dissociate the actors from the parts they were playing; the actors cannot be accused of being unconvincing.

Makeup and costuming contribute to the actor's world of make-believe. Often, however, inability to apply makeup properly or to wear a costume naturally prove stumbling blocks to an actor striving for convincingness. Makeup takes much study and practice; it varies with the lights and auditorium being used. A specific problem, especially in the noncommercial theatre, is presented by young actors or actresses playing middle-aged or older roles. One should make up for the middle of the house, but should not apply cosmetics too heavily, for the sake of those in the front rows. It is better to err with too little than too much.

The professional theatre, with its emphasis on typecasting, has greatly simplified the makeup problem, but makeup is still an exceedingly important factor in the actor's being believed by the audience. Makeup on the screen is an art in itself. The camera is most difficult to fool and, although typecasting eliminates the necessity for makeup much of the time, on occasion it is an important part of the total impression.

Both commercial and noncommercial players are often guilty of allowing their costumes to overpower them. It is most important to wear the costumes of a period play with ease. The Shakespearean ruff and cape, the tunic of the Greek theatre, the ruffles and breeches of the Restoration, the bustles and hoop skirts of the nineteenth century can wreak havoc on a production if the actors have not learned to wear them as well as they have memorized their roles. The mood of a Civil War play presented by a summer stock company was completely destroyed when a young lady caught the front of her hoop on the corner of a sofa, with the rear of the hoop hitting the back of her neck. Warm weather had caused the actress to reduce her undergarments to a pair of red shorts, and the audience suddenly had thrust before its eyes a sight like nothing so much as the Japanese flag.

A criticism often made of an actor is simply, "I did not believe him." To avoid this condemnation is a vital part of every artist's work, for belief is a prime requisite of dramatic enjoyment, and *truth* is the final test. At the risk of repetition, and because this simple list has often been most helpful to the authors, we present nine keys to this all-important quality of being convincing:

> *Movement*—Do movement, gesture, and all body action appear easy, smooth, and natural for the character, the mood, and the situation?
>
> *Concentration*—Is the character on stage always aware of: what he is doing, why he is there, what his goal is, and what is occurring on stage? At the same time, does he subconsciously give the audience adequate consideration with regard to whether they are hearing and seeing what is being said or done, and whether all points are being made clearly?
>
> *Communion*—Is each character talking *to* the other characters with the proper tone and feeling, so that all speech possesses a conversational quality and complete truthfulness?
>
> *Emotion*—Has each actor expressed the correct emotion, to the proper degree, and with the right inflections for each situation? Does he have proper restraint both vocally and physically?
>
> *Imagination*—Is each actor's conception of his character clear, and appropriate—in keeping with the spirit, goal, style, and mood of the play and the situation?

Identification—Does each actor convincingly identify himself with the character in voice, speech, dialect, movement, and gesture, whether his school be that of impersonator, interpreter, or personality actor?

Relaxation—Is he properly relaxed and at ease, yet sufficiently alive and vital to keep the play always moving?

Transitions—Is he aware of each new idea and of his own goals? Does his acting reflect the changes in the scene and in his character as the dramatic action progresses? Does his character grow and change?

Truth—Is he wholly believable in every aspect? Is he so right for his character, is each movement so perfectly executed, that the over-all impression is one of absolute verisimilitude?

Finally, on the subject of convincingness comes the matter of projection, for the actor must constantly think and work in terms of the audience and theatre size. He does not play on the same scale with an audience of one hundred or two hundred or five hundred or one thousand. Stages of the "arena," "proscenium," or any other type call for a generally different audience-actor relationship, as well as a varied projection. Every facet of an actor's form and technique is subject to constant surveillance in order to effect adjustment to each new situation.

6. *Does the actor fit into the production as an integral part of the whole?* Note how he "gives" a scene that does not belong to him as well as how he "takes" the scene that does. It is not always to an actor's credit to say that he stole the show. Many actors play to the audience in a bid for popularity rather than forming a part of the scene as the author had intended. Famous stars have been small enough to attract the attention of the audience by making a movement, coughing, or dropping a handkerchief, when the best interest of the play demanded that attention be on another player.

Sometimes the star in a professional production is guilty of upstaging the other members of the cast. This is unforgivable. The same error may be committed unintentionally by noncommercial players, although frequently with a little technique and some knowledge of the stage, they, too, have been known to steal scenes deliberately. Part of the critic's work is to study each actor and understand his importance in the scene, then to ascertain whether he is a selfish actor attempting to stand out from the group, or a cooperative one who is wholly conscious of just what contribution to the total picture he should make.

The preceding six questions must always be asked if we as theatregoers would meaningfully observe the art of the actors. Without asking them, and without observing how successfully each actor has met each challenge, we deny him his technique, and we rob him of his profession.

By now the reader may have discovered for himself an honest standard for his decision about an actor's contribution. Although acting grows out of nature and is based on biology and all the human attributes and characteristics, the average man without proper training is no better equipped to evaluate the actor's art than any other art. Without the right background he takes for granted that the actor's ultimate goal is to produce life so realistically that one could mistake the acting for reality. Such duplication in any art is only deception.

Our estimate of an actor's artistic worth should be based on an understanding of what he says *in addition to the lines he speaks*, for merely giving lines their literal meaning cannot be considered acting. He must, in addition, imply what *he and the character are thinking*; then he has, as an artist, begun to interpret. If he also portrays how *he and the character feel* concerning these lines, he is practicing what we may call the art of acting.

A superior description of good acting comes to us from John Dolman:

> Good acting is neither wholly realistic nor wholly unrealistic. It is sufficiently realistic to be intelligible and suggestive and to arouse the necessary empathy; it is sufficiently consistent to be convincing; and it is sufficiently unreal to preserve *aesthetic distance* and to leave something to the imagination.[5]

When we, as an audience, have come to appreciate the art of the actor we shall be able to distinguish between him, his art, and his role. With this artistic intelligence we shall rise above that group who insist that any character whose death occurred during the play's action should not appear in the curtain call.

[5]John Dolman, Jr., *The Art of Acting* (New York: Harper & Row, Publishers, 1949).

Questions for Discussion

1. A famous critic once said, "The playwright must interpret life artificially in terms of reality, while the actor must interpret life realistically in terms of artificiality." Explain.

2. Choose a motion picture, a stage production, and a television program, thinking as far back as you can when making the selection. Is it the story or the acting that you remember? Explain why the most memorable components stayed in your mind.

3. Give instances of actors who you feel have mastered only the technical areas of acting. List some who have largely mastered both the technical and the mental aspects. Have you ever been conscious of an actor who seemed to have reached the emotional or spiritual area? Explain.

4. Make a list of ten actors, and explain a special quality or aspect possessed by each that enhances his artistry or his popularity.

5. Describe the finest piece of acting you have ever seen. Explain why it so qualifies. Be specific in your analysis.

6. Make lists of actors you would consider to be: impersonators, interpreters, personality actors.

7. Assuming that the director is responsible for the "what" and the actor for the "how," separate and discuss the direction and the acting in a recent dramatic production.

8. Can you cite an actor who possesses evidence of talent as it is defined in this chapter, but who has done little or nothing to develop that talent?

9. Give examples of some actor's discipline and authority or the lack of it.

10. Do some research on what any prominent actor has said about acting, or on how he works in developing a role.

11. Review the four considerations: Is the actor fresh, easy, restrained, convincing? Then cite from your own experience as many examples as possible of the item listed under each. The examples may have been either positive or negative in their effect on the audience.

12. Explain what is meant when we speak of an actor as possessing three different entities, all of which must be recognized in criticizing his work.

Bibliography

For Supplementary Reading or Special Projects

Albright, H. D., William P. Halstead, and Lee Mitchell, *Principles of Theatre Art*. Boston: Houghton Mifflin Company, 1955.

Boleslavsky, Richard, *Acting: The First Six Lessons*. New York: Theatre Arts, Inc., 1933.

Cole, Toby, and Helen Krich Chinoy, *Actors on Acting: Theories, Techniques and Practices of the World's Great Actors*. New York: Crown Publishers, Inc., 1949.

Duerr, Edwin, *The Length and Depth of Acting*. New York: Holt, Rinehart and Winston Inc., 1962.

Eustis, Morton, *Players at Work*. New York: Theatre Arts, Inc., 1937.

Funke, Lewis, and John E. Booth, *Actors Talk About Acting*. New York: Random House, Inc., 1961.

Lewes, George, *On Actors and the Art of Acting*. New York: Grove Press Inc., 1957.

McGaw, Charles, *Acting is Believing*. New York: Holt, Rinehart and Winston, Inc., 1955.

Seyler, Athene, and Stephen Haggard, *The Craft of Comedy*. New York: Theatre Arts, Inc., 1946.

Sievers, W. David, *Directing for the Theatre*. Dubuque, Iowa: William C. Brown Company, Publishers, 1965.

Stanislavsky, Constantin, *An Actor Prepares*. New York: Theatre Arts, Inc., 1936.

———, *Building a Character*. New York: Theatre Arts, Inc., 1949.

———, *Creating a Role*. New York: Theatre Arts, Inc., 1961.

Whiting, Frank M., *An Introduction to the Theatre*, rev. ed. New York: Harper & Row, Publishers, 1961.

Young, Stark, *The Theatre*. New York: Hill and Wang, Inc., 1927.

5

The Technicians

and the

Background

Throughout history scenic background, costumes, and lighting have varied in importance. At times each has been utterly ignored; in other periods and productions one or more have overpowered both actors and play. The individual artists involved, with a few exceptions, have been forgotten, and only in comparatively recent times have we come to consider the work of the scene designer, the lighting designer, and the costume designer, who are today called the technicians of the theatre. Any conscientious analysis of a dramatic production must take into serious consideration the contributions of the technicians. Names such as Boris Aronson, Howard Bay, Edith Lutyena Bel Geddes, Lloyd Burlingame, William and Jean Eckart, Ben Edwards, David Hays, George Jenkins, Leo Kerz, Jo Mielziner, Motley, Donald Oenslager, Robert Randolph, Jean Rosenthal, Oliver Smith, J. Michael Travers are now known by intelligent playgoers. The work of these technicians who create the scenic background, the lighting, and the costumes should be recognized along with the contributions of the director, the actors, and the playwright.

In this chapter we shall consider very briefly the historical backgrounds of these technicians and, in more detail, their individual goals and techniques observable in any current dramatic production.

It is interesting to trace the development of the physical theatre from the campfire of primitive man and his unconscious drama, through the glorious sunlit outdoor theatre of the Greeks, the spectacular arenas of the Romans, the various stations in the liturgical plays performed in Catholic churches of the Middle Ages, the elaborate perspectives of the Renaissance, and the painted backdrops of the nineteenth and early twentieth centuries, to the "peep-hole" or "picture frame" stage with its realistic scenery.

It is a story that finds the playwright and the actor gradually losing their freedom both in space and emotional expression. The wide open-air stage of the Greeks, providing freedom for imagination and movement, has been traded for the tiny realistic stage cluttered with properties and furniture, forcing the actor to think in terms of littleness. He and his emotions have been imprisoned. The move toward realism almost eliminated contact between actor and audience. In the realistic theatre, the audience is little more than an eavesdropper. As more and more has been done in the way of portraying locale, it has likewise become less necessary for the audience and actors to be imaginative. The price of sharing the intimacy of our next-door neighbor's life has meant trading the majestic for the microscopic.

In Chapter Two, while discussing the play and the playwright, a play was defined as "a story devised to be presented by actors, on a stage before an audience." The phrase "on a stage" has undoubtedly governed the nature of the written drama. This fact, more than any other, has brought about the current debate on the relative merits of the proscenium versus the thrust or open stage. The open stage was prevalent until the late seventeenth or early eighteenth centuries. Since that time— for approximately three hundred years—plays have been written for the proscenium stage.

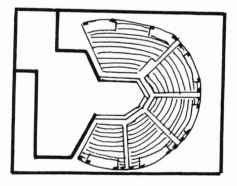

To judge any drama or production honestly, one should have a clear mental picture of the theatre and the stage equipment for which it was written. One should also be aware of the intended actor-audience rela-

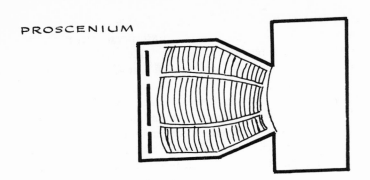

tionship, as discussed in Chapter Three. The following line drawings may serve to picture the evolution of this relationship, as well as the diminishing freedom of both the playwright and the actor.

GREEK

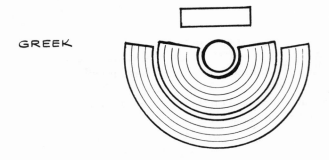

The Greek theatres, seating fifteen to twenty thousand persons, called for a particular style of play and performance. Out of it grew our classic style. The afternoon performances in Shakespeare's Globe Theatre, without scenery or authentic costuming, required that the lines of the play itself provide a far more detailed description of the setting. The appearance of the ghost of Hamlet's father, and Macbeth's murder of Duncan—both nocturnal events—had to be played in broad daylight on the stage of the roofless Globe. The appeal was to the ear rather than to the eye, and this was a drama of rhetoric. In his lines, and beautiful lines they were, Shakespeare set the time, season, and locale:

> But, look, the morn, in russet mantle clad,
> Walks o'er the dew of yon high eastward hill.

or

> How sweet the moonlight sleeps upon this bank!

How much greater the imagination of the audience had to be in 1600! Today most of this detail is left to the technical staff.

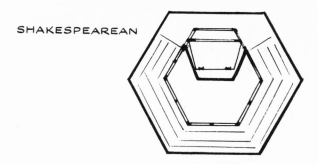

During the seventeenth century, in London's roofed theatres and on enclosed stages with painted wings to suggest locality or season, drama became less romantic in style. The drama of rhetoric gave way to a drama of conversation. Because the audience in the days of Charles II was made up of one social class, the theatre of the Restoration became a theatre of smart dialogue, clever repartee, and language often considered quite vulgar even today. The emphasis fell on writing the type of speech that might be heard in the best social circles of that day.

APRON

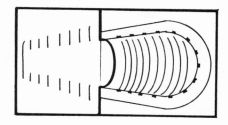

After the Restoration, playwriting in England fell to a very low ebb. The physical theatre was little changed, but plays were less vulgar as all classes were once more admitted to the playhouses. Between 1720 and 1860 only three notable plays were written in England—*She Stoops to Conquer* by Oliver Goldsmith and *The Rivals* and *The School for Scandal* by Richard Brinsley Sheridan. Each followed the Restoration pattern of prose conversation.

During the eighteenth and nineteenth centuries the stage apron became smaller, and the performance was pushed more and more back of the proscenium arch. The scenery put greater emphasis on the suggestion of locale, although it was still painted, very artificially, on wings and backdrops. It is always difficult to pinpoint the very beginning of a transition. The change begins in many places and in different ways. As we have noted, the "well-made," mechanically constructed play of France

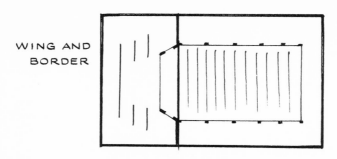

WING AND
BORDER

was attacked by Zola in his demand for a naturalistic theatre. He demanded that "a slice of life" be placed on the stage. In Norway the young Henrik Ibsen was beginning to write dialogue that sounded very like ordinary conversation. There were also changes in the settings. An exact date for the first box set is not known. It is referred to in Germany as early as 1804, and its first appearance in England is generally accepted as 1832. Greater realism in the scenic theatre was soon followed by a demand for a more lifelike dialogue. The mirror in this new theatre was expected to reflect life without those purely theatricalized embellishments so common to the plays of Scribe and Sardou, or the artificiality and sentimentality associated with Victorian England.

Arthur Wing Pinero named the three-sided room with the fourth wall missing "the peep-hole" stage, and with Henry Arthur Jones and Bernard Shaw he championed Henrik Ibsen and what was soon to be known as realistic drama. Once entrenched, the new style began its reign. Improvements in lighting (the electric light came into practical use in the last fifteen years of the century), improvement in scene-shifting devices such as the sliding or revolving stage, sound recordings, and countless other mechanical assets, all helped to give birth to the theatre as we know it.

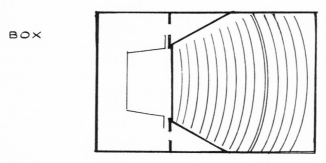

BOX

The last step in this evolution is the arena theatre, which puts the audience on four, or sometimes only three, sides of the stage.

Historically, then, and because of the physical theatre of his period, the dramatist has written for us in the majestic beauty of the Greeks, the

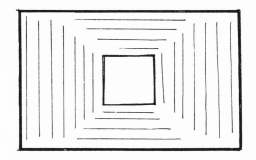

ARENA

poetic power of the Elizabethans, the brilliant and often vulgar dialogue of the Restoration, the artificial and extreme morality of the Victorians, and finally in the language spoken by the modern man in the street. Each playwright writes for the stage of his day, and we must know what it was physically if we are to understand his plays fully. This understanding makes clear the unfairness of comparing the dramas of one century with those of another.

The late Thomas Wood Stevens, famous Shakespearean scholar and director, said, "Shakespeare loses far more than he gains when one of his plays is taken out of the Elizabethan setting and given a modern production with all the accoutrements the twentieth century has at its disposal." Mr. Stevens's statement may be open to question, for it tends to limit the production of plays from the past in our modern theatres. However, it does emphasize a very important point. *We should always consider plays of the past not only in terms of the theatre in which they are being given, but also in terms of the theatre for which they were written.*

John Dolman made an interesting analysis of the scenic background, its evolution, and its various contributions on these various stages. His discussion is given brief consideration here because the artistic importance of scenery seems to have grown proportionately to its development.

Dolman pointed out that the one purpose of the *skene*—that small building in the background of the Greek theatre—was to serve as *concealment* for the actors while costume changes were being made, or when their presence on the stage was not necessary. It is only natural that the bare surface of such an enclosure would sooner or later call for some means of *decoration*. Undoubtedly the Greeks took some steps in this direction, but it is fair to assume along with Anthony Kadlec:

> Ever since the first Greek stepped in and out of the first *skene house,* the audience has been excited and pleased with the "embellishments." The first *skene house* gave the audience something tangible in locale. They knew that when that first actor made that first entrance, he was not just the actor coming out of the *skene house,* but a character coming through the opening of a cave or the gate of a palace.

243   THE TECHNICIANS AND THE BACKGROUND

Since that first entrance, the embellishments have had periods of complexity as well as simplicity. The important thing is, however, that the setting, the locale made tangible, has come to be expected. More important, it has been appreciated, and the word "appreciated" seems to do more to justify the existence of the designer than anything else. To the designer, it means creativity, satisfaction, service.[1]

The third use or purpose of scenery is *mood*, which became important during the Middle Ages. At this time the Roman Catholic Church, with nuns and choir boys as actors and the various stations of the cross as stages, turned to the theatre as its means of relating the great stories of the New Testament. It remained for Leonardo da Vinci, and later Inigo Jones in England to develop the perspective in scene painting that for the first time *suggested place*.

The element of suggestion reigned for more than two hundred years, with artificially painted backdrops that attempted to duplicate furniture, properties, and scenic detail. It was replaced only by the box set and the realistic interiors or exteriors that came to be a part of the theatre whose goal was to *portray place*. As scene-shifting devices, mechanical equipment, and modern lighting facilities came into existence it was almost a race to see which setting could be made the most like life itself. The peak was reached in this country during the days of David Belasco. His ultra-realistic settings dominated the stage for years, and his influence is still felt in some phases of our theatre.

One of the leaders in the opposition to this sort of realism was Gordon Craig, a champion of aesthetic unity in production, whom we have already mentioned as being responsible for the emergence of the director as a power in the theatre. Craig preferred a few simple pieces of scenery and a minimum of properties. His goals were a suggestion of locale and simplicity rather than imitation. His influence was felt in this country about 1915, when Robert Edmond Jones and Lee Simonson along with several others began to plead for a stage setting that was much more than a background. Robert Edmond Jones, one of the greatest artists in the American theatre, insisted that "a stage setting is not a background; it is an environment. Players act in a setting, not against it." By 1920 a new generation of scene designers had come into prominence, all influenced by Jones's philosophy, so very well stated in his epoch-making book, *The Dramatic Imagination*:

> The designer must always be on his guard against being too explicit. A good scene, I repeat, is not a picture. It is something seen, but it is something conveyed as well; a feeling, an evocation. Plato says somewhere: It is beauty I seek, not beautiful things. That is what I mean. A setting is not just a beautiful thing, a collection of beautiful

[1]Anthony L. Kadlec, "The Designer's Dilemma," *The Chorus*, program note of the University Theatre (Boulder, Colorado: University of Colorado, October, 1958).

things. It is a presence, a mood, a symphonic accompaniment to the drama, a great wind fanning the drama to flame. It echoes, it enhances, it animates. It is an expectancy, a foreboding, a tension. It says nothing, but it gives everything.[2]

Scenery and the Scene Designer

Before discussing the requirements of scenery, we should consider some of the modern trends in scenic design. Few stage settings fit into any single classification, for aesthetic freedom always permits borrowing from any source that will contribute to total effectiveness. The scene designer confers with the director and then proceeds to create the scenery that will best fit the needs of the play. Rarely does he think in terms of a particular scenic style. He does what he feels should be done, and after the set is completed the audience labels it. It is this labeling that presents one of our greatest problems in discussing scenery, and the difficulty lies in terminology. Unfortunately, few authorities are in full agreement as to the exact meaning of all the words they use to describe the settings in our modern theatre.

The six most commonly accepted scenic styles are realism, simplified realism, impressionism, expressionism, theatricalism, and formalism. The first four lean in the direction of imitating life and, in theory, propose to help the actor develop and project the mood and spirit of the play. The last two tend to suggest rather than portray, serving only as a satisfactory background and, in theory, help the actor by staying out of his way. In interpreting each style, we hope to show how that style makes use of line, mass, and color.

Realism The ultra-realistic set is an effort to portray place consistently, convincingly, and as completely as possible. There are plays, such as *Street Scene, Of Mice and Men,* and *The Diary of Anne Frank,* in which realism in the scenery is most necessary. Great attention is given to small detail, and every effort is used to give evidence of reality. David Belasco once imported the authentic furniture of Madame du Barry with which he set the stage of the play about her life. At other times he insisted upon running water, a stove that actually prepared food on stage, and such realistic details as knocking radiators. The sunsets he contrived through lighting are still praised for their naturalistic beauty by those who saw them in the theatre half a century ago.

Such duplication of life and such lack of suggestion always finds criticism among those who accept the premise that all art is selection

[2]Robert Edmond Jones, *The Dramatic Imagination* (New York: Duell, Sloan & Pearce, Inc., 1941), pp. 23–26.

rather than representation. Exciting as realism may be, and appropriate as it is for some plays, it is not considered as artistic or creative as certain other styles.

Simplified realism This is an effort to stylize so that the setting may meet more accepted aesthetic standards. In the simplified setting no effort is made to fool the audience. An unconvincing detail is eliminated; its discovery does not initiate a search for a substitute. Some evidence of unreality may appear—this is not a distraction, but an admission that the setting is only an illusion of reality. The goal of the artist is suggestion of the exact locale rather than representation.

Impressionism This gives only the impression of locale and carries simplification even further. It is what Jo Mielziner calls "implied scenery," and is more concerned with mood than detail, or any effort to do more than suggest place. It demands more imagination on the part of the audience. Because the element of exaggeration is almost inevitable, most impressionistic sets take on some form of stylization. An impressionistic set normally uses only partial walls and set pieces that are often silhouetted against a plain cyclorama. Doors, windows, and lesser details may be only indicated. This style of scenery is very effective in staging classical plays or, in fact, almost any style of drama with the exception of the ultra-realistic. It was used very effectively in conjunction with the simplified realism in *Death of a Salesman*, especially in the dream sequences that took place in Willy Loman's mind.

Expressionism This is the most difficult of all to describe, for it borrows from all the other arts by using music, rhythm, line, mass, color, and light. The designer distorts the lines of the scenery to express mental or emotional distortion of one or more characters. Plastic forms, levels, and sharp angles are frequently seen. It finds its greatest use in such plays as *Marat/Sade*, *The Adding Machine*, or the asylum scene in *Peer Gynt*.

Whereas impressionism appeals principally to emotion, expressionism appeals more to the intellect. Very common a few years ago, the latter is used less frequently now except in combination with other styles.

Theatricalism Until the realistic theatre came into existence, theatricalism was freely accepted in any theatre experience. This was especially true after the development of perspective in scene painting. It reached its height during the nineteenth century when wings and backdrops were frank admissions of unreality, even though they attempted to suggest the locale. A theatrical set today presents scenery as scenery. It may be decorated attractively and in the mood of the production, but it makes no pretense to be more than scenery. There is no attempt to convey an illusion of reality. Theatrical sets are found most frequently in musical revues. Actors perform in front of the scenery, for it serves more as background than as locale.

Formalism   Formalism makes use of the natural background belonging to the building, the theatre, or the auditorium where the play is being given. It employs neither representation nor suggestion. Perfect examples are simple draperies, a church pulpit, or an outdoor stage. Such a set is ideal for poetic tragedy. It was, of course, the only stage or setting used by the Greeks and Shakespeare. Background is only background; it is not expected to be considered as scenery. Formal backgrounds are very effective with the classics, or in modern unrealistic plays suited to the presentational form.

In the following illustrations Don Swanagan, New York designer, has envisioned a realistic setting for an imaginary script, and then shown how

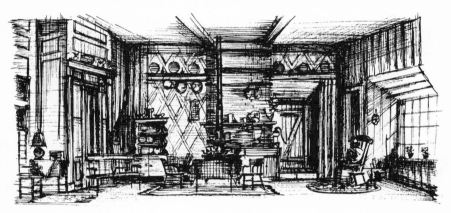

Realism

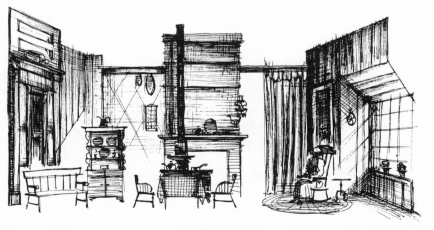

Simplified Realism

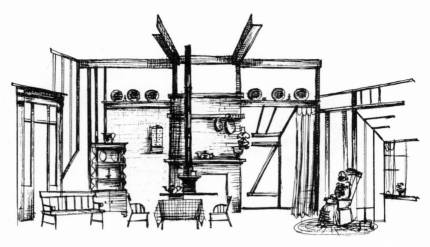

Impressionism

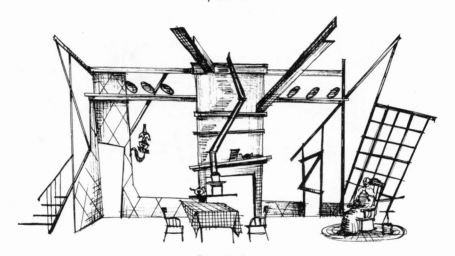

Expressionism

that same setting might appear if our generalizations concerning simplified realism, impressionism, expressionism, and theatricalism were carried out. Formalism does not appear, because that style would use the natural locale and, therefore, no scenery, as we have here defined it.

Three contributing factors may be used in conjunction with any one of the six scenic styles listed above. They are stylization, symbolism, and space staging. In the confusion of scenic terminology, the most abused word of all is "stylized." In this book we should like to think of it primarily as an adjective that modifies one of the major styles. The word seems to have a clearer meaning when used thus, in association with a specific scenic style.

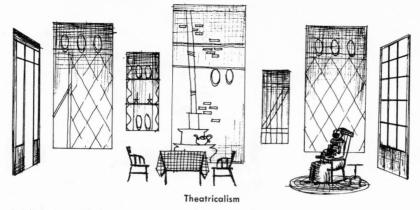

Theatricalism

Stylization works and depends on the imagination of the audience. It appeals to the emotion or to the intellect, as the scene designer may desire. Its chief technique is exaggeration, with a special treatment of an established scenic style, for it is not style in itself. The very term must imply illusion.

The scene designer may stylize according to the *period* of the play or the *mood* of the play. The first might involve designing a near replica of the old Globe Theatre stage for the production of a Shakespearean play. In Shakespeare's day this would have been a formal setting, but it would now be *stylized formalism*. An equally imaginative designer might conceive a series of backdrops and wings to represent the various settings in *Ten Nights in a Barroom* as it was done in 1890. This could be *stylized theatricalism*. In his approach to mood, another artist could paint a blown-up water color forest scene, depicting the wildest sort of trees and flowers to suggest the fantasy expressed by Bernard Shaw in *Androcles and the Lion*. This has been termed "artistic child's play," for such a design would give the artist's impression of the play's mood and could be called *stylized impressionism*.

Symbolism, too, often constitutes part of a setting. This involves the use of some object that, through its association, establishes the thought, locale, or mood. The imagination of the audience then fills in the remainder of the setting. Such symbols may be a judge's bench for a courtroom, a blackboard for a schoolroom, a figure of the Virgin Mary for a religious mood. A flag, a church window, or a jail door could also be used symbolically. Concrete symbols may become *symbolic impressionism*. Abstract motifs of a similar nature may thus lead to a *symbolic expressionism*. *Our Town* could be said to have used a basically formalistic background; but when the church window was projected on the back wall, or the soda fountain was implied by the use of two chairs and a plank, or the ladders suggested stairways, the scene designer was using a *symbolic formalism* or *symbolic impressionism*.

A reconstruction of the stage of the Globe Playhouse. Courtesy of the Folger Shakespeare Library, Washington, D.C.

Below. Stage and auditorium of the Tyrone Guthrie Theatre, Minneapolis, Minnesota.

250   THE PRODUCTION

The third contributing factor is called *space staging*, and if the director possesses sufficient lighting equipment and a satisfactory cyclorama, he can do remarkably artistic and imaginative work. Space staging involves a dark stage with a spotlight picking out the characters and scene successively required. The lighted area may indicate anyplace or everyplace. Space staging is usually found most practical and effective when a drama calls for a great many short scenes, or when it is necessary for the action to move from one locale to another very rapidly. As much or as little as the designer may wish in the way of properties and scenery may be used to indicate locale. When an effort is made to suggest an exact place through space staging, the scenery is referred to as a *simultaneous setting*, and more often than not is impressionistic in style. Any number of locales may be found on the stage—a country store, a church, a bedroom, an office—all adequately equipped to give a definite impression of place. Each can be brought into focus merely by concentrating the light on that particular area.

A second and somewhat simpler effect is known as *multiple setting*. The principle is the same except there is no effort to suggest exact locale. The stage may be practically bare of scenery or properties. It follows more nearly the staging in an Elizabethan theatre—outer and inner stage, balconies, etc. As then, the lines are depended on to indicate locale if that information is necessary. With multiple staging little more than light and characterization are used. Space staging can be used to advantage in many plays but is less effective in realistic plays.

We would emphasize that styles in scenic design are constantly changing. Thus audiences should no longer expect standard sets, but instead look for imagination and artistry on the part of the scene designer. Experimentation is exciting and audiences can encourage it. Much has already been done by the educational and community theatres in this direction, and the scenic contributions of the professional theatre have shown marked progress in the past decade. With this explanation of modern scenic trends, the chart on page 252 may help to summarize and further clarify the goals and means of the contemporary scenic artist.

These six modern trends in scenic art, plus the three contributing factors, and combinations of any or all, are the tools of the scene designer.

Borrowing from much that has been written on the subject of scenery, we may say that four rather generally accepted "musts" make up the basic requirements of stage scenery.

The scenery must fit the action of the play. Modern plays call for great detail and localization. The setting itself must tell much about the background, social position, and life of the people who are discovered in it. It must have the proper doors, windows, stairs, and furnishing to fit the

MODERN SCENIC STYLES

Realism (Naturalism)
Consistent—convincing—complete

Simplified Realism
No effort at completeness;
unconvincing details eliminated

Impressionism
Less detail—only essentials
to suggest locale and emotion

Expressionism
Still suggests, but by distortion;
tries to portray feeling
in physical set

Theatricalism
Background decorated and
used as background only

Formalism
Building or surroundings
as they are

PURPOSE or GOAL

Helps actor to
portray
mood—
spirit—
emotion
by assisting him.

Helps actor by
staying out
of his way.

CONTRIBUTING FACTORS

Stylization
Exaggeration to
suggest
period or mood

Symbolism
One object
represents another—
or a great deal more

Space Staging
A light picks a scene out of a void
and illuminates a portion of a multiple or simultaneous setting which
may suggest or represent a specific
or a generalized locale—anywhere
or everywhere.

action of the players. The décor may consist of the vast amount of litter found in *The Odd Couple* or the bare essentials of a hut.

In plays of another period, less emphasis is placed on detail. A Greek play may be done in front of a stone façade, with a set of natural drapes, or even more effectively in an outdoor theatre. Because of its formal style, it does not require much scenery. An imaginative scene designer may play around with the script and devise some steps, platforms, or pillars, but simplicity is always his keynote. Almost the same holds true for Shakespeare, although many interesting settings have been devised through the use of a unit set and varied multiple settings made up of arches, levels, pillars, or columns. The flexibility of these components permitted the suggestion of the various scenes demanded by the script. Here also simplicity is important.

In the production of plays from the Restoration through the eighteenth and nineteenth centuries the action invariably demands the use of the painted backdrop and wings with few furnishings, and great use of the front or apron of the stage.

It is the scene designer's first obligation to understand the action and the relative importance of all scenes so that his setting may be used more effectively by actors and director.

The setting must portray the type, style, spirit, and purpose of the play. At the curtain's rise, the scene designer's use of line, color, and light should give the audience a clear indication of whether the play is fundamentally tragedy or comedy, farce or melodrama. The setting should likewise suggest the style, whether it be realistic, classic, romantic, or fantastic, and the mood or spirit of the scene itself.

The scenery must help the actor to tell his story. The background should never get in the actor's way or distract from what he is trying to say, do, or make the audience feel. Background may assist the actor by contributing, or by staying out of his way. Either goal is accomplished only after the scene designer and the director have come to a clear understanding on the spirit and purpose or mood of the whole production. It is then that the designer chooses from the various methods we have described and decides exactly how he can use scenery to achieve the desired artistic impression.

The scenery must never attract attention to itself. The only time the audience should be conscious of the scenery is when the curtain first rises. The moment the play begins the scenery should "fade into the background" so completely that it is forgotten by the audience. Often the work of a scenic artist and his assistants is applauded at the rise of the curtain. This display of audience appreciation is commendable, but if at the end of the act we find the setting being discussed in the lobby rather than the play and the acting, we know that the setting is artistically wrong. This often happens with realistic settings, which the audience notices throughout the play in an effort to ascertain how the artist has either attained his effects or erred in his portrayal. Such distractions in themselves form the severest criticism of realistic stage settings.

Two examples of inartistic design may help to illustrate the point. The first concerns a production of *H. M. S. Pinafore*. Costumes were in the hands of the sewing class; the scenery was designed by the art department and constructed by the boys in manual training; the vocal instructor spent months in developing the solos, duets, and choruses; the women's physical education department devised dances; the physics teacher supervised the lighting; and the instrumental music director developed a thirty-six piece orchestra. Truly, it was a cooperative all-school event. The setting was perhaps as complete and realistic as that in any non-commercial production the operetta has ever had. A near-perfect replica of a ship was constructed on the stage, and the backdrop portrayed a skyline with almost photographic accuracy.

On the evening of production, just before the audience had begun to assemble, the scene designer and director made one final inspection of the setting. They agreed that it was most complete and effective. The scene designer felt that the total picture might be enhanced with one additional detail. He suggested punching a hole in the tower of the painted lighthouse on the backdrop and placing one of the stage crew on a ladder with a flashlight, to be turned on and off, suggesting a revolving light in the tower. This was done—and with it so was the artistry of the production. When that small light flashed on and off each thirty seconds during the evening, *H. M. S. Pinafore* all but ceased to exist.

When the performance was over there had been little mention of the music, the story, the costumes, the setting, and acting, or even the over-all production. The star of the evening was the boy with the flashlight. The effect was summed up most pointedly by a little old lady several weeks later, "I couldn't take my eyes off that lighthouse. It was so realistic. I timed that light, and it came on every thirty seconds. How on earth did you do it?" The elimination of this distracting detail in the scenery could have directed the emphasis where it belonged—on the production.

One more example of ultra-realism should thoroughly establish our point. One scene in Maxwell Anderson's *Winterset* takes place in the rain. In a college production of that play, a very ambitious senior boy, whose enthusiasm then surpassed his artistic evaluation, conceived the idea of arranging a series of pipes above the stage, attached to the water supply backstage. Holes were then made in the pipes to release the necessary rain. In the scene between Mio and Miramne in which Mio says, "I feel the rain in my face," the supreme artist at the water spigot let him have it. Rain, first in a sprinkle and later in a downpour, drenched the actors, whose real job it was to interpret the lines of Maxwell Anderson. The moment the water began to fall, the audience forgot what the actors were saying and began to think, "Why, that is real water!" "Where is it coming from?" "Those actors are getting soaking wet!" Then, with much craning of necks, they began to ask their neighbors, "Where is the water going to?" Many confessed afterward that they were unable to enjoy the remainder of the play because subconsciously they kept thinking, "It's pouring rain, and I didn't bring an umbrella."

The three great arguments against too much realism in the theatre are: (1) it detracts attention from the actors and the play; (2) it weakens illusion by challenging the audience to compare the make-believe of the set with life itself; and (3) it destroys aesthetic distance. We would point out, however, that these arguments against realism apply to the theatre far more than to the motion pictures, where scenery serves a different purpose.

As shown in earlier pages there has been—especially since the midfifties—a great reversal of trends. Realism steadily lost ground except in productions that demanded surface reality in all details. This has been and is a most healthy sign. Indeed, we have dealt at such great length on realism (and arguments against it) in the theatre only because many student readers are far more familiar with the mass media of motion pictures, where surface realism is of primary importance, and are prone to judge stage productions according to the same standards.

The chief requirement of all scenery is that it be functional and a part of the production itself. When Raymond Sovey designed the atmosphere and setting for *Our Town* in 1938, he put into it the most effective background for that script. It was a startling innovation, but Sovey was an advocate of the "atmosphere theory," and an associate and disciple of Robert Edmond Jones. He was determined to create a world that was absolutely "right" for what was to be said and done in Thornton Wilder's imagined world. The simplicity, truth, and universality of the script was reflected in the sparse background and properties of the production. Sovey's "locale" became so much a part of the imagined world that it has been copied in almost every production of that play around the world. For those familiar with any one of the more than one hundred-twenty "locales" that Sovey created for Broadway productions, his recognition of "truth" rather than realism is immediately evident.

When *Our Town* first opened there was great fear among the advocates of scenery—especially realistic scenery—that a trend might develop toward its elimination. A cartoon appeared in *The New Yorker* in which two of Helen Hokinson's characters were seen at the box office inquiring, "Is this a play with or without scenery?" Raymond Sovey once said: The real question should always be—"Is there any theatre in the scenery?" We should always ask ourselves—how theatrical, how helpful, how provocative—how meaningful or how detrimental is the atmosphere that has been created by the scenery?

Frequently professional productions have given their performances with the most elaborate and detailed scenery and décor. When the same production went on the road, it was necessary to simplify to the extreme. Scene designers who have at first felt that it would be impossible to eliminate details have been amazed, when by necessity the deletion was forced upon them, to find not only that the scenery was equally satisfactory in depicting locale but that it also enhanced the production.

Lighting and the
Lighting Designer

In our discussion of the scene designer, the lighting was frequently mentioned, and it is not uncommon for the scenery and lighting to be designed by the same artist. In any event, the electrician must work in close cooperation with the scene designer as well as with the actors and costumer; for the lights affect the settings, and they are often instrumental in altering the make-up and costumes of the actors.

Historically, the lighting designer is one of the youngest artists in the theatre. The Greeks and Romans, as has been shown, worked under the light of the sun. Even Shakespeare's theatre had no roof, and performances were given by day. After the theatre was taken inside, the candle was the only means of illumination. Color was supplied by placing bottles of different colored wine between the flame and the object illuminated. Later gas supplanted candles and various hues of silk gave the color. It was possible for the first time to alter the quantity of light on a given scene. (Neither the color nor the odor from these lights contributed much to the appearance of the actor or the pleasure of the audience.) It was discovered in the middle of the nineteenth century that a combination of burning chemicals placed on a cake of lime produced a strong white light, and this soon became an important part of stage illumination. The phrase "in the limelight" still suggests the actor who holds the brightest area of the scene.

Shortly before 1900 the arc light was invented. This was soon followed by the incandescent lamp and its development. Once again we must mention the name of Adolphe Appia—almost at the time that the electric light became a factor, he published *Die Musik und die Inscenierung*, calling for the same kind of reform in lighting that Gordon Craig was demanding of scenery. Appia made use of the new invention to enhance the work of the actor. Whereas before light had served only as illumination, Appia used it artistically for the very first time. It can safely be said that no single item has more affected the course of theatre art in the past century than the electric light. David Belasco and Steele McKaye did the most in adapting the invention to the American theatre, and since 1920 there have been so many improvements and refinements that lighting facilities and equipment now are a major factor in the design of any building that is to be used for theatre production.

In the lighting of its productions, the noncommercial theatre surpasses the professional more often than in any other single area. This is owing principally to restrictions encountered in the course of dealing with the professional electricians' unions. There are regulations regarding the equipment that may be used, and the number of personnel required to do a job. Base salaries are high, and the cost of overtime is exorbitant. The unions' strict rules and customs regarding membership have made it virtually impossible for persons especially trained in the art of stage lighting to "get a card."

Our theatre today offers three means of controlling lights—the quantity or amount of light that is being used, the color of that light, and its distribution over the stage. Each quality can affect the audience in countless psychological ways. Knowledge of human behavior and a feeling for the mood of a scene, coupled with artistic design, can lift a dramatic scene to an effectiveness never envisioned by our forefathers. The theatre electrician literally paints with light. It is not unusual for a production to have several hundred light changes during a performance, all of which, when done well, are so subtle that the audience is hardly aware that they are being made. Changes in lighting may serve to emphasize a character or a scene at appropriate moments, create or change the mood in numerous ways, shift the direction of the audience's attention, relieve eye or nervous tension, alter the color of costume or set, suggest weather or season, give an appearance of life and vitality to a weary actor, unify one group or set it off in opposition to another, or indicate fantasy or reality or a dream sequence. In the hands of a really good lighting designer, the possibilities of lighting in the modern theatre are limitless. Such an artist must have adequate equipment at his disposal, of course, and the faculty for taking infinite pains. To realize what has been done and how we have been affected by the lighting is one of the most fascinating phases in analyzing a modern theatrical production.

The stage must at all times be sufficiently lighted to make for visibility without strain. This does not mean that every square inch of the stage should be equally lighted, which was the effect of old-fashioned footlights. The walls and upper corners of the set, or any part of the stage that is not going to be used by the actors, should be given less illumination than areas where the action will take place. In this respect, visibility should always be selective. This is impossible with general illumination. It is attained only by the specific control afforded by the spotlight whose beam can be directed.

Good lighting selects and emphasizes that aspect of the production that needs pointing up at any given moment. It would be unnecessary to keep a doorway lighted throughout an entire act, but it may be highly important to light that opening just as an important character makes an entrance. In almost any modern play, the directing of attention by means of light is of fundamental importance. At the same time, the entire stage must be lighted evenly enough for the illumination on the darker area to eliminate distraction in the audience when the actor passes from one emphasized area to another.

Artistic lighting accentuates the proper emotional and psychological qualities of the play. Through the use of color, light, and shadow, a mood is established and an audience is affected accordingly. Mystery, impending disaster, the supernatural, time of day, and season of the year can all be suggested by lighting. Quite ordinary plays have been lifted almost into the realm of greatness by the effective use of lights. In the same way, a distinguished play could be robbed of its inherent greatness by ineffective lighting.

The electrician has the power to establish a mood even more quickly than the playwright or the actor. This was done especially well in an early production of *There Shall Be No Night.* The impression of the Finnish winter and deep snow was instantly established by the cold white light that streamed through the large window on that New Year's Day.

In *Rose of the Rancho* David Belasco so completely simulated the hot Mexican sun at siesta time that the audience became uncomfortable to the point that men loosened their collars and the women began to fan themselves.

In addition to adequate visibility, proper selection and emphasis, and the creation of a mood or atmosphere, the designer must choose between realistic lighting, which would represent nature, or lights used purely for their theatrical effect. If lighting is to represent nature, it must seem to have a natural source, such as a window, a lamp, or a fireplace. These areas must be in brighter light than other parts of the room, for the lighting must follow the laws of nature.

For basically theatrical plays, it is not necessary to consider the light source. Needless to say, such plays are the joy of the electrician. His imagination can go the limit, and with modern equipment tremendous effects are achieved in any nonrealistic play.

The theatrical use of lights is most valuable in the production of any style other than the realistic, where it may prove somewhat distracting unless reasonable motivation is supplied.

It is equally important that the electrician eliminate any distracting elements, such as a spill of light on the proscenium, teaser, or tormentor, or a light leak from backstage. A poorly illuminated room, supposedly just offstage and into which characters are to pass, can quickly destroy the illusion. An audience can be greatly disturbed by a lamp that flickers owing to a loose connection or the reflection of some light in a mirror or picture. Extreme care must be given to the light outside windows, or when the impression of distance or sky is required.

In our theatre the lighting designer is an artist, and each of his effects is the result of careful planning, knowledge of human emotions, the specific needs of the script, the flexibility and limitations of his instruments, and his own creative imagination. Not to recognize and appreciate his contribution is to miss some of the most artistic achievements of the modern theatre.

Costume and the Costume Designer

It was not until the eighteenth century, when David Garrick insisted that his actors dress in costumes appropriate to the role and the play, that any special thought was given to actors' apparel. The players of the Elizabethan period wore the cast-off clothes of the lords and ladies under whose patronage they were appearing. Consequently costumes were always contemporary with the period in which they lived. There are stories of audiences becoming almost hysterical with laughter when the actors in *Julius Caesar* first appeared in authentic Roman costumes. This occurred in both France and Germany well after 1750.

As an integral part of the unified production, however, the costumer now enjoys equal rank with the other technicians. He must realize the vast range of color meanings and their psychological effect on an audience. He must be conscious of various combinations as well as the effect of light on pigment. Color must be considered with an eye to harmony, unity, and contrast. Conflicting dramatic forces may wear opposing colors, either warm or cold, or those that clash. Whichever technique is used must, above all, be employed subtly. The good costumer knows that the actor must stand out against the set but that no actor, unless for a special purpose, must ever wear a costume or accessory that clashes with the set. In life we may not consider the color of the hostess's draperies in our choice of a tie or dress, but on the stage such factors must be taken into consideration.

The actor's personality—both as it is and as it is to be in the play— must be given special thought. The Chinese philosophical concept of Yin and Yang is relevant here, and is applicable to both men and women. The qualities represented by the Yin typify the sweet, quiet, sensitive, introverted individual; the Yang bespeaks the forceful, strident, confident, forward extrovert. The first may seem to embody the qualities we class as "feminine," and the latter, the "masculine." This theory further suggests that the proper dress for each personality emphasizes his own type—ruffles or softer hues for the Yin, and tailored styles or darker, positive colors for the Yang. At the same time, each should borrow from the other with a median as the goal. To go completely in either extreme might have comedy value, and in some instances be appropriate to portray the extremely masculine or feminine. The same femininity or masculinity could be lessened, given its proper status, or perhaps eliminated by the proper costumes in both color and design.

The costumer must possess great originality in designing and in styling, for pictures of clothes only suggest what others have already done, and exact copies have no place in the life of creative artists. Clothes are as personal as any other aspect of a character. Not only must they be agreeable to the temperament of the wearer, but they must also fit the part he is playing in all respects. They must have the proper effect on all the other costumes of the company, and, of course, on the audience.

The costumer of a period play is faced with further problems. There must always be ample evidence of characteristics associated with the costumes of the age to be evoked. The designer must be reasonably authentic, although he may sacrifice some authenticity for considerations of comfort and design. In period plays the emphasis is with centuries rather than with decades or shorter periods; however, frequent use must be made of elements associated with a specific period. These would include such details as the midline decoration of the Egyptians, the chin ruffs of the Elizabethans, the immaculate collars and cuffs of the Puritans, the hoop skirts of the Civil War, the bustles and leg-of-mutton sleeves of the late nineteenth century, and so on. The good costumer takes these constant elements and simplifies or exaggerates as his artistic nature and the demands of the play dictate.

The costumer, in the final analysis, must never forget one essential: every detail on the stage must possess dramatic significance. Like the other technicians, he must observe certain requirements.

All costumes must fit the period, season, locality, time of day, occasion, and mood of the scene. (Each detail has been discussed, or needs no further elaboration at this point.)

Each costume's line and color must do the most for character projection and for the person wearing it. The character may have to dominate, be dominated by, or blend with the others in the scene.

In this respect the costuming of a modern play is sometimes the most difficult. As an example, in staging a college dance scene in a university theatre production, it might seem logical to ask the girls in the cast to wear their own gowns. To do this would quickly show the director and the costumer how sharp is the demarcation between life and art. The result could be chaotic if the effects of color values in distinguishing between those with leading roles and those cast as supporting characters were lost, or if the general blending of colors and setting were unbalanced. To get the right costume for the right person and to blend them all into a balance of color that will tell the story dramatically in such a scene is a most formidable problem. Yet the same girls could wear gowns they had selected independently at a real dance with a highly pleasing effect.

Each costume must be stageworthy in that the lines and design are sufficiently exaggerated to convey the intended effects to the audience. A costume that might be considered very attractive for street wear could be completely unsuited to the stage. Either distance or lighting could eliminate or alter the design so that it lost all dramatic value. Rarely is it possible to use, on the stage, a costume that was actually worn in an earlier period. It may be very authentic, but probably lacks the theatrical or dramatic qualities so necessary in a production. Likewise, a costume that looks most attractive on the stage could appear too theatrical for street use.

The costumes must be worn with ease. We have already cited examples of occasions when actors, because of inadequate rehearsals, permitted the costumes to distract from the performance. It is essential that each actor have his apparel for a sufficient time to become accustomed to it. If even after such rehearsal the actor lacks the very important freedom of movement, the costumer must find some substitute. It is the costumer's problem to see that all costumes blend harmoniously into the performance.

Ultimately, an audience evaluating the work of the costumer must consider his originality in creation and execution as well as his understanding of the dramatic significance of each costume for the audience.

Regarding the work of the three technicians—the stage designer, the lighting designer, and the costumer—there is always the final question: Is there a technical smoothness and integration that makes the average audience wholly unconscious of these contributing elements? We would again emphasize that the technicians' work has made our theatre more and more a visual rather than an auditory experience. Some of this emphasis has grown out of our two visual media, the motion picture and television. They have influenced the stage to some extent just as they have been influenced by the stage. The importance of visual emphasis today is pointed up when we pause to look back. A blind man in Greek or Elizabethan theatres could have enjoyed a play and its beauty almost as much as a man who could see, for those plays were addressed primarily to the ear. A blind man in a modern theatre is greatly handicapped. In this sense it can be said that ours is less literary. Whereas the poetry of drama was once expressed in the lines, it is now found in the pictorial phases of the stage and the integration of its many parts. Our theatre calls for less imagination from the writer and the audience, but more from all other artists.

This change of emphasis, plus the unification of the whole, prompts many to say that now, even though the drama itself may have declined, the theatre (a separate institution), has the opportunity to display greater artistry than at any other time in its history. The basis of this argument lies in our contention that poetry is that happiness which overcomes us when we become suddenly aware of the presence of the beautiful. With this definition in mind, we readily understand that our modern theatre need not have lost its poetry; that all poetic beauty did not die with Ben Jonson.

There can be just as much poetry in our theatre as there was in the theatre of Shakespeare. Only the emphasis has been changed. The poetry of the Elizabethan theatre lay in the drama, in the spoken line; the poetry of the modern theatre lies in the coordination of all the many theatre elements. Without any control of lighting or sound, minus scenery or authentic costumes, and with a noisy, uneducated audience in the pit, the Elizabethan theatre attempted to create its illusion, and we know that it did so with a considerable measure of success. The modern theatre possesses all these technical embellishments, and a far more educated audience. Much has been learned about the psychology of audiences and the nature of man. Theatre workers have been able to learn much more about the theory of their craft. Furthermore, the theatre itself has become a more cooperative project with a single artist to balance and coordinate the efforts of all the other artists. What may have been lost is the beauty of the word, but this can be compensated for, at least to some extent, by the unity of the total production. Beauty and truth are still possible in the theatre.

Questions for Discussion

1. From your experience in theatre, give several examples of ultra-realism distracting from the main point of production.

2. Give an example of the work of a technician that added materially to the success of a production. When has the work distracted in some way? Who was specifically responsible?

3. Give some examples of realistic lighting and of theatrical lighting; of a simultaneous setting or a multiple setting.

4. Explain how a costume or a stage setting can have dramatic significance. The following negative criticisms of these technical aspects are typical. "It's a beautiful costume, but it does nothing for the actor"; and "The setting is attractive, but it has no theatre in it." Explain how each statement might be true.

5. How can a stage designer affect or help a production?

6. Distinguish between scenery as an environment and scenery as a background.

7. Choose any play from Chapter Two. Draw a floor plan for one of the acts. Describe the type of scenery that would best fit its type, style, spirit, and purpose.

8. Write an essay on the contributions of Adolphe Appia, Gordon Craig, or Robert Edmond Jones.

9. From a newspaper or a magazine clip pictures that could be used as illustrations of the Yin and Yang theory for both men and women.

10. Bring to class pictures of stage sets that most satisfactorily fit the six modern scenic styles.

11. Choose from magazines or design yourself the most appropriate costumes for a man and a woman in any play of your choice. Remember this is for a *stage* performance.

12. From books on costuming, history, or other sources bring to class examples of costumes from at least three periods in history.

Bibliography

For Supplementary Reading or Special Projects

Appia, Adolphe, *The Work of Living Art and Man in the Measure of All Things*. Coral Gables, Fla.: University of Miami Press, 1960.

Bellman, Willard F., Lighting the Stage: *Art and Practice*. San Francisco: Chandler Publishing Co., 1967.

Craig, Edward Gordon, *On the Art of the Theatre* (2nd ed.). Boston: Small Maynard, 1924.

Flugel, J. C., *The Psychology of Clothes*. London: The Hogarth Press Ltd., 1950.

Gorelik, Mordecai, *New Theatres for Old*. New York: Samuel French, Inc., 1940.

Hatlen, Theodore W., *Orientation to the Theater*. New York: Appleton-Century-Crofts, 1962.

Jones, Robert Edmond, *The Dramatic Imagination*. Des Moines, Iowa: The Meredith Publishing Co., 1941.

Mielziner, Jo, *Designing for the Theatre*. New York: Atheneum Publishers, 1965.

Nicoll, Allardyce, *The Development of the Theatre* (3rd ed.). New York: Harcourt, Brace & World, Inc., 1937.

Oenslager, Donald, *Scenery Then and Now*. New York: W. W. Norton & Company, Inc., 1936.

Oxenford, Lyn, *Playing Period Plays*. London: Garnet Miller Ltd., 1958.

Simonson, Lee, *The Stage is Set*. New York: Harcourt, Brace & World, Inc., 1932.

Young, Stark, *The Theatre of Robert Edmond Jones*. Middletown, Conn.: Wesleyan University Press, 1958.

6

Experimentation

Today

Recent movements in the theatre, particularly the experimental plays of the sixties, are worth a special glance. What is successful in the avant-garde will eventually have an effect on the old guard, and together they may produce tomorrow's classic. The new and the different, the far out, may be exciting but it may well be dull and boring. The theatre, fortunately, ultimately weeds out the latter and holds on to the former.

In a provocative but perhaps lengthy and strident book, *A Theater Divided*, Martin Gottfried places the American theatre and its professional critics in two wings—right and left—which are the conventional and established on the one hand and the experimental and fringe on the other. He deplores the lack of interaction between the wings (even while investigating rather frequent examples of such interaction) and predicts the "imminent death of the Broadway stage." In this judgment he thereby joins the obituary critics of drama as well as of the other arts.

The gulf between experimental theatre and established professional theatre is not a local, New York, American phenomenon. The right and left bank theatres in Paris and their equivalents in Rome, Berlin, and London have long had a similar problem of coexistence and interaction. Innovations are not always as new as they appear to the young or to persons with a limited historical perspective. Recent experimentation, from roughly the middle of the twentieth century, seems to fall generally into three simplified categories: *reduction, addition,* and *improvisation.* Most of what is new may be subsumed under one or more of these impulses, for even reduction and addition are not as mutually exclusive as they appear.

265

Reduction has been most effective when it has been an imaginative cutting away of the expected, particularly a hacking away at realistic-naturalistic stagecraft. For instance, to an audience brought up on the overfurnished living room, the stage without furniture produces some shock or heightened awareness. When the sets have been overdone, the bare stage can give the effect of originality. Reduction may take the form of cutting down, or out, visual effects as in the basically aural *Under Milkwood* of Dylan Thomas or, in reverse, cutting down the aural and heightening the visual in the increased use of pantomime in a play. The reductive has more recently operated as an attack on story or plot or on character or on the theatre itself mixing actors and audience, although this is more properly an improvisational device. The absurdists have overused the originality of reduction. With the theory that communication is impossible, they have attempted to dramatize this impossibility with a bare stage, no characters, no story, and almost no language. This subtraction probably cannot successfully go much beyond *Waiting for Godot* and still be theatre.

Addition or accretion or substitution, of course, refers simply to adding something to the usual mixture in search of the new and different. This has been very often a contribution of the imaginative director or stage designer or of technicians. Gottfried makes much of the innovation in the American musical, at about the time of *Oklahoma!* and *West Side Story*, of a new concept of total dramatic choreography rather than the inserted dance routine. This was, no doubt, the major factor in the revitalization of a moribund form, and choreography has been imaginatively applied to the nonmusical play as well. This seems to be new, but it has its base in the ancient Greek theatre as can be seen in the original meaning of the word "orchestra," a place for dance. A large part of the impact of the Living Theatre's production of *The Brig* in 1963 was apparently in the staging—Julian Beck's set of the wire screen across the stage, a kind of pictorial expressionism, and Judith Malina's direction with its choreographed blocking and rhythm. The Kenneth H. Brown script reads much like naturalism, but the theatre production lifted this "concept for theatre" or play without a story from the outworn mode.

Improvisation must be an elastic term that covers everything from apparently scriptless spontaneity, the "theatre of chance," the intrusion of the relevant or irrelevant, of the jumbled revue numbers to the "happening" or apparently uncontrolled action. It is interesting to note that the Living Theatre, in its early experimentation, did Pirandello's *Tonight We Improvise*, 1930, which uses improvisation for particular dramatic effect.

The "happening," a current concept, may be of three types. One is the attempt to place what is *happening* on the world stage on the coffeehouse stage or wherever two or three persons are gathered. Recently, the events that have occupied this type have been either Viet Nam or Black Power. It makes a cry of its modernity—*Viet Rock*, for instance—but is strongly reminiscent of the Living Newspaper experiments of the nineteen thirties, the Works Progress Administration sponsored Federal Theatre and its productions of *Triple-A Plowed Under* or *One Third of a Nation*, a Living Newspaper about housing, which is not so dated an issue. Both current issues are modern forms of the old problem play at the roots of naturalism.

The second kind of happening is more personal and may depict publicly a trip of a drug addict, or it may be other personal problems acted out, including the therapeutic use of role-playing for the mentally ill. This is but a dramatic extension of the ballad singer, with or without protest and electric guitar, or the poet reciting his own work, even composing it as he goes along, in cafe atmosphere. A dramatic performance of any kind that refuses to rely on script control must suggest the Italian *commedia dell' arte* of a much earlier era. That these dramatic techniques may be fruitful for more conventional drama is indisputable. Such playwrights as Molière and Beckett, Peter Weiss and Jean-Claude van Itallie, among others, prove the proposition.

The third kind of happening is more esoteric, the Happening with the capital letter appropriated by spokesmen for a very "in" group of painters-sculptors turned playwrights. Michael Kirby in his book of *Happenings* ostensibly closes the circle around Allan Kaprow, Red Grooms, Robert Whitman, Jim Dine, and Claes Oldenburg; he places the very first Happening in 1959 with Allan Kaprow's *18 Happenings in 6 Parts*, at which point he indicates the word would be coined. This implies that the word is a neologism, which it is not, even though Kirby makes a good case for its being very close to Dadaism in Europe, 1916 through the twenties. When Kirby struggles with definition, he works with a jargon that obscures rather than clarifies, as exemplified in the summary statement: "Happenings might be described as a form of theatre in which diverse elements, including nonmatrixed performing, are organized in a compartmented structure."[1]

We can, however, pick out certain concepts that may be useful from his critical introductory essay, the relationship to the plastic arts, for instance. "Happenings are a new form of theatre, just as collage is a new form of visual art." They have a physical crudeness due to their connection with "action painting" and "junk sculpture." It seems strange that the possibilities of looking at a play in terms of painting should not be carried back at least to its twentieth-century beginnings in Gertrude Stein, under the influence of Picasso. Julian Beck could have told Allan

[1] Michael Kirby, *Happenings* (New York: E. P. Dutton & Co., Inc., 1966), p. 21.

Kaprow this much. "It was during this winter," writes Gertrude in *The Autobiography of Alice B. Toklas,* and the Yale *Catalogue* establishes the winter as 1913, "that Gertrude Stein began to write plays. They began with the one entitled, *It Happened a Play.* She says a landscape is such a natural arrangement for a battlefield or a play that one must write plays." In the 1922 edition of *Geography and Plays* appeared *What Happened. A Play in Five Acts.* Here are two early happenings, even if they are not happenings as so called today. And the Stein-Thompson *Four Saints in Three Acts* must have made some impact on the artists-sculptors with its New York revival in 1952. Michael Kirby returns to the idea of *collage* (a surrealist art of various objects pasted together in incongruous relationship for symbolic or suggestive effect) as it moved toward an environment where painting "took over the room itself, and finally, as sort of an Environment-with-action, became a Happening."

Other characteristics include the nonverbal aspect of happenings, as sounds—noise, music, tapes—predominate the normal use of language. The structure can be called insular or compartmented, contiguous, hermetic, like "a three-ring circus using simultaneous and sequential 'compartmentalization.' " Time-place-character matrices do not necessarily exist for happenings, which freedom gives them the reputation of being improvised, but the action is often indeterminate rather than improvised. The "script" is action written down within a pattern, not dialogue, with the performer frequently treated as a prop or stage effect. Performers and things change places, and happenings might simply be called "theatre of effect."

Happenings are *alogical* (presumably not subject to logic), whereas traditional theatre is logical and the Theatre of the Absurd is illogical. Symbolism may be either very private or very obvious. There is a definite relationship to Artaud's Theatre of Cruelty, as well as similarity in details to Dada, Surrealist and Expressionist plays, including those by Lorca; but in those plays "the dream elements always exist in a matrix . . . . : time, place and character change with the fluidity of thought, but they are always present, and a continuous information structure exists. They cling to story chronology."[2] It is inferred that this is non-happening.

This "in" kind of happening can ultimately contribute to theatre only when it breaks out, as it apparently does in *America Hurrah.* Some kind of matrix must be found to hold the material together or you will not get beyond the Kaprow-Oldenburg kind of thing, which limits communication to the very, very few.

Most of the dramatic experimentation in New York City since 1950 has

[2] Michael Kirby, *Happenings* (New York: E. P. Dutton & Co., Inc., 1966), p. 39.

taken place Off-Broadway and more recently Off-Off-Broadway in garages, churches, restaurants, art galleries, or anywhere except a conventional playhouse. Off-Broadway used to be centered in and around Greenwich Village where one could see the Ibsen and O'Neill plays not being done anywhere else and something as different and new as the 1958 Burgess Meredith-Zero Mostel production of *Ulysses in Nighttown*.

Off-Off-Broadway lies mainly on the fringes of Off-Broadway, with "plays that range from the bilious to the brilliant." It has been called the "pass the hat" theatre circuit, seldom reviewed, often reviled, badly attended, run on nothing, but a "comer." A typical young member of its audience is supposed to have said, "The plays? Man, they're alive. Even when they stink, they're alive!"

This kind of theatre has an appeal to the off-beat groups and to the larger mass of young people who are influenced by the beat generation. Actors and audience often seem equally preoccupied with drugs, hallucination, rock music, withdrawal, and pure sensation. It's a wild world, but out of it can be seen emerging two major contributions to dramatic art, even if not fully emerged: the Beck-Malina Living Theatre company productions and the combination of playwright Jean-Claude van Itallie and director Joseph Chaikin.

Judith Malina and Julian Beck developed the Living Theatre as a company oriented toward experiment and repertory, in opposition to Broadway. Their early work in the 1950's was experimental enough but relied on plays that were not entirely new—Pirandello, Brecht, William Carlos Williams, and Gertrude Stein (*Dr. Faustus Lights the Lights*, for instance, a 1938 script) among others. Their greatest New York successes were with two original plays: Jack Gelber's *The Connection* on narcotics addiction and in 1963 Kenneth H. Brown's *The Brig*, a combination of photographic, factual duplication of life in a Marine Corps prison in Japan. The imaginative setting and direction of this play have been referred to above. In style, its intention was to arouse; its tone is violent and its method is assault. Edith Oliver in *The New Yorker* gave high praise to the production, noting that the background *is* the play—no plot, little characterization, but a "probing documentary." Her final questions are significant and summary. "Is it interesting or boring, or is it even a play? Does it have anything beyond shock value? Who knows?" At least, the residue is important. It does have shock value. That is, the 1963 production had it. The Malina-Beck company contribution was greater than the text seems to call for.

Of course, the story of the Living Theatre's difficulties with the Internal Revenue Service and its subsequent departure for Europe has been often and almost too fully told by the *Tulane Drama Review* and others. The company was making its third tour of Italy in 1967 with repertory including its version of *Frankenstein, Mysteries,* and Miss Malina's version of Brecht's *Antigone,* an adaptation of Hölderlin's version of Sophocles' play. The distance from Sophocles requires a very elastic imagination to be conceived. The *Mysteries* was created for the American Students and Artists Center in Paris. Being hardly a play, without a script and with little dialogue, it was the Becks' reaction to Antonin Artaud; even if delayed, it was extreme theatre of cruelty, now called "gut theatre," agonizing, physical, almost hysterical, theatrical. The *Frankenstein* was a pastiche, referred to less pejoratively as "free form work," including portions of Mary Shelley, Artaud, and Goethe's *Faust.* One of its innovations is supposed to be overlapping languages—multilingual German, English, French, Italian side-by-side without translation—which was done in films some twenty years before, the Italian *Open City* and the Swiss *Dernière Chance.* For that matter, Shakespeare did very nicely with the French-English mixture in *Henry V.* Potentially, the demand is for considerable audience sophistication.

In such productions, Martin Gottfried reports: "The Living Theater intends to entirely eliminate the playwright and the director from the theater," which seems impossible and improbable. One scene takes place entirely within the head of Frankenstein's monster. "The dialogue is limited and much of the sound is just sound—on tape and in partly extemporized chanting by the actors."[3] The tape recorder, whether it is Krapp's last or not, has joined the newsreel and magic lantern of epic theatre effects. We have addition and improvisation in large doses in the new Living Theatre.

Among reductive techniques Gottfried notes Lanford Wilson's *This Is the Rill Speaking* as "an early example of a movement away from the intelligibility of dialogue . . . the feel and rhythm of human conversation." Of course, Harold Pinter has been doing this and Gertrude Stein did it earlier, and perhaps its beginnings were in Chekhov. *The Rill* is characterized as "a dramatic collage of back porches, cars—everywhere," a "sugar-free *Our Town*" set in the author's own native Ozark mountains. The happening has pushed its influence here and elsewhere.

Perhaps the most important single development out of left-wing New York theatre has been the Joseph Chaikin Open Theatre Off-Broadway production of Jean-Claude van Itallie's *America Hurrah,* three one-act plays: "Interview," "TV," and "Motel"—which are also three acts of a single satire on modern America. Short stories used to be just short stories in a collection until Joyce's *Dubliners* and Sherwood Anderson's *Winesburg, Ohio* proved they could be something more in sequence, a new form of the novel set in mosaic. *America Hurrah* is a new form that is

---

[3] Martin Gottfried, *A Theater Divided* (Boston: Little, Brown and Company, 1967), p. 299.

born of many things like the vaudeville revue, the one-acter, the satire of *This Is the Week That Was*, the cartoon, the circus, and the chamber of horrors—the happening raised to a level of intelligibility.

America Hurrah opened November 6, 1966, and ran for 634 performances at the Pocket Theatre. Some of the most understanding criticism of this play came from normally "right-wing" sources. Walter Kerr, for example, wrote in *The New York Times* for November 7, 1966:

> A whisper in the wind . . . . There's something afoot here. And it's nothing as simple as the subtitle on the program—"3 Views of the U.S.A." suggests . . . .
>
> Take a slippery, and in the end rather chilling, moment in the first 'view.' We've watched a handful of unemployed persons sit wistfully on square blocks while bland masked interviewers, sugared with smiles, hurl impertinent questions at them. We've watched the stage dissolve into the city streets, the players dissolve into wailing sirens, whispered folk songs, the jumpy cacophony of marionettes rattling through a recording tape at the wrong speed. We've noticed that the lurching through sound and space has an interior urgency about it that is odd indeed, especially since there isn't the least trace of obvious narrative to lure us on. We lurch along willingly, bidden to do so by something original and personal in playwright Jean-Claude van Itallie's restrained voice.
>
> Now a moment comes when a full-throated siren alerts us to a corner accident. Someone's been killed. The labored inhale-exhale of artificial respiration, made into a musical continuation by the same malleable actors who are saying all the lines, fails.
>
> A pretty girl—a girl with a strong sense of obligation—leaves the accident to go on to a party. She would like to tell everyone at the party about the accident, though no one will listen. Above all, she would like to apologize for being late. No accident is enough to make a person late for a party.
>
> Slowly, subtly and with a sense of having been slapped in the face, we do grasp that it is the girl herself who has been killed and that she is apologizing for having been killed at so inopportune a moment. The dead must never be inconveniently dead. Not in America, not just now.
>
> In his second and third bits of spying on the way it *feels* to be on this continent these days, the playwright offers us two strong, plain contrasts that are quietly and deftly kept from turning obvious.
>
> In a television studio, three very normal workers glance at the monitor now and then, where busy performers with striped faces . . . go through all of the violent, cloying, synthetic motions that pass for companionable entertainment on the national airwaves. But there is no relation between the workers and the work; a yawning gulf, big enough to drown us all, has opened between the real concerns of real people and the imaginary concerns of our imaginary archetypes.
>
> One of the real workers nearly strangles to death on a bone in his chicken-salad sandwich. But the burly chanteuse, who pours affection across the land as though she were an open fire hydrant of boundless goodwill, goes right on beaming her thousand good nights. Disaster is irrelevant in a time of eternal delight.

In a "respectable, decent, and homey" motel...a massive Mother Hubbard made of very clammy clay revolves and revolves like a warning beacon, welcoming the transient to a haven filled with the books of John Galsworthy and "toilets that flush of their own accord." Meantime, two oversize grotesques, male and female, enter a paid-for room to strip to their flesh-tinted Band-Aid bodies and then to destroy the room wantonly, book by book, toilet by toilet.

None of this is didactic. It is simply observant. None of it is absurd. For the most part, Mr. van Itallie treads gently across the sorrowing inattentive earth. If some of the evening sounds as though the verse of E. E. Cummings has been rearranged by Kenneth Fearing and then set to the intrusive rhythm of "Turkey in the Straw" it's no mistake.... These deliberate "primitives" come to seem a valid, perhaps necessary, first try—almost as though we were Greeks again, searching out a right sound for the stage. Perhaps that is why there are so many garish Greek masks and even elevated Greek boots, puffing up the players at the Pocket.[4]

There is a sense of having come full circle in Mr. Kerr's most perceptive review to the reappearance of the Aristophanic monkeys and nightingales. The new is here, even in the uses of the past. The masks are now plastic and the faces are cartoon faces.

Time Magazine in the November 18 issue and in its most unfortunately characteristic style nevertheless wrote that *America Hurrah* is a "three-playlet wedding between pop art and the theater of cruelty. It is an Off-Broadway trip through an air-conditioned blightmare towards an icy emptiness at the core of American life, the land of the deepfreeze and the home of the rave, of the neon smile and the plastic heart." And in the February 21, 1967, issue of *Look* magazine, *America Hurrah* was called "the season's most hair-raising play,... using ancient stage devices to lampoon modern institutions."

There is less discontinuity between the parts of this play than might be expected. The blah-blah-blab of the interviewer passes easily into the inane conversation of the cocktail party into the typical TV formulaic sound patterns. And the artificiality of the motel guests (including the transvestism of padded bras and wigs) is just that produced by a rather literal interpretation of TV advertising. That "Interview" had originally been called "Pavanne" may suggest through Pavanne for a Dead Princess the central figure of the young girl who gets to the party though dead, who tries, unsuccessfully, to communicate. Here, perhaps, is the pity of it all. The matrix of the van Itallie play is quite simply an idea; this is American life at its emerging worst.

Megan Terry's *Viet Rock*, which also appeared in 1966, elicited a greater variety of critical reception. In more or less revue form it presented a far left position on American involvement in Viet Nam. Similar

4 Walter Kerr, *The New York Times*, November 7, 1966, p. 66, cols. 1-3.

technical devices, choreography, music, "mixed sound and rolling mias-
mic structure" gave Henry Hewes the opportunity to couple *Viet Rock*
with *America Hurrah* both as "frequently exciting in the originality of
their stage craft."

But Walter Kerr in *The New York Times* for November 27, 1966, under
the rubric "One Succeeds, the Other Fails. Why?" wrote:

> *America Hurrah* beckons you straight through the surface cacaphony
> of shrill night noises on the city streets, the hum and buzz of the
> daily round as it is danced in the electronic age, the blare of the eve-
> ning news broadcast and the shriek of the thriller that follows it, deep
> into the cool pool of quiet self-contradiction which contemporary man
> has accepted as his natural environment. Inside the clatter there is
> essential composure: the author has listened for, heard, and precisely
> reported the address of that womb-away-from-the-womb in which
> most of us spend our hours now.
>
> The other, Megan Terry's anti-war incantation, *Viet Rock*, makes
> all of the same sounds, except the clear sound of talent . . . . There is
> no real "in" . . . . She has simply hurled a style at the wall, and let
> it splatter.[5]

Of course, there were many to disagree, chiefly perhaps Richard
Schechner, editor of the *Tulane Drama Review.*

There has always been an avant-garde, and the developments we have
been considering are ours. What is new and good today will become the
old and good tomorrow. Only something that is really good will ever get
into the main stream, which, after all, is our primary concern.

[5] Walter Kerr, *The New York Times*, November 27, 1966, Sec. 2, p. 1, col. 1.

Questions for Discussion

1. Reduction as a technique is most effective when the imagination of the audience is called upon to supply what is theatrically missing. For example, when you read Dylan Thomas' *Under Milkwood*, which was once called *A Play for Voices Perhaps*, you tend to supply the visual picture from dialogue and sound effects—as in any radio drama. List the "pictures" that appear from a page of *Under Milkwood* or from a page of any radio drama script.

2. One reason for the multiple interpretations for *Waiting for Godot* is that the imagination is required to supply a story line and a theme. Collect three different imaginative interpretations from reviews and critics. Which seems best to you and why?

3. The Broadway productions of Tennessee Williams's *The Glass Menagerie* and of Arthur Miller's *Death of a Salesman* used settings that suggested paintings, impressionistic and expressionistic. What did the addition of this technique contribute to each play?

4. Painting and sculpture are most obviously "added" to improvisational theatre in the "happening" as described by Michael Kirby. This happening has a lot in common with underground films. The underground film from New York City called *Jan* with trick photography shows paintings appearing on various parts of a girl's body. Select several examples of surrealistic techniques and show how they are used in film or play. (You can begin as far back as Strindberg, *The Dance of Death*, 1901, or *The Dream Play*, 1902.)

5. What elements of the "happening" have appeared on television?

6. Compare the new musical *Hair* with either *West Side Story* or *My Fair Lady* and point out the innovational differences.

7. Consider the use of the tape recorder in recent drama (*Krapp's Last Tape*, the beginning of each *Mission Impossible* television sequence, and any others you can think of). To what degree does it represent mechanization and dehumanization? Why is it so often jarring, ironic, yet capable of tender effects?

8. What reasons can you advance for the effectiveness of the satire in *America Hurrah* and for at least the possibility of opposite opinion about the satire in *Viet Rock*?

Bibliography

For Supplementary Reading or Special Projects

Brown, Kenneth H., *The Brig*. New York: Hill and Wang, 1965.

Gottfried, Martin, *A Theater Divided*. Boston: Little, Brown and Company, 1967.

Kirby, Michael, *Happenings*. New York: E. P. Dutton & Co., Inc., 1966.

Van Itallie, Jean Claude, *America Hurrah*. New York: Coward-McCann, Inc., 1967.

IV

The

Professional

Critic Speaks

7

Summary and
Examples of
Professional
Criticism

With the assumption that "theatre" includes, for our purposes, cinema and television as well as the living stage, this book set out to outline and explain one theory of theatre understanding and evaluation. The concepts and principles on which this theatrical approach to the theatre is based were used in an effort to set up criteria for the beginner to apply, temporarily at least, in determining why he has or has not enjoyed a given stage, motion picture, or television experience. Beliefs and prejudices of the authors have been presented as such, with the full realization that any playgoer with further experience and reading may modify or even discard much of what he finds on these pages. This is inevitable—the point is that *in so doing he will have set up his own standards of judgment.* This is our first goal.

It is said that Shakespeare first stated what he was going to say, then said it, and finally pointed out that it had been said. Whether or not this generalization can be substantiated, the purpose of this chapter is to complete a similar cycle, examining this book in retrospect.

We have from the beginning conceived the fine arts to exist primarily for the purpose of aesthetic pleasure. The theatre has been considered a synthesis or meeting ground of the arts because it is composed of all

279

their elements. We have supposed that theatre belongs to the people and that audiences attend primarily to have their emotions touched. We have concluded that audiences are different from the individuals of which they are composed, and that accordingly the art of the playwright is the most difficult of all literary work. We have insisted that each artist be ever aware of the fact that the theatre must *entertain* its audience in the fullest meaning of that term; that all entertainment is not art but that all art is entertainment; and that there is something wrong with so-called art that does not entertain. In addition to its entertaining function, the theatre must, in its capacity as teacher, challenge the audience mentally, improve its taste, increase its knowledge of life and art, and clarify its thinking. In so doing it will thus *create a better audience which will in turn demand better theatre*. This is the second major goal of the book.

All this must be done while the spectators are being entertained, for the theatre has the right to expect only involuntary attention, attention that comes without effort on the part of the audience. It is the obligation of the theatre as an art to give the audience more than it could have lived in the same period. It must suggest life rather than imitate it, presenting an illusion of *seeming* real rather than *being* real. This is accomplished through theatrical reality, commonly called theatricalism, which we define as *exaggeration under control* and which is found in every phase of a production. This bigger-than-life quality must not cease to be believed by the audience while it is in the theatre.

The vast importance of the audience, its reactions, and its contributions to a production must never be forgotten by any of the theatre's artists, or by those who would consider themselves critics. For this reason our first chapter considered the audience and the development of a critical standard. The theatre is in one sense similar to a five-ring circus, with each ring contributing an essential part to the whole production. The five areas are the audience and its reaction, the play and the playwright, the director and the directing, the actor and the acting, the technicians and the background they create.

Poetry can be as vital and as alive in the twentieth century as it was at any time in the past; it has only changed its appearance, and may be found in the unity, harmony, emphasis, proportion, balance, rhythm, and grace that the artist director can bring to the well-coordinated production. We have accepted the belief that all art is selection and that it consists of substance, form, and technique. We have defined technique as the artist's means of accomplishing his end. It is the measure of his own creative powers for bringing together the substance and form. We have tried to explain some of the accepted theatre forms and to point up some of the most obvious techniques of each artist. The artist works not only in the hope of sharing his own aesthetic experience with the audience, but of receiving its approbation for his efforts. Finally, we have considered that all art is life seen through the personality of an artist as he creates, interprets, portrays, or suggests some segment of life.

Although stage, motion pictures, and television are not analogous in all respects, the fact remains that they work with much the same material, employ most of the same artists, and strive for a common goal—moving their audiences emotionally, through communication. Therefore, we may evaluate the total effectiveness of each with much the same general standards, which were presented here as ten commandments of dramatic criticism.

The way in which each individual is moved emotionally or aesthetically depends on the stimulus, his personal background, and his experience. Unanimity of opinion is neither expected nor desired.

This book was planned in the hope that it might make the reader understand and demand more of these media of entertainment, education, and communication. It is further hoped that he might view them all with a greater degree of imaginary puissance, always considering Goethe's three significant and valid principles for evaluating any work of art: What is the artist trying to do? How well has he accomplished his goal? Is it worth the doing? Such an approach demands that our dramatic criticism exist on three levels—the *literary*, which emphasizes the written drama; the *theatrical*, stressing the creation of beauty through sheer theatre magic; and the level of pure *escape* or entertainment commonly referred to as "show business." Criticism so balanced will permit each artist the freedom to create, and in turn will *produce a fairer and more honest* evaluation of his work.

If, then, these pages have (1) helped the playgoer to create his own standards of dramatic criticism, (2) provided a fairer judgment of the artists' work, and (3) laid the foundation for building better audiences who will eventually demand better theatre, a contribution will have been made in the realm of dramatic understanding, discrimination, and theatre appreciation.

A Defence of the

Professional Reviewer[1]

JOSEPH WOOD KRUTCH

If the Man from Mars should ever actually make his long expected visit to our earth, nothing would puzzle him more than the continued toleration accorded to various occupations and institutions which seem to be universally condemned. Very few things—and almost no "good things"—have ever been said in favor of marriage or the professions of law and medicine. Yet century after century men continue to get married and doctors and lawyers are not only permitted to exist but actually are paid—rather well, at that—by the very people who have exposed their essentially pernicious activity.

The existence of professional critics of literature and the theatre affords, as the Man from Mars would discover, a minor but very extreme example of the same paradox. In the English-speaking world, literary criticism has been a paying trade for about two hundred and fifty years; play reviewing for a somewhat shorter period—for though "the critics" begin to be contemptuously referred to toward the end of the Seventeenth Century, the reference then was to amateurs, and plays were not regularly reviewed in periodicals until about a century later. Yet, during all this time, few words have been said in favor of critics of any kind. As nearly everyone knows, Dryden first embodied in words one standard reproach against them when he defined a critic as something generated out of the corruption of a poet. The friends of Samuel Johnson were already questioning the right of any man who could not compose a tragedy, to presume to criticize one, and the play reviewer had no sooner appeared than playwright, producer and spectator agreed in referring to him in terms of bottomless contempt. Nevertheless, the play reviewer persisted and flourished. He outgrew shame-faced anonymity; he became

[1]Reprinted from the 1943 *Theatre Annual* with permission of the author and that publication.

increasingly prosperous despite contempt, and on the newspapers of today he is not only one of the most highly paid members of the staff but also one of the comparatively few who are deliberately publicized by their employers. With the critic's enthusiastic consent, the dramatic editor working under him, devotes considerable space to the protests against, and the denunciations of, critics in general as well as of his critic in particular, which pour in from actors, playwrights, producers, and the public.

Various charges are perennially leveled against him. Nowadays he is seldom accused of being open to bribery, but he is periodically denounced as too blasé to recognize merit when he sees it, too frivolous to appreciate anything except light entertainment, and so anxious to show off that he gladly sacrifices fairness to epigram. Yet these charges, grave as they are, are not the most fundamental. A good play reviewer might, in theory at least, avoid all of them. Fundamentally, most protestors imply a doubt that there is any such thing as a good critic of plays. His trade, so it seems to them, involves a double impertinence. He tells his betters (the authors and the actors) what they should do and he tells his equals (the spectators) what they should like. Why, they unite in asking, should they stand for it? If critics do not like a certain play and a certain production why don't the critics write a better one and act in it themselves?

Yet it is these same people who enable the critic to continue to draw pay for his impertinence. The managers send him tickets. The spectators buy the papers in which his "worthless opinions" are set forth. After an opening night, most of those concerned with the new production sit up until dawn waiting for the first editions, and if the "worthless opinion" happens to be favorable, it reappears within a few hours in the form of a gigantic photographic enlargement outside the lobby of the theatre in which the play was produced. Even the law joins the curious conspiracy to encourage the critic in his arrogance by protecting his right to express commercially damaging opinions (which are demonstrably no more than opinions) despite the fact that any similar criticism of almost any other product offered for sale would bring a prompt and successful suit for damages.

As I understand it, the legal theory is, that when a producer sends the critics a free ticket he invites an opinion and thus forfeits any right to protest. From time to time exasperated producers have refused to send certain individual critics their usual tickets and have even attempted (unsuccessfully in recent years, though a test case is still before the courts) to refuse to sell them admissions. But so far as I am aware, no one has ever tried the really interesting experiment of bringing a suit for damages against a critic, who has bought rather than been given a ticket, based upon his expressed opinion which is commercially damaging but which cannot be supported by objectively verifiable facts.

Probably no responsible manager will ever make that experiment—for fear that it might be successful. No responsible manager, in other words, would really like to see the profession of drama critic abolished because, whatever his opinion of the competence of critics in general, he knows that once newspapers and magazines stopped taking it for granted that plays must be reviewed and news of the theatre presented, a considerable portion of the public would almost simultaneously stop taking it for granted that "sophisticated" people cannot continue to qualify as "sophisticated" unless they have seen and can discuss the latest theatrical productions. He knows, further, that as things now go, no inconsiderable part of his prosperity depends upon this general assumption that the theatre is part of sophisticated metropolitan life.

Thus, the paradox involved in the fact that constantly irritated managers continue to tolerate the critics may be resolved without any real defence of the critic himself. Even were he as impertinent and as incompetent as he is frequently held to be, he would still be useful to the theatrical entrepreneur. But the case of the general public is somewhat different. It obviously does not really resent the critic as unreservedly as it thinks that it does. Would it be possible, one wonders, to describe his function in terms acceptable to his audience?

One must begin by assuming that criticism, in the highest sense of the term, is bound to constitute, at best, only a small portion of all the writing which any professional critic publishes. If by such criticism we mean profound generalizations concerning works of permanent artistic value, then no man ever lived who was capable of producing it in sufficient quantity to earn himself a livelihood as a working journalist; and if such a hitherto unparalleled genius were to appear, he would not find in the course of the best theatrical seasons very many opportunities to exhibit his powers. If, even, within the limits of any drama critic's ability, he were to attempt to try each new offering by the highest artistic standards; if he were to resolve to view everything from the aspect of eternity; to call nothing good which was not absolutely so; then, masterpieces being rare as they are, it is obvious that he might pass his whole professional life without once deviating from an invariable judgment which would read "By the standards which Sophocles, Shakespeare and Molière have established—even by the standards set by Ibsen and Shaw—this play is a failure."

That he does nothing of the sort and that not one of his readers expects him to, is evidence enough that a tacit understanding exists. "Good," "bad," even "great," are used relatively. The reviewer means, and is understood to mean, "relative to the standards set by the prevailing level of the dramatic and theatrical art." If he is a good reviewer, he occasionally reminds his readers and himself that this tacit understanding does exist and he makes some attempt to estimate just how low or how high the assumed standards are; but this is the material for an occasional essay, not something which needs to be or could be repeated every time an interesting drama or an amusing comedy makes its appearance.

Discuss with any working drama critic his theory or his practice, and you will find him very soon making some distinction between the routine reviews and "my Sunday piece." That does not mean, usually at least, that he considers even this Sunday piece criticism for the ages, but it does mean that he takes pleasure in distinguishing between the perspective appropriate to a weekly as opposed to a daily judgment, and that he thinks of a review as something essentially different in its nature from even the informal critical essay.

To say this, however, is not to imply that reviewing is merely irresponsible criticism. The so-called drama critic is, most of the time, a reviewer rather than a critic; and it is only as a reviewer that he can, as a rule, usefully employ his talents, however great they may be. The real justification for his existence lies in a proper understanding of the nature of reviewing rather than in any consideration of criticism in the more exalted and formal sense. That a reviewer may occasionally write such criticism is beside the point. Others may write it also, and at best the professional reviewer will not and cannot write it often enough to make it the activity for which his magazine or newspaper pays him a living wage. But he can and often does make of reviewing a useful and difficult art with aims and principles of its own. And it is as reviewer that he finds a public large enough to give him his important place on the staff of the publication which employs him.

What, then, is good reviewing and what is the task to which a good reviewer sets himself? Extremists have sometimes maintained that good reviewing is merely good reporting. On occasion they have gone so far as to deny the reviewer the right to any opinions or judgments of his own and have urged him to limit himself to a detached account of what happens in the play plus a report on the reaction of the audience. That, of course, would be a preposterous program, but a new play *is* new, it *is* something which most of the reviewer's readers know nothing about when they begin to read his piece, and that fact, by making it necessary for him to be a reporter among other things, establishes immediately one of the fundamental differences between the good review and the good critical essay. The latter normally assumes that the reader is familiar with the work about to be criticized, that he is in possession of all the obvious facts, and that the critic's judgments or interpretations can begin at the level where he is aware of insights not assumed to be necessarily shared by every ordinarily competent reader. The reviewer, on the other hand, can assume nothing of the sort. He cannot pass a convincing judgment nor undertake any sort of criticism, properly so called, until he has given the reader a working equivalent of the experience which is to be interpreted and judged. In all, he will have a thousand, or fifteen hundred words at most, for his review and of these he will have available for any kind of criticism only those left over after he has told the reader what it is that he is criticizing.

Obviously the preliminary task is formidable. In a few hundred words the reviewer must manage to convey the effect of a play lasting two hours and a half. The reader will expect no less since he turns to the review first of all, not because he will accept without question the yes or no of the reviewer, but because he expects to judge for himself, on the basis of the account, whether or not the play is one which he wants to see. The reviewer can aim at no less, not only because he must give the reader what the reader expects, but also because, if the reader is to pass an intelligent judgment, he must be in possession of something which will take the place of a direct experience with the play being reviewed.

No mere summary of the plot or statement of the theme will do. A fair summary of *Hamlet* can, as Voltaire proved, make it seem like one of the most preposterous dramatic compositions ever offered any public. Not an account, but an equivalent, of the spectator's experience must be presented, and to do that the reviewer must practice, not reporting, but the art of re-creating in descriptive terms the effect of a narrative. That particular art is essentially the one used and abused by certain nineteenth-century writers who undertook to present "the adventures of the soul among the masterpieces." It has more recently fallen into disrepute as a method of criticism and has been described by T. S. Eliot, in his lofty way, as the result, not of a genuinely critical impulse, but of a "weak creative impulse." Perhaps Mr. Eliot is right. But however unacceptable as a method of criticism in the most exalted sense of the term, it is a *sine qua non* of really good reviewing since the reviewer, though not merely a reporter of the external circumstances of a new play and of its reception by the public, must nevertheless be first of all a reporter of aesthetic experiences. Insofar as every such experience is personal and not identical with the experience of any other spectator, the reporter is also an interpreter and a champion of the justness of his own reactions. But only insofar as he is convincing, only insofar as he succeeds in making the reader assume that he would have reacted in substantially the same manner, will the reviewer either be accepted as a guide or become capable of rendering significant any genuinely critical observations which he may finally get around to making.

No two reviewers go about the accomplishment of this very special and highly difficult task in the same way, but every first-class review is like every other in at least this one respect: every sentence contributes not only its obvious content but also something toward the creation of an atmosphere from which the mood of the reviewer and, by implication therefore, the effect of the play under discussion, is communicated to the reader. Once it has been decided how much or how little of the plot must be told (and that may vary from almost nothing) then that much must be recounted in such a way as to suggest, at the same time, its effectiveness or ineffectiveness, its logic or its lack of logic, its novelty or its staleness. And so with every other aspect of the whole which is reported—for what must always be given is not merely the fact but the effect of the fact. One must not recount a plot and then say that it is strong. One must manage somehow to make the strength apparent, and one must also do even more difficult things, especially since one's space is limited. One must catch and reflect in one's own manner the weightiness of the tragedy or the insouciance of the comedy. Since only if one does so, will the reader catch, as he must if the review is to be successful, his indirect glimpse of what the experience of witnessing that performance would be like. Thus it is only after he has, in these various indirect ways, been put into some sort of possession of the work itself that he can profit from any genuinely critical observations which the reviewer may have it in him to make.

An ideal review contains, then, at least three things, essentially distinct things, though ordinarily they are so mingled that the reader is hardly aware that they are distinct. Such a review is, first of all, a report of an item of news—such and such a play, by such and such an author, was first performed at a certain theatre with a certain cast and deals, tragically or comically or farcically, with certain situations. With this news report —this simple account—is mingled an impressionistic re-creation of the work itself, complete enough to entertain and to convince a reader. Complete enough, also, to make possible the final element, namely, a judgment based upon whatever genuinely critical convictions the reviewer may have revelant to the play under discussion.

Such a piece of writing, whether the genre which it constitutes be an important or an unimportant one, is obviously of a specialized sort. It constitutes a relatively new form and it has been to an extraordinary extent so taken for granted that it has seldom been analyzed or even recognized for the distinct thing which it is. Nearly every playgoer assumes that he would make a good reviewer, and of the dozens of young men who have consulted me concerning the possibility of entering the profession, not one has ever assumed that any special ability or experience was necessary or that his problem involved anything beyond the question of how one went about getting a job which anyone could fill and a great many people would like to have. Yet, as Max Beerbohm once remarked, "Theatrical reminiscence is the most terrible weapon in the armory of age," and there are few people who have not suffered that torture, which is usually the only result of the attempt on the part of most nonprofessionals, old or young, to tell their friends about the wonderful play they have just seen. A reviewer, whether he is a good critic or not, must at the very least find willing listeners while he discourses on a topic nearly everybody likes to talk about but almost nobody likes to hear discussed by his friends.

That the professional reviewer wields an enormous immediate and practical influence is plain enough from the growing tendency of managers to close, at once, any production which has received generally unfavorable notices. To what extent reviewers have influenced for good or ill the general development of playwriting during the last decade or so, it would be difficult to judge. Comparatively few have made themselves crusaders, as Shaw did in the Eighteen Nineties, and their influence has for the most part been hard to measure. None has evolved a *Hamburgische Dramaturgie* in the course of his reviewing; many have set an example of intelligent and enlightened commentary which has probably imperceptibly moulded the taste of the average theatregoer to a considerably greater extent than he is aware. And it ought to be remembered that the narrowly crusading critic, however important the function he may perform, is a bad reviewer—as Shaw frankly admitted of himself in the preface to his *Dramatic Opinions and Essays.*

I prefer to rest the defence of my colleagues and of myself on our practice of the art of reviewing as I have attempted to describe that art. I doubt that we have actually done much to assist our leading playwrights to find themselves. On the other hand, our record has, I think, been pretty good so far as our ability to recognize and applaud important talents as they have appeared is concerned. And by giving the theatregoing public reviews which it found interesting, I think we have probably helped to find an audience for those playwrights whom we have not called into being and probably not greatly aided in the solution of their own artistic problems.

A View of Some Professional Critics

Henrik Ibsen's social problem plays were not received kindly when they first appeared. *The Doll's House* first appeared in its original form in this country in 1891. (An earlier version with a happy ending had been done by Helen Modjeska.) In 1894 *Ghosts* was presented in the Garden Theatre in New York, unleashing a torrent of abuse. William Winter, one of the leading critics, reported on the production. His criticism, which follows, is typical.

The Wallet of Time

WILLIAM WINTER[2]

Moral obliquity and mental failure, sequent on inherited physical disease, resulting from sexual vice, is the subject of that play, and platitudinous gabble is the form. A youth, by name Oswald Alving, who has inherited a permeative taint from his profligate father, deceased, and whose condition is verging toward some unrecognizable form of mania, is shown as a suitor of his half-sister, a vulgar beauty named Regina, putatively the child of a drunken carpenter, actually the offspring of Alving's blackguard sire and a female servant. The devoted, widowed mother of that youth is shown as the long-suffering victim of precedent years of horror and of the circumstances thus indicated, and, incidentally, as the renounced idol of a clerical ass, named Manders—with whom, however, she signifies her willingness to cohabit. The climax of this noxious postulate is the collapse of young Alving under his mysterious disease, and his afflicted mother's removal of him from this vale of suffering by means of a poisonous dose of morphine. This revolting fabric is tendered for public approval as being freighted with a "lesson," and it has been accepted and extolled as though it were new—notwithstanding the fact that centuries before the Prophet of Corruption emerged in Christiania it was recognized and recorded that the sins of the father are visited on the children, and that the human heart is deceitful and desperately wicked.

Objection to this choice gem of decadence has subjected the objectors to much contumely. Its admirers announce it as "tragic" and "terrific." It is, in fact, an indefensible and shameful vagary of a diseased fancy. Objection to it cannot be invalidated, because that objection rests on incontestable grounds. Conduct consequent on disease may be, incidentally, admissible as an expedient in drama—as much so, for example, as conduct resultant on a broken leg. But exposition of loathsome disease

[2]William Winter, *The Wallet of Time* (New York, 1913) Moffat, Yardin & Co., II, 567–71.

resultant from sexual immorality is not a proper subject for theatrical display. Furthermore, Ibsen's presentment of it is not dramatic but didactic, and it is prolix and drearily barren. And, finally, his treatment of the subject is distorted, radically false, and misleading, imparting no reliable information, but, in its totality of effect, befouling the mind, dejecting the spirit, and doing no sort of good. Thus it lacks even the scant justification of being a sound, scientific clinical treatise. For those reasons the work is radically immoral.

The apostles of Ibsenism are continually blarting about "truth" and "frankness." They ought, accordingly, to be favored with both. No reasonable person doubts or denies the existence of frightful "social diseases." It has long been recognized that those diseases work incalculable harm, blast thousands of lives, cause suffering, death, and, worse than death, madness; worst of all, that their consequences often fall heaviest upon unsuspecting, helpless innocence. No one disputes the need of extirpating them. The day will come, and it will not now be long in coming, when authentic information about them will be widely disseminated, through proper channels and in a wise manner, among all classes, and when individual cooperation will do much to eradicate the social injuries fluent from them. Meantime such subjects as are treated in *Ghosts* are peculiarly unfit for "discussion," of any kind, before the miscellaneous theatrical audience of both sexes, all ages, and widely varying degrees of intelligence.

The Ibsen drama seldom affords opportunity for acting—a chief reason being that most of the characters in it are so radically false to nature, so entirely arbitrary creations of the author's perverse and morbid fancy, that they cannot be impersonated. The interlocutors walk in and talk till they are tired, telling each other what, generally, they already know, and then walk out; and presently they come back and talk some more. Persons accustomed to the stage can readily perform such tasks. Miss Mary Shaw, who is the chief performer on our stage of Mrs. Alving, in this obnoxious piece, has long been known as an actress of distinct but not exceptional talent and of much vigor.[3] In that part she displayed the proficiency and repose of an old actress; the ability to murmur softly, to make a good simulation of middle-aged maternal tenderness, deftly to employ the stare of abject misery, and to speak scorn with a nice inflection. Indeed, Miss Shaw did more with such a word as "pitiful" than ever the sonorous parson did with "Mesopotamia"—but no admirer of talent could fail to grieve at seeing a woman so clever engaged in a work so noxious and so absurd. From the beginning of her activity as a

[3]Winter had just seen Mary Shaw's revival of *Ghosts*, produced at the Manhattan Theatre, January 26, 1903. The audience was composed, he contemptuously notes, of "a small and sad assemblage, chiefly female."

theatrical mentor of society, Miss Shaw has shown signs of taking a more serious view of herself than anybody else ever has taken or ever will take. Her purpose in producing Ibsen's *Ghosts* according to her published proclamation on the subject (so eminently coherent and rational, insofar as common sense can appreciate and weigh it), was "to educate the public palate up to an appreciation of mankind's real inconsistency," and to make the drama "an engrossing form of instruction in the vital truths of life"—those vital truths being that "the world is a sordid, narrow-minded, pinchbeck little world"; that society wears "a grinning mask" to cover a state of seething corruption; that the weakness of humanity was never, till the arrival of Miss Shaw, fully comprehended; that under the surface of things there are "awful facts," and that "truth," when "naked" (as, of course, it never is and never has been, except in the plays of Ibsen), is "a horrible, distorted Hyde, which reflects perfectly the immutable course of nature." Such a purpose of instructive benevolence—so sane, so original, so suitable to the theatre, and so likely, when prosperous, to diffuse so much comfort—could only be viewed with the homage of grateful acceptance.

Brooks Atkinson wrote of a more recent production of *Ghosts* in *The New York Times.*

At the Theatre

BROOKS ATKINSON[4]

Let's consider that Eva Le Gallienne has done her duty by Ibsen's drama about duty. She plays the leading character in *Ghosts* as intelligently as Ibsen wrote the part. With the assistance of Margaret Webster, who directed the performance, she has mounted the play respectfully at the Cort, where it opened last evening. But nearly seventy years have slipped away since *Ghosts* shocked and outraged respectable people in Europe, although the British were not shocked and enraged until a little later. For critical judgments worse than those you are getting today, see the collection of noisome abuse William Archer put together and Shaw included in *The Quintessence of Ibsenism.*

Since *Ghosts* is planned and written by a master craftsman of the old school, it can still be made exciting by great acting or by a novel point of view. Nazimova gave it size and the aura of malevolence in her revival in 1935. Long ago Mrs. Fiske, overburdened with mischief, made a comedy out of it, which was obviously incorrect, though rather ingratiating.

Miss Le Gallienne is an honest actress with a lucid style. She knows Ibsen as thoroughly as she knows Chekhov, and the Mrs. Alving she plays is no doubt Ibsen's character. But his ponderous assault upon duty seems more like history now than a criticism of life. With the help of Shaw a couple of decades later Ibsen won that revolution. No one has ever done anything from a sense of duty since Ibsen and Shaw destroyed middle-class culture.

As the chief prioress of intelligence in our theatre, Miss Le Gallienne gives us a liberated Mrs. Alving, who is no longer humbugged by polite superstitions. Working in a small compass, as becomes her, she makes a

[4]Brooks Atkinson, *The New York Times*, February 18, 1948.

carefully wrought design out of the character. A nod, a gleam, a fleeting gesture, a hurried step or two, a limp manner of sitting on the divan while the parson roars virtuous bombast—she designs a full-length character out of these and other bits of eloquence. She also speaks uncommonly well. But for a play that needs so much drive and strength to compensate for hardened arteries, Miss Le Gallienne's performance is weak. She leaves it well inside the grounds of the old folks' home.

And isn't the pace unnecessarily torpid? Everything else about the performance seems excellent. Alfred Ryder does a particularly good job with young Oswald, describing the whole progress of the character from filial affability through mounting terror to madness. As the pious stuffed shirt, Herbert Berghof gives a forceful performance that catches the sanctimonious stupidity of the part. Jean Hagen's scheming servant girl is well played also—the commonness harshly breaking out of the demure reserve in the last scene. And Robert Emhardt's obsequious knavery is amusing.

In designing and lighting the setting, Watson Barratt has achieved complete illusion without crowding the stage with manufacturing and construction. His nineteenth-century drawingroom, stuffy without being dull, is one of his best pieces of work. There is a lot of good work in this revival of *Ghosts*. But it does not conjure the dullness out of the script. Respectability can be as pernicious as duty. After a violent birth in 1881, *Ghosts* is respectable now.

At the Theatre

BROOKS ATKINSON[5]

Arthur Miller has written a superb drama. From every point of view *Death of a Salesman,* which was acted at the Morosco last evening, is rich and memorable drama. It is so simple in style and so inevitable in theme that it scarcely seems like a thing that has been written and acted. For Mr. Miller has looked with compassion into the hearts of some ordinary Americans and quietly transferred their hope and anguish to the theatre. Under Elia Kazan's masterly direction, Lee J. Cobb gives a heroic performance, and every member of the cast plays like a person inspired.

Two seasons ago Mr. Miller's *All My Sons* looked like the work of an honest and able playwright. In comparison with the new drama, that seems like a contrived play now. For *Death of a Salesman* has the flow and spontaneity of a suburban epic that may not be intended as poetry but becomes poetry in spite of itself because Mr. Miller has drawn it out of so many intangible sources.

It is the story of an aging salesman who has reached the end of his usefulness on the road. There has always been something unsubstantial about his work. But suddenly the unsubstantial aspects of it overwhelm him completely. When he was young, he looked dashing; he enjoyed the comradeship of other people—the humor, the kidding, the business.

In his early sixties he knows his business as well as he ever did. But the unsubstantial things have become decisive; the spring has gone from his step, the smile from his face, and the heartiness from his personality. He is through. The phantom of his life has caught up with him. As literally as Mr. Miller can say it, dust returns to dust. Suddenly there is nothing.

This is only a little of what Mr. Miller is saying. For he conveys this elusive tragedy in terms of simple things—the loyalty and understanding

[5]Brooks Atkinson, *The New York Times,* February 11, 1949.

of his wife, the careless selfishness of his two sons, the sympathetic devotion of a neighbor, the coldness of his former boss's son—the bills, the car, the tinkering around the house. And most of all: the illusions by which he has lived—opportunities missed, wrong formulas for success, fatal misconceptions about his place in the scheme of things.

Writing like a man who understands people, Mr. Miller has no moral precepts to offer and no solutions of the salesman's problems. He is full of pity, but he brings no piety to it. Chronicler of one frowzy corner of the American scene, he evokes a wraithlike tragedy out of it that spins through the many scenes of his play and gradually envelops the audience.

As theatre *Death of a Salesman* is no less original than it is as literature. Jo Mielziner, always equal to an occasion, has designed a skeletonized set that captures the mood of the play and serves the actors brilliantly. Although Mr. Miller's text may be diffuse in form, Mr. Kazan has pulled it together into a deeply moving performance.

Mr. Cobb's tragic portrait of the defeated salesman is acting of the first rank. Although it is familiar and folksy in the details, it has something of the grand manner in the big size and the deep tone. Mildred Dunnock gives the performance of her career as the wife and mother—plain of speech but indomitable in spirit. The parts of the thoughtless sons are extremely well played by Arthur Kennedy and Cameron Mitchell, who are all youth, brag, and bewilderment.

Other parts are well played by Howard Smith, Thomas Chalmers, Don Keefer, Alan Hewitt, and Tom Pedi. If there were time, this report would gratefully include all the actors and fabricators of illusion. For they all realize that for once in their lives they are participating in a rare event in the theatre. Mr. Miller's elegy in a Brooklyn sidestreet is superb.

Lunt, Fontanne Open
"Their" Playhouse

BROOKS ATKINSON[6]

After squandering their time on polite trivialities for a number of years, Alfred Lunt and Lynn Fontanne are appearing in a devastating drama, *The Visit*, which opened, appropriately enough, at the Lunt-Fontanne Theatre Monday evening.

Whether *The Visit* suits them or they suit *The Visit* is beside the point. For when Friedrich Duerrenmatt, the author, gets seriously down to work in the savage last act, our two most gifted comic actors look like our most gifted dramatic actors. Under Peter Brook's ingenious direction, they give an unforgettable performance.

When the curtain goes up *The Visit* promises to be an amusing European drama. When the author states his premise, it seems to be settling down into a sort of Ionesco satire. The point is this: Güllen, a poverty-stricken European town, is about to welcome its richest émigré —Claire Zachanassian. Everyone hopes that she will generously endow Güllen.

She proposes to give Güllen one billion marks on one condition: that they murder their fellow townsman, Anton Schill. When she was a girl in Güllen he had seduced her and also denied the paternity of their child. All she asks now is justice.

The proposal is so fantastic that everyone rejects it, and the audience shares the attitude of the people of Güllen. But not Herr Duerrenmatt. He means it, both as an observer of life and as a dramatic craftsman. For the second half of *The Visit* consists in a slow, macabre pressing on to a ghoulish climax. Everything has its price. Put the price high enough and society can find a way to make murder moral. Village democracy finally demands the death of Anton Schill, since village democracy is concerned with the good of the greatest number of people.

If Maurice Valency's adaptation is a faithful interpretation of the

[6]Brooks Atkinson, *The New York Times*, May 7, 1958.

German original, Herr Duerrenmatt is a sufficiently powerful dramatist to make an unpalatable theme acceptable. He writes with wit and humor when he is setting his snares. But he writes with cold fury when he gets to the core of his theme. The slow disintegration of character, the hypocritical turning on Anton Schill by his neighbors, the community malevolence of the town meeting when the awful vote is taken—are written with a calculated cruelty that proves Herr Duerrenmatt's cruel theme.

Production and performance are superb. Teo Otto has designed a skeletonized series of settings that carry the play forward swiftly; and Paul Morrison has lighted the production vividly. The cast is long and uniformly excellent. As the village burgomaster, Eric Porter gives a remarkably effective performance, his bluff good humor drifting off into sanctimonious evil at the end. As the village schoolmaster, Peter Woodthorpe is also admirable, tracing the corruption of a good man into a traitor with sensitivity and a dash of pity.

But the triumph of the evening is the acting of our two most illustrious drawingroom comedians in the harshest roles they have played in a quarter of a century. As Anton Schill, Mr. Lunt plays a haggard, futile provincial who begins the drama in a gay mood and finishes it as a corpse. Mr. Lunt manages to invest a crumpled part with dignity and character.

As the wealthy, worldly Claire Zachanassian, Miss Fontanne has a part that more closely resembles those she has latterly been playing. She is as glamorous as ever, slow, undulating and artful. But there is hardness in the center of the character; although the manners are casual, the desire for revenge is terrifying. Miss Fontanne portrays the whole character with great insight and implacable force.

The Lunt-Fontanne Theatre, which also opened Monday evening, is the daintiest and most luxurious in town. It must have been shocked by the play it found on the stage when the gorgeous curtain rolled up. But it must have been proud of the actors whose name it bears. They are devoting their genius to a bold, grisly drama of negativism and genius is what they have.

Theater: A.P.A. Stages
Pirandello's 'Right You Are'

WALKER KERR[7]

There are no second-rate performances in *Right You Are* but there are two performances so far above the ordinary that to call them first-rate would be downright stingy.

Donald Moffat and Helen Hayes are the players doing the work in question, and to watch them take center stage at the Lyceum is like stepping into a cool, serene garden after a day of hard work. We are soothed and exhilarated in the same deep breath.

Not that both are playing serenely. One is, one isn't. Mr. Moffat is the truly composed figure of the play, a benign gentleman who has obviously spent time in the lap of the gods and has never felt the slightest dis-composure since. For he has decided to accept life precisely as it is—which is to say indecipherable.

Smiling at mystery and embracing every form of madness as just so much more sanity, the actor plainly relishes his role as stand-in for Pirandello. In this particular artifice Pirandello has posed for a neighbor-hood—and for all the rest of us—one of his knottier small questions. Is the elderly lady who has moved in downstairs quite out of her mind in thinking her daughter alive? Or is the daughter's ravaged husband dream-ing in thinking her dead? Or, perhaps, is there no daughter at all, just a phantom slipping in and out of two heads from time to time, now dead, now alive, always elusive?

Mr. Moffat, curled up catlike and contented and with just a bit of brandy for company, listens most attentively as a half-dozen busybodies furiously pursue the "truth." But you watch him, waiting for him to spring, and when he does spring you know that the leap will be sheer pleasure. For he is quite past caring what "truth" may turn out to be, having swallowed down so many truths that he knows their taste is

---

[7]Walter Kerr, *The New York Times*, November 24, 1966.

single. What he has now is appetite, relish for all flavors, and he smacks his lips for joy when two accounts of the same affair cancel each other out.

Gracefully embracing each new contradiction as it comes from the mouths of eyewitnesses, he puts the shadow dance through its paces like a wry and witty ringmaster, facing down the human menagerie with charm, good cheer and unruffled resignation.

Miss Hayes, as the newcomer to the neighborhood who may be deluded or who may be precisely what she claims to be, achieves her control in another way. Badgered as she is by too many amateur detectives, made the center of the puzzle when she wishes only to be left in peace, she must fight for self-assurance, find her poise through fiercely clenched fingers.

The double effect is immaculately achieved. Like a trapped bird behaving cautiously in a jungle of snares, she lifts her chin firmly listens with her ears but not her eyes, and dominates every inquisition with a conviction that is as stern as silence.

Every now and again she permits a whisper of panic to slip out. Beating her breast without raising her voice, she lets anguish roam the room, though on a leash. Suddenly impersonating the man who disbelieves in her daughter, she can make his terror real, too, for the moment. Perhaps no one in our theater can make bared teeth flash so imperceptibly, so fleetingly, as Miss Hayes can, revealing what is hidden and hiding what had best be kept quiet. Between a fire that is raging inside, and a firm refusal to display it fully, lies the peculiar and magically satisfying tension of the actress's work.

A close third in the company that the Association of Producing Artists has assembled is Sydney Walker, husband of the ghost who haunts them all. Mr. Walker has broadened his effects a bit since the play was performed at the Phoenix several seasons ago; his perspiration is more real, less suggestive. But in his quick, rattled cough, and in the kneaded handkerchief he grips in one fist, there is still a teasing power to lure us along.

In all other ways the production that Stephen Porter has directed is now richer in detail, quicker to suggest the confusing buzz and hum of the human spirit's baffling contrariness. *Right You Are*, as a conceit, still seems to me less than perfect Pirandello; it presses its argument too literally at times, burdening us occasionally with a concrete world that will not easily dissolve into illusion. It is a fascinating parlor game of Lies and No Consequences nonetheless, and we must continue to bow before the prophetic insights of the man who best anticipated the mid-twentieth century's state of mind.

Particularly helpful in sustaining the now-you-see-it-oh-no-you-didn't air of turning the familiar world inside out are Keene Curtis as a fellow who simply can't be quieted until he has facts tucked safely in his pocket, Richard Woods as a splendidly obtuse investigator, Anita Dangler as a gypsylike snoop who stomps out her opinions with her feet, and Gordon Gould as a thoroughly relaxed diplomat who seems to have been modeled in wax. James Tilton's single setting—with three receding draped arches to suggest that we are all nearing the vanishing point—is as handsome as it is appropriate.

In short, you can't go wrong on *Right You Are*. It's being played in repertory, and before you pay it a visit you'd best check the company's calendar.

Philadelphia,
Here I Come!

WALTER KERR[8]

As the season has progressed—that is surely the wrong word for what has been happening to the season—I have come to feel less and less like a reviewer and more and more like a common scold. You may be as relieved as I am to know that this morning the sun shines brighter.

Producer David Merrick has gone window-shopping in Dublin and brought us back a fine new play. *Philadelphia, Here I Come!* is a funny play, a prickly play, finally a most affecting play, and the pleasure it gives is of a most peculiar kind. Author Brian Friel has set all of his cranky, fond, and obstinately shy people to searching for the one word that is everlastingly on the tip of everyman's tongue, and everlastingly not spoken. He has written a play about an ache, and he has written it so simply and so honestly that the ache itself becomes a warming-fire.

It has taken craft as well as truthfulness to do the trick. Hero Patrick Bedford is a man with a misbegotten past, a yearning present, and a dubious future. He has failed to speak in time for the girl he loved. He cannot prod the father he shares his meals with to so much as ask if he happens to be tired of an evening. He is leaving the tiny town of Bally-beg to fly on a shiny jet to a possibly shinier America, but he already knows the American Irish he will share life with there. They have, for all their ceaseless chirping about ground-floor apartments and the latest in air-conditioning, less to say than the folk at home. "It's the silence that is the enemy," our hero cries as he stands between two worlds knowing that he can enter neither.

But it is not Mr. Bedford who sounds the cry. In order to make his baffled man articulate, author Friel has given him an alter ego to slip about the stage with him, now in lockstep, now dancing away in spite, mocking his every thought and pouring out all of the invective and all

[8]Walter Kerr, *The New York Herald Tribune*, February 17, 1966.

of the imprisoned love that chokes him dry. Donal Donnelly plays this second presence and plays him as fetchingly, as elusively, quite as brilliantly as the playwright has written him. Mr. Donnelly is no mere Voice of Conscience to his strangled master; there is no trace here, you will be happy to know, of the woodenness O'Neill imposed upon his split central figure in *Days Without End.* Instead we are listening to the skipping, sassy, candid, tormenting back-talk all of us give ourselves when we know we are behaving like the chuckleheads we are, listening to the running argument we keep up with ourselves every furious, fumbled day of our lives.

Mr. Donnelly sings half of the songs Mr. Bedford is trying to cheer himself up with, supplying a taunt in the lyrics and a rippling irony in the rhythms. He can chant "Bless This House" through his teeth, do a devastating fashion-commentator's report on an old man's undressing habits, clutch his elbows with glee at the futility of trying to provoke a new thought out of a neighbor's arthritic mind. With the effrontery of Donald Duck, he quacks the whole world back into the bog.

But the play is no wake for all of the solitary souls in the universe. For it has enough of the habit of poetry in it to slip inside solitariness and find the gentle fire, the suppressed fire, that is there. Playwright Friel can turn a scene inside out, without warning, and supply glancingly the moving truth you hadn't counted on.

A trio of old pals come, rather reluctantly, to see the emigrant off. Hearing them prate about their nonexistent sexual prowesses and remember ravishing moonlit evenings on the beach, the twin hero knows them—and hates them—for the clods they have become. "The boys— they weren't always like this, were they?" he anguishes to himself. Before the scene is done one clod has made the one gesture that could transform the lie into glowing light. A drunken schoolmaster brings warm wishes and a request for a loan never to be repaid; but the fraud in him is also a friend. An aunt from America, with the jaw of a petulant pekinese, becomes—in her cups—a cascade of shattering vulgarity. But the aunt has a transparent skin, too, and cannot completely conceal the wounds that have made her the blathering trash she is.

Lights go on and off within the breathing, blustering, edgy moments that follow one another. Behind the glare there is shadow, and the players at the Helen Hayes are able to find the imperceptibly shifting colors of both. Eamon Kelly, as the father, has only to lean back on his chair and raise his head slightly to let you see the quality of a man who cannot be drawn out. Mairin D. O'Sullivan as a crone hoping a new child will be named for her, Lanna Saunders as a girl who couldn't love a man into declaring himself, Mavis Villiers as the Philadelphia-adapted aunt and Eamon Morrissey as a dense and redheaded spiritual stand-in for

Stan Laurel are all excellent under Hilton Edward's perceptively modulated stage direction.

The kitchen setting is standard, as though the Abbey had never torn it down. The mood is rueful, dissipating itself only very slightly in the last act; perhaps it is closest in intention and feeling to the final sequences of *Our Town*. The speech is plain, decently earthy, holding its quiet sentiment close. The play is without pretense and it never cheats, doing exactly what it means to do very simply and very well.

Homecoming
Unfathomable

NORMAN NADEL[9]

The peculiar merit of *The Homecoming*—and perhaps this applies in varying degrees to all of Harold Pinter's plays—is that it exists only on the stage. In other words, it has nothing in common with the short story, novel poetry, reporting, or philosophical discourse. To approach it on the printed page is to miss its strange aura altogether. And it certainly has no counterpart in life. Many other plays can be read, measured against life, or transposed to other literary forms, but not *The Homecoming*.

So if this quality of uniqueness, of immutability, is to be counted a virtue, then this must be interpreted as praise for the fascinating but unfathomable comedy that arrived last night at The Music Box, following a long run in Pinter's native England.

Peter Hall's direction and the performances by six members of the Royal Shakespeare Company appear to be as firmly welded to the spirit and atmosphere of the play as the dialogue itself. The combination of distinctive and incredibly deft actors in six utterly unpredictable roles is enough to give the evening a stinging and special quality.

This doesn't mean that everybody is going to enjoy *The Homecoming*. On the contrary, I suspect its greatest appeal will be to the adventurers among theatergoers, and of them, only those with a taste for enigmas. Many people will be outraged at having been "put on," or exasperated by Pinter's blithe abandonment of either logic or reality. Even those of us who found last night's experience stimulating had to wait patiently through maddeningly deliberate conversations that descended into tedium.

As part of its studied illogic, John Bury has designed a London sitting room about sixty feet wide, that looks like the lobby of an ancient, decrepit hotel. The furniture sits about like malevolent prehistoric beasts,

[9]Norman Nadel, *World Journal Tribune*, January 6, 1967. Reprinted by permission of the author.

while a massive horror of a floor lamp stares at the action. In its dimensions, its décor and its sepulchral atmosphere, it is a nightmare room, which is as it should be, because this is a nightmare play.

Paul Rogers is Max, the father—old and still oozing the black hatred that apparently goes back to his infancy. He remembers despising his father for dandling him on his knee and tossing him lovingly into the air.

Even when he speaks affectionately of his late wife, his speech is vicious: "She wasn't such a bad woman, even if it made me sick to look at her ugly, stinking face." This is one of the more refined and lyric of his several hundred comments during the evening. He is a tyrant and a monster of a senior citizen.

Son Lenny (Ian Holm) at first seems merely nasty, but he has unlimited reserves of covetousness, viciousness, and slyness, all revealed as we get to know him. Joey (Terence Rigby), the second of Max's sons, is a thick-talking beast of a boxer who doesn't know how to defend himself or to attack, according to his contemptuous old father.

The only decent member of this household is mild-mannered Uncle Sam (John Normington), a chauffeur who drives satisfied customers about in a Humber Super-Snipe but comes home to endure unbelievable vituperation from his brother.

It is into this "home" (how alien the word seems) that the third son, Teddy (Michael Craig), brings his wife, Ruth (Vivien Merchant—Mrs. Pinter in private life). He is a Ph.D. teaching at a university in America.

For only a little while you think that these two will be the reasonable, the sensible ones. They're both attractive. Craig is distinguished and poised. Miss Merchant moves with a grace both feline and ladylike, which somehow gives off overtones of sexuality. But they appear wholly proper.

We begin to see that they belong in this weird situation when a small argument about going to bed is turned around and repeated—he saying her words and she his. This, however, barely hints at the unconventionalities to come. Before the evening is spent she is involved in love-play with the thick-witted brother, while the husband and the others watch (it later continues for two hours more privately upstairs). And she blandly considers a proposal that she go into prostitution there, rather than go home to her children, meanwhile making herself available to all of the family except one who has dropped dead, understandably enough.

Throughout, speeches hang in space like furniture that floats a few inches off the ground; it is dehumanized conversation, even in its most sex-saturated passages.

Punctuating this eerie dialogue are monolithic silences, a Pinter characteristic. Nothing seems to have roots, and you suspect that the great, grim room itself exists somewhere in a glowering void.

The humor of *The Homecoming* is dark, biting, and unexpected. There surely hasn't been a more unconventional approach to comedy in a long time.

Bibliography

For Supplementary Reading or Special Projects

Atkinson, Brooks, *Broadway Scrapbook*. New York: Theatre Arts, Inc., 1947.

Brown, Kenneth H., *The Brig*. New York: Hill and Wang, 1965.

Ewen, David, *Complete Book of the American Musical Theatre* (revised). New York: Holt, Rinehart & Winston, Inc., 1959.

Gibson, William, *The Seesaw Log: A Chronicle of the Stage Production with Text*. New York: Alfred A. Knopf, Inc., 1959.

Gottfried, Martin, *A Theatre Divided*. Boston: Little, Brown and Company, 1966.

Kirby, Michael. *Happenings*. New York: E. P. Dutton & Co., Inc., 1966.

Marowitz, Tom Mine, *The Encore Reader*. New York: D. B. S. Publications, 1965.

Oppenheimer, George, *The Passionate Playgoer*. New York: The Viking Press, Inc., 1958.

Smith, Cecil, *Musical Comedy in America*. New York: Theatre Arts Books, 1950.

Van Itallie, Jean-Claude, *America Hurrah*. New York: Coward-McCann, Inc., 1967.

Young, Stark, *Immortal Shadows*. New York: Charles Scribner's Sons, 1948.

V

Appendix

Glossary
of Theatre
Terms

Most of the following terms are frequently used in discussions involving the theatre. A knowledge of their meaning is essential. Generally, those which were defined or discussed in the text have not been included here.

Abstract set ... Drapes, single units of doors or windows arranged for music or ballet numbers. No effort at realism or locale. Common in television.

Absurd, theatre of the ... Contrary to most schools of thought that there is meaning of some kind in life, the avant-garde of the fifties saw living as illogical, irrational, unreasonable, formless, and a mass of contradictions. In France where absurdism had its greatest strength, Eugene Ionesco, Samuel Beckett, and Jean Gênet were the leaders. In England N. F. Simpson and Harold Pinter, and in America Edward Albee, Arthur Kopit, and Jack Gelber were part of the movement.

Actors' Equity Association ... Union of professional legitimate theatre actors with headquarters in New York City.

Ad lib ... Generally, improvised or added words and gestures that are not written in the script or rehearsed.

Angel ... Individual who furnishes financial backing for a production, but whose name rarely appears in connection with it.

311

A.N.T.A. . . . American National Theatre and Academy. Congressionally chartered organization for serving the theatre in all its branches. Supplies advice and various services. Offices in New York City.

Annie Oakley . . . A pass or complimentary ticket to the theatre, so called because of the habit of punching holes in such a ticket before rubber stamp days.

Antagonist . . . The character most in opposition to main character (protagonist) of the play.

Antoinette Perry Awards . . . "Tonies," awarded each season for outstanding work in writing, acting, and design in the New York theatre. An award in honor of Antoinette Perry, actress and director.

Apron . . . Space on stage in front of main curtain; very wide in Restoration and eighteenth century. Much of the play took place here. (See "Forestage.")

Arena stage . . . A form of center staging with audience on three or four sides. (See "Theatre-in-the-round" and "Penthouse theatre.")

Arras setting . . . Half circle of neutral draperies that serve as formal background for the stage. (See "Cyclorama.")

Artistic failure . . . Play that may have artistic qualities but has received poor notices and is a failure at the box office.

Aside . . . Words spoken by the actor in a lower tone. The audience is supposed to hear them, but not the other characters of the play.

Backdrop . . . Large flat surface at rear of stage, painted to suggest locale and used with wings in seventeenth, eighteenth, and nineteenth centuries. In present-day theatre usually represents sky. (See "Sky-drop")

Backing . . . A series of flats or drops placed behind doors and windows to mask backstage area. Also used to denote money that helps to produce a play. (See "Angel.")

Backstage . . . The entire area behind the proscenium arch, but normally during the action of the play that area which is not seen by the audience.

Bit part . . . Very small role, described by one actor as "two speeches and a spit."

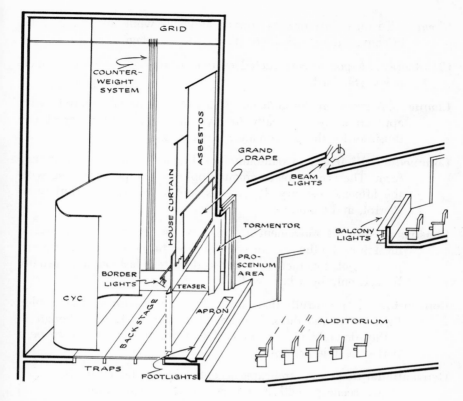

Blackout ... A sudden extinguishing of the lights on the stage, usually at end of act. Used mostly for skits, short acts in a variety show.

Blooper ... Error by some member of cast or crew.

Border ... A short curtain hung above the stage to mask the flies when a ceiling piece is not being used.

Borderlights ... A series of lights above and at front of stage to light the acting area with general illumination.

Box set ... Standard setting of today with back wall, two side walls, and usually a ceiling to represent the interior of a room.

Broad comedy ... Slapstick bordering on farce or burlesque. Overdone for sake of contemporary "groundlings," (q.v.) and lacking subtlety.

Burlesque ... Character traits, stage business, or movement, so exaggerated that the sense of reality or its illusion are destroyed. Emphasizes humor.

Cheat...To turn body or play toward audience while appearing to be in conversation with other players on the stage.

Clambake...A poorly constructed or rehearsed program that is much below standard.

Claque...A group in the audience (friends or, especially, hired) who applaud or react vocally to give the impression of great enthusiasm for the performance or an actor.

Commedia dell' arte...A pantomime or drama without any set literary form. The theatre of common people in Europe beginning with the fifteenth century. It gave us such characters as Harlequin, Pierrot, and Columbine.

Constructivism...A movement in Russia whose proponents objected to illusion in the theatre, for scenery substituting ladders, platforms, planes put together in a most distorted fashion and usually backed only by a bare wall.

Convention...An untruth that the public accepts—for example: blue light for moonlight and yellow light for sunlight, although in reality daylight is more blue. Something that has come to be a part of a style or form.

Conventional theatre...Indicates accepted theatre building with raised stage, scenery, lights, and proscenium, with auditorium and audience out front as we know it.

Create a role...To perform a role in the very first production of a script.

Critic's Circle...A group composed of first-line New York critics for newspapers and magazines (about twenty) who by secret ballot award prizes to best American and foreign play and musical each spring.

Cue...The final words, business, or movement of one character before another begins his own.

Cut...To delete a line or omit certain business.

Cyclorama or "cyc"...Curtain or canvas usually hung in half-circle to cover back and sides of stage. May represent blue of sky or be plain drape setting. (See "Arras setting.")

Décor...Furnishings, properties, drapers, and decorations of setting. (See *Inscenierung.*)

Denouement ... The moment when the last suspense is eliminated. —Literal translation of the French "untying of the last knot." Usually comes with or after climax and before conclusion.

"Deus ex machina" ... See "God from the machine."

Downstage ... The part of the stage nearest the audience.

Dramatic action ... Term used to describe the action that takes place within the play—Oedipus' search for the slayer of Laius—Hamlet's search to discover if the ghost has spoken the truth, then his efforts to right the wrong. What happens in the play to the characters beyond physical action.

Dramatic time ... The period that elapses in the action of a script. (See "Physical time.")

Dressing the house ... Scattering the audience by leaving pairs or more of seats empty to give impression of a larger attendance.

Drop ... The name given the curtains that are hung from the flies.

Emmy ... Television award given annually. (See "Oscar.")

Epic drama ... The work of Bertolt Brecht (1898–1956) Brecht called all drama before his own "Aristotelian" and described it as aiming to enthrall the audience by building to a climax—arousing and then purging their emotions. His drama sought to arouse the spectator's *thoughts* as it strove to prevent emotional involvement. It was made up of short and disconnected scenes, the emphasis on society rather than the individual.

Flat ... A piece of scenery composed of muslin, canvas, or linen stretched over a wooden frame. Used for walls or backing of a set.

Flies ... The whole area above stage back of the proscenium where borders, drops, and small pieces of scenery are hung.

Floor plan ... A bird's-eye view from above with walls, entrances, and furniture all shown in proper place.

Fluffed line ... A stammer, stutter, twisting of words, or other faulty delivery by the actor.

Fly ... To raise scenery above the floor of the stage by use of ropes, battens, etc.

Fly catching . . . Movement, business, or sound made by an actor to attract attention to himself when emphasis should be elsewhere.

Forestage . . . Part of stage nearest audience when an inner proscenium is used. Sometimes used interchangeably with "apron."

47 Workshop . . . Playwriting course originally at Harvard and later at Yale under George Pierce Baker from which many leading playwrights of the twentieth century emerged.

Fourth wall . . . An imaginary wall at the proscenium through which the audience sees the play.

Freeze . . . To stand completely still as if for a picture.

George Spelvin . . . Name often used by an actor for the second or lesser role he is playing. This alias is generally thought to have been used first in 1907 in Winchell Smith and Frederic Thompson's play, *Brewster's Millions*. An actor chose the name for his second role. The critics praised "George Spelvin" for his work and the play was a hit. Smith always insisted on listing the same name on future programs, for luck.

Ghost walks . . . Term used by actors since days of Shakespeare to denote payday. (The actor who played the Ghost in *Hamlet* went to the manager and said the actors refused to go on unless payment for past performances had been made. He returned with money in hand and announced: "The Ghost walks tonight.")

Gimmick . . . A device or trick used for a special effect, usually in an effort to get a laugh, although it may seek to elicit any emotion.

God from the machine . . . Translation of Latin, *deus ex machina*——when Fate (or the author) intercedes to save the action from the logical conclusion.

Good theatre . . . A quality that makes a play especially effective when presented before an audience.

Grand drape . . . A curtain above the stage and at the top of the proscenium arch; it hangs in front of the main curtain and decorates the top of the stage and reduces the height of the opening.

Gridiron or grid . . . Framework of wood or steel above the stage. Used to support and fly scenery.

Ground cloth . . . Waterproof canvas covering usually used to cover the entire stage floor.

Groundlings ... Term used by Shakespeare to indicate the uneducated and untrained theatregoers who sat in the pit, and were highly entertained by broad comedy.

Ground row ... Profile at the back of stage representing trees, shrubbery, hills, etc. Masks the meeting of stage floor and cyclorama.

Ham acting ... An exaggerated and insincere performance, notable for noise rather than honest feeling or sincerity. Extravagant gestures, choking sounds, and trickery are used for their effect alone. Should not be confused with broad acting or projection.

Hokum ... Deliberate simulation of emotion by artificial means. Also, the means used—sure-fire but time-worn theatrical tricks.

House seats ... Seats retained by the management to cover errors or to be given to distinguished guests. Released just before curtain time.

Ingenue ... The actress who plays the role of an innocent young woman.

Inner stage ... In Elizabethan theatre the small area upstage and enclosed by curtains. It localized action that moved forward to outer stage after the scene was underway.

Inscenierung ... German term to indicate the whole visual stage picture, including lighting. (See "Décor.")

Juvenile ... Young actor; counterpart of ingénue.

Legitimate drama ... The term comes from eighteenth-century England when theatres had to hold a license from the king. Term signified that a play was spoken rather than an "illegitimate" musical entertainment, which could be played in theatres that held no license. In modern times "legitimate" denotes the live stage as opposed to motion pictures and television which are the result of mating art with science (the camera and all it involves).

Light leak ... Light that can be seen through a crack or opening in the set.

Light spill ... Light that strikes the proscenium or set and thus "spills over" in a distracting manner, rather than striking just the area it is supposed to cover.

Live ... Actually present on stage in studio, as opposed to filmed or recorded.

Lock ... Term indicating elements that prevent a character from escaping the results of the conflict.

Mask ... To cover from view of the audience with some type of scenery.

Moscow Art Theatre ... Established by Constantin Stanislavsky in the last decade of the nineteenth century; until the Stalin regime, considered one of the finest theatres in the world.

Muff ... To mispronounce or transpose words or syllables.

Musical comedy ... A light story with spoken dialogue interspersed with music and dances.

Obligatory scene ... The scene that the playwright has led us to expect and without which the audience would be disappointed. Sometimes referred to as *"scène-à-faire"* (literally, "scene to do").

Oscar ... Motion Picture Academy Award, given each year for the outstanding achievement in all phases of the cinema.

Outer stage ... Forestage of Elizabethan theatre, used especially for soliloquies and most dramatic scenes. Historically preceded the apron, (q.v.).

Paper ... Complimentary tickets given out free or at reduced rates to bring in a larger audience. Issuing these in quantity is sometimes called "papering the house."

Penthouse theatre ... Name given to the first arena theatre of this century when it opened at the University of Washington.

Peripeteia or peripety ... A reversal of circumstances that leads to a result contrary to our expectation.

Physical time ... The actual minute length of the production, as opposed to the dramatic time.

Plant ... Apparently casual insertion of an idea, character, or property to be used more significantly later in the play.

Plastic scenery ... Built in three dimensions rather than painted on a flat surface.

The Poetics ... Written by Aristotle (360–322 B.C.). The earliest critical treatise extant dealing with dramatic practice and theory.

Point of attack ... That arbitrary point where the writer has chosen to begin his script.

Practical ... Scenery that is usable; a door or window that will open, etc.

Première ... First public performance of an art work.

Producer ... In America the individual or group who raises the money or underwrites the production financially. In England usually considered to be the director as well.

Project or projection ... To increase size of voice, movement, and gesture so as to be visible and audible in the rear of the auditorium. It "theatricalizes nature," so to speak, by increasing the feeling, but all is done with sincerity. Sometimes called "playing broadly," but not to be confused with "ham acting."

Properties or props ... Any article or piece of furniture used by the actor.

Proscenium ... The wall that separates the audience from the backstage.

Proscenium arch ... The opening in the proscenium through which the audience sees the stage; the picture frame.

Protagonist ... The leading character in the play—the one in whom the audience is most interested.

Pulitzer Prize ... Award given each year to the best play on an American theme.

Rake ... To place the set on a slant. Usually applied to side walls.

Repertoire, repertory ... A list of dramas, operas, parts, etc., that a company or person has rehearsed and is prepared to perform.

Repertory company ... Theatrical group that has and performs alternately the pieces in a repertoire.

Resolution ... Method of solving all conflicts presented in the play.

Return ... A flat used at extreme right and left of stage and running off stage behind the tormentor (q.v.). Sometimes it serves as the tormentor.

Revue ... A series of unrelated songs, skits, dances, very loosely tied together by the title—the subject is usually topical. There is no pretense of plot.

Scène-à-faire ... (See "Obligatory scene.")

Schmaltz ... Overly sentimental material, usually with the use of music in the background. Sometimes applied to overacting or production.

Screen Actors' Guild ... Union of motion picture actors.

Script ... The written drama from which the play is built.

Set pieces ... Scenery that will stand without support. Used especially in nonrealistic productions.

Show business ... Name applied to theatre productions pandering to a nondiscerning audience and emphasizing escape or box-office appeal rather than literary or theatrical merit.

Skeleton setting ... Rudiments of a setting, appealing largely to the imagination of the audience.

Skene ... A small hut in the Greek theatre, used for concealment during a change of costume. It has given us the English word "scene."

Skit ... A short scene of dialogue or pantomime, usually in a satirical or humorous vein.

Sky-drop ... A drop painted blue to represent sky and to mask rear of stage; hangs from the flies. (See "Cyclorama.")

Sneak ... To bring in music, sound, or voices at an extremely low level of volume.

Soliloquy ... A speech delivered by the actor when alone on the stage. There are two types:

> **Constructive**—explains the plot to the audience, as in many of Shakespeare's prologues.

> **Reflective**—shows personal thought or emotion, as in *Hamlet*.

Stage right, left ... Right or left side of the stage from the actor's point of view.

Static play ... One in which very little happens and the characters and situations are essentially the same at the end as in the beginning.

Steal ... Getting from one part of the stage to another without its being noticed. Can also mean pre-empting a scene that really belongs to another.

Sting ... To punctuate with a sudden musical phrase, shout, or some other emphatic sound.

Stock, stock company ... A resident company presenting a series of plays, each for a limited run, but not repeated after that engagement.

Tag . . . Final line of the play.

Teaser . . . Border just upstage and back of the front curtain. Masks the flies and determines the height of the proscenium opening during the performance.

Theatre Guild . . . Producing organization in New York. It works on a subscription series there and in many other large cities.

Theatre-in-the-round . . . (See "Arena stage.")

The Théatre Libre . . . Free theatre in France established in Paris in 1887. Headed by André Antoine, it introduced naturalism and freedom from artificiality of the nineteenth century.

"The method" . . . Name applied to the Russian or Stanislavsky approach to acting: very subjective, introspective, and individualistic.

Tormentors . . . Flats at extreme down right and left of stage near proscenium and masking backstage area. (See "Return.")

Trap . . . Opening in stage floor, permitting entrances or exits from under the floor.

Turkey . . . Name indicating a dramatic production that has utterly failed.

Twofer . . . A coupon which gives two tickets for the price of one. Issued toward the end of a play's run.

Type-cast . . . To cast people of the same age, appearance, size, or nature as the character in the play. Mostly an outgrowth of the realistic theatre.

Unit setting . . . Pieces of scenery—flats, pillars, doors, pylons, arches, etc., that can be put together in various combinations to furnish different settings.

Upstage . . . Toward back of stage. For many years the stage was higher in the back and slanted down toward the footlights and audience. This is still true in some European theatres.

Vaudeville . . . Production consisting of several acts—singing, dancing, dialogue, acrobatics, etc.—all unrelated but offering a variety of entertainment. Called "music hall" in England. Extremely popular in America until the mid-thirties. To play "The Palace," the leading vaudeville house in New York, was the goal of every act.

Victorian . . . Applied to the second half of the nineteenth-century in England coincident with the reign of Queen Victoria and noted for prudery and ostentation in art.

Washington Square Players . . . Amateur group that grew into the most successful Theatre Guild in New York City.

Well-made . . . Term applied to scripts written in mid-nineteenth century that followed a set pattern or formula in their construction. Scribe and Sardou were most prominent exponents of this approach. The term is often used in a derogatory sense.

Wings . . . Off stage space to left and right. Sometimes refers to wing pieces used in a series of two or three on either side of the stage as part of a wing and backdrop set.

Index

Index

Index

325

12.50